Recommender System with Machine Learning and Artificial Intelligence

Scrivener Publishing
100 Cummings Center, Suite 541J
Beverly, MA 01915-6106

Machine Learning in Biomedical Science and Healthcare Informatics

Series Editors: Vishal Jain and Jyotir Moy Chatterjee

In this series, the focus centers on the various applications of machine learning in the biomedical engineering and healthcare fields, with a special emphasis on the most representative machine learning techniques, namely deep learning-based approaches. Machine learning tasks are typically classified into two broad categories depending on whether there is a learning "label" or "feedback" available to a learning system: supervised learning and unsupervised learning. This series also introduces various types of machine learning tasks in the biomedical engineering field from classification (supervised learning) to clustering (unsupervised learning). The objective of the series is to compile all aspects of biomedical science and healthcare informatics, from fundamental principles to current advanced concepts. Submission to the series: Please send book proposals to drvishaljain83@gmail.com and/or jyotirchatterjee@gmail.com

Publishers at Scrivener
Martin Scrivener (martin@scrivenerpublishing.com)
Phillip Carmical (pcarmical@scrivenerpublishing.com)

Recommender System with Machine Learning and Artificial Intelligence

Practical Tools and Applications in Medical, Agricultural and Other Industries

Edited by

**Sachi Nandan Mohanty,
Jyotir Moy Chatterjee, Sarika Jain,
Ahmed A. Elngar and Priya Gupta**

Scrivener
Publishing

WILEY

This edition first published 2020 by John Wiley & Sons, Inc., 111 River Street, Hoboken, NJ 07030, USA and Scrivener Publishing LLC, 100 Cummings Center, Suite 541J, Beverly, MA 01915, USA
© 2020 Scrivener Publishing LLC
For more information about Scrivener publications please visit www.scrivenerpublishing.com.

Wiley Global Headquarters
111 River Street, Hoboken, NJ 07030, USA

For details of our global editorial offices, customer services, and more information about Wiley products visit us at www.wiley.com.

Library of Congress Cataloging-in-Publication Data

ISBN 978-1-119-71157-5

Cover image: Pixabay.Com
Cover design by Russell Richardson

Set in size of 11pt and Minion Pro by Manila Typesetting Company, Makati, Philippines

10 9 8 7 6 5 4 3 2 1

To our Parents & Well Wishers

Contents

Preface   xix

Acknowledgment   xxiii

Part 1: Introduction to Recommender Systems   1

1   An Introduction to Basic Concepts on Recommender Systems   3
Pooja Rana, Nishi Jain and Usha Mittal
1.1   Introduction   4
1.2   Functions of Recommendation Systems   5
1.3   Data and Knowledge Sources   6
1.4   Types of Recommendation Systems   8
     1.4.1   Content-Based   8
         1.4.1.1   Advantages of Content-Based
                 Recommendation   11
         1.4.1.2   Disadvantages of Content-Based
                 Recommendation   11
     1.4.2   Collaborative Filtering   12
1.5   Item-Based Recommendation vs. User-Based
     Recommendation System   14
     1.5.1   Advantages of Memory-Based Collaborative Filtering   15
     1.5.2   Shortcomings   16
     1.5.3   Advantages of Model-Based Collaborative Filtering   17
     1.5.4   Shortcomings   17
     1.5.5   Hybrid Recommendation System   17
     1.5.6   Advantages of Hybrid Recommendation Systems   18
     1.5.7   Shortcomings   18
     1.5.8   Other Recommendation Systems   18
1.6   Evaluation Metrics for Recommendation Engines   19
1.7   Problems with Recommendation Systems
     and Possible Solutions   20

	1.7.1	Advantages of Recommendation Systems	23
	1.7.2	Disadvantages of Recommendation Systems	24
1.8	Applications of Recommender Systems		24
	References		25

2 A Brief Model Overview of Personalized Recommendation to Citizens in the Health-Care Industry   **27**
Subhasish Mohapatra and Kunal Anand

2.1	Introduction		28
2.2	Methods Used in Recommender System		29
	2.2.1	Content-Based	29
	2.2.2	Collaborative Filtering	32
	2.2.3	Hybrid Filtering	33
2.3	Related Work		33
2.4	Types of Explanation		34
2.5	Explanation Methodology		35
	2.5.1	Collaborative-Based	36
	2.5.2	Content-Based	36
	2.5.3	Knowledge and Utility-Based	37
	2.5.4	Case-Based	37
	2.5.5	Demographic-Based	38
2.6	Proposed Theoretical Framework for Explanation-Based Recommender System in Health-Care Domain		39
2.7	Flowchart		39
2.8	Conclusion		41
	References		41

3 2Es of TIS: A Review of Information Exchange and Extraction in Tourism Information Systems   **45**
Malik M. Saad Missen, Mickaël Coustaty, Hina Asmat, Amnah Firdous, Nadeem Akhtar, Muhammad Akram and V. B. Surya Prasath

3.1	Introduction			46
3.2	Information Exchange			49
	3.2.1	Exchange of Tourism Objects Data		49
		3.2.1.1	Semantic Clashes	50
		3.2.1.2	Structural Clashes	50
	3.2.2	Schema.org—The Future		51
		3.2.2.1	Schema.org Extension Mechanism	52
		3.2.2.2	Schema.org Tourism Vocabulary	52
	3.2.3	Exchange of Tourism-Related Statistical Data		53

3.3	Information Extraction	55
	3.3.1 Opinion Extraction	56
	3.3.2 Opinion Mining	57
3.4	Sentiment Annotation	57
	3.4.1 SentiML	58
	3.4.1.1 SentiML Example	58
	3.4.2 OpinionMiningML	59
	3.4.2.1 OpinionMiningML Example	60
	3.4.3 EmotionML	61
	3.4.3.1 EmotionML Example	61
3.5	Comparison of Different Annotations Schemes	62
3.6	Temporal and Event Extraction	64
3.7	TimeML	65
3.8	Conclusions	67
	References	67

Part 2: Machine Learning-Based Recommender Systems   71

4 Concepts of Recommendation System from the Perspective of Machine Learning   73

Sumanta Chandra Mishra Sharma, Adway Mitra and Deepayan Chakraborty

4.1	Introduction	73
4.2	Entities of Recommendation System	74
	4.2.1 User	74
	4.2.2 Items	75
	4.2.3 Action	75
4.3	Techniques of Recommendation	76
	4.3.1 Personalized Recommendation System	77
	4.3.2 Non-Personalized Recommendation System	77
	4.3.3 Content-Based Filtering	77
	4.3.4 Collaborative Filtering	78
	4.3.5 Model-Based Filtering	80
	4.3.6 Memory-Based Filtering	80
	4.3.7 Hybrid Recommendation Technique	81
	4.3.8 Social Media Recommendation Technique	82
4.4	Performance Evaluation	82
4.5	Challenges	83
	4.5.1 Sparsity of Data	84
	4.5.2 Scalability	84

	4.5.3	Slow Start	84
	4.5.4	Gray Sheep and Black Sheep	84
	4.5.5	Item Duplication	84
	4.5.6	Privacy Issue	84
	4.5.7	Biasness	85
	4.6	Applications	85
	4.7	Conclusion	85
		References	85

5 A Machine Learning Approach to Recommend Suitable Crops and Fertilizers for Agriculture   **89**
Govind Kumar Jha, Preetish Ranjan and Manish Gaur

	5.1	Introduction	90
	5.2	Literature Review	91
	5.3	Methodology	93
	5.4	Results and Analysis	96
	5.5	Conclusion	97
		References	98

6 Accuracy-Assured Privacy-Preserving Recommender System Using Hybrid-Based Deep Learning Method   **101**
Abhaya Kumar Sahoo and Chittaranjan Pradhan

	6.1	Introduction	102
	6.2	Overview of Recommender System	103
	6.3	Collaborative Filtering-Based Recommender System	106
	6.4	Machine Learning Methods Used in Recommender System	107
	6.5	Proposed RBM Model-Based Movie Recommender System	110
	6.6	Proposed CRBM Model-Based Movie Recommender System	113
	6.7	Conclusion and Future Work	115
		References	118

7 Machine Learning-Based Recommender System for Breast Cancer Prognosis   **121**
G. Kanimozhi, P. Shanmugavadivu and M. Mary Shanthi Rani

	7.1	Introduction	122
	7.2	Related Works	124
	7.3	Methodology	125
	7.3.1	Experimental Dataset	125
	7.3.2	Feature Selection	127

| | 7.3.3 | Functional Phases of MLRS-BC | 128 |

7.3.3 Functional Phases of MLRS-BC 128
7.3.4 Prediction Algorithms 129
7.4 Results and Discussion 131
7.5 Conclusion 138
Acknowledgment 139
References 139

8 A Recommended System for Crop Disease Detection and Yield Prediction Using Machine Learning Approach 141
Pooja Akulwar
8.1 Introduction 142
8.2 Machine Learning 143
8.2.1 Overview 143
8.2.2 Machine Learning Algorithms 145
8.2.3 Machine Learning Methods 146
8.2.3.1 Artificial Neural Network 146
8.2.3.2 Support Vector Machines 146
8.2.3.3 K-Nearest Neighbors (K-NN) 147
8.2.3.4 Decision Tree Learning 147
8.2.3.5 Random Forest 148
8.2.3.6 Gradient Boosted Decision Tree (GBDT) 149
8.2.3.7 Regularized Greedy Forest (RGF) 150
8.3 Recommender System 151
8.3.1 Overview 151
8.4 Crop Management 153
8.4.1 Yield Prediction 153
8.4.2 Disease Detection 154
8.4.3 Weed Detection 156
8.4.4 Crop Quality 159
8.5 Application—Crop Disease Detection and Yield Prediction 159
References 162

Part 3: Content-Based Recommender Systems 165

9 Content-Based Recommender Systems 167
Poonam Bhatia Anand and Rajender Nath
9.1 Introduction 167
9.2 Literature Review 168
9.3 Recommendation Process 172
9.3.1 Architecture of Content-Based Recommender System 172
9.3.2 Profile Cleaner Representation 175

9.4   Techniques Used for Item Representation and Learning
User Profile   176

     9.4.1   Representation of Content   176

     9.4.2   Vector Space Model Based on Keywords   177

     9.4.3   Techniques for Learning Profiles of User   179

         9.4.3.1   Probabilistic Method   179

         9.4.3.2   Rocchio's and Relevance Feedback Method   180

         9.4.3.3   Other Methods   181

9.5   Applicability of Recommender System in Healthcare
and Agriculture   182

     9.5.1   Recommendation System in Healthcare   182

     9.5.2   Recommender System in Agriculture   184

9.6   Pros and Cons of Content-Based Recommender System   186

9.7   Conclusion   187

     References   188

10   Content (Item)-Based Recommendation System   197

R. Balamurali

   10.1   Introduction   198

   10.2   Phases of Content-Based Recommendation Generation   198

   10.3   Content-Based Recommendation Using Cosine Similarity   199

   10.4   Content-Based Recommendations Using Optimization
Techniques   204

   10.5   Content-Based Recommendation Using the Tree
Induction Algorithm   208

   10.6   Summary   212

     References   213

11   Content-Based Health Recommender Systems   215

*Soumya Prakash Rana, Maitreyee Dey, Javier Prieto
and Sandra Dudley*

   11.1   Introduction   216

   11.2   Typical Health Recommender System Framework   217

   11.3   Components of Content-Based Health
Recommender System   218

   11.4   Unstructured Data Processing   220

   11.5   Unsupervised Feature Extraction & Weighting   221

     11.5.1   Bag of Words (BoW)   221

     11.5.2   Word to Vector (Word2Vec)   222

     11.5.3   Global Vectors for Word Representations (Glove)   222

   11.6   Supervised Feature Selection & Weighting   222

11.7	Feedback Collection	225
	11.7.1 Medication & Therapy	225
	11.7.2 Healthy Diet Plan	225
	11.7.3 Suggestions	225
11.8	Training & Health Recommendation Generation	226
	11.8.1 Analogy-Based ML in CBHRS	227
	11.8.2 Specimen-Based ML in CBHRS	227
11.9	Evaluation of Content Based Health Recommender System	228
11.10	Design Criteria of CBHRS	229
	11.10.1 Micro-Level & Lucidity	230
	11.10.2 Interactive Interface	230
	11.10.3 Data Protection	230
	11.10.4 Risk & Uncertainty Management	231
	11.10.5 Doctor-in-Loop (DiL)	231
11.11	Conclusions and Future Research Directions	231
	References	233
12	**Context-Based Social Media Recommendation System**	**237**
	R. Sujithra Kanmani and B. Surendiran	
12.1	Introduction	237
12.2	Literature Survey	240
12.3	Motivation and Objectives	241
	12.3.1 Architecture	241
	12.3.2 Modules	242
	12.3.3 Implementation Details	243
12.4	Performance Measures	243
12.5	Precision	243
12.6	Recall	243
12.7	F- Measure	244
12.8	Evaluation Results	244
12.9	Conclusion and Future Work	247
	References	248
13	**Netflix Challenge—Improving Movie Recommendations**	**251**
	Vasu Goel	
13.1	Introduction	251
13.2	Data Preprocessing	252
13.3	MovieLens Data	253
13.4	Data Exploration	255
13.5	Distributions	256
13.6	Data Analysis	257

13.7	Results	265
13.8	Conclusion	266
	References	266

14 Product or Item-Based Recommender System   **269**
Jyoti Rani, Usha Mittal and Geetika Gupta

14.1	Introduction	270
14.2	Various Techniques to Design Food Recommendation System	271
	14.2.1 Collaborative Filtering Recommender Systems	271
	14.2.2 Content-Based Recommender Systems (CB)	272
	14.2.3 Knowledge-Based Recommender Systems	272
	14.2.4 Hybrid Recommender Systems	273
	14.2.5 Context Aware Approaches	273
	14.2.6 Group-Based Methods	273
	14.2.7 Different Types of Food Recommender Systems	273
14.3	Implementation of Food Recommender System Using Content-Based Approach	276
	14.3.1 Item Profile Representation	277
	14.3.2 Information Retrieval	278
	14.3.3 Word2vec	278
	14.3.4 How are word2vec Embedding's Obtained?	278
	14.3.5 Obtaining word2vec Embeddings	279
	14.3.6 Dataset	280
	14.3.6.1 Data Preprocessing	280
	14.3.7 Web Scrapping For Food List	280
	14.3.7.1 Porter Stemming All Words	280
	14.3.7.2 Filtering Our Ingredients	280
	14.3.7.3 Final Data Frame with Dishes and Their Ingredients	281
	14.3.7.4 Hamming Distance	281
	14.3.7.5 Jaccard Distance	282
14.4	Results	282
14.5	Observations	283
14.6	Future Perspective of Recommender Systems	283
	14.6.1 User Information Challenges	283
	14.6.1.1 User Nutrition Information Uncertainty	283
	14.6.1.2 User Rating Data Collection	284
	14.6.2 Recommendation Algorithms Challenges	284
	14.6.2.1 User Information Such as Likes/ Dislikes Food or Nutritional Needs	284

14.6.2.2   Recipe Databases   284
14.6.2.3   A Set of Constraints or Rules   285
14.6.3   Challenges Concerning Changing Eating
Behavior of Consumers   285
14.6.4   Challenges Regarding Explanations
and Visualizations   286
14.7   Conclusion   286
Acknowledgements   287
References   287

Part 4: Blockchain & IoT-Based Recommender Systems

291

**15 A Trust-Based Recommender System Built on IoT Blockchain
Network With Cognitive Framework**   **293**
S. Porkodi and D. Kesavaraja
15.1   Introduction   294
15.1.1   Today and Tomorrow   294
15.1.2   Vision   294
15.1.3   Internet of Things   294
15.1.4   Blockchain   295
15.1.5   Cognitive Systems   296
15.1.6   Application   296
15.2   Technologies and its Combinations   297
15.2.1   IoT–Blockchain   297
15.2.2   IoT–Cognitive System   298
15.2.3   Blockchain–Cognitive System   298
15.2.4   IoT–Blockchain–Cognitive System   298
15.3   Crypto Currencies With IoT–Case Studies   299
15.4   Trust-Based Recommender System   299
15.4.1   Requirement   299
15.4.2   Things Management   302
15.4.3   Cognitive Process   303
15.5   Recommender System Platform   304
15.6   Conclusion and Future Directions   307
References   307

**16 Development of a Recommender System HealthMudra
Using Blockchain for Prevention of Diabetes**   **313**
Rashmi Bhardwaj and Debabrata Datta
16.1   Introduction   314
16.2   Architecture of Blockchain   317

16.2.1   Definition of Blockchain   318
16.2.2   Structure of Blockchain   318
16.3   Role of HealthMudra in Diabetic   322
16.4   Blockchain Technology Solutions   324
16.4.1   Predictive Models of Health Data Analysis   325
16.5   Conclusions   325
References   326

Part 5: Healthcare Recommender Systems   **329**

17 **Case Study 1: Health Care Recommender Systems**   **331**
    Usha Mittal, Nancy Singla and Geetika Gupta
    17.1   Introduction   332
    17.1.1   Health Care Recommender System   332
    17.1.2   Parkinson's Disease: Causes and Symptoms 333
    17.1.3   Parkinson's Disease: Treatment and Surgical
              Approaches   334
    17.2   Review of Literature   335
    17.2.1   Machine Learning Algorithms for Parkinson's Data 337
    17.2.2   Visualization   340
    17.3   Recommender System for Parkinson's Disease (PD)   341
    17.3.1   How Will One Know When Parkinson's
              has Progressed?   342
    17.3.2   Dataset for Parkinson's Disease (PD)   342
    17.3.3   Feature Selection   343
    17.3.4   Classification   343
              17.3.4.1   Logistic Regression   343
              17.3.4.2   K Nearest Neighbor (KNN)   343
              17.3.4.3   Support Vector Machine (SVM)   344
              17.3.4.4   Decision Tree   344
    17.3.5   Train and Test Data   344
    17.3.6   Recommender System   344
    17.4   Future Perspectives   345
    17.5   Conclusions   346
    References   348

18 **Temporal Change Analysis-Based Recommender System
    for Alzheimer Disease Classification**   **351**
    S. Naganandhini, P. Shanmugavadivu and M. Mary Shanthi Rani
    18.1   Introduction   352
    18.2   Related Work   352
    18.3   Mechanism of TCA-RS-AD   353

18.4   Experimental Dataset   354
18.5   Neural Network   357
18.6   Conclusion   370
        References   370

19 Regularization of Graphs: Sentiment Classification   373
    R.S.M. Lakshmi Patibandla
19.1   Introduction   373
19.2   Neural Structured Learning   374
19.3   Some Neural Network Models   375
19.4   Experimental Results   377
        19.4.1   Base Model   379
        19.4.2   Graph Regularization   382
19.5   Conclusion   383
        References   384

**20 TSARS: A Tree-Similarity Algorithm-Based Agricultural
    Recommender System   387**
    *Madhusree Kuanr, Puspanjali Mohapatra
    and Sasmita Subhadarsinee Choudhury*
20.1   Introduction   388
20.2   Literature Survey   390
20.3   Research Gap   393
20.4   Problem Definitions   393
20.5   Methodology   393
20.6   Results & Discussion   394
        20.6.1   Performance Evaluation   394
        20.6.2   Time Complexity Analysis   396
20.7   Conclusion & Future Work   397
        References   399

**21 Influenceable Targets Recommendation Analyzing Social
    Activities in Egocentric Online Social Networks   401**
    Soumyadeep Debnath, Dhrubasish Sarkar and Dipankar Das
21.1   Introduction   402
21.2   Literature Review   403
21.3   Dataset Collection Process with Details   404
        21.3.1   Main User's Activities Data   405
        21.3.2   Network Member's Activities Data   405
        21.3.3   Tools and Libraries for Data Collection   405
        21.3.4   Details of the Datasets   406
21.4   Primary Preprocessing of Data   406

21.4.1 Language Detection and Translation 406
21.4.2 Tagged Tweeters Collection 407
21.4.3 Textual Noise Removal 407
21.4.4 Textual Spelling and Correction 407
21.5 Influence and Social Activities Analysis 407
21.5.1 Step 1: Targets Selection From OSMs 408
21.5.2 Step 3: Categories Classification of Social Contents 408
21.5.3 Step 4: Sentiments Analysis of Social Contents 408
21.6 Recommendation System 409
21.6.1 Secondary Preprocessing of Data 409
21.6.2 Recommendation Analyzing Contents of Social Activities 411
21.7 Top Most Influenceable Targets Evaluation 413
21.8 Conclusion 414
21.9 Future Scope 415
References 415

Index **417**

Preface

This book comprehensively covers the topic of recommender systems, which provide personalized recommendations of items or services to the new users based on their past behavior. Recommender system methods have been adapted to diverse applications including social networking, movie recommendation, query log mining, news recommendations, and computational advertising. This book synthesizes both fundamental and advanced topics of a research area that has now reached maturity. Recommendations in specific domains and contexts, the context of a recommendation can be viewed as important side information that affects the recommendation goals. Different types of context such as temporal data, spatial data, social data, tagging data, and trustworthiness are explored. In industry point of view, for an individual item or product recommendation system can help to developed for better selling.

Chapter 1 discusses about pros and cons of method like cold-start, scalability, sparsity is explained in detail in terms of recommender systems. Various other approaches of recommendation systems are explained like multi-criteria-based recommender systems, risk-aware recommender systems, mobile recommender system, hybrid recommender system, healthcare recommender system, etc.

Chapter 2 provides an insight into the implementation of the recommender system in both tangible and non-tangible products as well as the service care industry.

Chapter 3 discusses both of data exchange and extraction processes with respect to Tourism Information System. Authors described about the importance of these processes and review how these are being dealt by researchers currently.

Chapter 4 deals with different concepts and challenges of recommendation systems, and how artificial intelligence and machine learning can be used for them. The chapter mainly focuses on the concepts and techniques used by the recommendation system for better suggestion.

Chapter 5 provides a recommender system based on a machine learning approach may be developed which could suggest the type of crop and the fertilizer may be used to increase their productivity and consequently, their income.

Chapter 6 proposes Restrictive Boltzmann Machine Approach (RBM) and hybrid deep learning method i.e. RBM with Convolutional neural network (CNN) (CRBM).

Chapter 7 proposed "Machine Learning-based Recommender System for Breast Cancer Prediction (MLRS-BC)" aims to provide an accurate recommendation for breast cancer prognosis, through four distinct phases namely: Data collection; Preprocessing; Training, testing and validation; and Prediction/Recommender.

Chapter 8 deliberates the concepts of content-based recommender systems by including different aspects in their design and implementation.

Chapter 9 discuss about the various methods to recommend item based on contents.

Chapter 10 The Content-Based Health Recommender System and associated popular Machine Learning algorithms are discussed in this chapter, including their usefulness to enhance profile health records (PHR) solutions.

Chapter 11 proposed context attributes along with the services provided by the social media for achieving better recommendation called as context-based social media recommendation system.

Chapter 12 provides analysis based on the challenge that Netflix offered to the data science community. The objective in this analysis is to train multiple machine learning algorithms using inputs from one data set to predict movie ratings in another data set.

Chapter 13 provides different types of products/items-based recommendations systems have been explained.

Chapter 14 introduced a trust-based recommender system is built to make a detailed review on the applicability of proposed system, where trust is the key in decision making process.

Chapter 15 introduced a Recommender System HealthMudra Using Blockchain for Prevention of Diabetes in details.

In Chapter 16 various health care recommender systems have been discussed. Different technologies to design recommender system are explained.

Chapter 17 describes about a new composite and comprehensive recommender system named Temporal Change Analysis-based Recommender System for Alzheimer Disease Classification (TCA-RS-AD) using deep learning model.

Chapter 18 provides an effective model has been discussed in egocentric OSN by incorporating an efficient influence measured Recommendation System in order to generate a list of top most influenceable target users among all connected network members for any specific social network user.

Chapter 19 aims at developing a recommender system based on tree data structure for farmers. The proposed system recommends seeds, fertilizers, pesticides and instruments based on farming and farmers' location preferences when buying seeds online.

Chapter 20 describes a new composite and comprehensive recommender system named Temporal Change Analysis-based Recommender System for Alzheimer Disease Classification (TCA-RS-AD) using a deep learning model.

Chapter 21 describes the case study on "Crop Disease Detection and Yield prediction". The study includes identification of crop condition, disease detection, prediction about production of specific crop and recommendation. The various machine learning techniques or algorithms can be used to monitor, disease detection and predict appropriate crop cultivation.

We like to thank all the authors for their valuable contribution which make this book possible. Among those who have influenced this project are our family and friends, who have sacrificed a lot of their time and attention to ensure that we remained motivated throughout the time devoted to the completion of this crucial book.

The Editors
May 2020

Acknowledgment

I would like to acknowledge the most important people in my life, my father Aloke Moy Chatterjee, my uncle Mr. Moni Moy Chatterjee & my late mother Nomita Chatterjee. This book has been my long-cherished dream which would not have been turned into reality without the support and love of these amazing people. They have continuously encouraged me despite my failing to give them the proper time and attention. I am also grateful to my friends, who have encouraged and blessed this work with their unconditional love and patience.

Jyotir Moy Chatterjee
Department of IT
Lord Buddha Education Foundation (APUTI)
Kathmandu
Nepal-44600

Part 1

INTRODUCTION TO RECOMMENDER SYSTEMS

1

An Introduction to Basic Concepts on Recommender Systems

Pooja Rana, Nishi Jain and Usha Mittal*

Department of Computer Science and Engineering, Lovely Professional University, Phagwara, India

Abstract

In today's world, we find a wide range of possibilities of any search that we do online and we might find difficulties in choosing what we actually need. To address these issues, recommendation System plays a major role. A recommender system is a filtering system that filters the data using different algorithms and recommends the most relevant data to the user. For instance, a recommender system for e-commerce requires a past history of the site and if the user is not having any past history then the recommender system recommends the bestselling product or most popular product present in the market. Recommendation systems are effective tools for personalization, are always up-to-date, and gives a recommendation based on actual user behavior. Besides being useful in buying products it has a few disadvantages like it is difficult to set up and get running as they are database-driven. Sometimes recommendations are wrong which makes customers unsatisfied. Recommender system is used in different areas like recommendation for entertainment such as movies, songs etc., e-learning web site recommendation, newspaper recommendation and e-mail filters.

In this chapter, various recommendation techniques with their pros and cons and different evaluation metrices has been discussed.

Keywords: Recommendation, item-based, rating, artificial intelligence

Corresponding author: usha.20339@lpu.co.in

Sachi Nandan Mohanty, Jyotir Moy Chatterjee, Sarika Jain, Ahmed A. Elngar and Priya Gupta (eds.) *Recommender System with Machine Learning and Artificial Intelligence: Practical Tools and Applications in Medical, Agricultural and Other Industries*, (3–26) © 2020 Scrivener Publishing LLC

1.1   Introduction

A recommender system is a sub-category of an information extraction system that helps to find the ranking or user preference for a particular item. Recommendation systems are dedicated software and methods that give ideas related to things that are used by different users [1, 2]. Many decisions can be made by considering recommendations like which product to purchase, type of music to listen, or what and where to read online news.

The things that are suggested by the system are known as "Item". A recommender system generally concentrates on a particular form of item like DVDs, or articles and thus its proposal, its graphical user interface (GUI), and the primary method used to make the suggestions are adapted to give beneficial and real recommendations for a particular form of item.

Consider an example of toy recommendation system that assists customers to select a toy to buy. The popular e-commerce web site i.e. Amazon.com also uses a recommendation system to identify the online store for every user [3]. As suggestions and choices are generally personalized, different users or user groups get different suggestions. In case of magazines and newspapers, non-personalized suggestions are produced, which are very easy to generate. Consider the example of selecting best ten books or CDs.

To make the personalized suggestions, ranked lists of items are produced. User's preferences and constrains are considered for generating the ranking to extract the most suitable products and services. For computing the most similar products and services, user's preferences are collected implicitly or explicitly by understanding the users' actions.

The fast development and diverse data existing on the web and existence of new e-business services like purchasing goods, comparing items, auction, etc. often stunned customers, leading them to make wrong choices. Thus, rather than giving benefit to customers, it starts decreasing the well-being. Actually, choice, with its insinuations of liberty, independence, and self-determination can become dangerous; generating a sense that independence may come to be observed as a kind of misery-inducing dictatorship [4].

These days, use of recommender systems has widely increased, indicated by the following facts:

1. In high-rated internet sites, recommendation systems have a vital role like Yahoo, Amazon.com, Netflix, YouTube, TripAdvisor and IMDB. Now, RSs as a part of service have

been provided to the subscriber by many media companies. For instance, Netflix, the online movie rental service, has paid a great price i.e. one million dollars as prize to the group that first successfully improved the accuracy of its recommendation system [3].

2. ACM Recommender Systems (RecSys) has been established in 2007 dedicated for conferences and workshops.

1.2   Functions of Recommendation Systems

Recommender system offers suggestions to the user about a particular item that user wants to use. Now this definition can be refined by representing the different roles that a system can play. Recommender system plays different roles according to the user for example; a recommender system used by travel intermediary is usually used to increase the revenue like Expedia.com and Visitfinland.com while the customer's objective for using the systems is to find an appropriate hotel and interesting events/attractions when visiting a destination.

The following are different reasons to exploit RS technology by service providers:

1. Increase the sale of product: The major objective of a commercial RS is to increase its sale, or in other words to sell those products also which can't be sold without recommendations. Recommendations are provided considering that suggested products and services meet the customer's requirements. Non-commercial recommendations are used for similar objectives. Consider an example of a content writer who wants to increase the number of news reader on his site. The goal of the service provider to use the recommender system is to increase the users that opts the products or services as compared to users surf the site.

2. Selling variety of products: RS also help a user to find items that might be difficult to find without a particular reference. For example, the recommender system used in Netflix has the goal of renting maximum movies in the list, rather than the most popular movies. Making such recommendations could be hard without a recommender system because the service provider cannot take the risk of suggesting videos

which do not meet the user's taste. In this way, the recommender system also suggests movies which are not even popular.

3. User satisfaction. The recommender system helps in improving the experience of the person with the application or web site. It provides interesting, significant and, relevant recommendations as well as provides better human–computer interaction. The effective recommendations i.e. accurate as well as interactive user interface increases usage of the system and the chances that the suggestions will be acknowledged.

4. User loyalty. A customer always prefers to use a web site or application which identifies its old users and treats him as a respected/valuable customer. It is a common feature of a recommender system as it computes recommendations/suggestions, considering the data attained from the user in earlier interactions such as his ratings of products. Therefore, the more the customer uses a particular site, the better his model becomes, i.e., output will be more customized to user's preferences.

5. Better understand of user needs: The recommender system is acting as an active learner to user's preferences by collecting explicitly or predictions made by the system. The business holders may then re-use this information for improving the stock management or production of items.

1.3 Data and Knowledge Sources

Recommender systems are knowledge extraction systems that actively collect different types of information to make the suggestions. Facts are mostly related to things to be recommended and the consumers who will get such suggestions. Available data sources are very large and diverse, their use for making recommendations are largely depends upon the recommendation techniques to be used.

1. Items: Products and services that a recommender system recommends are referred to as items. The recommendation of an item is considered positive if the suggested product is beneficial for the consumer. If the product is not meeting

user requirements and the customer took a wrong decision while choosing it, then recommendation is negative.

2. For example, a news recommender system designer must consider structure of news, the textual representation, and the time significance of any news. As while reading news, no monetary cost is associated but cognitive cost is there. If the system makes a positive recommendation, then cost of searching and reading news is dominated by the benefit of getting relevant and valuable knowledge. But if recommendation is negative, then the user's time is wasted which restricts the user to use the system again. In other areas, like mobile phones, or business investments, actual monetary cost is associated which becomes significant component to take into account while choosing the most suitable recommendation techniques.

3. Examples of items having low difficulty and value are news, web articles, e-books, DVDs, and movies. Items having high complexity and value are laptops, LCDs, mobile phones, digital cameras, electrical appliances, PCs, etc. Insurance policies, travel plans, financial investments and jobs are considered as most complex items [10]. According to the basic recommendation approach, recommender systems use a variety of properties and characteristics of the products and services. For instance, in a movie recommendation, the genre like comedy, thriller, etc., as well as the actors, and directors can be used to define a movie.

4. Users: Users of a recommender system may have very diverse aims and features. In order to make positive recommendations, the system should exploit a variety of data about the users. This data can be organized in several means and again the usage of data depends upon the recommendation approach.

5. Transactions: Any recorded communication between a recommender system and user is referred to as transaction. These are logs that collect essential information generated at the time of interaction and these are valuable for the recommendation technique. The log may also have an explicit feedback given by the user like ranking to the particular product.

6. Ratings are the most common method of transaction data that a recommender system gathers. These rankings may be

collected explicitly or implicitly. There different types of ratings as follows:

- Ranking can be a numerical value like 1–5 given in the items related with e-commerce sites like Amazon.com.
- Ranking can be an ordinal value like "strongly agree, agree, neutral, disagree, strongly disagree" normally used in surveys.
- Ranking can be a binary value in which feedback is taken from user as product is useful or not.

1.4   Types of Recommendation Systems

Different types of recommendation system are available that differ in terms of problem domain, Information used, and importantly recommendation algorithm used to make prediction. There are mainly two types of recommendation systems as shown in Figure 1.1 i.e. content-based RS and Collaborative filtering methods.

1.4.1   Content-Based

Based on the previous responses submitted by the user, the system learns to make recommendations by analyzing the feature similarity among items. For example, based upon the rating of a user for different genre of movies, the system will learn to recommend the genre which is positively rated by the user. A content-based recommendation system builds a user profile based upon the previously rated items by the user. A user profile represents the user interests and is able to adapt to new interest also. Matching of user profile against the features of content object is basically the recommendation process. Result of this process is a judgment that signifies the user interest in the object. A highly accurate profile of user interests will result

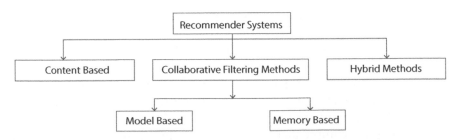

Figure 1.1 Different recommendation techniques.

in usefulness of an information access process. For instance, it might be used to filter the web results by determining whether a user is interested in the specific page or not.

The recommendation process comprises of 3 steps, each of which is handled separately.

    a. *Content Analyzer:* If data is non-structured, some pre-processing is required in order to obtain relevant information. The main responsibility of a content analyzer is to represent the contents coming from the source in a relevant form for the next processing steps. Feature extraction techniques are used to modify item structure from original to the targeted (e.g. web pages represented as keyword vectors). This representation is input to the next component.

    b. *Learner:* This module constructs the user profile by generalizing the data obtained from the previous component. Machine learning techniques are used to learn the generalize strategy, which are able to construct a model based upon user preferences in the past, both positive and negative. For example, profile learner of a web page recommendation system will implement a relevance feedback method which combines positive and negative feedback into a prototype vector representing the user profile.

    c. *Filtering Component:* This module makes use of the user profile to derive related items. This is done by matching the profile alongside items to be recommended. Based upon the similarity metrics, a relevant judgment is produced either binary or continuous.

Content Recommendation systems acquire the recommendation idea from the past data of a user based on what items a user has purchased or liked. Both user and item attributes are of equal importance in terms of making a prediction. Consider the example of news recommender, features like categories (Finance, Sports, Health, Technology, Politics, Entertainment, Automobile, etc.) or location (local, national or international) etc. are required to find the similarity index between news. To extract features like sentiment score, TF-IDF scores are used. In this approach, the profile of each user as well as each item is created and two vectors are created.

a. *Item vector:* A vector of length N and contains value 1 for words having high TF-IDF and 0 otherwise.
b. *User vector:* A 1 × N vector containing probability of occurrence of word of every word in the article. The user vector is based in the attributes of item.

After that, similarity between user and article is computed using following methods:

a. *Cosine similarity:* It is used to measure similarity between user and item. This way gives user–item similarity. This method is best when we have high dimensional features especially in information retrieval and text mining. The range of this is between −1 and 1 and there are two approaches:
   - Top-n approach: According to this, top n best products are recommended and value of 'n' is decided by user [5].
   - Rating scale approach: In this, a prefixed threshold is fixed and all the items having value greater than threshold are suggested as given in Equation 1.

$$Cosine(x, y) = \frac{\sum_{i=1}^{n} x_i y_i}{\sqrt{\sum_{i=1}^{n} x_i^2} \sqrt{\sum_{i=1}^{n} y_i^2}} \qquad (1)$$

c. *Jaccard Similarity:* This similarity is computed using Equation 2. This method is used to compute item–item similarity. It compares item vectors with each other and returns the most similar item. This is only useful with binary vectors. If any ratings or rankings having multiple values then this method is not applicable.

$$J(X,Y) = \frac{|X \cap Y|}{|X \cup Y|} \qquad (2)$$

c. *Euclidean Distance:* It is computed using the formula given in Equation 3.

$$Euclidean\ Distance = \sqrt{(x_1 - y_1)^2 + \cdots + (x_N - y_N)^2} \qquad (3)$$

d. *Pearson's Correlation:* It is computed using the formula given in Equation 4. It tells the correlation between the two items. Higher correlation means higher similarity.

$$sim(u,v) = \frac{\sum (r_{ui} - \bar{r}_u)(r_{vi} - \bar{r}_v)}{\sqrt{\sum (r_{ui} - \bar{r}_u)^2} \sqrt{\sum (r_{vi} - \bar{r}_v)^2}} \qquad (4)$$

1.4.1.1   Advantages of Content-Based Recommendation

a. *User Independence*—Content-Based Recommendation system build a user profile only based upon the rating or purchased done by the user in the past. No neighbor is considered for building the profile of the user who has same interest as of user.
b. *Transparency*—Explanation facility of content-based recommendation system is transparent to the user which means it provides explanations of the recommendations.
c. *New Item*—It does not suffer from the first rater problem which means if an item is not rated by any user it is still able to recommend that item to the user.

1.4.1.2   Disadvantages of Content-Based Recommendation

a. *Limited content analysis*—One of the shortcomings of content-based recommendation system is limited content associated with the item in terms of number of features and type of features. Domain Knowledge is also crucial to make a recommendation. For example, making a movie recommendation system requires knowledge of actors and directors of the movie. Proper differentiation cannot be done between the item's user likes and items user dislikes if available data is insufficient. Representation sometimes is able to capture only certain aspects of user choice but not all. For example, Web pages, feature extraction techniques from text completely overlook visual qualities and additional multimedia information.

b. *Over-specialization*—Content-based recommendation system does not have any essential method to explore something unpredicted. System can recommend only those items which result in high score while matching with the user profile. It is also called serendipity problem which shows the limit of recommendations that can be made by content based. A "perfect" content-based technique would hardly provide anything new, limiting the range of applications for which it would be beneficial.

c. *New user*—To make recommendation system to learn about user preferences, sufficient ratings need to be collected. System is not able to provide reliable recommendations to the new users as no past data is available.

1.4.2   Collaborative Filtering

This approach uses 'user behavior' for recommendations. In this approach, there is no feature corresponding to users or items. It uses a utility matrix and most commonly used in industries as it is independent from any additional information.

Limitation of content-based recommendation system can be overcome by the collaborative approach for instance it can make prediction for those items for which content is not available. It uses the feedback of other users to recommend such items. These systems evaluate the quality of an item based on peer review. It can also suggest products with different content as long as other users have shown the interest in the content.

There are 2 categories of collaborative filtering as shown in Figure 1.2:

a. *Memory-based (neighborhood) approach:* In this, utility matrix is learnt and suggestions are given by asking the given user with rest of the utility matrix [9]. Let's suppose we have 'm' movies and 'u' users. To find out how much user likes movie 'k' Equation 5 is used:

$$\bar{y}_i = \frac{1}{|I_i|} \sum_{j \in I_i} y_{ij} \tag{5}$$

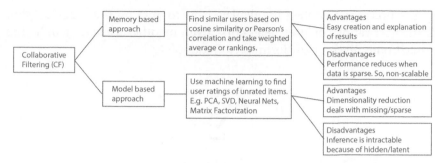

Figure 1.2 Different techniques of collaborative filtering.

The above formula will give the average ranking that customer 'i' has specified to all the items. Rating of product can be estimated as given in Equation 6:

$$\hat{y}_{ik} = \overline{y}_i + \frac{1}{\sum_{a \in U_k} |w_{ia}|} \sum_{a \in U_k} w_{ia}(y_{ak} - \overline{y}_a) \tag{6}$$

It is easy to compute, but if data becomes sparse, performance becomes poor. Now the similarity between users 'a' and 'i' can be calculated using the methods like cosine similarity, Pearson's correlation, etc.

Memory-Based Collaborative Filtering is further divided into two categories i.e. user-based filtering and item-based filtering [7].

b. User-Item filtering: In this method, for a new item 'i' for a particular user 'u' rankings of nearest neighbors of user 'u' are used to compute the ranking rui of the user 'u' but only those neighbors are considered who have already given a ranking for the item 'i'. The rating rui can be estimated as shown in Equation 7.

$$\hat{r}_{ui} = \frac{1}{|N_i(u)|} \sum_{v \in N_i} r_{vi} \tag{7}$$

Above equation does not consider the different level of similarity can occur among neighbors.

The prediction of item is calculated by computing the weighted sum of the user ratings of 'user-neighbors' given by other users to item 'i'. The prediction is given by the formula in Equation 8.

$$P_{u,i} = \frac{\sum_v (r_{v,i} * s_{u,v})}{\sum_v s_{u,v}}$$

(8)

Where $P_{u,i}$ is the prediction of an item, $R_{v,i}$ is the rating given by a user 'v' to an item 'i' and $S_{u,v}$ is the similarity between users.

What will happen if a new user or new item is inserted in the dataset? There is term known as cold start which is of two types:

a. *Visitor cold start:* When a new consumer is presented to the knowledgebase, as system is not having any past data of the user, it becomes difficult to suggest any product to him. To resolve this issue, overall or regionally most popular products are recommended.

b. *Product cold start:* When a new item comes in the market or given to the system, user' actions are required to decide its value. Higher the reviews and ratings product got from users, the easier it becomes for the system to suggest to appropriate consumer.

1.5   Item-Based Recommendation vs. User-Based Recommendation System

Five points need to be considered in order to make a choice between user-based and item-based neighborhood recommendation system. Points are as follow:

a. *Accuracy:* Ratio of users and items is typically responsible for the accuracy of neighbourhood recommendation system. In user-based recommendation system, similarity between two users is calculated by analysing the scores given by the users for the same item. Item-based approaches compute the similarity between two items by analyzing the scores given by the same user.

b. *Efficiency*: Efficiency in terms of memory and computational power also depends upon ratio of users and items. So, if the users are more than items that happen in most of the cases, item-based recommendation systems are more reliable in terms of memory and time required to calculate the similarity. On the other hand, time complexity is same for both because it depends upon the number of users and number of items.

c. *Stability*: Stability of user-based and item-based system is related to occurrence and change in number of users and items in the system. If items are static then we should use item-based recommendation system because similarity weights of items can be computed at irregular time intervals. On the opposite hand, if the list of items is changing then user-based system are most preferable.

d. *Justifiability*: Based upon preferences, whether justification is required or not, item-based or user-based recommendation system is selected. Item-based methods can simply be used to explain why a recommendation is made. As an explanation to the user a list of neighbor items and their similarity weights can be shown to the user which are used for making the recommendation. User can also participate in the process by modifying the neighbours. On the other hand, user-based methods can't explain the recommendation process because the user is not aware about other's preferences.

e. *Serendipity*: Problem of serendipity occurs in item-based recommendation system because it recommends only those items to the users which have been liked by the user in the past. For example, in the movie recommendation system only that movies will be recommended to the user whose genre or actors are same as of previously liked. On the contrary, user based can make unexpected recommendation by analysing the neighbors who have made same rating to the item as the user and checks the ratings on different items by the neighbor user which are yet not rated by the user.

1.5.1 Advantages of Memory-Based Collaborative Filtering

a. *Easiness*: Neighborhood-based approaches are instinctual as well as easy to implement. Only one parameter requires tuning i.e. how many neighbors to be considered for final evaluation.

b. *Justifiability*: Memory based collaborative filtering approaches also offer a crisp explanation for the calculated results. Item-based methods can simply be used to explain why a recommendation is made. As an explanation to the user a list of neighbor items and their similarity weights can be shown to the user which are used for making the recommendation. User can also participate in the process by modifying the neighbours.

c. *Efficiency*: In terms of efficiency, neighborhood-based system is more preferable. As compared to others, model-based systems do not require expensive training phases as well as memory consumption is low.

d. *Stability*: Memory based collaborative systems are slightly affected by the continuous insertion of consumers, products and rankings. For example, once the similarity between items has been calculated, model can generate suggestions. Once new ranking is added, only similarities between the items need to be computed.

1.5.2   Shortcomings

- These systems are fully dependent on the rankings provided by the users.
- These systems are not able to handle the sparse data which result in performance degradation.
- Recommendation cannot be made for new customers and new products.
- System is not scalable.

a. *Model based approach:* This model represents users and items using utility matrix i.e. utility matrix is decomposed into A and B matrix where A signifies user and B denotes the items [9]. For matrix decomposition, different techniques like SVD, PCA are used. Rating of each item is computed and product with highest rating is recommended. This model is beneficial when available data is large in volume.

This approach is further divided into 3 sub-types:

a. Clustering based algorithm.
b. Matrix factorization-based algorithm.
c. Deep learning/Neural Nets.

1.5.3   Advantages of Model-Based Collaborative Filtering

- It helps to resolve the problem of sparsity and scalability.
- Prediction accuracy is better.

1.5.4   Shortcomings

- Implementation cost is high.
- There is trade-off between scalability and efficiency of model.
- Due to dimensionality reduction methods, it may loss valuable information.

1.5.5   Hybrid Recommendation System

In this, two or more techmiques are combined like content-based and collaborative fltering. Limitations of one techniques can be overcommed by other technique. There are several classes of Hybrid Recommendation Systems:

- Mixed—In this, number of different techniques are combined together to design a system. Here the generated item lists of each technique are added to produce a final list of recommended items. Recommendations made by all techniques are combined and final result is presented to user.
- Weighted—In these, weighted linear functions are used to compute the rank of products by aggregating the output ranks of all systems. P- Tango is the first weighted hybrid system for online newspaper recommender system.
- Cascade—These systems work in stages. First method is used to make a rough rating of products and then generated list is refined by second method. In these systems, order of processes matters a lot.

- Feature augmentation—In feature augmentation systems, output of one system acts as input to other system. These are also order-sensitive.
- Switching—In this, system switches among various recommending methods depending on some conditions. For instance, a CF-CBF method may shift to the content-based recommender if collaborative filtering method doesn't offer sufficient reliable results.

1.5.6   Advantages of Hybrid Recommendation Systems

- Overcome the limitations of collaborative filtering, content-based and other systems.
- Recommendation results have been improved.
- Can work on sparse data also.

1.5.7   Shortcomings

- Expense have been increased.
- Complexity has been increased.
- External information is required which is not always available.

1.5.8   Other Recommendation Systems

a. *Demographic Filtering:* These systems use demographic data like age, gender, education, etc. for classifying groups of users. New user problem does not exist in such systems as they do not consider ratings for making recommendations. Though, it is hard today to gather sufficient demographic information due to online privacy concerns. These can be used with other systems as a hybrid model for better results.

b. *Knowledge-Based Filtering:* These systems use knowledge about users and their requirements/preferences to make suggestions [4]. Constraint-based systems belong to knowledge-based systems which recommend products that are seldom bought like car, house, etc.

1.6   Evaluation Metrics for Recommendation Engines

To evaluate the recommender system, different metrics are used like mean absolute error, root mean square error, precision, recall, F1 score, etc. [6, 8].

1. *Recall:* It is defined as percentage of products actually user liked and products actually suggested.

$$Recall = \frac{t_p}{t_p + f_n} \tag{9}$$

Here, in Equation 9 t_p refers to the number of products suggested by RS to a user and $t_p + f_n$ refers to the total products liked by users. Higher the value of recall better is the recommendation result.

2. *Precision:* It is defined as total number of products actually liked by user from all the products recommended by system.

$$Precision = \frac{t_p}{t_p + f_p} \tag{10}$$

Here, in Equation 10 t_p refers to the number of products suggested by RS to a user and $t_p + f_n$ refers to total products suggested. Higher the precision better is recommendation.

3. *Root Mean Squared Error (RMSE):* It is used to measure the error in the predicted values.

$$RMSE = \sqrt{\frac{\sum_{i=1}^{N} (Predicted_i - Actual_i)^2}{N}} \tag{11}$$

Here, in Equation 11 'Predicted' is the value given by the model and 'Actual' is the original value. Lower the RMSE value better is the recommendation.

4. *Mean Absolute Error (MAE):* It is used to compute the difference between actual and predicted value as given in Equation 12.

$$MAE = \frac{1}{N} \sum |Predicted - actual| \tag{12}$$

The smaller the *MAE* value better is the recommendation.

The below mentioned metrics considers the order of the product recommended so they are the ranking metrics:

MAP at *k* (Mean Average Precision at cutoff k): It is computed by selecting the subset of suggestions given by RS from rank 1 to rank *k* as given in Equation 13.

$$MAP_i = \frac{1}{|R_i|} \sum_{k=1}^{|R_i|} P(R_i[k]) \tag{13}$$

Higher the *MAP* value better is the recommendation.

1.7   Problems with Recommendation Systems and Possible Solutions

1. *Cold start problem:* When a new customer uses the system or new products are added to it, then this problem arises. The reason behind the problem is neither the system is able to predict the taste of the new users nor system contains the ratings of new products leading to unacceptable results. This issue can be resolved in many ways:
   a. By taking the ranking of some products from the customer at the beginning.
   b. By taking the users preferences and requirements explicitly.
   c. Recommending products to the customer depending on the gathered demographic information.
   User demographic information can be used to identify about the place, zip-code along with interactions of the new user with the system so that recommendations can be made on the basis of rankings given by other customers having similar demographic information. The products which are useful and good but are not rated yet are known as sleepers. To handles

the sleepers, different methods can be used like item popularity, linked open data, entropy and content-based methods.

2. *Synonym:* Two or more different words which represents to same object or meaning is known as synonym. But recommendation systems are not able to differentiate these words. For example, "comedy movie" and "comedy film" both words are considered different by a memory-based CF approach. Excessive use of synonyms reduces the performance of recommender system. To remove the synonym problems, many techniques like ontologies, Latent Semantic Indexing (LSI) and Single Value Decomposition (SVD) could be used.

3. *Shilling Attacks:* If a malicious user or competitor provides untruthful rankings to some products either to increase product visibility or to reduce the popularity, this type of attack is known as shilling attack. These attacks reduce the performance and quality of recommender system as well as break the faith of customers. CF based techniques are more prone to this threat as compared to the item-based CF approach. Bandwagon, average, random are different recommender systems attacks. To detect the attacks, various methods such as generic, hit ratio, model specific attributes and prediction shift are used. Different parameters to categorize the attack are aim of attack, size of attack, and prerequisite data to initialize the attack.

4. *Privacy:* Providing personal data to the recommender systems may increase the system performance but may lead to problems of data privacy and security. Users are reluctant to feed data into recommender systems that suffer from data privacy issues. Therefore, a recommender system, whether CB or CF, should build trust among their users, however CF recommenders are more prone to such privacy issues. In CF technique, user data including ratings are stored in a centralized repository which can be compromised resulting in data misuse. For this purpose, cryptographic mechanisms can be used by providing personalized recommendations without involving third parties and peer users. Other techniques include using randomized perturbation techniques, allowing users to publish their private data without exposing their identities, and using Semantic Web technologies especially ontologies in combination with NLP techniques

to mitigate the unwanted exposure of information. Limited Content Analysis and Overspecialization: Content-based recommenders rely on content about items and users to be processed by information retrieval techniques. The limited availability of content leads to problems including overspecialization. Here, items are represented by their subjective attributes, where selecting an item is based mostly on their subjective attributes. Features that represent user preferences in a better way are not taken into account. For many domains, content is either scarce such as books or it is challenging to obtain and represent the content such as movies. In such cases relevant items cannot be recommended unless the analyzed content contains enough information to be used in distinguishing items liked/disliked by the user. This also leads to representation of two different items with same set of features, where, e.g., well-written research articles can be difficult to distinguish from bad ones if both are represented with same set of keywords. Limited content analysis leads to overspecialization in which CB recommenders recommend items that are closely related to user profile and do not suggest novel items. In order to recommend novel and serendipitous items along with familiar items, we need to introduce additional hacks and note of randomness, which can be achieved by using genetic algorithms that brings diversity to recommendations being made. The problem is relatively small in CF recommenders where unexpected and novel items may get recommended.

5. *Grey Sheep:* Grey sheep is a scenario in which views of a customer do not match with any group and so, is not able to take advantages of suggestions. Pure CB filtering can resolve this issue where items are suggested by exploiting user personal profile and contents of items being recommended. Similarly, sparse rating and first rater in CF filtering can also be resolved by CB filtering. Integrating CB with CF techniques may also yield more serendipitous and novel suggestions. Grey sheep users can be identified and separated from other users by applying offline clustering techniques including k-mean clustering. This way performance gets better and recommendation error is minimal.

6. *Sparsity:* Due to large data set about the items, the catalogue and user unwillingness to make ratings about items cause

a profile which is dispersed in nature and will make wrong recommendation. In this method we use nearest neighbors but few ratings make it very hard to compute the results. Different techniques can be used like multi-dimensional recommendation model, demographic filtering, SVD methods, and using content-boosted CF algorithm to cope with this situation.

7. *Latency Problem:* CF based recommendation systems face latency problem when new products are added more often to the knowledgebase, in which the system recommends to already ranked products and newly inserted products are not yet ranked. With the help of CB filtering method waiting time of items can be reduced but it may lead to overspecialization. To handle this problem, the category-based method and user stereotype can be used. Various clustering methods can also be used to improve performance. To increase the scalability and accuracy of the system, model-based CF methods can also be utilized.

8. *Evaluation and the Availability of Online Datasets:* Quality of the recommender system can be determined by evaluating the system. Deciding the evaluation criteria and choosing appropriate metrics is the major challenge. Mostly systems estimate system results and procedures by considering test dataset and use metrics such as mean average error (MAE), Precision, and F-Measure for evaluation.

9. *Context-Awareness:* It uses all the information in which system is installed, e.g., time, the current location and the current activity. It is intended that data collected from mobile services is used for designing recommender systems and will contain the user's personal data collected from social networks. Collecting preferences of users and context-related information is the significant components to generate appropriate suggestions for the user. Information can be collected by detecting facial expressions, speech interpretations and physiological signals analysis.

1.7.1 Advantages of Recommendation Systems

1. It helps in increasing the average order value by displaying personalized options.
2. It helps in engaging shoppers.

3. It helps in increasing the number of items per order.
4. It can bring traffic to your site.
5. It helps in transforming the shoppers to clients.
6. It lowers the work and overhead.

1.7.2   Disadvantages of Recommendation Systems

1. Customer can make wrong choices, if biased recommendations are made by RS.
2. Sometimes, RS suggests wrong products and services by analyzing little or incomplete user information.

1.8   Applications of Recommender Systems

The most popular applications of recommender systems are as follows:

- Entertainment—making suggestions for videos, movies and music.
- Content—making suggestions for news, web articles, e-books, e-learning sites, etc.
- E-commerce—making suggestions for products and items likes electrical and electronic appliances [10].
- Services—making suggestions for different services like travel, houses to rent/sell, or match-making services.

Other detailed applications are:

- Search valuable products: RS provides a list of ranked products that meets best to user's requirements or satisfies all the user standards.
- Suggest a sequence: RS provides s list of the items that does not exactly match user criteria but it may be of user interest.
- Suggest a package: RS also provides a list of interrelated products like with the recommendation of camera; it recommends memory card and a cover.
- Only net-surfing: RS provides content of user interest to help people that browse without any objective.

References

1. Abbar, S., Bouzeghoub, M., Lopez, S. Context-aware recommender systems: A service-oriented approach, in: *3rd International Workshop on "Personalized Access, Profile Management, and Context Awareness in Databases"*, PersDB 2009 - In Conjunction with VLDB 2009.

2. Adomavicius, G., Sankaranarayanan, R., Sen, S., Tuzhilin, A., Incorporating contextual information in recommender systems using a multidimensional approach. *ACM Trans. Inf. Syst.*, 23, 1, 103–145, 2005.

3. Arazy, O., Kumar, N., Shapira, B., Improving social recommender systems. *IT Prof.*, 11, 4, 38–44, 2009.

4. Balabanovic, M. and Shoham, Y., Content-based, collaborative recommendation. *Commun. ACM*, 40, 3, 66–72, 1997.

5. Deshpande, M. and Karypis, G., Item-based top-n recommendation algorithms. *ACM Trans. Inf. Syst.*, 22, 1, 143–177, 2004.

6. Herlocker, J.L., Konstan, J.A., Terveen, L.G., Riedl, J.T., Evaluating collaborative filtering recommender systems. *ACM Trans. Inf. Syst.*, 22, 1, 5–53, 2004.

7. Linden, G., Smith, B., York, J., Amazon.com recommendations: Item-to-item collaborative filtering. *IEEE Internet Comput.*, 7, 1, 76–80, 2003.

8. McLaughlin, M.R. and Herlocker, J.L., A collaborative filtering algorithm and evaluation metric that accurately model the user experience, in: *Proc. of SIGIR '04*, SIGIR '04: Proceedings of the 27th annual international ACM SIGIR conference on Research and development in information retrieval, pp. 329-336, 2004.

9. Schafer, J.B., Frankowski, D., Herlocker, J., Sen, S., Collaborative filtering recommender systems, in: *The Adaptive Web*, pp. 291–324, Springer, Berlin/Heidelberg, 2007.

10. Sharda, N., *Tourism Informatics: Visual Travel Recommender Systems, Social Communities, and User Interface Design*, Information Science Reference, IGI-Global, 2009.

A Brief Model Overview of Personalized Recommendation to Citizens in the Health-Care Industry

Subhasish Mohapatra[1*] and Kunal Anand[2]

[1]Adamas University, Kolkata, West Bengal, India
[2]Kalinga Institute of Industrial Technology, Bhubaneswar, Odisha, India

Abstract

The Recommender System is one of the aspiring domains in today's information and communication technology world. The recommender system does a metric analysis and determine if the recommended product is relevant or not for a user. A recommender system analyzes a large amount of unstructured data for intelligent mining. In recommender system, the procedure of delivering an explanation is based on an intelligent collaborative filtering process for decision making. In this context, the collaborative filtering-based recommendation system model has become an indispensable tool for future decision insemination to end-user. The recommender system avails valuable information from citizens, doctors, pharmacists, and market analysts to create a datastore where the decision logic and collaborative filtering can be applied to disseminate recommendation to the citizens for the service they need in due course of time. This chapter provides an insight into the implementation of the recommender system in both tangible and non-tangible products as well as the service care industry. With the implementation of this recommender system model, the remedial solution for citizens will gain a new momentum. The recent research needs a large volume of products or medical data to ensure its quality and trustworthiness. By the advancement of research, this model will derive valuable outcome. This model is a context-specific recommendation system that will grow further after data collection and learning. In this chapter, we provide the detailed theoretical framework of the flow chart-based recommender system in the health care model that strongly supports transparency, trustworthiness, and validity.

Corresponding author: mohapatra.subhasish@gmail.com

Sachi Nandan Mohanty, Jyotir Moy Chatterjee, Sarika Jain, Ahmed A. Elngar and Priya Gupta (eds.)
Recommender System with Machine Learning and Artificial Intelligence: Practical Tools and Applications in Medical, Agricultural and Other Industries, (27–44) © 2020 Scrivener Publishing LLC

Keywords: Recommendation system, intelligent mining, context-based, collaborative filtering

2.1 Introduction

To visualize the implementation details of a recommender system, we need to use case analysis that can suggest different domain-specific analyses for different sets of problems in real-life scenarios. Let's dwell upon some common recommendation models with a variety of contents. Some of them are as discussed below.

1. To watch which movie: Nowadays, it is the area of suggestion on social networking sites. It takes the sentiment analysis of users in word count format and classifies them as good, average or bad by doing case analysis in machine learning. The common set of machine learning principle is used for binary classification, decision tree, random forest, etc. [15, 24, 31].

2. To buy which stock: This is a useful recommendation for mutual fund investors who need stock market recommendations before buying or selling the product. It is based on historical analysis of stocks in year wise manner and it affects the mutual fund buying pattern by the investor. Stock market behavior and growth of mutual fund in cascading year is being analyzed by different machine learning principles. For example, random forest, support vector machine, regression analysis, etc. It tremendously looks into different aspects of stock market data i.e. growth pattern, buying behavior of people, and predicts the mutual funds that will give a handsome amount of return in the long term or short term as it can affect the buyer's financial transaction [3, 11, 21, 29].

3. Which product we buy: Here, the system will analyze the number of transactions for a specific product and consumer satisfaction rate that controls the frequent purchase behavior. A product is considered as good if it carries high demand. It has a great impact on the profit margin for a company as in the past many products abolished from the market due to lag in proper recommendations by the user. Further, it can control the peer to peer consumer buying

behavior. The consumer care products range from baby care products to personal care, from medicine to garment, from electronic products to application over the internet, etc. This paradigm shift can motivate a set of people for any particular product. It is the new era of marketing. The segment analysis by researchers, rather, show that only casing movie star for the product advertisement will not give it a hike if it is not being understood by the owner. The novelty pattern lies if more consumers share the satisfaction story after using any product and it tremendously makes an impact on the market share of a company [1, 19, 26].

In all these domains, one thing is common that we will discuss over here. Every company wants to increase customer satisfaction to maximize the sale of their product for more market penetration. Irrespective of use case, the data set is taken in this format Customer-Id, Product-Id, Number of transactions in units, Consumer rating, Transaction date, Demographic, psychographic, and cultural shift that can affect the recommendation system. Here, we focus on the following facts in the recommendation system:

1. The methods used for demonstrating the recommendation system: content-based, collaborative filtering, and clustering [17].
2. How the evaluation metrics work? We give a clear-cut insight upon statistical accuracy metric, and decision support accuracy metric.
3. Changing the behavior pattern of users and study of the attributes that can shift the buying behavior of a consumer.

2.2   Methods Used in Recommender System

2.2.1   Content-Based

There are two vital methods which are the pillars of building recommendation system: content-based and collaborative filtering. In this subsection, we discuss the merit of each one of them in real-life scenarios and why it is suitable for building a recommender system model. The new age recommender system extracts the best features of the recommendation systems and termed it as a hybrid recommendation system [24].

In content-based techniques, as shown in Figure 2.1, we find to match the same set of users and the content they visit or loved to buy. Though in this mechanism we collect attribute field of users and products, we take the highest score of similarity into account. In a movie recommender system, we identify the attribute fields like the direction team, actors, period of movie, movie length, movie genre like periodical, romantic, comedy, suspense thriller, adult content, or family, etc. To establish the similarity between movies, the feature named audience experience after watching the movie, is extracted and then the sentiment analysis of word count is performed on data profile. This is collectively taken as a movie review. The idea behind content-based system is to create a profile for each user and each item base of the Tf-idf score (term frequency-inverse document frequency). It further reflects the weight factor for information retrieval. It is used in text data mining in search engine optimization for scoring and ranking a document. Term frequency is conceptualized as how many times a term occurs in a document. Inverse document frequency is a measure of how much information the word provides. The amount of information provided by a word can be measured by inverse document frequency, idf. Following example discusses the concept of term frequency and inverse document frequency [23].

Example-1: (Tf-idf)
Document-1 (d1)

that	1
Are	1
An	2

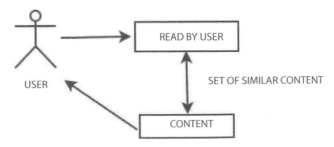

Figure 2.1 Content-based recommendation.

fruit	1

Document-2(d2)

that	1
Are	1
rather	2
example	3

Tf ("that", d1) =1/5=0.2

Tf ("that", d2)1/7=0.14

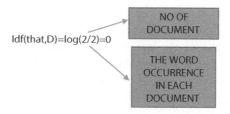

So, the (Tf-IDF) for the word "that" implies that from mining point of view, this particular word do not provide much information.

Tf-idf ("that", d1, D) = 0.2 * 0 = 0, Tf-idf ("that", d2, D) = 0.4 * 0 = 0.

There are multiple ways to do a user-profile analysis to determine the similarity between users and items. We must have to give impeccable attention to this phenomenon. The enigmatic feature extraction used in this is Cosine similarity and Jaccard similarity.

$$\text{Cosine}(x,y) = \frac{\sum_{i=1}^{n} x_i y_i}{\sqrt{\sum_{i=1}^{n} x_i^2} \sqrt{\sum_{i=1}^{n} y_i^2}} \qquad (1)$$

The similarity between user and item that delivers the user-item similarity pattern is established by Cosine similarity. The beauty of cosine similarity lies in its high dimensional feature mapping in the domain of information retrieval and text mining.

$$\text{Jacard}(x, y) = mod \frac{x \cap y}{x \cup y} \tag{2}$$

It is an equation that is used to derive item–item similarity. Here we analyze the item vector with each other and return a most similar item. It is well suited for item-item similarity for ranking establishment [20].

2.2.2   Collaborative Filtering

The recommender system uses this technique more frequently to establish social filtering by collecting user experiences. It can analyze the similarity pattern among users or items in a very sensible way.

The first approach under collaborative filtering is item to item approach where we concentrate on the neighborhood analysis, as shown in Figure 2.2. Consider that the user-1 has the same opinion about a product as of user-2 then the behavior content of the emotion of both the users is suitable for establishing the collaborative filtering.

Another approach is the classification filtering. It is a learning method that is used to determine which class the product will lie after classifying its behavior attributes more collaboratively. In a broad sense, collaborative filtering is divided into memory-based (calculating neighborhood) and

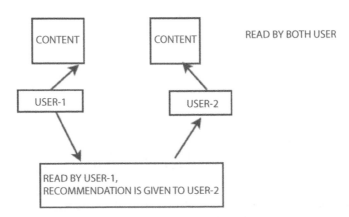

Figure 2.2 Collaborative filtering.

model-based (Using different data mining techniques: Bayesian network, clustering, semantic analysis).

2.2.3   Hybrid Filtering

A huge number of online users have trust in recommender systems. It delivers an explanation about an item that why is it recommended for a specific set of users. This technique has gathered attention in helping users with quality decision making. The working mechanism relies upon the accuracy of the model. So, before implementing, the author must recommend to study the theoretical aspect of the proposed model and must instantiate its effectiveness in a real-world environment. Nowadays, the recommender system hugely impacts people's lives. So, the growing need of users upon the recommendation system must ensure its ability to explain, its consistency and diversity. Hybrid filtering leverages the beauty of both content and collaborative data. This method has the potential to tackle both content and collaborative data in its term and combine the efforts of both to produce a system from their strategic advantage. It uses accuracy metric techniques for more user centrist evaluation for delivering recommendations. The proposed model described in Figure 2.5, concentrates on collecting user argument, like or dislike attribute list, demographic data, range of financial reimbursement, product/person choice, category, etc. Adhering to those attribute lists, we must build a suggestion-explanation metric window for the user. It must ensure lucid presentation quality in explanation. It tied closely to domain-specific attributes and characteristics of specific data available. A hybrid filtering based explanation in the recommender system calculates the product affinity with a similar set of users that can further emerge as a better-matched pair.

2.3   Related Work

Numerous studies from the past about various research aspects have gathered the effect and impact of explanation in the performance of the recommender system. The transparency, trust, effectiveness, and satisfaction of the recommender system is controlled by its explanation characteristics [14].

The Collaborative filtering technique explains the various facets of the recommender environment. That further evaluates several explanation attributes like satisfaction, efficiency, product review, success recovery rate of patients by a specific doctor, medicine review by a user and its impact either positive or negative feedback, which can completely compensate the explanation style of recommender systems [12].

In this section, we explain a theoretical prototype framework of doctor and medicine explanation model to a user in real-time scenarios. Allocating the recommender system and its effect on social networking platform tremendously impacts the decision-making behavior of other users. For example, App reviews, consumer care reviews, movie reviews can shift the behavior pattern of a user after they visit the review status of peer members in the group. Explanation in the recommender system can be termed as a bit of information that serves for a variety of goals such as the need for explanation in commercial product transaction and medicine recommendation after realizing the patient's need. Explanation increases the performance of the recommender system. It was also noticed that the recommender system with an explanation enhances the user acceptance rate. Explanation can span across several disciplines such as intelligent systems, chat-bots, human–machine interactions. The major objective of this chapter is to give an overview of the area of explanation in recommender systems. The utility of explanation in the recommender system will witness as an effective and reliable remote solution for end-users. In this section, we go through different explanation techniques used for making predictions in recommender systems. Most of the techniques use machine learning for simulating user behavior. Nowadays, people are more aware of the information available online while selecting a product or service. Mostly, they select things based on the explanation based ranking system. The logic of the recommender system has already been discussed in section-I. Moreover, this ranking criteria for any service the citizen seeks to use is a novel adoptive machine learning technique that delivers a suitable recommendation with the explanation to the service seeker. It is a concrete mechanism that enhances the coverage and quality of service of any product over digital media. Here, we contribute to an explanation-based recommender system theoretical framework for the health care domain for an easy understanding of explanation in the recommender system. Moreover, the explanation routine in recommender system opens a new channel i.e. innovative form of ICT to address the need of people and encompassing substantial service deployment in real-time. Most notably, in developing countries like India mobile penetration to remote geographical jurisdiction overcome the problem of inaccessibility of recommender system service [7, 16].

2.4   Types of Explanation

The fundamental exploration of the recommender system is still at the nascent stage. For this, it needs a unified essence theory for classification that is described below.

1. Functional explanation: This explanation that deals with the functional and behavioral study of the system.
2. Causal explanation: This variety of explanation deals with the event tracking and establishing causal relationship among them.
3. Intentional explanation: It deals with the cognitive study of human behavior analysis.
4. Scientific explanation: It is used to do speculative analysis in the scientific field.

Explanation for categorizing the users based on the item purchased falls into following three varieties as discussed below:

1. Item-based: Item is the primary focus of categorization that classifies the user based on, what item the user is likely to buy.
2. User-based: Based on user behavior, the explanation controls event for the recommender system.
3. Feature-based: The impact of the product upon the user is a major criterion of explanation in this segment.

The explanation for operating a recommender system is categorized as below.

1. User triggered explanation: When the user seeks request or response about any specific product then this explanation has the potential to resolve this request scenario.
2. Spontaneous explanation: The user has no control over it. It establishes an analogy with the progress of the event as per the time demand.
3. Knowledge-based explanation: It is the method of giving a hypothetical explanation for quick learning [9, 13, 33].

2.5 Explanation Methodology

Some well-known algorithms influence the style of the recommender system. These algorithms deliver the implicit method of explanation to trigger the execution of an explanation in a module. The style of explanation is coupled with an aspect of advice to give a thoughtful impact upon user selection. The primary objective of the explanation method is given in Figure 2.3. In this section, we overview the explanation styles.

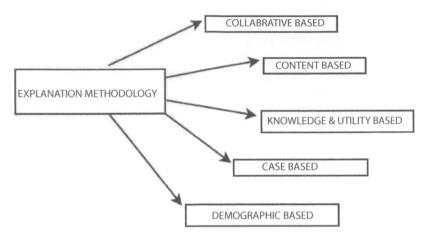

Figure 2.3 Category of explanation.

2.5.1   Collaborative-Based

The insight of a collaborative-based algorithm strives to represent behavior that helps visitors over the internet for their product selection. It gives input to the recommender system in the form of users' ratings about any item. So, this algorithm searches for users with the same set of ratings about any specific product. The nearest neighborhood technique explains the behavior of this algorithm. Here, a similar set of users are represented as neighbors. Most commercial website uses this approach to increasing the sale of their product over the internet. For example, when a customer visits a watch section then the probable accessories list of the watch is recommended to the user. Moreover, it also recommends the item which the user has viewed recently [21, 33].

2.5.2   Content-Based

This explanation style incorporates quality and content dimensions before making the recommendation to the user.

It conceptualizes the similarity between items. The keyword style explanation (KSE) and tag style explanation (TSE) is included in this type. Generally, it drags the user's sentiment towards their preference over any product based on the nature of tag. Here, the tag plays a driving factor in the selection of any item. The content-based technique relies upon data i.e. the user provides either explicitly (by giving rating or feedback) or implicitly by navigating to any link. It is based on the relevance of data ordering in a user profile. Based on the above method, the user profile is generated which is then used to deliver suggestions to the user. Here we come across two terms named item and attribute. Item refers to the content whose attributes are used in the recommender system i.e. movies, books, etc. The attribute is coined as the properties of an item i.e. well-known movie tag, motivating catch line for any product. Here Tf-idf is used to generate a data profile for learning purposes in data science. Tf-idf is explained with an example in section-1 [22, 28, 37].

2.5.3   Knowledge and Utility-Based

This algorithm is well suited for a particular type of recommender system that depends upon the explicit knowledge of the item assortment, user preference. Knowledge acquisition plays a vital role in this algorithm.

It came into existence were collaborative and content filtering were unable to provide a suitable explanation. The major strength of this algorithm is, it can efficiently work in complex domain i.e. for real estate purchase, car, tourist destination, or any luxury expensive item. Though Ratings and reviews deliver efficiency in the above two algorithms but it can't meet the criteria for the above two products. To articulate user experience, this algorithm proposed a strong analogy to increase the user's trust.

It creates a knowledge domain to analyze user response. It catches the user's experience through some tricky questions, and it builds a strong analogy to enhance the user's trust. It creates a knowledge domain to collect user interaction experience and catches user's data through a conversational platform. The variant data set of user argument in knowledge base mine the user for the specific product based on previous successful learning i.e. given in Figure 2.4. As per matching data, ranking is done for this algorithm [15, 23, 26].

Constraint satisfaction graph is used for sorting user preference and generate a DAG (direct acyclic graph) to compose a chain of user argument.

2.5.4   Case-Based

It adopts a proactive technique of persuasiveness for the case analysis which is composed of too many queries and responses. Here, the case indicates a similar item set for a group of users. It is used to deliver a recommendation that rely upon the product getting high score, rather it is an influential style of recommendation. It counts similarity in the domain-independent approach. It is a form of content-based recommendation which is well suited for many recommendation engines. This approach makes a judicious explanation of product similarity to improve quality.

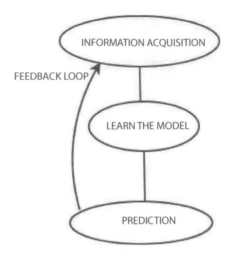

Figure 2.4 Information acquisition in knowledge-based explanation.

It adheres to case-based reasoning (CBR) in which piles of cases (previously solved cases and solutions) play a major role when any new case comes for analysis. Mostly, in this approach one learning technique is used where a similar case with a solution that has acclaimed highest user response or score, is used to solve the newborn case. CBR is a multi-step reasoning strategy that is based on problem specification and retrieval. It catches user query or response as problem specification and retrieves the knowledge that has received the highest score for a similar set of cases. A case-based technique adopts the best matching estimation to explain [33].

2.5.5   Demographic-Based

This algorithm categorizes the users depending on the selection of attributes and further the recommendations are established that are based on demographic classes. Age, sex, area is known as demographic information. For example, if it is given in a site that 70% of people of your age use this product and getting benefits. Many commercial sites and industries have adopted this strategy as it is not too complex and the implementation is also simple. In demographic-based recommender system, a proper market research is needed along with the cultural value of citizens in the specified region, accompanied by a short survey report to accumulate data for categorization. Though, demographic techniques use different data, it forms "people-to-people" correlations like collaborative ones. As compared with the collaborative and content-based recommender systems, the demographic approach does not require a history of user ratings, which makes it more beneficial. This approach focuses on demographic contextual information before explaining [28].

2.6   Proposed Theoretical Framework for Explanation-Based Recommender System in Health-Care Domain

Nowadays, the health-care based recommender system is gradually gaining acceptance among users. An understandable flowchart is needed to elaborate the explanation-based recommender systems to the users.

This collaborative case-based explanation system in health-care provides an effective and acceptable explanation to the user as a conceptual model. To address the necessity of explanation in the recommender system the flow chart is given in Section 3.1. In Figure 2.4, we have already explained the working principle behind the recommender system.

In this chapter, we performed a survey upon explanation in the recommender system. Moreover, in this section, a theoretical framework has been represented that organizes the human–computer interface (HCI) and machine learning perspective for explainable recommendation analysis. Explain ability and effectiveness are the two divergent dimensions for better explain ability in complex recommendation model. So, the proposed framework will serve an attractive dimension in explain ability for a personalized recommendation to the user.

Health-care recommendation explanation is generated here by collecting information from three sources i.e. patients, doctors, and pharmacists given as in Figure 2.5. Here, in this model, HCI is the kiosk through which the doctor, user, and patient can give their information and a machine learning algorithm works beneath this model for data mining by decision tool and delivers personalized information to the user.

2.7   Flowchart

Step-1

This is the kiosk that is enabled over the internet. Here, the patients, pharmacists, and doctors can register themselves to access the attributes over health interface.

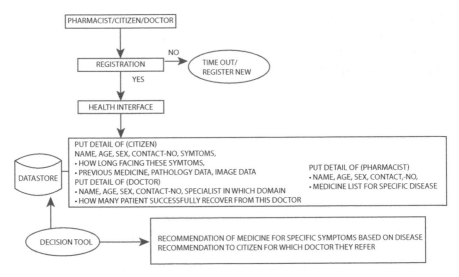

Figure 2.5 Online explanation-based recommender system for health-care.

Step-2

When the registration is successful, the person can access the health interface and submit their details. A unique-id will be generated for each person in a hospital/or network of hospitals if they follow this pattern of data acquisition in an explanation-based recommender system.

Step-3

The details from each person are stored in a data store. It is a conglomeration of a variety of data. Decision logic (classification, fuzzy IF-Then rule, decision tree) will recommend the explanation to the users for doctor selection or intake of medicine remotely. Decision-making philosophy is a cognitive process in the artificial intelligence domain. it is a separate application module i.e. classifying disease, from the User entry (symptom list, X-ray, pathology report, etc.). Decision tree logic gives doctor allocation to the patient after analyzing the symptoms. Maximum recovery rate of patient from a doctor is decided by the rank function model fidelity rate as mentioned below:

Model Fidelity = |explainable items ∩ recommended items|/ |recommended items|

It controls the quality of explanation in model. It is a futuristic model that controls the autonomy in the health-care sector, and the middlemen can't influence any citizens exorbitantly.

Step-4

It provides personalized support to online users. It exploits domain knowledge more transparently. In this model, explanations like which disease, what symptoms, and the medications they have to continue till they have not recovered fully, are provided to the patients. Item matches for a particular disease and the corresponding medical professional with the highest success rate is recommended to the patient for treatment.

2.8   Conclusion

There exist multiple perspectives to explore an explanation-based recommendation system, which works for different application scenarios either actively or passively. The emerging research environment of the recommender system needs an explanation for the system's trustworthiness. So, in this aspect, we provide a brief overview of the explanation-based recommender system for the health-care domain. This is a kiosk-based theoretical framework that can serve explanation significantly for user queries. Explanation plays a major role in recommender systems. The lack of explain ability in the recommendation system decreases user persuasiveness, rather it is a support for retrieving information with evidence. Recently, deep neural network has been used in many scenarios of explanation. The complexity behind many recommendation systems should be further highlighted. In this survey, we provide an outlook on the future of explainable recommendation model in health-care. A recommendation model would not only be effective by providing high-quality recommendations but also qualitative explanation.

References

1. Van Barneveld, J. and Van Setten, M., Designing usable interfaces for TV recommender systems, in: *Personalized Digital Television*, pp. 259–285, Springer, Dordrecht, 2004.
2. Bilgic, M. and Mooney, R.J., Explaining recommendations: Satisfaction vs. promotion, in: *Beyond Personalization Workshop*, vol. 5, p. 153, IUI, International Conference on Intelligent User Interfaces, 2005.
3. Friedrich, G. and Zanker, M., A taxonomy for generating explanations in recommender systems. *AI Mag.*, 32, 3, 90–98, 2011.

4. Gedikli, F., Ge, M., Jannach, D., Understanding recommendations by reading the clouds, in: *International Conference on Electronic Commerce and Web Technologies*, Berlin, Heidelberg, Springer, pp. 196–208, 2011.
5. Gönül, M.S., Önkal, D., Lawrence, M., The effects of structural characteristics of explanations on use of a DSS. *Decis. Support Syst.*, 42, 3, 1481–1493, 2006.
6. Herlocker, J.L., Konstan, J.A., Riedl, J., Explaining collaborative filtering recommendations, in: *Proceedings of the 2000 ACM Conference on Computer supported Cooperative Work*, ACM, Cambridge University Press, pp. 241–250, 2000.
7. Jannach, D., Zanker, M., Felfernig, A., Friedrich, G., *Recommender systems: an introduction*, New York, Cambridge University Press, 2010.
8. Mandl, M., Felfernig, A., Teppan, E., Schubert, M., Consumer decision making in knowledge-based recommendation. *J. Intell. Inf. Syst.*, 37, 1, 1–22, 2011.
9. Pu, P. and Chen, L., Trust building with explanation interfaces, in: *Proceedings of the 11th International Conference on Intelligent User Interfaces*, ACM, pp. 93–100, 2006, January.
10. Sharma, A. and Cosley, D., Do social explanations work? Studying and modeling the effects of social explanations in recommender systems, in: *Proceedings of the 22nd International Conference on World Wide Web*, ACM, pp. 1133–1144, 2013, May.
11. Symeonidis, P., Nanopoulos, A., Manolopoulos, Y., MoviExplain: a recommender system with explanations. *RecSys*, 9, 317–320, 2009.
12. Tintarev, N. and Masthoff, J., Effective explanations of recommendations: user-centered design, in: *Proceedings of the 2007 ACM Conference on Recommender systems*, ACM, pp. 153–156, 2007, October.
13. Tintarev, N. and Masthoff, J., The effectiveness of personalized movie explanations: An experiment using commercial meta-data, in: *International Conference on Adaptive Hypermedia and Adaptive Web-Based Systems*, Berlin, Heidelberg, Springer, pp. 204–213, 2008, July.
14. Tintarev, N. and Masthoff, J., A survey of explanations in recommender systems, in: *2007 IEEE 23rd International Conference on Data Engineering Workshop*, IEEE, pp. 801–810, 2007, April.
15. Tintarev, N. and Masthoff, J., Designing and evaluating explanations for recommender systems, in: *Recommender Systems Handbook*, pp. 479–510, Springer, Boston, MA, 2011.
16. Tintarev, N. and Masthoff, J., Effective explanations of recommendations: user-centered design, in: *Proceedings of the 2007 ACM Conference on Recommender Systems*, ACM, pp. 153–156, 2007, October.
17. Tintarev, N. and Masthoff, J., Evaluating the effectiveness of explanations for recommender systems. *User Model. User-Adap.*, 22, 4–5, 399–439, 2012.
18. Tintarev, N. and Masthoff, J., Over-and underestimation in different product domains, in: *Workshop on Recommender Systems associated with ECAI*, Springer, Boston, MA, Recommender Systems Handbook, pp. 14–19, 2008.

19. Vig, J., Sen, S., Riedl, J., Tagsplanations: explaining recommendations using tags, in: *Proceedings of the 14th International Conference on Intelligent User Interfaces*, ACM, pp. 47–56, 2009, February.

20. Sharma, R. and Ray, S., Explanations in recommender systems: an overview. *IJBIS.*, 23, 2, 248–262, 2016.

21. Mohamed, M.H., Khafagy, M.H., Ibrahim, M.H., Recommender Systems Challenges and Solutions Survey, in: *2019 International Conference on Innovative Trends in Computer Engineering (ITCE)*, IEEE, pp. 149–155, 2019, February.

22. Aciar, S., Zhang, D., Simoff, S., Debenham, J., Recommender system based on consumer product reviews, in: *Proceedings of the 2006 IEEE/WIC/ACM international Conference on Web Intelligence*, IEEE Computer Society, pp. 719–723, 2006, December.

23. Shobana, V. and Kumar, N., A personalized recommendation engine for prediction of disorders using big data analytics, in: *2017 International Conference on Innovations in Green Energy and Healthcare Technologies (IGEHT)*, IEEE, pp. 1–4, 2017, March.

24. Zhong, Z. and Li, Y., A Recommender System for Healthcare Based on Human-Centric Modeling, in: *2016 IEEE 13th International Conference on e-Business Engineering (ICEBE)*, IEEE, pp. 282–286, 2016, November.

25. Zhang, Y. and Chen, X., Explainable recommendation: A survey and new perspectives, 2018. https://arxiv.org/abs/1804.11192v8.

26. Wang, N., Wang, H., Jia, Y., Yin, Y., Explainable recommendation via multitask learning in opinionated text data, in: *The 41st International ACM SIGIR Conference on Research & Development in Information Retrieval*, ACM, pp. 165–174, 2018, June.

27. Wang, W. and Benbasat, I., Recommendation agents for electronic commerce: Effects of explanation facilities on trusting beliefs. *JMIS.*, 23, 4, 217–246, 2007.

28. Wang, X., He, X., Feng, F., Nie, L., Chua, T.S., Tem: Tree-enhanced embedding model for explainable recommendation, in: *Proceedings of the 2018 World Wide Web Conference*, International World Wide Web Conferences Steering Committee, pp. 1543–1552, 2018, April.

29. Wang, X., Chen, Y., Yang, J., Wu, L., Wu, Z., Xie, X., A Reinforcement Learning Framework for Explainable Recommendation, in: *2018 IEEE International Conference on Data Mining (ICDM)*, IEEE, pp. 587–596, 2018, November.

30. Wu, L., Quan, C., Li, C., Wang, Q., Zheng, B., Luo, X., A context-aware user-item representation learning for item recommendation. *ACM T. Inform. Syst. (TOIS)*, 37, 2, 22, 2019.

31. Wu, Y., DuBois, C., Zheng, A.X., Ester, M., Collaborative denoising autoencoders for top-n recommender systems, in: *Proceedings of the Ninth ACM International Conference on Web Search and Data Mining*, ACM, pp. 153–162, 2016, February.

32. Wu, Y. and Ester, M., Flame: A probabilistic model combining aspect-based opinion mining and collaborative filtering, in: *Proceedings of the Eighth ACM*

International Conference on Web Search and Data Mining, ACM, pp. 199–208, 2015, February.

33. Xian, Y., Fu, Z., Muthukrishnan, S., de Melo, G., Zhang, Y., Reinforcement Knowledge Graph Reasoning for Explainable Recommendation, 2019. https://doi.org/10.1145/3331184.3331203

34. Zhang, Y., Ai, Q., Chen, X., Wang, P., Learning over knowledge-base embeddings for recommendation, 2018. https://arxiv.org/pdf/1803.06540.pdf.

35. Costa, F., Ouyang, S., Dolog, P., Lawlor, A., Automatic generation of natural language explanations, in: *Proceedings of the 23rd International Conference on Intelligent User Interfaces Companion*, ACM, p. 57, 2018, March.

36. Jang, E., Gu, S., Poole, B., Categorical reparameterization with gumbel-softmax, 2016. https://arxiv.org/abs/1611.01144.

37. Lillicrap, T.P., Hunt, J.J., Pritzel, A., Heess, N., Erez, T., Tassa, Y., Wierstra, D., Continuous control with deep reinforcement learning, 2015. https://arxiv.org/abs/1509.02971.

38. Zheng, L., Noroozi, V., Yu, P.S., Joint deep modeling of users and items using reviews for recommendation, in: *Proceedings of the Tenth ACM International Conference on Web Search and Data Mining*, ACM, pp. 425–434, 2017, February.

39. Chen, J., Zhang, H., He, X., Nie, L., Liu, W., Chua, T.S., Attentive collaborative filtering: Multimedia recommendation with item-and component-level attention, in: *Proceedings of the 40th International ACM SIGIR conference on Research and Development in Information Retrieval*, ACM, pp. 335–344, 2017, August.

40. Chen, X., Zhang, Y., Xu, H., Cao, Y., Qin, Z., Zha, H., Visually explainable recommendation, 2018. https://arxiv.org/pdf/1801.10288.

41. Zhang, Y. and Chen, X., Explainable recommendation: A survey and new perspectives, https://arxiv.org/abs/1804.11192, 2018.

42. Lee, D.D. and Seung, H.S., Algorithms for non-negative matrix factorization, in: *Advances in Neural Information Processing Systems*, Massachusetts Institute of Technology Press, pp. 556–562, 2001.

43. Wang, H., Wang, N., Yeung, D.Y., Collaborative deep learning for recommender systems, in: *Proceedings of the 21th ACM SIGKDD International Conference on Knowledge Discovery and Data Mining*, ACM, pp. 1235–1244, 2015, August.

2Es of TIS: A Review of Information Exchange and Extraction in Tourism Information Systems

Malik M. Saad Missen[1]*, Mickaël Coustaty[2], Hina Asmat[1], Amnah Firdous[3], Nadeem Akhtar[1], Muhammad Akram[4] and V. B. Surya Prasath[5]

[1]*Department of Computer Science and Information Technology, The Islamia University of Bahawalpur, Pakistan*
[2]*Laboratoire Informatique, Image et Interaction (L3i), Facultès des Sciences et Technologies, University of La Rochelle, France*
[3]*Department of Computer Science, COMSATS University, Islamabad, Pakistan*
[4]*Virtual University of Pakistan, Lahore, Pakistan*
[5]*Department of Electrical Engineering and Computer Science, University of Cincinnati, Ohio, United States*

Abstract

Tourism industry could be one of the largest sources of revenue for any country. After the emergence of Web 2.0, it is also one of the largest data intensive industries in the world. Tourism-rich countries often use Tourism Information Systems (TIS) for management of tourism-related data. These systems are used are used on several levels of tourism stakeholder's hierarchy from data generation and exchange to intelligent decision making. Data exchange and extraction are core tasks that a generic TIS is supposed to perform. In this chapter, we discuss both of these processes with respect to TIS. We describe the importance of these processes and review how these are being dealt by researchers currently. Further, we highlight the limitations of current approaches of data exchange and extraction and identify potent future solutions that can enhance the performance of TIS in many aspects can drive future recommender systems.

Keywords: Information extraction, opinion extraction, information exchange, tourism information system, tourism tecommender system

*Corresponding author: saad.missen@iub.edu.pk

Sachi Nandan Mohanty, Jyotir Moy Chatterjee, Sarika Jain, Ahmed A. Elngar and Priya Gupta (eds.) *Recommender System with Machine Learning and Artificial Intelligence: Practical Tools and Applications in Medical, Agricultural and Other Industries,* (45–70) © 2020 Scrivener Publishing LLC

3.1   Introduction

Tourism industry makes up 9% of the world's GDP (World Tourism and Tourism Council—https://www.wttc.org). It is considered an umbrella industry because it incorporates many related industries like culture, sports, agriculture, etc. Besides this, tourism helps development of small and medium scale industry development hence contributing to economic growth of local population. Taking example of European Union, local hotels, bars, motels and restaurants makeup almost 8.5% of the world's enterprises, and 95.5% of these enterprises are small. Generally, the objective of the tourism-related SME's is to promote the tourism in their region and help the government to increase the number of tourists each year. Taking example of France for the year 2013, the number of foreign tourists to France reached 84.7 million which represented a 2% increase from the previous year 2012 when 83 million visited the country. France is aiming to bring this number to 100 million for the year 2014–2015. With this increasing number of tourists each year, the volumes of data generated by these tourists (by using mobile application, online reservations, currency exchange, etc.) and relevant tourism agencies (i.e. online reservation web sites, online tourism recommendations, sites for recommending packages and deals for tourists, etc.) is increasing exponentially.

Tourism Information Systems (TISs) are used by tourism related stakeholders to monitor all pertinent information. A particular TIS may target the tourists [20, 32], tourist administrators (like tourism offices or ministry of tourism etc.) [45] or both as its users [47]. In this work we discuss the textual data challenges of TIS's with respect to tourism administrators (we call management TIS's onwards). Few examples are given in Table 3.1 of tourist information (or recommendation) systems. For further details we refer the reader to the survey works by [3] and [23].

The specific objectives and functions of these management TISs could change from organization to organization but main objectives generally remain same and are listed below:

- To add tourism related information in TIS.
- To extract information from the current data available which can help administrators to form better tourism policies and take better decisions.
- To prepare data for data exchange with other TISs.
- To perform information extraction tasks to seek knowledge from the data available.

Table 3.1 Examples of available tourist information systems (TIS).

No.	Title	Description	Web reference
1	AMBISENSE	Objective of this system is to design and implement technology that is context-sensitive i.e. adaptive to its users	www.ambiesense.com
2	CAPITALS ITTS	This system was developed to provide a single platform for integration of all tourism related services to users of five EU capitals	www.eu-capitals.net
3	CRUMPET	Targeted its mobile audience i.e. its aim was to provide tourism related services for all users accessing it through mobile	www.ist-crumpet.org
4	DIETORECS	A recommendation system to guide its users with its intelligent destination decision making	dietorecs.itc.it
5	LiveCities	This system uses user's context i.e. location, personal information to provide relevant information to its users. Provided information can be plain text, audio, video or HTML	8wires.io/opensource/livecities
6	PersonalTour	Used by travel agencies to provide the best and economical packages to their customers according to their preferences	www.igiglobal.com/chapter/personaltour-multi-agentrecommender/56441
7	VISIT	Applies sentiment analysis techniques on information collected from Facebook and Twitter to recommend "must visit places" to its users	Scisweb.ulster.ac.uk/kevin/pgnet12-kevin.pdf

- To provide statistics relevant to tourism on region level.
- To provide a user-friendly graphical user interface to its users (tourism administrators).
- To enable the tourist destinations administrators in managing as well as incorporating a sustainable tourism with respect to related local industries.
- To enable the stakeholders by including an appropriate response mechanism for the fluid market environment which is the common norm nowadays.
- To provide strong foundation to enhance the management structure capability by using available information infrastructure.

Generally, management TISs are structured to serve on both levels i.e. at national and regional levels. Mostly, a management TIS contains the following main three aspects:

- Performance—Yearly economic indicators, record of flights, statistics of how the travel systems performs, etc.
- Product Inventory—Record of accommodations, along with carriers, cruise, attractions within the systems. This also includes information about the tourist's destinations
- Marketing—Current market trends, information status of market, etc.

There has been lot of research in development of TISs since 1990s focusing on different challenges. However, the challenges for development of TIS evolved with the passage of time. In this chapter, we discuss two major aspects of TIS i.e. information exchange and information extraction. We simply highlight current techniques being used for these purposes and discuss challenges associated with these techniques and we also propose the techniques regarding future perspectives of these aspects of TIS.

We discuss these aspects of TIS in following salient topics:

- Information Exchange
  1. Exchange of Tourism Objects Data.
  2. Exchange of Statistical Data.
- Information Extraction
  1. Sentiment Extraction.
  2. Time and Event Extraction.

We organized the chapter in the following way. In Section 3.2 we discuss the information exchange aspect of TIS. In Section 3.3 we discuss information extraction aspect with details on opinion and temporal (along with event) extractions. In Section 3.4, we discuss the sentiment annotation, and we conclude our chapter with remarks in Section 3.5.

3.2   Information Exchange

Information exchange is an important concept in Information System Architecture [14]. There are two parties that are required for accomplishing exchange of information, one acts as a sender while the other receives it. In general information systems these two parties can be systems, organizations, humans [17]. A TIS is also supposed to communicate with other TISs for exchanging data among them. It is one of the most important functions of a TIS which helps collecting more data and validating its current data. Generally, TISs are supposed to exchange two kinds of data:

- Tourism related data about tourism objects (like hotels, museums, lakes, etc.) which includes text and multimedia (photos, audios and videos).
- Tourism statistical data.

3.2.1   Exchange of Tourism Objects Data

Tourism in its tendency is an industry firmly reliant on data exchange. Data exchange is principally difficult because of the heterogeneity of information sources. The issue of uniting heterogeneous data sources is known as the interoperability issue. The information heterogeneity is a big problem. Currently, researchers are dealing with this problem by writing some information interface programs. It has been observed that maintenance of these programs is expensive in terms of both time as well as economy. However, ontology-based document exchange is a good alternative to solve this scalability issue [16].

Many have embraced XML (eXtensible Markup Language) for information exchange over the Web. In France, for example, national traveler associations follow the TourInFrance (TIF) format (http://www.tourinfrance.net) which utilizes XML for depiction of its components. Generally, XML structure is defined by XML Schema, but it does not give a uniform way for representing semantics of the data. It has been noticed that two kinds of problems appear when an XML file is to be transformed from one format to other.

3.2.1.1   Semantic Clashes

Semantic conflicts occur as a result of mismatch of concepts in different standards. Use of totally different concepts, different concept names or different levels of granularity are few examples of semantic conflicts when we talk about data exchange using XML. Researchers have identified eight categories of semantic conflicts [16], see Figure 3.1 for an example in terms of naming, position, and scope.

3.2.1.2   Structural Clashes

Heterogeneity of XML representation often result into what we call structural clashes. In XML, same concept can be referred to in different ways even though XML Schema is used to constrain XML documents, but XML schema has been designed to constrain XML document content and not concepts. Structural clashes in XML usually are caused by different usage of specific elements. For example, one representation might use attributes rather than embedded elements or some other might express concepts in enumeration values [16], see Figure 3.2.

It happens often with XML documents that the semantics associated with it are hard coded within the application and not available for further processing. Same case is also observed where documents are provided with XML Schema, but XML Schema fails to represent their meanings.

Vocabulary supported solutions are also in use where all systems being part of a consortium use same defined vocabulary but there are problems with such solutions:

- These vocabularies are not supported by other web systems like search engines.
- Often such vocabularies do not afford to extend themselves with changing requirements of a domain.
- Most of them are limited to a certain domain.

Different Naming	<PostCode> Vs <PostalCode>
Different Position	<PostCode> in <Address> element rather than in <ContactInfo> element
Different Scope	<TelephonePrefix> and <TelephoneNumber> separated vs. <PrefixTelephoneNumber> as single concept

Figure 3.1 Examples of semantic clashes [16].

```
<ContactInformation>
<Address PostalCode="X-1220">
Wannaby Street 59, Dreamtown
</Address>
</ContactInformation>
```

```
<ContactInformation>
<Address>
<Street>Wannaby Street 59</Street>
<City>Dreamtown</City>
<PostalCode>X-1220</PostalCode>
</Address>
</ContactInformation>
```

```
<ContactInformation>
<Address> Wannaby Street 59,
<PostalCode>X-1220</PostalCode>
Dreamtown
</Address>
</ContactInformation>
```

Figure 3.2 Examples of structural clashes [16].

In this scenario, there is a need for something which has the capability of overcoming all these challenges as described in this section for a safe information exchange between systems. Schema.org could be the future of information exchange.

3.2.2   Schema.org—The Future

Schema.org (www.schema.org) is an effort on vocabularies founded by Google, Microsoft, Yahoo, and Yandex. It was announced in June 2011 used to build and support a universal set of structured data markup rules that can be used to identify objects and relationships between them. The vocabulary defined by Schema.org finds its support on web as well as on other information systems. Its ever-evolving vocabulary is something that can be used for information exchange among systems with ever changing scope and information needs. It will give rise to extended version of semantic web whose aim is to extend the standard data formats of the World Wide Web to other applications and technologies. The overall goal of Schema.org is to provide a single standard resource for developers for a more effective and semantically intelligent information exchange between information systems.

3.2.2.1 Schema.org Extension Mechanism

Many web applications seek to have support of structured data represented using a single standard vocabulary (like schema.org) but knowing the scope and requirements of structured data, it is hard to imagine for vocabulary like schema.org to represent everything available. This is the reason, schema.org has an extension mechanism (https://schema.org/docs/extension.html) i.e. a process that can be followed by researchers and developers to add new or improve existing vocabularies present in schema.org. If the proposed additions get a sufficient level of acceptance from the community, they can be made part of the core schema.org vocabulary.

We argue that schema.org having support for web as well as other information systems and having an extendable and domain-independent vocabulary is the most suitable choice for Information exchange among tourist information systems. In the next sub-section, we highlight some aspects of Schema.org vocabulary that can be exploited for tourist information exchange.

3.2.2.2 Schema.org Tourism Vocabulary

Having discussed above that Schema.org is very rich to represent and exchange information of all domains, we discuss its application to tourism domain for information representation. Currently, many different standards are being used for this purpose in different parts of the world. For example,

- In France institutional tourism stakeholders have adopted TourInFrance (TIF), while tour operators and distributors gathered within XFT (For Travel eXchange) to create a common language "directed journey".

- In Europe several countries come together in an association called Harmonet.
- At the World level providers (hotel groups, airlines, etc.), producers and travel distributors gathered in OTA (Open Travel Alliance).

For simplicity, we only discuss TourInFrance here. French National Tourism Organizations (NTOs) have to respect the TourInFrance (TIF) format for description of tourism objects. TIF adapted XML (Extensible Markup Language) for description of its elements in September 2004. TIF focuses on 19 types of sources in tourism including natural resources, hotels, activities, restaurants, etc., and defines several constructs to characterize them. Using TIF can be useful to provide a detailed objective description. However, the use of related data sources, for e.g. terminological resources, are also often required to optimize data search and management. Table 3.2 lists the Schema.org equivalent elements for TIF elements used to describe different tourism objects. Knowing the extensible nature of Schema.org, it is easier to make additions wherever needed.

3.2.3   Exchange of Tourism-Related Statistical Data

Currently, tourism stakeholders do not use any standard format for the exchange of statistical data. Generally, data is created using any statistical software and is transferred to other TIS assuming that other system supports processing of transferred file. Situation becomes severe in case of heterogeneous systems. To avoid this problem, we propose to adopt the standard Statistical Data Model exchange (SDMX) [4].

SDMX provides a framework to organize and exchange data. It provides guidelines to shape the data for international data exchange. Overall, SDMX (http://ec.europa.eu/eurostat/data/sdmx-data-metadata-exchange) includes the following aspects:

- Statistical data described using a logical modeling, along with structure guidelines.
- A standard for automated data exchange.

Finally, the difficulty of using this standard is in its implementation. Hence, tourism stakeholders at national level need to be working together to identify and share the same tourist terminology SDMX (concepts, code lists, defining data structures). The use of SDMX will have impacts on both

Table 3.2 Example of mapping from TIF to Schema.org.

TourInFrance	Schema.org
01. Activit sportive	TourismEntity/Sports
02. Droit du tourisme	TourismEntity/Tourism Legislation
03. Cologie du tourisme	TourismEntity/Ecology of Tourism
04. Conomie du tourisme	TourismEntity/Economy of Tourism
05. Quipement touristique	TourismEntity/Tourism Facilities
06. Flux touristique	TourismEntity/Visitor Flows
07. Formation et employ	TourismEntity/Training and Employment
08. Hbergement	TourismEntity/Accommodation
09. Loisirs	TourismEntity/Leisure Activities
10. Manifestation touristique	TourismEntity/Tourism Events
11. Patrimoine touristique	TourismEntity/Tourism Heritage
12. Politique du tourisme	TourismEntity/Tourism Policy
13. Prestation touristique	TourismEntity/Tourism Services
14. Professionnel du tourisme	TourismEntity/Tourism Professionals
15. Promotion touristique	TourismEntity/Tourism Promotion
16. Science et information	TourismEntity/Science and Information
17. Sociologie des loisirs	TourismEntity/Sociology of Leisure
18. Tourisme sectorial	TourismEntity/Tourism Sectors
19. Transport	TourismEntity/Transport
20. Pays et groupement de pays	TourismEntity/Countries and Country Groupings

i.e. data providers and data users. Adopting SDMX as standard for statistical data will enable them [4].

- To import/export data from questionnaires.
- To compare responses across years.
- To improve metadata provisions.

Similarly, SDMX will positively affect data users [4]. For example,

- Data will have greater coherence across agencies.
- Metadata will be more available.
- Data will be of a higher quality.
- Timeliness will be improved.

The link—http://www.ecb.europa.eu/stats/services/sdmx/html/tutorial.en.html—can be helpful at understanding what exactly needs to be done if someone wants to develop an application based on SDMX information model.

3.3   Information Extraction

Information extraction (IE) refers to the process of detecting, predicting, and identifying instances in text for specified classes of entities [19]. Considering the complexity of this task, various aspects of related information extraction tasks have been considered in the previous literature, from machine learning to information retrieval with different databases, and to analysis of different documents [38]. In short, extraction task was mainly concerned with identification of named entities and relationship between them from natural language text but with the passage of time it has evolved according to the task requirements and user needs. TIS also seek support of information extraction for their intelligent decision making. Earlier TIS used to play with structured data because most of the information used to come through manual interface. However, with the emergence of online social networks, the challenge of extracting useful information from unstructured data is a daunting task. Online tourism data includes opinions, temporal and event information. Opinions on different tourism objects or services like hotels, traveling, museums, etc. are generally expressed on review sites (like TripPlanner etc.). Similarly, temporal and event information available on informative web sites of different tourism web sites (like web sites of tourism offices, travel agencies, tourism planners, etc.) is also very important in tourism context. Generally, temporal information is associated with event information and hence, we will discuss them together. In this section, we will discuss some existing work already been done in the domain of tourism. We also discuss some challenges of dealing with opinion and temporal/event information.

3.3.1   Opinion Extraction

An opinion is simply subjective to the person whom it belongs i.e. it shows his/her personal beliefs about something. Opinions help decision making in individuals, societies and also in big enterprises [27, 49]. This process is required to be fast as well as accurate so that decisions can be made with the available concise information. In the real world, people engage in discussions to illustrate their points of view. However, a significant boost in this phenomenon is seen after the emergence of online social networks. On the web, people give their opinions on products, news articles, political issues, etc. Anyone's opinion about something can either be positive or negative (i.e. polarity of opinion) [21]. This phenomenon of posting their opinions on the web has generated huge volumes of opinion data on the web. Many researchers have worked on extraction of opinions from text, a process which is called opinion mining or opinion extraction. Most of the proposed extraction approaches revolve around the definition by Liu [27] and therefore, we can find work extracting opinion holders [8, 11] opinion targets [22, 42], sentiment [10] and time of the opinion [24, 28, 31]. Note that we can mathematically define an opinion as a quadruple represented as a vector (g, s, h, t), with g—the opinion (or sentiment) target, s—the sentiment about the target, h—the opinion holder, t—the time when the opinion was expressed.

Globally, there are two types of approaches that have been used i.e. machine learning approaches and sentiment lexicon or knowledge-based approaches. The purpose of this chapter is not to present a review of opinion extraction approaches because there are already many such detailed surveys [21, 28, 30, 36, 48] that can be consulted for details. However, we will highlight few works that relate to opinion extraction in tourism domain.

Most of the opinion extraction work relating to tourism falls within the category of aspect-based opinion extraction approaches (also called feature-based opinion extraction). Aspect-based opinion extraction techniques divide input texts into features pertinent to the topic or product being described in the given document [28].

Latent Dirichlet Allocation (LDA) based approach for feature-based opinion extraction was proposed in [46] similar to the approach proposed in the pioneer work of [41]. These kinds of approaches fall in the category of unsupervised topic-modeling techniques similar to the one proposed in [13] where a trend detection framework has been proposed. Another example of using unsupervised technique for opinion extraction for tourism includes [18].

3.3.2   Opinion Mining

Generally, opinion mining approaches performance differ with the changes in the topic or domain i.e. when we change the queries and the relevant data collection, results of a particular approach might change drastically. Cruz *et al.* [9] compute the importance of the topic or domain in opinion mining. Since various topics have differing issues and features inherent to topics, they proposed to build a system that can perform across different domains with human intervention. Namely, they utilized annotation data collection specific to each domain under consideration. Other types of approaches for opinion mining that proved to be successful in aspect-oriented opinion extraction that are based on the concept-level sentiment analysis. Main tools for such approaches are knowledge bases, web ontologies or semantic networks, that permit to extract additional information needed for a particular concept [5, 7]. Cambria *et al.* [6] provided a library for concept-level sentiment analysis. Their approach gives additional information (semantic) and sentics for various concepts involved. These concept-level sentiment analyses can include high-level tasks as well. For example, summarization of opinions, adaptation to various domains, and multimodal sentiment analysis that requires. the analysis of audio, linguistic, and visual features.

Besides these machine learning methods, lexicon-based natural language processing techniques, a method that can be very effective on extraction of opinion is the annotation of sentiments. For a very effective opinion extraction, it is necessary to have an effective and complete opinion annotation. In next section, we discuss existing opinion annotation schemes and give a comparison between them and point-out the drawbacks with existing annotations.

3.4   Sentiment Annotation

Web is full of resources in the form of texts, images, movies, and sounds and web search engines are good at retrieving all these resources to their users within seconds. While our current systems are good at bringing or retrieving relevant information, they are not fully capable of understanding the semantics of information they are retrieving [35]. Note that, this retrieval to obtain a large amount of data alone is not sufficient for machines, they will need to learn it with passage of time because they are used to retrieve it. If we want to make our machines understand semantics of data they are fetching, augmentation with the metadata are required. Metadata tags are utilized to mark the contents of a given data collection is called an annotation over the input. However, precision of annotation is very important for accurate and effective results. For this reason, the annotations play a clinical role in developing intelligent human language technologies. The importance of annotation can be estimated from the fact that currently there exist many annotations schemes for opinion extraction. In what follows section, we briefly discuss about *SentiML*, *EmotionML* and *OpinionMiningML* and provide a comparison in the context to represent opinions for text documents.

3.4.1   SentiML

Conventional sentiment annotation style is utilized in the SentiML annotation [12]. In this schema, we can find target tags for the object for the expressed sentiments, and modifier tags encases the expression providing the sense of sentiments. Further, such a scheme incorporates in the vocabulary a much-needed appraisal type tag. This tag does a grouping of the two tags, target and modifier, as well as describes the eventual polarity of the grouped expression. In addition to these tag-based usages, the scheme of SentiML utilizes a robust linguistic theory to form its Appraisal Framework (AF). This AF helps to determine various appraisal types for e.g. judgments, affect, and appreciation within the modifier tag. This is a positive apect of SentiML. Since SentiML is a simple annotation schema it attracts the researchers working in this domain to adapt it without hesitation because they do not need to learn domain specific commands to adapt this annotation scheme. However, further work is required to solve some issues related the style of SentiML.

3.4.1.1   SentiML Example

In the example annotations of SentiML, one sentence is given as below:
"The U.S. State Department on Tuesday (KST) rated the human rights situation in North Korea "poor" in its annual human rights report, casting dark clouds on the already tense relationship between Pyongyang and Washington."

Relevant annotations are given below:

Listing 1: SentiML example.

```
<APPRAISALGROUP id="A0" fromID="T0" fromText="situation" toID="M0" toText="poor"
    orientation="negative"/>

<APPRAISALGROUP id="A1" fromID="M1" fromText="dark" toID="T1" toText="clouds" orientation
    ="negative"/>
<APPRAISALGROUP id="A2" fromID="M2" fromText="tense" toID="T2" toText="relationship"
    orientation="negative"/>

<MODIFIER id="M0" start="201" end="205" text="poor" attitude="appreciation" orientation="
    negative" force="normal" polarity="unmarked"/>

<MODIFIER id="M1" start="250" end="254" text="dark" attitude="appreciation" orientation="
    negative" force="normal" polarity="unmarked"/>

<MODIFIER id="M2" start="277" end="282" text="tense" attitude="appreciation" orientation=
    "negative" force="normal" polarity="unmarked"/>

<TARGET id="T0" start="175" end="184" text="situation" type="thing" orientation="neutral"
    />

<TARGET id="T1" start="255" end="261" text="clouds" type="thing" orientation="ambiguous"/
    >

<TARGET id="T2" start="283" end="295" text="relationship" type="thing" orientation="
    neutral"/>
```

In this example above, the annotated sentence has three phrases that are different and SentiML notation has been used to identify them. Note in particular that words such as the "situation", "clouds", and "relationship" are identified. These are targets words that represent the opinion in the sentence. Targets such as these are identified on phrase level, however at the global level target of opinion, North Korea is not identified anywhere.

3.4.2   OpinionMiningML

OpinionMiningML [37] provides tagging attitude expressions of features and objects in different textual segments based on a XML formalism. This OpinionMiningML corresponds to the feature-based opinion expression models globally in the opinion mining literature. However, this is only a proposal of an annotation schema. The main ideas in OpinionMiningML schema is to illustrate features or facets from various segments of text to form ontology based on these features. Definitions of relations between these features are givn using tags such as the <SERVED-AT> and <FEATURE-OF>. Further, meta tags are defined such as the <OBSERVATIONS>, <APPRIASAL>, that capture the expressions about these features. This particular separation approach as well the capturing various relations between features, expressions along with their polarity, for demarking features facilitates a modular approach for this annotation scheme and is one of the positive points of this formalism. In terms of drawbacks, this formalism can be cumbersome for annotators are meta information which includes expressive statement (ES) need to be captured. Moreover, the formalism structure introduced by this approach can be hard to discern. This can provide a roadblock for automatic tagger developments since the feature and relations extraction challenges associated with the annotations scheme.

3.4.2.1   OpinionMiningML Example

We present the annotation of the same previous example using OpinionMiningML syntax:

Listing 2: OpinionMiningML example.

```
<COMMENT id="1" ontologyreference="1">
<FRAGMENT id="1"> The U.S. State Department on Tuesday (KST) rated the human rights
    situation in North Korea "poor" </FRAGMENT>
<FRAGMENT id="2"> in its annual human rights report, casting dark clouds on the already
    tense relationship between Pyongyang and Washington.</FRAGMENT>

<APPRAISAL polarity="negative" intensity="medium">
    <FACETREFERENCE>1</FACETREFERENCE>
        <FRAGMENTREFERENCE>1</FRAGMENTREFERENCE>
        <FRAGMENTREFERENCE>2</FRAGMENTREFERENCE>
</APPRAISAL>
<APPRAISAL polarity="negative" intensity="medium">
    <FACETREFERENCE>2</FACETREFERENCE>
        <FRAGMENTREFERENCE>1</FRAGMENTREFERENCE>
        <FRAGMENTREFERENCE>2</FRAGMENTREFERENCE>
</APPRAISAL>
</COMMENT>
```

In this example above, we note that this annotation scheme requires a meta tagging domain ontology, hence meta tags such <FACET> or <ONTOFACET> are not defined for the example.

3.4.3   EmotionML

EmotionML [39] was conceived to elucidate emotion theories from a wide variety of contexts from different technologies.

EmotionML uses the fact that there is not a single common representation for effective states in the sciences, and also there is no single vocabulary to utilize for the emotion's extraction. Hence, state of emotions <emotion> is given by four types that describe <dimension>, <action – tendency>, <category>, and <appraisal> with the particular vocabulary used identified.

Three use cases of EmotionML are considered [40]:

1. Manual/human annotation of emotion-related data
2. Automatically recognizing emotions
3. Emotional systems behavior generation

To satisfy all the three use cases above, a plug-in language formalism is used in EmotionML scheme that depends on the different context scenarios. Based on the W3C draft on this subject, the EmotionML needs to be defined along with one or more particular vocabularies driven representations that are used for defining emotion-based states. This nonexistence of a default vocabulary is a drawback of EmotionML specifications since there is no single vocabulary set as a standard in the community for emotions. This means, the user is left with the choice of selection of emotion vocabulary. Thus, as noted in [40] the EmotionML formalism is striving to strike a balance, thereby providing a selected set of recommended vocabularies for emotions as well provides documentations of usages. Other complications with EmotionML is in defining beyond emotional states such as the "emotion dimension sets". These are qualitative emotions with different attributes, e.g. intensity, and how they are experienced differently e.g. negative or positive.

3.4.3.1   *EmotionML Example*

We present the annoation the same previous example using EmotionML syntax.

Listing 3: EmotionML example.

```
<emotionml xmlns="http://www.w3.org/2009/10/emotionml" xmlns:meta="http://www.example.com
    /metadata" category-set="http://www.w3.org/TR/emotion-voc/xml#acc-categories">
<info>
        <meta:doc>Example taken from annotation of SentiML
        </meta:doc>
</info>
The U.S. State Department on Tuesday (KST)
<emotion>
< category   name="reproach"/>
        rated the human rights situation in North Korea "poor"
</emotion>
        in its annual human rights report
<emotion>
        < category   name="disappointment"/>
        casting dark clouds
</emotion>
 on the already
<emotion>
        < category   name="disappointment"/>
        tense relationship between Pyongyang and Washington.
</emotion>
</emotionML>
```

3.5   Comparison of Different Annotations Schemes

The above annotations schemes can be compared based on various perspectives. We provide these contrasting perspectives below for the SentiML, OpinionMiningML, and EmotionML considered here, and refer to [50] for detailed analysis:

- Scope: The W3C standard based EmotionML covers various emotions and their aspects across fields whereas OpinionMiningML, SentiML are limited to the NLP and IR domains. We contend that, compared to OpinionMiningML, the SentiML provides bigger scope, since OpinionMiningML is limited to only feature-based analysis of sentiments.
- Complexity: In terms of complexity, EmotionML is higher due to its large scope than the other two annotation schemes and thus is less user friendly than the others. Overall, OpinionMiningML is complex than the easy to use SentiML which makes use of vocabulary with concepts e.g. target, modifier, holder as we have seen above.

- Vocabulary: OpinionMiningML, and SentiML are tied with specific vocabularies whereas EmotionML text annotation can be equipped with newer and broader vocabulary from the users. OpinionMiningML focus is on features and relevant sentiments to the features and uses meta tags whereas SentiML uses modified and targets of sentiments concepts.

- Structure: OpinionMiningML contains more granularity than the other two annotations schemes and uses it upto the feature levels. All three schemes use XML based formalisms.

- Contextual Ambiguities: SentiML provides a solution to the contextual ambiguities that plague the opinion mining and remains a challenge. All three annotations schemes define expression semantics, e.g. suggestion, appreciation.

- Theoretical Grounds: In contrast to an appraisal framework driven SentiML or the W3C standard based EmotionML, the OpinionMiningML is does not have a theoretical footing. Also, the EmotionML is a W3C recommendation after a lengthy discussion process that involved stakeholders and experts. SentiML is also based on stronger linguistic driven theory which are lacking in OpinionMiningML scheme.

- Granularity Level: All three schemes act distinctively on granularity levels. OpinionMiningML and SentiML consider sub-sentence levels whereas EmotionML is operated at sentences level. Note that though, it is compulsory to go to subsentence or even words level to find appropriate sentiments, it is the sentence that eventually provides a logical unit of conducted discourse.

- Name: Another interesting comparison that can be seen in these three annotation schemes is in their name. All three annotations schemes utilize interchangeable words for opinions e.g. emotion, opinion, sentiment.

- Flexibility: In terms of flexibility, EmotionML provides complete freedom to choose an appropriate vocabulary for the domain under consideration so as to suit emotional states of that particular domain. While SentiML does not have such flexibility, the OpinionMiningML is similar to the EmotionML in this regard. OpinionMiningML provides, based on requirements, choice of building a domain-based ontology in the annotation scheme usage.

From the points of comparisons, it is evident that current annotation schemes are not able to meet demands of today's information needs related to opinions. They seem to be more adaptive towards specific domains but there is a need of an annotation scheme which represents all information relevant to opinions in all domains. An annotation standard providing support for semantic web technologies (like Linked Data) and having the ability to deal with contextual ambiguities is needed. An effort in this regard can be consulted in the extension of SentiML scheme named SentiML++, see [29, 50].

3.6   Temporal and Event Extraction

Extracting temporal information has become one of the most demanding information needs of current recommender systems. For many web related tasks like fresh news retrieval, novelty detection, information aggregation, etc., temporal extraction comes into play. Earlier, researchers did not exploit all temporal information present in a document for several IR related tasks [26]. However, lately researcher groups have started exploring this information dimension [2]. It is worthy to know the temporal structure of text in a document by knowing the temporal relations between events and related temporal evidences [15, 43, 44].

Currently, lot of temporal evidences are being used for extracting temporal information from text. These evidences include tense, aspect, temporal adverbials, conventions for pragmatism, relations for rhetorical elements, and knowledge of the background. Exploring such temporal structure of the documents is one of the most interest temporal related tasks. For example, finding the order of events in multi-document summarization is a very interesting task and temporal information plays its role in this task. Similarly, in question answering systems, sometimes it is needed to locate events on the timeline, or to determine the event occurring prior to some event or date.

Contrary to sentiment annotation which suffers from the availability of several annotation schemes, temporal annotations mostly seek support of a common standard known as TimeML [33]. Although its name refers to only time in its capacity, but it is the most widely used annotation scheme for temporal as well as for event annotation. In the following section, we give a brief overview of TimeML.

3.7   TimeML

An annotation scheme for representing events and time in natural language is provided by TimeML [33]. Generally, it addresses following problems of even and time annotations:

- Identifying events in natural language text and associating time with it.
- Relative ordering of events.
- Resolving contextual ambiguities in temporal expressions.
- Reasoning about the duration of events.

AQUAINT workshops and projects played a vital role in development of TimeML [33]. TimeBank was the first annotated data collection annotated with TimeML. Later a graphical annotation tool was developed in TANGO workshop. The original TimeML specification has developed into more recent versions and has been approved as an international standard in 2009 known as ISO-TimeML language.

TimeML Example Sentence: "The TERQAS Workshop will resume Monday, July 15. The session will start at 9:00 a.m."

Listing 4: TimeML time annotation example.

```
The TERQAS Workshop will resume

<TIMEX3 tid="t1" type="DATE" value="2002-07-15">

Monday, July 15

</TIMEX3>

. The session will start at

<TIMEX3 tid="t2" type="TIME" value="T9:00"

temporalFunction="true" anchorTimeID="t1">

9:00 a.m.

</TIMEX3>
```

TimeML supports many languages (English, Italian, French, Portuguese, Chinese, Korean, Romanian...) with very little modifications needed from one language to other. Although TimeML addresses many problems but it has some limitations (i.e. it does not cover all needs pf temporal annotation sin NLP) because it was meant to be increased performance of answering systems by focusing on temporal identification of events, time stamps corresponding to events, contextually underspecified temporal expressions reasoning, and reasoning over the persistence of events [25].

Similar to temporal expressions, by annotating a representative of the event expressions all the event expressions are marked. The example below provides an example of event annotation using TimeML [34].

Listing 5: TimeML event annotation example.

```
All 75 passengers <EVENT eid="1" class="OCCURRENCE" tense="past" aspect="NONE"> died
</EVENT>.
```

The event categories supported by TimeML consists of reporting, occurrence, perception, aspectual and further categories such as the state, intentional state, intentional action, as well as modal.

Lefeuvre-Halftermeyer *et al.* [25] summarized some major limitations of TimeML and they also proposed some modifications to tackle with those limitations that are listed below:

- Well identified features of the norm enrichments: such as the temporal function of TIMEX time expressions, and TLINK temporal relation's additional types.
- Concerning the units or features annotated with deeper modifications: Between time and tense for EVENT units, clarity is required. Between temporal signals (the SIGNAL unit) and TIMEX modifiers (the MOD feature), coherence of representation is required.
- Perform temporal annotation further on top of a syntactic, instead of lexical, layer is recommended which is temporal annotation on a treebank.

Similar to time annotation, currently TimeML is the only annotation scheme for annotating events so it cannot be compared to any other annotation scheme. However, TimeML model can be compared to ACE for modeling of events [1]. In one hand, in TimeML, an event is a word that points to a node in a temporal relations network. On the other hand, in ACE, an event is part of a complex structure where arguments relations that are themselves complex structures. In ACE, ancillary temporal information as in the form of temporal arguments that are only noted when explicitly given. In contrast, in the TimeML, all events are annotated since all events form temporal network. In ACE model, only 'interesting' events are annotated [1], and these events in a set of 34 predefined categories. Considering the complexity aspect, ACE model of events is difficult to process than TimeML model.

3.8   Conclusions

In this chapter, we reviewed discussed tourism information systems with a particular focus on exchange and extraction in the context of tourism information system (TIS). We highlight current approaches, their limitations and possible alternatives for compensating those limitations. We discussed the limitations of XML and locally used data formats for data exchange. We have demonstrated that how schema.org—can prove itself a standard for data exchange for tourism industry. Currently, tourism industry lacks the standardization which is hurting it a big way and schema.org can be a solution to its problems. Similarly, we focus on the very important dimensions of information extraction where we see how current opinion annotation approaches fail to meet our requirements. We also compare different opinion annotation schemes i.e. SentiML, EmotionML and OpinionMiningML. Our review work in this chapter is important for information extraction driven recommender area researchers new to this domain. Further, such annotations schemes need to be used for devising robust recommender systems in the tourism application domain.

References

1. Ahn, D., The stages of event extraction, in: *Proceedings of the Workshop on Annotating and Reasoning about Time and Events*, pp. 1–8, 2006.
2. Alonso, O., Strötgen, J., Baeza-Yates, R.A., Gertz, M., Temporal Information Retrieval: Challenges and Opportunities. *TWAW, volume 813 of CEUR Workshop Proceedings*, CEUR-WS.org, pp. 1–8, 2011.
3. Borràs, J., Moreno, A., Valls, A., Intelligent tourism recommender systems: A survey. *Expert Syst. Appl.*, 41, 16, 7370–7389, 2014.
4. Gregory, A. and Heus, P., DDI and SDMX: Complementary, not competing, standards. Paper, *Open Data Foundation*, 2007.
5. Cambria, E., An introduction to concept-level sentiment analysis, in: *Mexican International Conference on Artificial Intelligence*, Springer, Berlin, Heidelberg, pp. 478–483, 2013.
6. Cambria, E., Gelbukh, A., Poria, S., Kwok, K., Sentic API: A common-sense based API for concept-level sentiment analysis. Paper presented at CEUR Workshop Proceedings, pp. 19–24, 2014.

7. Cambria, E., Schuller, B., Liu, B., Wang, H., Havasi, C., Knowledge-based approaches to concept-level sentiment analysis. *IEEE Intell. Syst.*, 28, 2, 12–14, 2013.
8. Chen, C.L., Liu, C.L., Chang, Y.C., Tsai, H.P., Mining opinion holders and opinion patterns in US financial statements, in: *IEEE International Conference on Technologies and Applications of Artificial Intelligence*, pp. 62–68, 2011.
9. Cruz, F.L., Troyano, J.A., Enríquez, F., Ortega, F.J., Vallejo, C.G., 'Long autonomy or long delay?'The importance of domain in opinion mining. *Expert Syst. Appl.*, 40, 8, 3174–3184, 2013.
10. Dave, K., Lawrence, S., Pennock, D.M., Mining the peanut gallery: Opinion extraction and semantic classification of product reviews, in: *Proceedings of the 12th International Conference on World Wide Web, ACM*, pp. 519–528, 2003.
11. Deng, L. and Wiebe, J., Recognizing Opinion Sources Based on a New Categorization of Opinion Types, in: *IJCAI*, pp. 2775–2781, 2016.
12. Di Bari, M., Sharoff, S., Thomas, M., Sentiml: Functional annotation for multilingual sentiment analysis, in: *Proceedings of the 1st International Workshop on Collaborative Annotations in Shared Environment*: Metadata, Vocabularies and Techniques in the Digital Humanities, ACM, p. 15, 2013.
13. Dueñas-Fernández, R., Velásquez, J.D., L'Huillier, G., Detecting trends on the Web: A multidisciplinary approach. *Inf. Fusion*, 20, 129–135, 2014.
14. Eriksson, O. and Axelsson, K., Its systems architectures-from vision to reality, in: *Proceedings of the 7th World Congress on Intelligent Systems*, 2000.
15. Floris, R. and Campagna, M., Social media data in tourism planning: analysing tourists' satisfaction in space and time, in: REAL CORP 2014. Plan it Smart. *Clever Solutions for Smart Cities Proceedings of 19th International Conference*, pp. 997–1003, 2014.
16. Fodor, O., Dell'Erba, M., Ricci, F., Spada, A., Werthner, H., Conceptual normalisation of XML data for interoperability in tourism. Transformation for the Semantic Web KTSW 2002, vol. 21, p. 69, 2002.
17. Forsman, A., Information exchange between information systems supported by standardization, in: *Promote IT 2001*, Ronneby Brunn, Sweden, pp. 49–52, 2001.
18. Goyal, M. and Bhatnagar, V., Classification of Polarity of Opinions Using Unsupervised Approach in Tourism Domain. *IJRSDA*, 3, 4, 68–78, 2016.
19. Grishman, R., Information extraction: Techniques and challenges, in: *International Summer School on Information Extraction*, Springer, Berlin, pp. 10–27, 1997.
20. Hinze, A. and Junmanee, S., Advanced recommendation models for mobile tourist information, in: *OTM Confederated International Conferences "On the Move to Meaningful Internet System*, Springer, Berlin, pp. 643–660, 2006.
21. Khan, K., Baharudin, B., Khan, A., Ullah, A., Mining opinion components from unstructured reviews: A review. J. King Saud Univ. *Comp. Info. Sci.*, 26, 3, 258–275, 2014.

22. Kim, H.D. and Zhai, C., Generating comparative summaries of contradictory opinions in text, in: *Proceedings of the 18th ACM Conference on Information and Knowledge Management*, *ACM*, pp. 385–394, 2009.

23. Kirilenko, A.P., Stepchenkova, S.O., Kim, H., Li, X., Automated sentiment analysis in tourism: Comparison of approaches. *J. Travel Res.*, 57, 8, 1012–1025, 2018.

24. Ku, L.W., Liang, Y.T., Chen, H.H., Opinion Extraction, Summarization and Tracking in News and Blog Corpora, in: *Proceedings of AAAI*, pp. 100–107, 2006.

25. Lefeuvre-Halftermeyer, A., Antoine, J.Y., Couillault, A., Schang, E., Abouda, L., Savary, A., Maurel, D., Eshkol-Taravella, I., Battistelli, D., Covering various needs in temporal annotation: A proposal of extension of ISO TimeML that preserves upward compatibility. *LREC 2016*, Portorož Slovenia. ffhalshs-01318792f, 2016.

26. Ligozat, G., Extracting, Annotating and Reasoning about Time and Space in Texts and Discourse. Master's thesis, University of Paris Sud, Paris, France, 2011.

27. Liu, B., Sentiment analysis and subjectivity, in: *Handbook of natural language processing*, vol. 2, pp. 627–666, 2010.

28. Liu, B., Sentiment analysis and opinion mining, in: *Synthesis lectures on human language technologies*, vol. 5(1), pp. 1–167, 2012.

29. Missen, M.M.S., Attik, M., Coustaty, M., Doucet, A., Faucher, C., Sentiml++: An extension of the sentiml sentiment annotation scheme, in: *European Semantic Web Conference*, Springer, Cham, pp. 91–96, 2015.

30. Missen, M.M.S., Boughanem, M., Cabanac, G., Opinion mining: reviewed from word to document level. *SNAM*, 3, 1, 107–125, 2013.

31. O'Connor, B., Balasubramanyan, R., Routledge, B.R., Smith, N.A., From tweets to polls: Linking text sentiment to public opinion time series, in: *Fourth International AAAI Conference on Weblogs and Social Media*, 2010.

32. Pröll, B. and Retschitzegger, W., Discovering next generation tourism information systems: A tour on TIScover. *J. Travel Res.*, 39, 2, 182–191, 2000.

33. Pustejovsky, J., Castano, J.M., Ingria, R., Sauri, R., Gaizauskas, R.J., Setzer, A., Katz, G., Radev, D.R., TimeML: Robust specification of event and temporal expressions in text, in: *New directions in question answering*, vol. 3, pp. 28–34, 2003.

34. Pustejovsky, J., Hanks, P., Sauri, R., See, A., Gaizauskas, R., Setzer, A., Radev, D., Sundheim, B., Day, D., Ferro, L., Lazo, M., Lazo, M., The timebank corpus, in: *Corpus linguistic*, p. 40, 2003.

35. Pustejovsky, J. and Stubbs, A., *Natural Language Annotation for Machine Learning: A guide to corpus-building for applications*, O'Reilly Media, Inc, CA, USA, 2012.

36. Rana, T.A. and Cheah, Y.N., Aspect extraction in sentiment analysis: comparative analysis and survey. *Artif. Intell. Rev.*, 46, 4, 459–483, 2016.

37. Robaldo, L. and Di Caro, L., Opinionmining-ml. Comput. Stand. Inter., 35, 5, 454–469, 2013.
38. Sarawagi, S., Information extraction. *Foundations and Trends® in Databases*, 1, 3, 261–377, 2008.
39. Schröder, M., Baggia, P., Burkhardt, F., Pelachaud, C., Peter, C., Zovato, E., EmotionML—An upcoming standard for representing emotions and related states, in: *International Conference on Affective Computing and Intelligent Interaction*, Springer, Berlin, pp. 316–325, 2011.
40. Shankland, S., Emotionml: *Will computers tap into your feelings?*, https://www.cnet.com/news/emotionml-will-computers-tap-into-your-feelings/. Retrieved 30 November 2019.
41. Titov, I. and McDonald, R., A joint model of text and aspect ratings for sentiment summarization, in: proceedings of ACL-08: *HLT*, pp. 308–316, 2008.
42. Turney, P.D., Thumbs up or thumbs down? semantic orientation applied to unsupervised classification of reviews, in: *Proceedings of the 40th Annual Meeting on Association for Computational Linguistics*, ACL, pp. 417–424, 2002.
43. Varga, A., Puscasu, G., Orasan, C., Identification of temporal expressions in the domain of tourism. *KEPT*, 1, 29–32, 2009.
44. Weiser, S., Laublet, P., Minel, J.L., Automatic Identification of temporal information in tourism web pages, in: *LREC*, 2008.
45. Wöber, K.W., Information supply in tourism management by marketing decision support systems. *Tour. Manag.*, 24, 3, 241–255, 2003.
46. Xu, X., Cheng, X., Tan, S., Liu, Y., Shen, H., Aspect-level opinion mining of online customer reviews. *China Commun.*, 10, 3, 25–41, 2013.
47. Zografos, K.G. and Madas, M.A., A travel and tourism information system providing real-time, value-added logistical services on the move, in: *Proc. First International Conference on Mobile Business*, 2002.
48. Husnain, M., Missen, M.M.S., Akhtar, N., Coustaty, M., Mumtaz, S., Prasath, V.B.S., A systematic study on the role of SentiWordNet in opinion mining. *Front. Comput. Sci.*, 2019.
49. Missen, M.M.S., Coustaty, M., Choi, G.S., Alotaibi, F.S., Akhtar, N., Jhandir, M.Z., Prasath, V.B.S., Salamat, N., Husnain, M., OpinionML—Opinion Markup Language for Sentiment Representation. *Symmetry*, 11, 4, 545, 2019.
50. Missen, M.M.S., Coustaty, M., Salamat, N., Prasath, V.S., SentiML++: an extension of the SentiML sentiment annotation scheme. *New Rev. Hypermedia M.*, 24, 1, 28–43, 2018.

Part 2
MACHINE LEARNING-BASED RECOMMENDER SYSTEMS

4

Concepts of Recommendation System from the Perspective of Machine Learning

Sumanta Chandra Mishra Sharma*, Adway Mitra and Deepayan Chakraborty

Centre of Excellence in Artificial Intelligence, IIT Kharagpur, Kharagpur, India

Abstract

Recommendation systems evolved as an independent research area in the last decade of the twentieth century. With the popularity of the internet and online services, the number of internet users increases gradually. So, to predict the customer's need and to suggest the relevant information to the customer, companies use different information filtering mechanism. Such information filtering mechanism is called the recommendation system [1, 2]. It is a software module that predicts the user's choice based on the past data of the user or related data of similar users. It helps the companies to boost their business and get customer satisfaction towards their product and services [1, 3].

This chapter deals with different concepts and challenges of recommendation systems, and how artificial intelligence and machine learning can be used for them. The chapter mainly focuses on the concepts and techniques used by the recommendation system for better suggestion. It also contains the challenges and applications or recommendation system.

Keywords: Recommendation system, content-based system, collaborative filtering, hybrid recommendation

4.1 Introduction

Have you ever thought of how social media gives a new friendly suggestion? Why online shopping sites suggest different items to buy? Why we get various video suggestions on YouTube? We get these things because of an

---

*Corresponding author: sumantamishra22@gmail.com

Sachi Nandan Mohanty, Jyotir Moy Chatterjee, Sarika Jain, Ahmed A. Elngar and Priya Gupta (eds.)
Recommender System with Machine Learning and Artificial Intelligence: Practical Tools and Applications in Medical, Agricultural and Other Industries, (73–88) © 2020 Scrivener Publishing LLC

underlying software that continuously analyses the data and recommend the suggestion. That underlying software module is the recommendation system.

A recommendation system is an information filtering system that helps the user to make proper decision [4–7]. This filtering system keeps track of the user activity, and with the help of its intelligent algorithms [4, 13–16], it predicts the future choice of a user.

The recommender system is treated as an application of machine learning system [13–16] that recommends the most relevant product and services to the user. With such suggestions, it helps both the user and the vendor for the proper transaction of services. These algorithms find the relativeness of the user's past choice with the current available products and suggest accordingly. To provide a better suggestion the underlying algorithm checks the likelihood of web content, information about social media interaction, frequent search topics of user, prior knowledge about the user, similar users interest for some item, and so on.

Now a day, the world wide web contains a considerable amount of information related to different fields. So, to filter this information and to predict the user interest, a recommendation system is used. This software module predicts users' choice based on the past data of the user or related data of similar users.

This chapter mostly focuses on different aspects of the recommendation system. The further sections of the chapter deal with the entities, techniques, applications, and challenges of the recommendation system.

4.2   Entities of Recommendation System

In general, the recommendation systems mainly deal with three things, i.e., the users, the items, and the actions [4]. The users are the customers, whereas the items refer to the objects or the information recommended to the customer. The action is nothing but interaction between the customer and the recommender system, that helps the recommender system for future suggestions. These three components are interrelated and treated as an essential component of the recommendation system (Figure 4.1). In this section, we will discuss them briefly.

4.2.1   User

The user is called the primary component or primary entity of the recommendation system. The need for a recommendation system comes into

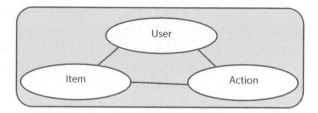

Figure 4.1 Entities of recommendation system.

existence because of the presence of users who needs different services of personal interest [11, 12]. A user can be a viewer of the YouTube videos or a buyer of online product or a researcher on some specific research domain [17] etc.

The recommender system takes different information about the user to create a user profile or user model. This profile helps to filter the suggestion provided to the user. A user profile includes the searching activity and behavior of the user. The rating provided by the users for a particular item, the web pages searched by the users, etc. are the components to build the user profile or user log for item recommendation.

4.2.2   Items

Item is a valuable entity recommended to the user. The value of a recommendation is treated as positive if the user has interest on the recommended item otherwise it is treated as negative [18]. Items always associated with a cost which includes the time spent on searching the item and money spent to get that item. So, it is the responsibility of the recommendation system to have a better suggestion for customer to reduce the cost of searching.

The recommendation system uses different features of the item for its evaluation and suggestion. Some feature values are fixed, while some feature values vary with time. If we consider the item mobile phone, then its brand, color, etc. are fixed for a particular product, but ratings and suggestions for that product change from time to time. When an item has more specific features, then it is treated as a complex one, while if the item has more general features, then it is treated as a simple item by the recommendation system.

4.2.3   Action

Actions are the transactions carried out by the user while interacting with the system for some item. The action can be a search for an item or a feedback for an item. These actions are stored in an action log of the recommendation system.

In a recommendation system, the feedback provided by the user can be of different forms, such as unary, binary, numeric, and suggested text. The unary system stores only the positive value; for example, if a user purchases an item, then the items purchased feature gets incremented; otherwise, there is no change in the feature value [4]. In the binary system, the user will give a positive or a negative feedback such as like or dislike for a product. Similarly, in numeric feedback, the worth of an item is analyzed by a numeric value within some range. The five-star rating system is a numeric feedback system. The last form of feedback is the suggestion provided by the user for a particular product, which helps others to make better decisions while selecting the product. The transaction log takes all this information to have a better classification of products and services and to identify the user's interest.

The underlying mechanism of a recommendation system is shown in Figure 4.2. It indicates that out of N number of items, the recommender system selects few items based on the log information associated with the particular user and items. It also considers the action log to decide on relevant suggestion.

4.3   Techniques of Recommendation

The recommendation system applies different techniques based on different business needs and targeted customer. When the targeted user is concerned,

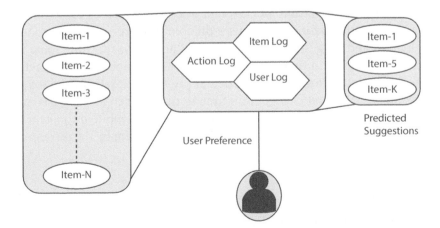

Figure 4.2 Recommendation mechanism.

then the recommendation can be divided into two categories, such as personalized and non-personalized recommendation system [11, 12]. Similarly, when the evaluation or filtering of information is concerned, then the recommendation system can be classified into content-based and collaborative approach [9, 10]. Apart from these, there are also different other techniques of recommendation [7, 8] that we will discuss in this section.

4.3.1   Personalized Recommendation System

Based on the intended user, a recommendation system can be of two types i.e., personalized and non-personalized recommendation system. The personalized recommendation system relies on a single-user perspective, and here the suggestions are based on the individual user activity [11]. The activity can be users rating for similar item, users' buying habits, etc. Personalized recommender also takes similar user activity into account for better suggestion. The online shopping sides use personalized recommendation methods to suggest different items to different users depending on their business.

4.3.2   Non-Personalized Recommendation System

In the case of non-personal recommendation, the websites give a general item preference based on the feature evaluation of the items by different types of users [11, 12]. One such non-personal recommendation is the news suggestion by online news agencies. The non-personal recommendations do not have a direct impact on the users' buying habits and personal interest, so such type of systems have less concern in recommendation system research.

4.3.3   Content-Based Filtering

Recommendation systems may be broadly classified into a content-based approach and a collaborative filtering approach [1–5, 9]. Figure 4.3 represents different types of filtering mechanism used in recommendation system.

The content-based approach recommends an item to a user based on the past actions of the user towards a similar kind of item. Here the similarity is measured by the contents of the items. The movie recommendation that we get on different websites is an example of a content-based recommendation.

Content-based system needs well-organized item descriptions to make proper predictions. Let us consider a book recommendation system, as shown in Figure 4.4. It shows that a user has shown his interest in book 'A' and purchased it. Now the content-based recommender finds another book 'B' with similar content or features as that of 'A' and suggests it to the user.

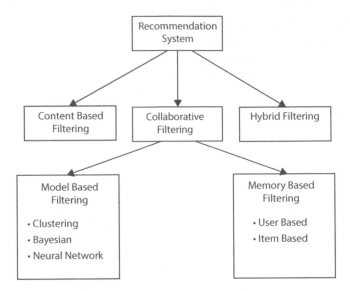

Figure 4.3 Recommendation techniques types based on information filtering.

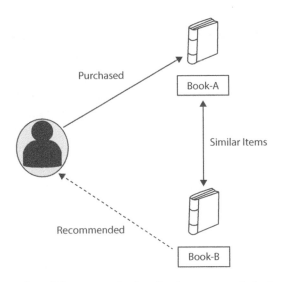

Figure 4.4 Content-based filtering mechanism (book recommendation).

4.3.4   Collaborative Filtering

The collaborative filtering method uses model-based [13–16] and memory-based approaches [3, 4, 18] to make accurate decision of the user's need. In this method, items are suggested to a new user based on the behavior and preferences of other users towards those items. An example of this approach is seen in shopping websites like Amazon or Flipkart, where the recommendation system suggests some item that the user may like or purchase. This suggestion is based on the shopping behaviors of other customers and product specifications [5].

To have a better understanding, let us consider the information depicted in Figure 4.5. It shows that there are three customers and three books. Here the solid arrow from customer to book indicates that the customer has purchased the book. Similarly, the dashed arrow from the book to the customer indicates that the book is recommended to the customer. Initially, customer-1 has purchased Book-A, and the system wants to recommend a new book to customer-1. The system checks the similarity between customer-1 and other customer and finds that customer-2 has similar book interest as customer-1, and customer-2 has purchase Book-A and Book-C. So, it recommends Book-C to customer-1.

In collaborative filtering, the similarity between users can be computed by using the correlation and cosine technique [18]. The correlation between two users P and Q depends upon the number of items for which both P and Q have given similar feedback or rating. If there are n items, then the ratings of P and Q can be represented by two vectors

$$P_{rating} = [p_1, p_2, \ldots\ldots, p_n] \text{ and } Q_{rating} = [q_1, q_2, \ldots\ldots, q_n]$$

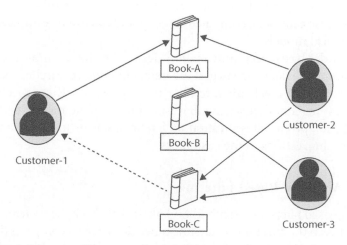

Figure 4.5 Collaborative filtering mechanism (book recommendation).

If the respective mean value of these ratings is p_m and q_m, then the correlation between P and Q is given by,

$$K_{\text{correlation}}(P,Q) = \frac{\sum_{i=1}^{n}(p_i - p_m)(q_i - q_m)}{\sqrt{\sum_{i=1}^{n}(p_i - p_m)^2}\sqrt{\sum_{i=1}^{n}(q_i - q_m)^2}} \qquad (1)$$

In the similar fashion the cosine similarity is calculated by using the Euclidean dot product method. It is represented as,

$$K_{\text{cosine}}(P,Q) = \cos(\theta) = \frac{\sum_{i=1}^{n}(p_i)(q_i)}{\sqrt{\sum_{i=1}^{n}(p_i)^2}\sqrt{\sum_{i=1}^{n}(q_i)^2}} \qquad (2)$$

In the above equation Θ is the angle between P and Q in n dimensional space.

4.3.5   Model-Based Filtering

The recommendation system uses different machine learning and Artificial intelligence algorithms [13–16] for better prediction, taking into account the user's history, product features, and behaviors of other customers. Many of these cannot be computed directly, and have to be estimated using mathematical models.

The model-based recommendation deals with the learning algorithms that examine the data and suggest the item. Different researchers have suggested a different mechanism to filter the suggestion. These mechanisms use nearest neighbor clustering, Bayesian probabilistic model, and neural networks for proper classification and refinement of information before providing suggestions to the customers.

4.3.6   Memory-Based Filtering

Memory based filters are neighborhood filters that check the preference similarity between the current user and the other users. It also compares the user's likeliness towards a set of products or services to give a healthy suggestion. It depends upon the users respond to an object. This approach mainly relies upon the availability of past data. It refines the recommendation with time, as with time, the available data volume increases, so suggestion becomes better.

Consider a memory-based filtering example with five users (User-1, User-2, User-3, User-4, and User-5) and three items (Item-1, Item-2, and Item-3), as shown in Table 4.1. The preferences of different users towards different items are represented in binary yes/no values.

For the first four users, we have the preference information for all items. Let the new user, which we call as User-5, has preferred Item-1. Now the filtering mechanism will use the available data to decide which item will it suggest to User-5 to prefer or purchase.

Initially, it checks the preference of other users towards Item-1, and the users having similar choices as User-5 is be considered. So, for decision making, the data of User-1 and User-3 is considered since they have the same preference as User-5 for Item-1. Now it takes voting for Item-2 and Item-3 by checking the yes/no value, where yes is treated as 1 and no as 0. It is observed that for Item-2, the vote is 1, and for item-3, the vote is 2. Since Item-3 has the highest vote, so it will be suggested to User-5.

The above approach is called a user-based approach since the similarity between users is considered for suggestion. Similarly, when the similarity between items is found, then it is called item-based approach.

4.3.7   Hybrid Recommendation Technique

Now a day's companies use a mixture of multiple recommendation technique, which is called a hybrid recommendation technique [2]. The hybrid approach [7, 18] takes the advantages of both content-based and collaborative filtering. It helps to improve the overall performance of the recommendation. This approach can be applied to our earlier example of book

Table 4.1 User-preference information for memory based filtering.

User	Preference		
	Item-1	Item-2	Item-3
User-1	Yes	Yes	Yes
User-2	No	Yes	No
User-3	Yes	No	Yes
User-4	No	Yes	Yes
User-5	Yes	?	?

recommendation system where the recommendation of a book can be made by considering the similarity of customers and correlation between customers and book.

4.3.8   Social Media Recommendation Technique

Apart from all the above recommendation techniques, some methods use the social networking behavior [10] of the individual and provides new friend and group suggestions to the user. Such techniques are called a social network recommendation technique. The recommendation system used by Facebook is a type of social network recommendation system.

4.4   Performance Evaluation

The performance of a recommendation technique can be evaluated by using prediction accuracy and classification accuracy metrics [3, 18].

In prediction accuracy we check the Mean Absolute Error (MAE) and Root Mean Square Error ($RMSE$) to analyze the performance of a method. If there are N number of items and X_i represents predicted rating of item i and Y_i represents the actual rating of item i then the MAE and $RMSE$ can be calculated by using Equation 3 and 4 respectively. Lower the MAE or $RMSE$ better the performance.

$$MAE = \frac{\left(\sum_{i=1}^{N} |X_i - Y_i| \right)}{N} \tag{3}$$

$$RMSE = \sqrt{\frac{\sum_{i=1}^{N} (X_i - Y_i)^2}{N}} \tag{4}$$

The classical accuracy approach uses confusion matrix (Table 4.2) to check performance. It takes the Precision, Recall and F-Measure value to evaluate the accuracy. These values can be calculated by using the following formulas.

$$Precision = \frac{TP}{TP + FP} \tag{5}$$

Table 4.2 Confusion matrix.

		Actual value	
		Positive	Negative
Predicted value	Positive	TP	FP
	Negative	FN	TN

$$Recall = \frac{TP}{TP + FN} \tag{6}$$

$$F - Measure = \frac{2 * Precision * Recall}{Precision + Recall} \tag{7}$$

4.5   Challenges

In this twenty-first century, the world wide web contains a huge amount of data, and it becomes a challenging job for the recommendation system to find a proper user-item match [5, 10]. Figure 4.6 list outs different

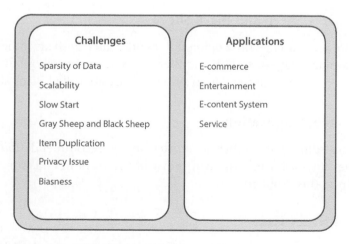

Figure 4.6 Challenges and applications of recommendation system.

challenges of recommendation system. It also shows the application of recommender in various industries.

4.5.1   Sparsity of Data

Data sparsity is one of the major challenges for e-commerce recommendation system. For a very large item set the user–item metric becomes sparse. It causes poor recommendations for some items. New items recommendation becomes dependent upon the old users to rate them. Lack of preference history causes poor recommendation for the new users. Many techniques have been proposed to solve the issue including dimensionality reduction, probabilistic matrix factorization etc.

4.5.2   Scalability

The increasing size of data affects the performance of the algorithm. That happens due to the fact that the computational capability goes out of practical limit.

4.5.3   Slow Start

When the user is new or the item is not rated then the recommendation system needs some amount of time to get some more information for starting [18, 19]. There are some networks which gives some information for the user to recommendation system to start.

4.5.4   Gray Sheep and Black Sheep

There are some users whose opinion does not match with any others. They are known as Gray sheep [20] and there are some users whose distinctive behavior causes recommendation system failure are called Black sheep.

4.5.5   Item Duplication

There are some items which is enlisted in the recommendation system multiple times with its synonym. Most of the recommendation systems suffer from this problem.

4.5.6   Privacy Issue

The recommendation system always leaks information of user. When evaluating the customer, the issue arises.

4.5.7   Biasness

People use to give positive feedback for their own product and negative feedback for competitors. It causes bad recommendation. The recommendation systems should handle them.

4.6   Applications

There are several applications for recommendation system in several websites. More over several researches are going on to improve the recommendation system in terms of its practical usability. With time the recommendation system evolved a lot. Some important applications of recommendation system are:

E-commerce: Most e-commerce site use recommendation system to build up user-item relationship through reviews, ratings and tagging. Some of them are Amazon, e-Bay, iTunes, etc.

Entertainment: Video sites like Netflix, YouTube, etc. use recommendation system to personalize videos according to the user's taste. This makes the sites easy to use for the users.

E-content System: Recommendation system is used by e-content systems to design e-mail filtering, personalized web pages etc.

Service: Some service-oriented websites like matrimony sites, tourist recommendation, consultancy, travel services use recommendation system.

4.7   Conclusion

The recommendation system helps to reduce the problem of information overloading and make our life easy. With the advancement of new techniques, the performance of recommender increases gradually. This knowledge of recommender techniques will empower researchers and will help them to come up with a new technique with better performance.

References

1. Bai, X., Wang, M., Lee, I., Yang, Z., Kong, X., Xia, F., Scientific paper recommendation: A survey. *IEEE Access*, 7, 9324–9339, 2019.

2. Erion, C. and Maurizio, M., Hybrid Recommender Systems: A Systematic Literature Review. *Intell. Data Anal.*, 21, 6, 1487–1524, 2017.
3. Isinkaye, F.O., Folajimi, Y.O., Ojokoh, B.A., Recommendation systems: Principles, methods and evaluation. *Egypt. Inform. J.*, 16, 261–273, 2015.
4. Ricci, F., Rokach, L., Shapira, B., Introduction to Recommender Systems Handbook, in: *Recommender Systems Handbook*, pp. 1–35, Springer, New York, 2011.
5. He, C., Parra, D., Verbert, K., Interactive recommender systems: A survey of the state of the art and future research challenges and opportunities. *Expert Syst. Appl.*, 56, 9–27, 2016.
6. Bobadilla, J., Ortega, F., Hernando, A., Gutierrez, A., Recommender systems survey. *Knowl-Based Syst.*, 46, 109–132, 2013.
7. Kunaver, M. and Pozrl, T., Diversity in recommender systems—A survey. *Knowl-Based Syst.*, 123, 154–162, 2017.
8. Parra, D. and Sahebi, S., Recommender Systems: Sources of Knowledge and Evaluation Metrics, in: *Advanced Techniques in Web Intelligence-2*, pp. 149–175, Springer, Berlin, Heidelberg, SCI 452, 2013.
9. Balabanovic., M. and Shahom, Y., Fab: content-based, collaborative recommendation. *Commun. ACM*, 40, 3, 66–72, 1997.
10. Basu, C., Hirsh, H., Cohen, W., Recommendation as Classification: Using Social and Content-Based Information in Recommendation. *Recommender Systems, Papers from Workshop Technical report WS-98-08*, AAI Press, 1998.
11. Micarelli, A., Gasparetti, F., Sciarrone, F., Gauch, S., Personalized Search on the World Wide Web, in: *The Adaptive Web*, pp. 195–230, Springer, Berlin, Heidelberg, LNCS 4321, 2007.
12. Mobasher., B., Data Mining for Web Personalization, in: *The Adaptive Web*, pp. 90–135, Springer, Berlin, Heidelberg, LNCS 4321, 2007.
13. Zhang, S., Yao, L., Sun, A., Tay, Y., Deep Learning Based Recommender System: A Survey and New Perspectives. *ACM Comput. Surv.* (CSUR), 52, 1, 5, 1–38, 2019.
14. Zhu, H., Li, X., Zhang, P., Li, G., He, J., Li, H., Gai, K., Learning Tree-based Deep Model for Recommender Systems, *Proceedings of the 24th ACM SIGKDD International Conference on Knowledge Discovery and Data Mining*, pp. 1079-1088, 2018.
15. Agrawal, R., Gupta, A., Prabhu, Y., Varma, M., Multi-Label Learning with Millions of Labels: Recommending Advertiser Bid Phrases for Web Pages. *Proceedings of the 22nd international conference on World Wide Web*, pp. 13–24, 2013.
16. Sembium, V., Rastogi, R., Tekumalla, L., Saroop, A., Bayesian Models for Product Size Recommendations. *Proceedings of the 2018 World Wide Web Conference*, WWW'18, pp. 679–687, 2018.
17. Beel, J., Gipp, B., Langer, S., Breitinger, C., Research-paper recommender systems: a literature survey. *Int. J. Digit. Libr.*, 17, 305–338, 2016.

18. Raghuwanshi, S.K. and Pateriya, R.K., Recommendation Systems: Techniques, Challenges, Application, and Evaluation, in: *Advances in Intelligent Systems and Computing*, vol. 817, pp. 151–164, Springer, Singapore, 2019.

19. Rana, M.C., Survey paper on recommendation system. *Int. J. Comput. Sci. Inf. Technol.*, 3, 2, 3460–3462, 2012.

20. Mahony, M.O., Hurley, N., Kushmerick, N., Silvestre, G., Collaborative recommendation: a robustness analysis. *ACM Trans. Internet Technol.*, 4, 4, 344–377, 2004.

A Machine Learning Approach to Recommend Suitable Crops and Fertilizers for Agriculture

Govind Kumar Jha[1]*, Preetish Ranjan[2] and Manish Gaur[3]

[1]Dept. of CSE, BCE Bhagalpur, Bhagalpur, Bihar, India
[2]Dept. of CSE, Amity University Patna, Patna, Bihar, India
[3]Centre for Advanced Studies, AKTU, Lucknow, UP, India

Abstract

Agriculture and allied sectors contribute more than 53% of GDP in India and 50% of the workforce is involved with it. Besides being the first and foremost contributor to the economic development of India, this sector is facing many problems and has the lowest per capita productivity. Despite the huge size of the agricultural sector, yields per hectare of crops are low compared to international standards. People are quite reluctant to choose it as their occupation and sometimes confused about their investment in agriculture. This is due to lack of information about their land, nutrition in the soil, level of water, composition of fertilizers required by soil and many others. This kind of very particular information may be availed to farmers through the internet and communication technology. By applying machine learning-enabled programs may provide rich insights for farmer decision support. A recommender system based on a machine learning approach may be developed which could suggest the type of crop and the fertilizer may be used to increase their productivity and consequently, their income.

Keywords: Machine learning, soil health card, recommendations, random forest, yield predictions

*Corresponding author: gvnd.jha@gmail.com

Sachi Nandan Mohanty, Jyotir Moy Chatterjee, Sarika Jain, Ahmed A. Elngar and Priya Gupta (eds.) Recommender System with Machine Learning and Artificial Intelligence: Practical Tools and Applications in Medical, Agricultural and Other Industries, (89–100) © 2020 Scrivener Publishing LLC

5.1   Introduction

India is an agriculture-based country and it plays a major role in the economic growth of the country. Most of the Indians are directly or indirectly depending on agriculture. Some are directly attached to the farming and some are involved in doing business with these agricultural products. The Indian agriculture sector accounts for 18% of India's gross domestic product (GDP) and provides employment to 50% of the countries workforce. Agriculture is the primary source of livelihood for 58% of India's population. Gross Value Added by agriculture, forestry, and fishing is estimated to be Rs. 18.53 trillion in FY18. The Indian food industry is poised for huge growth, increasing its contribution to world food trade every year. It has immense potential for value addition, particularly for the food processing industry. The Indian food and grocery market is the world's sixth-largest, with retail contributing 70% of the sales. The Indian food processing industry accounts for 32% of the country's total food market, which is ranked fifth in terms of production, consumption, and export. It contributes around 8.80 and 8.39% of Gross Value Added (GVA) in the manufacturing and agriculture sector respectively. Therefore, India as a country is dependent potentially on agriculture for its economic development.

Agriculture is a source of livelihood and source of income in India. Comparing the performance of this sector with other parts of the world, we still lack the basic infrastructure support for the farmers. We do not have enough water, fertilizer, good quality seeds and effective pesticides. India has a very big agricultural area. It is very problematic to reach every corner of the country even for the government and solve specific problems. Green revolution solved some of the problems by introducing chemicals, fertilizers, and pesticides to increase agricultural productivity. Technology may play a major role to strengthen our farmers.

India's agriculture is composed of many crops, with the foremost food staples being rice and wheat. Indian farmers also grow pulses, potatoes, sugarcane, oilseeds and non-food items as cotton, tea, coffee, rubber, and jute. India is the world's largest producer of pulses, rice, wheat, spices, and spice products. Apart from these, the other agriculture-based businesses are dairy, meat, poultry, and fisheries. India has also emerged as the second-largest producer of fruits and vegetables in the world. Therefore, India has a wide range of agricultural products depending on varied environments.

Soil Health Card is prepared by an agricultural scientist under the Soil Health Card scheme of Govt. of India. Figure 5.1 is the Soil Health card, issued by Govt. of India, does not have much useful information that

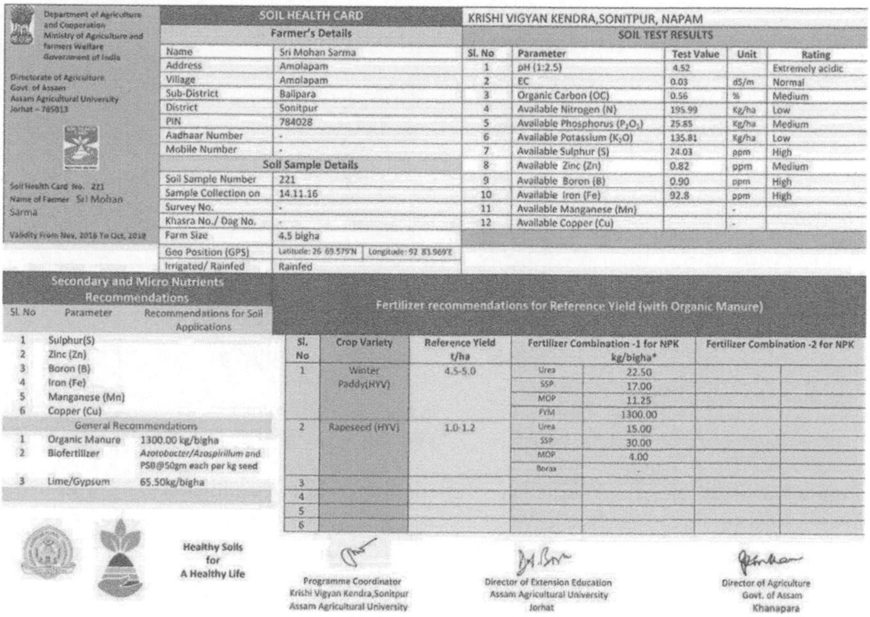

Department of Agriculture and Cooperation
Ministry of Agriculture and farmers Welfare
Government of India

Directorate of Agriculture
Govt. of Assam
Assam Agricultural University
Jorhat – 785013

Soil Health Card No. 221
Name of Farmer Sri Mohan Sarma
Validity From Nov, 2016 To Oct, 2018

SOIL HEALTH CARD

Farmer's Details	
Name	Sri Mohan Sarma
Address	Amolapam
Village	Amolapam
Sub-District	Balipara
District	Sonitpur
PIN	784028
Aadhaar Number	-
Mobile Number	-
Soil Sample Details	
Soil Sample Number	221
Sample Collection on	14.11.16
Survey No.	-
Khasra No./ Dag No.	-
Farm Size	4.5 bigha
Geo Position (GPS)	Latitude: 26 69.579'N Longitude: 92 83.969'E
Irrigated/ Rainfed	Rainfed

KRISHI VIGYAN KENDRA,SONITPUR, NAPAM

SOIL TEST RESULTS

Sl. No	Parameter	Test Value	Unit	Rating
1	pH (1:2.5)	4.52		Extremely acidic
2	EC	0.03	dS/m	Normal
3	Organic Carbon (OC)	0.56	%	Medium
4	Available Nitrogen (N)	195.99	Kg/ha	Low
5	Available Phosphorus (P_2O_5)	25.85	Kg/ha	Medium
6	Available Potassium (K_2O)	135.81	Kg/ha	Low
7	Available Sulphur (S)	24.03	ppm	High
8	Available Zinc (Zn)	0.82	ppm	Medium
9	Available Boron (B)	0.90	ppm	High
10	Available Iron (Fe)	92.8	ppm	High
11	Available Manganese (Mn)		-	
12	Available Copper (Cu)		-	

Secondary and Micro Nutrients Recommendations

Sl. No	Parameter	Recommendations for Soil Applications
1	Sulphur(S)	
2	Zinc (Zn)	
3	Boron (B)	
4	Iron (Fe)	
5	Manganese (Mn)	
6	Copper (Cu)	
	General Recommendations	
1	Organic Manure	1300.00 kg/bigha
2	Biofertilizer	*Azotobacter/Azospirillum* and PSB@50gm each per kg seed
3	Lime/Gypsum	65.50kg/bigha

Fertilizer recommendations for Reference Yield (with Organic Manure)

Sl. No	Crop Variety	Reference Yield t/ha	Fertilizer Combination -1 for NPK kg/bigha*		Fertilizer Combination -2 for NPK	
1	Winter Paddy(HYV)	4.5-5.0	Urea	22.50		
			SSP	17.00		
			MOP	11.25		
			FYM	1300.00		
2	Rapeseed (HYV)	1.0-1.2	Urea	15.00		
			SSP	30.00		
			MOP	4.00		
			Borax	-		
3						
4						
5						
6						

Healthy Soils for A Healthy Life

Programme Coordinator
Krishi Vigyan Kendra,Sonitpur
Assam Agricultural University

Director of Extension Education
Assam Agricultural University
Jorhat

Director of Agriculture
Govt. of Assam
Khanapara

Figure 5.1 Sample of Soil Health Card (Source-https://soilhealth.dac.gov.in).

farmers can use directly. So various ML algorithms leverage Soil Health Card information for farmers.

Farmers should be encouraged to use technology through ICT in every process associated with farming. Soil quality is an important factor that affects the productivity of crops. Online application may produce SHC to the farmers showing the status of nutrient in soil with respect to 12 parameters, namely N, P, K (Macro-nutrients); S (Secondary-nutrient); Zn, Fe, Cu, Mn, Bo (Micro-nutrients); and pH, EC, OC (Physical parameters). Based on this, the SHC will also recommend fertilizers and soil amendments required for the farm to attain maximum profit with minimum investment. Using this ML based approach, we predict the yield and predicted profit to farmer. The complete status of soil samples collected, tested and SHC cards printed and distributed reports given in Figures 5.2 and 5.3.

5.2 Literature Review

Soil testing mechanism in India is a very tedious job and it really takes time as different samples of soil are collected from farming land. This is sent to the laboratories, tested and reported back to the farmers. Different

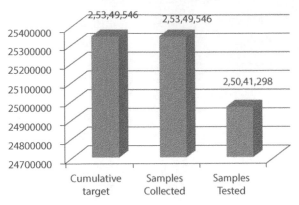

Figure 5.2 Status of SHC Collected and Tested (Source: https://soilhealth.dac.gov.in).

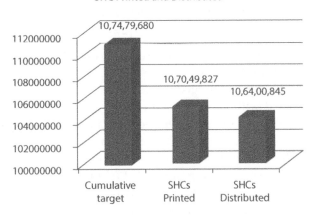

Figure 5.3 Status of SHC Printed and Distributed (Source: https://soilhealth.dac.gov.in).

methodologies and machine learning (ML) algorithms have been implemented for soil analysis. Ambarish *et al.* have used experimental NPK
dataset from ICAR to develop a Random Forest-based decision tree for the
prediction of required NPK for the crop and soil specific agriculture land.
Random forest is a collection of tree predictors where the trees are constructed using various random features. Random vectors are generated to
represent the growth of trees where the trees are never being pruned. The
web interface based on the random forest algorithm is tested using four

types of soils and crops. They observed that the predicted required amount of soil NPK content has minimum deviations from the target level and also having minimum RSME. This will help farmers to estimate the required NPK content without manual calculations. Panchamurthi *et al.* has collected more than 300 datasets for Tiruvallur district from the department of horticulture and agriculture. The data is related to the different types of crops, vegetables, fruits, and oilseed grew in that area. Fertilizer and nutrient requirement are recommended on the results of the soil test analysis. Every year crop yield suffers due to lack of knowledge on the soil being used and same old practices followed by farmers due which farmers may end up paying more for certain utilities such as irrigation, fertilizers. The Soil Health card, issued by Govt. of India does not have much use for information that farmers can directly use. It contains information like the variety of crops and intercrop that can be grown on a farmer's land based on its agro-climatic region and value of N, P, K ratio of farmer's land. This info is pretty rudimentary considering farmer's view. So, our objective is to use this SHC information and make it directly useful to farmers. Canada is one of the largest agricultural producers and exporters in the world. But it is noticed that there is a common problem faced amongst the farmers while farming, that they don't choose the right crop based on their soil requirements and location. Due to this, they face a serious setback in productivity. This problem of the farmers has been addressed through precision agriculture. Precision agriculture is a modern farming technique that uses research data of soil characteristics, soil types, crop yield data collection, and suggests the farmers the right crop based on their site-specific parameters.

5.3   Methodology

There are various machine learning algorithms that have been implemented for the analysis of soil data. Machine learning algorithms involve a learning process with the objective to learn from training to perform a task. After the end of the learning process, the trained model can be used to classify, predict, or cluster testing data using the experience obtained during the training process. Training data is described by a set of attributes, also known as features or variables. A feature can be nominal (enumeration), binary (i.e., 0 or 1), ordinal (A+ or B−), or numeric (integer, real number, etc.). ML tasks are typically classified into different broad categories depending on the learning type (supervised/ unsupervised), learning models (classification, regression, clustering, and dimensionality reduction), or the learning models employed to implement the selected task. Tasks of Learning ML tasks are classified into two main categories, that is, supervised and unsupervised learning, depending on the learning signal of the learning system. In supervised learning, data are presented with example input and the corresponding outputs, and the objective is to construct a general rule that maps inputs to outputs. In some cases, inputs can be only partially available with some of the target outputs missing or given only as feedback to the actions in a dynamic environment (reinforcement learning). In the supervised setting, the acquired expertise (trained model) is used to predict the missing outputs (labels) for the test data. In unsupervised learning, however, there is no distinction between training and test sets with data being unlabeled. The learner processes input data with the goal of discovering hidden patterns. This method is characterized by a soil data collected from the farm, crop provided by agricultural experts, the achievement of parameters such as soil through soil testing lab dataset. The data from soil test given to recommender system, it will use the collected data and do ensemble model and other ML-based approaches to recommend a crop for a site-specific parameter with high accuracy and efficiency. There are various methods related to agriculture for providing solutions to the problem of farmers, but they provide mostly generalized solutions to the farmers. Also, sometimes they are dealing with only one or two components of farming only. So we are trying to integrate these entire components into one and give detailed and scheduled solutions to farmers, integrating packages of practices. In this application real-time info will be given to farmers from field preparation to their predicted yield.

Various ML algorithms have been applied over the dataset are as follows:

1. Naïve Bayes: This classification is popularly used to categorize the document on the basis of a sequence of words, relationships and other assumptions in the multinomial distribution of words. This kind of supervised learning is studied from a probabilistic point of view which is regarded as estimating the class posterior probabilities given test example. Bayesian models (BM) are a family of probabilistic graphical models in which the analysis is undertaken within the context of Bayesian inference. This type of model belongs to the supervised learning category and can be employed for solving either classification or regression problems. Naive Bayes [1], Gaussian Naive Bayes, multinomial Naive Bayes, Bayesian

network [2], a mixture of Gaussians [3], and Bayesian belief network [4] are some of the most prominent algorithms in the literature.

2. Bayes Net: It is a graphical model that uses Bayesian inference for probability calculations. It aims to model conditional dependence through the edges of the acyclic directed graph. Each edge corresponds to a conditional dependence and each node corresponds to a unique random variable. These variables are conditionally independent of their descendants.

3. Logistic Regression: It is used to measure the probability of a certain class using a logistic function. A binary logistic model has a dependent variable with two possible values labeled as 0 and 1. The basic characteristics of the logistic model are that increasing the independent variables scales the odd of the given output at a constant rate.

4. Multilayer Perceptron: It is a class of feedforward artificial neural network. It consists of at least three-layer of nodes. The layer of nodes in the input layer, hidden layer, and output layer. Each node act as a neuron except the input nodes which uses an activation function for training. It finally distinguishes the data that is not linearly separable.

5. Random Forest: As the name suggests, this supervised classification algorithm creates a forest with a number of trees. The more trees in the forest make the forest more robust. Similarly, the higher the number of decision trees produces higher accuracy in the result.

Therefore, it is an ensemble learning method of classification by constructing a multitude of a decision tree with controlled variance. Ensemble Learning (EL) models aim at improving the predictive performance of a given statistical learning or model fitting technique by constructing a linear combination of a simpler base learner. Considering that each trained ensemble represents a single hypothesis, these multiple-classifier systems enable hybridization of hypotheses not induced by the same base learner, thus yielding better results in the case of significant diversity among the single models. Decision Trees are classification or regression models formulated in a tree-like architecture [5]. With DT, the dataset is progressively organized in smaller homogeneous subsets (sub-populations), while at the same time, an associated tree graph is generated. Decision trees have been typically used as the base learner in EL models, for example, random forest

[9], whereas a large number of boosting and bagging implementations have been also proposed, for example, boosting technique [10], adaboost [11], and bootstrap aggregating or bagging algorithm [12]. Each internal node of the tree structure represents a different pairwise comparison on a selected feature, whereas each branch represents the outcome of this comparison. Leaf nodes represent the final decision or prediction taken after following the path from the root to leaf (expressed as a classification rule). The most common learning algorithms in this category are the classification and regression trees [6], the chi-square automatic interaction detector [7], and the iterative dichotomiser [8]. The main focus would be generating accurate models and provide useful recommendations.

5.4   Results and Analysis

We intended to use data from various soil surveys and then develop Machine Learning models which will answer different questions from farmers. A database is maintained which has cumulative data from different surveys on which machine learning algorithms are executed. The problem we'll solve is a classification task with the goal of predicting an individual's health. The dataset which has been considered contains 12 parameters, namely N, P, K (Macro-nutrients); S (Secondary- nutrient); Zn, Fe, Cu, Mn, Bo (Micronutrients); and pH, EC, OC (Physical parameters) temperature and yield as attributes and some label is set for the health of soil samples. This dataset was collected from farmers SHC.

The machine is trained from the dataset using various Machine Learning (ML) algorithms. The performance of the different machine learning algorithms such as Naïve Bayes, Bayes Net, Logistic Regression, Multi-Layer Perceptron (MLP) and Random Forest is measured on the basis of Weighted ROC (WtROC), True Positive (TP), False Positive (FP), Precision and Recall. The following values of Table 5.1 have been obtained corresponding to different algorithms.

Output has been compared and analyzed from the graph plotted from the values from Table 5.1.

From Figure 5.4, it can be concluded that Random Forest is leading among all algorithms with reference to the different performance indicators. The random forest model achieved 1.0 ROC, which illustrates the highest true positive rate against false positive. This algorithm has the highest recall and precision values with respect to other algorithms which reflects the accuracy of results. Hence, it may be concluded that random forest is the highest sensitivity towards the classification of supplied soil dataset as input. This algorithm

Table 5.1 Performance indicators of algorithms.

	Naïve Bayes	Bayes Net	Logistic Regression	MLP	Random Forest
WtROC	0.542	0.5	0.535	0.608	1
TP	0.388	0.349	0.367	0.447	1
FP	0.315	0.349	0.325	0.29	0
Precision	0.386	0.122	0.359	0.471	1
Recall	0.388	0.349	0.367	0.471	1

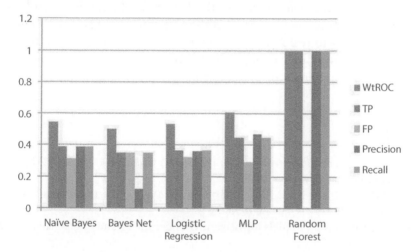

Figure 5.4 Comparative results.

is most suitable for the classification of soil data in comparison to other algorithms. Feature importance can give us insight into a problem by telling us what variables are the most discerning between classes. This increases the rate of accuracy in making the correct choice of machine learning algorithm will give better recommendations and thus proliferate the productivity.

5.5 Conclusion

Data analytics and machine learning models have been used for determining soil health. This can provide recommendations aiding the farmer to make well-informed decisions regarding the best-suited crops for a particular area. It has been concluded that the random forest algorithm produces the most accurate yield prediction under given soil conditions. Therefore, a farmer can plan his investment accordingly taking into consideration the predicted yield hence the forecasted profit. Farmers can plan the sowing rate, spacing and fertilizers to be used on the basis of the soil health card. Giving suggestions to farmers for planting the best crop can minimize their risk factors involved with this occupation. This gives targeted results to farmers analyzing their Soil Health Card and predicting their yield per hectare if they follow few suggestions. We can predict the yield and predicted profit to the farmer using the random forest model. It can be used to publish an advisory based on the soil nutrient status of a farmer's holding. It can show recommendations on the dosage of different nutrients needed. It will also advise the farmer on the fertilizers and their quantities he should apply, and also the soil amendments that he should undertake, so as to realize optimal yields. Our work will help the farmers by recommending them an appropriate crop based on their soil type and land assists them in making better decisions regarding farming.

References

1. Pearl, J., *Probabilistic reasoning in intelligent systems*, vol. 88, p. 552, Morgan Kauffmann, San Mateo, 1988.
2. Duda, R.O. and Hart, P.E., *Pattern classification and scene analysis*, vol. 7, Wiley, Hoboken, NJ, USA, 1973.
3. Neapolitan, R.E., Models for reasoning under uncertainty. *Appl. Artif. Intell*, 1, 337–366, 1987.
4. Fix, E. and Hodges, J.L., Discriminatory Analysis–Nonparametric discrimination consistency properties. *Int. Stat. Rev.*, 57, 238–247, 1951.
5. Atkeson, C.G., Moorey, A.W., Schaalz, S., Moore, A.W., Schaal, S., Locally Weighted Learning. *Artif. Intell.*, 11, 11–73, 1997.
6. Kohonen, T., An introduction to neural computing. *Neural Networks*, 1, 1, 3–16, 1988.
7. Belson, W.A., Matching and Prediction on the Principle of Biological Classification. *Appl. Stat.*, 8, 65–75, 1959.
8. Breiman, L., Friedman, J.H., Olshen, R.A., Stone, C.J., *Classification and regression trees*, vol. 19, Routledge, Abingdon, UK, 1984.
9. Suykens, J.A.K., Van Gestel, T., De Brabanter, J., De Moor, B., Vandewalle, J., *Least squares support vector machines*, World Scientific, Singapore, 2002.
10. Galvão, R.K.H., Araújo, M.C.U., Fragoso, W.D., Silva, E.C., José, G.E., Soares, S.F.C., Paiva, H.M., A variable elimination method to improve the parsimony

of MLR models using the successive projections algorithm. *Chemometr. Intell. Lab.*, 92, 83–91, 2008.

11. Breiman, L., Random forests. *Mach. Learn.*, 45, 1, 5–32, 2001.

12. Schapire, R.E., A brief introduction to boosting, in: Proceedings of the IJCAI International Joint Conference on Artificial Intelligence, Stockholm, Sweden, 31 July–6 August 1999, vol. 2, pp. 1401–1406, 1999.

13. Freund, Y. and Schapire, R.E., Experiments with a New Boosting Algorithm, in: *Proceedings of the Thirteenth International Conference on International Conference on Machine Learning, Bari, Italy, 3–6 July 1996*, Morgan Kaufmann Publishers Inc., San Francisco, CA, USA, pp. 148–156, 1996.

14. Breiman, L., Bagging predictors. *Mach. Learn.*, 24, 2, 123–140, 1996.

Accuracy-Assured Privacy-Preserving Recommender System Using Hybrid-Based Deep Learning Method

Abhaya Kumar Sahoo* and Chittaranjan Pradhan

School of Computer Engineering, KIIT Deemed to be University, Bhubaneswar, India

Abstract

Recommender System is an efficient information filtering system which has been used in different fields to customize applications by predicting and recommending various items. Collaborative Filtering (CF) is most well-known technique of recommender system which is used to find a new one among various items that correspond to user's choice by measuring similar users' interest shown on other similar items. Recommender system is decision making system which is used in various fields to personalize applications by recommending different kinds of items. CF is a famous filtering technique in recommender system which is used in cross domain applications to predict and recommend an item to a particular user. Here Privacy and accuracy are two main factors which play major role for recommender system. There are different machine learning and deep learning based collaborative filtering methods used in recommender system. In this chapter, we propose Restrictive Boltzmann Machine Approach (RBM) and hybrid deep learning method i.e. RBM with Convolution neural network (CNN) (CRBM). These two proposed approaches provide better accuracy of the movie recommender system as compared to other existing methods. The proposed CRBM (RBM with CNN method) is best method which provides less mean absolute error (MAE) than all methods.

Keywords: CNN, collaborative filtering, CRBM, deep learning, matrix factorization, RBM, recommender system, singular value decomposition

**Corresponding author*: abhaya.sahoofcs@kiit.ac.in

Sachi Nandan Mohanty, Jyotir Moy Chatterjee, Sarika Jain, Ahmed A. Elngar and Priya Gupta (eds.) *Recommender System with Machine Learning and Artificial Intelligence: Practical Tools and Applications in Medical, Agricultural and Other Industries*, (101–120) © 2020 Scrivener Publishing LLC

6.1   Introduction

Today's scenario, people is connected through the internet in all aspects of life. When people use the internet for buying any product, they first look for the reviews and comments on that product. Recommender system plays a main role which predicts and recommends a particular product which will be preferable by the user in the e-commerce site. This system behaves as the decision-making system which is designed based on the user's preferences, features and item attributes [1, 6].

Based on the user's profile, recommender system has the ability to predict whether a particular product would be preferred by the user or not. This information filtering system can be developed using item's profile or user's profile. This chapter discusses mainly item based collaborative filtering used in recommender systems [6, 14]. Now-a-days, e-commerce websites generate high revenues with the help of recommender system that predicts and recommends the preferable product for the user [4, 24, 26].

Many challenges along with problems are seen as the growth of user data is increased when people visit the various e-commerce websites. The main problem in the recommender system is the information overload, sparsity and privacy which can be resolved by using machine learning approaches. To achieve better accuracy of recommender system, different approaches such as matrix factorization (MF), basic singular value decomposition (BSVD) and weight based singular value decomposition (WBSVD) etc. are used. Different metrics such as Mean absolute error (MAE) and Root Mean Square Error (RMSE) are widely used to compute the performance of recommender system. The main objective is to decrease RMSE value of the model which will provide high accuracy. MAE is another measurement technique of accuracy by computing the difference between the predicted ratings and the real ratings, so the smaller MAE, the better recommendation quality. In the above approaches, we get different RMSE and MAE value. As compared to above approaches, different neural network based deep learning methods such as restricted Boltzmann machine and convolution neural networks which gives better accuracy to recommend right item to user in recommender system. In this chapter we propose RBM along with CRBM hybrid approach which provides better accuracy result than above all approaches.

The rest of the chapter is organized as follows: Section 2 describes about the overview of recommender system. Section 3 presents the CF based recommender system. Section 4 presents various methods used in recommender system. Section 5 introduces proposed RBM and CRBM based recommender system along with experimental result and analysis. Section 6 contains the conclusions and future work.

6.2   Overview of Recommender System

A. Recommender system and its fundamental theory
Recommender system takes user–item matrix as input. There are various types filtering techniques used in recommender system i.e. content-based filtering, collaborative filtering, and hybrid filtering. Recommender systems address the issue of information overload by generating suitable information from a massive quantity of dynamically produced information in accordance to the taste, interest, or past behavior of the user regarding an item [2, 15, 25, 30]. On the basis of the user's profile, recommender system acquires the capability to predict if or not a specific user would favor an item, which is shown in Figure 6.1.

B. Phases of Recommender system
To build an efficient Recommender system, different phases should be followed. These phases consist of input and output phases along with learning phase. Figure 6.2 shows the phases of recommendation process. The whole design of recommender engine goes through three phases such as information gathering, learning information through a model and testing the model to recommend and predict in efficient manner.

The different phases of recommender system are shown in Figure 6.2.

1. Information Collection: In this process, we collect appropriate user information and create a profile or model for each user including the user's meta-data, behavior or attributes of

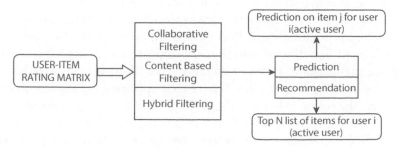

Figure 6.1 Block Diagram of a recommender system.

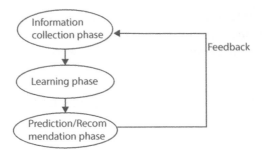

Figure 6.2 Phases of the recommender system.

the assets accessed by him/her for the task of prediction. The system requires learning as much as possible from the user to make sensible recommendations straight from its inception. Recommender systems depend upon various kinds of input that can be classified into explicit feedback where users express their interest for an item or implicit feedback where the system infers a user's choices indirectly by monitoring his behavior or hybrid feedback attained by employing a mix of the other two feedback methods [3].

2. Learning Phase: This phase implements a learning algorithm to filter and utilize the properties of the user from the gathered feedback of the previous phase [1, 15].

3. Prediction/Recommendation Phase: This phase recommends or predicts what type of items the user might like. It can be done either via memory based or model-based techniques directly applied on the collected data-set in the first phase of the recommendation process or can be achieved based on the previous activities of the user recorded by the system [1].

C. Various Filtering techniques used in Recommender system

Data collected in the previous phases needs to be filtered for the process of recommendation. Filtering can either be content-based filtering which utilizes the information about past choices made by the user and the meta data of items or collaborative filtering (CF) which functions by creating a user-item matrix that specifies the choice of items made by the users or hybrid filtering which is a combination of one or more filtering techniques. CF can either be model-based or memory based. Recommendations generated by CF can either be a prediction or recommendation.

Various filtering techniques are shown in Figure 6.3.

1. Content based Filtering: A content-based filtering technique
   used items features and behaviors which help to predict better
   in the recommender system. This filtering technique is mainly
   based on a user's history and profiles that deal with various
   attributes of items. Users give their ratings, which may be different in nature, such as positive, negative and neutral. Usually
   positive rated items are recommended by the system [1].
2. Collaborative Filtering: This technique calculates similarity among items based on the user's ratings using different
   methods such as Pearson's coefficient, Jaccard's distance and
   cosine distance etc. [5, 6, 23].
3. Hybrid Filtering: This approach uses both content filtering
   and collaborative filtering to enhance the quality of recommender system. Different hybrid methods are used in the
   hybrid filtering based recommender system such as weighted
   hybrid, switching hybrid and cascade hybrid etc. [1].

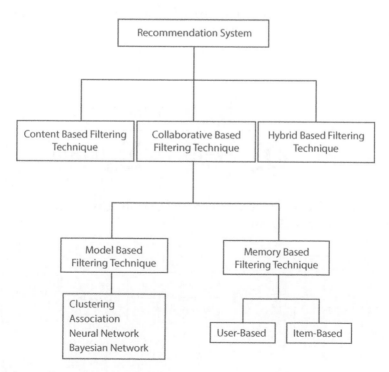

Figure 6.3 Different filtering techniques used in recommender system.

6.3   Collaborative Filtering-Based Recommender System

Collaborative filtering technique finds the correct outcomes using user–item matrix of the user's preferences towards the items. Comparing among user–item matrix and users' preferences calculates the similarities of user profile. By applying similarity concept, neighborhood among users is created [9]. The Unrated item by the user gets the recommendation to the item with the help of positive ratings of the others in his neighborhood. This collaborative filtering-based recommender system helps in both prediction and recommendation. This filtering technique can be applied in either memory based or model based. Figure 6.4 shows the different activities involved in collaborative filtering technique [5, 6, 10–12].

A. Memory based Collaborative filtering
In the filtering technique, both user and item play main role in case of user based collaborative filtering and item based collaborative filtering. Predication depends on similarity coefficient which can be computed in three ways. These are correlation-based cosine-based and Pearson's correlation coefficient-based similarity measures.

Pearson's coefficient among users' p and q given rating on item can be defined as:

$$t(p,q) = \frac{\sum_{i=1}^{n}\left(r_{p,i} - \overline{r_p}\right)\left(r_{p,i} - \overline{r_p}\right)}{\sqrt{\sum_{i=1}^{n}\left(r_{p,i} - \overline{r_p}\right)^2}\ \sqrt{\sum_{i=1}^{n}\left(r_{q,i} - \overline{r_q}\right)^2}} \tag{1}$$

Cosine similarity is used to compute the similarity between two users which is depicted in Equation 2.

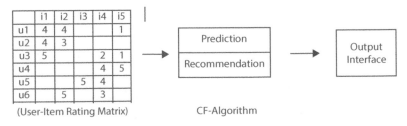

	i1	i2	i3	i4	i5
u1	4	4			1
u2	4	3			
u3	5			2	1
u4				4	5
u5			5	4	
u6		5		3	

(User-Item Rating Matrix)   CF-Algorithm

Prediction

Recommendation

Output Interface

Figure 6.4 Process flow of collaborative filtering.

$$s\left(\vec{u},\ \vec{v}\right)=\ \frac{\vec{u}.\vec{v}}{\left|\vec{u}\right|*\left|\vec{v}\right|}=\frac{\sum_{i}r_{u,i}r_{v,i}}{\sqrt{\sum_{i}r_{u,i}^{2}}\ \ \sqrt{\sum_{i}r_{v,i}^{2}}} \tag{2}$$

Jaccard Similarity of sets M and N is |M∩N| / |M∪N|, that is the quotient between the size of the intersection and the size of the union of M and N. This is shown in Equation 3.

$$S\left(M,N\right)=\left|M\cap N\right|/\left|M\cup N\right| \tag{3}$$

User–user similarity is measured by computing ratings on ten same items in user-based collaborative filtering. This method predicts the rating which is mainly based on weighted average user item rating. These three methods are very much required to find similarity between the two products.

B. Model based Collaborative filtering
It works on the basis of previous users' ratings to develop a model which is based on different machine learning algorithms [3–5, 7, 27–29].

6.4 Machine Learning Methods Used in Recommender System

Machine learning and deep learning techniques play the main role in recommender system that helps towards prediction and recommendation. Information security along with privacy is the main factor in the recommender system [8]. The objective of recommender system is to provide better accuracy along with high level of privacy. To achieve this objective, we use different machine learning based privacy preserving algorithms such as matrix factorization, singular value decomposition and variable weighted singular value decomposition method etc.

A. Matrix Factorization
To solve high sparsity issues in recommender systems, we use matrix factorization method which uses latent factors [2, 11, 16, 17, 29]. This method correlated both user and item to latent factors which help to hide the internal information behind the data. The item is identified by vector q_i whereas the user is identified by vector p_u. The dot product $q_i^T p_u$ shows the correlation among user and item which is shown in Equation 4.

$$u_i = q_i^T p_u \tag{4}$$

B. Singular Value Decomposition

Singular Value Decomposition is used for finding latent factors in recommender system that helps towards privacy [4, 14]. This method divides a × b matrix Y into three matrices as $Y = PSQ^T$ where P and Q are two orthogonal matrices of size a × c and a × z, respectively; z represents rank of the matrix Y. S denotes a diagonal matrix of size c × c. Singular values are shown in the diagonal of the matrix [19]. This is shown in Equation 5.

$$\hat{Y} = PSQ^T \tag{5}$$

To fill up the sparse locations in routing matrix, the average value of user ratings is used to provide the privacy towards a recommender system. This method also helps to hide the matrix structure which leads to better feature detection of item and user [9, 10].

C. Variable Weighted BSVD (WBSD)

This method is the improved version of the Singular Value Decomposition method which provides better accuracy with high level of privacy. The variable weight plays a main role in this method [20]. Active users can disturb the data to provide privacy by using variable weight. This change in weight can be calculated by using Equation 6.

$$\omega_i = e^{\delta_{max} - \delta_i} \tag{6}$$

Where σ_i, σ_{max} and ω_i denote disturb weight, highest disturb weight and variable weight of user i respectively. The range of ω_i lies among 0 and 1. The new B_m can be computed as per Equation 7.

$$B_m = BS_m S_m^T \tag{7}$$

Where B_m shows the disturbed matrix where each row denotes the data whereas column corresponds to the item.

C_w is computed which is shown in Equation 8:

$$C_\omega = \sum_{I=1}^{m} \omega_i x_i^T x_i \tag{8}$$

Where x_i represents the rating of user i, and the x_i^T represents the transposition of x_i.

D. Deep Learning Method used in Recommender System

Deep learning is the subset of machine learning field where different models of deep learning approach can be used in prediction and recommendation of recommender system such as Multilayer Perceptron (MLP), Restricted Boltzmann Machine (RBM), Convolution Neural Network (CNN) and Recurrent Neural Network (RNN) etc. [8, 18, 19, 20–22].

1. MLP with Auto-encoder

MLP is based on a feed forward neural network that uses multiple hidden layers. Each layer uses a different transfer function as activation function arbitrarily. Auto-encoder (AE) is a deep learning model, i.e. based on back propagation technique that finds the gradient of the error function w.r.t. the weights of the neural network. This model is depicted in Figure 6.5.

Auto-encoders are normally used for dimensionality reduction, data compression and data reconstruction for unsupervised learning.

2. Convolution Neural Network

CNN is a deep learning model that based on feed-forward network. This neural network uses a different convolution layer which finds the local and global features of the input data.

3. Restricted Boltzmann Machine

This model is usually working on probability distribution over the inputs, which consists of two layers such as visible layer and hidden layer [7]. No layer is communicated among the visible and hidden layer. This RBM based deep learning model uses a contrastive divergence approach that extract attributes and features. RBM model is energy-based model that uses binary-valued hidden and visible units which are depicted in Figure 6.6. A matrix of weights W represents the strength of the connections among hidden and visible units V_i, and H_g, respectively. It includes bias weights for these units. Performance of the model mainly depends on the number of hidden units.

4. Adversarial Networks

Adversarial Network is a kind of neural network, which is generative in nature and this network has main two parts such as discriminator and generator.

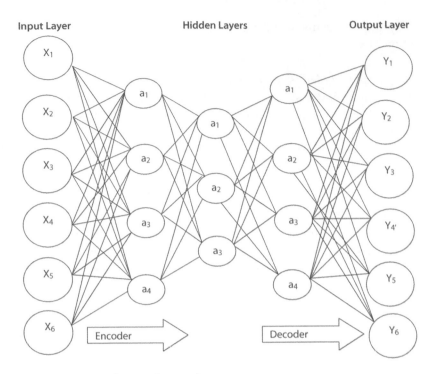

Figure 6.5 Auto-encoder neural network.

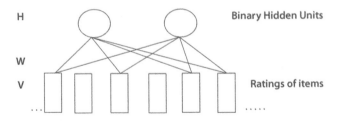

Figure 6.6 RBM neural network.

6.5 Proposed RBM Model-Based Movie Recommender System

This method is implemented using python with TensorFlow and algorithm of this method is described in Algorithm 1.

Algorithm 1

1. Load the dataset of movies and ratings

2. Correct the data and convert the dataset into a specific format
3. Merge movie ID with movie ratings
4. Create the training set
   4.1. For each user in the group for userID
      4.1.1. Create temp that stores every movie's rating
   4.2. For each movie in currentUser's movie list
      4.2.1. Divide the rating by 5
      4.2.2. Add the list of ratings into training set
      4.2.3. Verify the adding of users for training set and set the model parameters
5. Train the model using RBM with 15 epochs, each epoch using 10 batches with size 100.
6. Calculate the error by epoch size.
7. Input the user and reconstruct the input
8. Find the output for input user.

Experimental Result of Above Approach

Experiment analysis is done by using MovieLens data set. This dataset consists of 10,000 ratings of 943 users and 1,682 movies [13]. In this dataset, Movie.dat file contains movie names along with genres. The ratings given by the users range between 1 and 5. Preferred value is highest rating value.

Parameters

We use parameter 'k' that denotes number of nearest neighbors. This 'k' value should be selected properly so that privacy of data will not be lost. Accuracy of the recommender system is computed by the use of Root Mean Absolute Error (RMSE) as a measurement parameter. RMSE is normally used measure the quality of recommender system as it is very easily calculated.

Figure 6.7 shows that RMSE of the proposed RBM model varies with variable k. RMSE value becomes minimum when k becomes 10. Accuracy and quality of recommendation of the model mainly depends on low value of RMSE.

Table 6.1 depicts that RBM based CF is more preferable when k becomes 10. The experimental results indicate that RBM technique is most efficient in terms of measuring accuracy of movie recommender system.

Therefore, RBM based Recommender system which uses collaborative filtering technique, provides the best result in calculating RSME value. Different metrics are used to measure the quality of recommender system such as Precision, Recall and ROC etc. By using no. of epochs, we evaluate our RBM based model by considering mean absolute error (MAE). Table 6.2 shows the comparison result among no. of epochs and MAE value of different methods. Figure 6.8 shows that the increase in

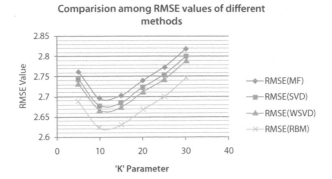

Figure 6.7 Comparison among 'k' and RMSE value.

Table 6.1 Differentiation between K and RMSE using various methods.

K	MF	SVD	WSVD	RBM
5	2.76137	2.74313	2.73219	2.68828
10	2.69592	2.67776	2.66688	2.62337
15	2.70339	2.6852	2.67413	2.63062
20	2.74089	2.72274	2.71169	2.66818
25	2.77257	2.75391	2.74288	2.69937
30	2.81879	2.80047	2.78935	2.74584

Table 6.2 Comparison among K and MAE of different methods.

No. of epochs	MF	SVD	WSVD	Proposed RBM
0	0.14412752	0.13432652	0.12912452	0.12286516
2	0.08904246	0.07924146	0.07403946	0.06778010
4	0.07580589	0.06600489	0.06080289	0.05454353
6	0.06872800	0.05892700	0.05372500	0.047465640
8	0.06597785	0.05617685	0.05097485	0.04471549
10	0.06439402	0.05459302	0.04939102	0.04313166
12	0.063298018	0.053497018	0.048295018	0.042035658
14	0.062187785	0.052386785	0.047184785	0.040925425

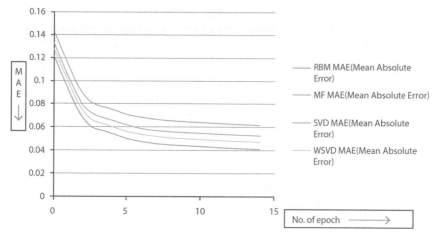

Figure 6.8 Comparison graph between MAE and no. of epochs.

the number of epochs that leads to high accuracy of the model. This leads to better recommendation quality by using proposed RBM based CF technique.

6.6 Proposed CRBM Model-Based Movie Recommender System

RBM model fails to extract global features for large image, convolution RBM (CRBM) is used to resolve the problem. Two factors such as locality and neighborhood play main role in the CRBM model. The connections between hidden and visible units are local and weights are used among clusters of the hidden units. As CRBM uses both features of RBM and CNN, so CRBM provides better results than RBM. This method is implemented using python with TensorFlow and also described in Algorithm 2. The CRBM approach is also depicted in flowchart manner which is shown in Figure 6.9.

Algorithm 2

1. Load the dataset of movies and ratings
2. Correct the data and convert the dataset into a specific format
3. Merge movie ID with movie ratings
4. Create the training set

4.1. For each user in the group for userID
    4.1.1. Create temp that stores every movie's rating
4.2. For each movie in currentUser's movie list
    4.2.1. Divide the rating by 5
    4.2.2. Add the list of ratings into training set
    4.2.3. Verify the adding of users for training set and set the model parameters
5. Train the model using RBM-CNN with 15 epochs, each epoch using 10batches with size 100.
6. Calculate the error by epoch size wise.
7. Input the user and reconstruct the input
8. Find the output for input user.

Flow Chart of Above Approach

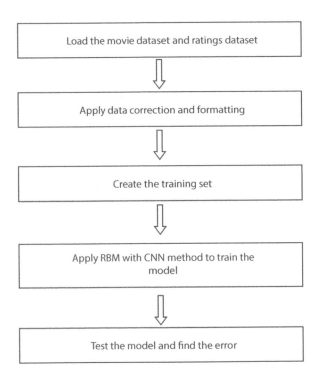

Figure 6.9 Flowchart of proposed CRBM approach.

Experimental Result and Analysis

Deep learning based collaborative filtering model framework combines the work of two operations. One operation is related to deep learning for the content information and other one is related to CF for the ratings. We use MovieLens dataset for training the model. RBM with the CNN model that is based on similar interest of neighboring users, is used for CF recommendations.

Dataset

Experiment analysis is done by using MovieLens data set. This dataset consists of 10,000 ratings of 943 users and 1,682 movies [13]. In this dataset, Movie.dat file contains movie names along with genres. The ratings given by the users range between 1 and 5. Preferred value is highest rating value. For developing model, 80% of dataset is treated as training set and the rest 20% is treated as test dataset.

Parameters

We need to choose parameter 'n' (number of nearest neighbors) for determining recommendation quality. Here value of n is the main factor on which data privacy depends. Therefore, we should select parameter n properly. Here we consider different parameter such as MAE, precision, recall and F-score to measure the quality of movie recommender system.

Performance Evaluation

Table 6.3 shows different parameter values by using different approaches while considering number of nearest neighbors. In Table 6.3, our proposed CRBM method provides better quality of movie recommender system by considering precision, recall and F-score. Table 6.4 shows the proposed CRBM method gives less MAE value among all other methods by considering no. of epochs.

Figure 6.10 depicts that the proposed CRBM (RBM-CNN) based CF movie recommender system gives least MAE value among existing methods by providing better accuracy of the system.

6.7   Conclusion and Future Work

The Item based collaborative filtering recommender system is very efficient in use when user space is large. This approach can be applied in

Table 6.3 Comparison among different parameters of different methods and no. of nearest neighbors.

Methods	MF			SVD			BSVD			RBM			Proposed CRBM		
N	Precision	Recall	F-Score	Precision	Recall	F-Score	Precision	Recall	F-Score	Precision	Recall	F-Score	Precision	Recall	F-Score
1	0.25	0.01	0.02	0.26	0.013	0.02	0.27	0.01	0.02	0.28	0.01	0.02	0.29	0.01	0.03
3	0.21	0.02	0.04	0.22	0.02	0.04	0.23	0.02	0.05	0.24	0.02	0.05	0.25	0.03	0.05
5	0.18	0.04	0.06	0.19	0.04	0.06	0.20	0.04	0.07	0.21	0.04	0.07	0.22	0.04	0.07
10	0.15	0.07	0.10	0.16	0.07	0.10	0.17	0.07	0.10	0.18	0.08	0.10	0.19	0.08	0.11
15	0.14	0.09	0.11	0.15	0.09	0.11	0.16	0.10	0.12	0.17	0.10	0.12	0.18	0.10	0.13
20	0.14	0.12	0.12	0.15	0.12	0.12	0.16	0.12	0.13	0.17	0.12	0.14	0.18	0.12	0.14

Table 6.4 Comparison among no. of epoch and MAE value of different methods.

No. of epoch	MF	SVD	WSVD	RBM	Proposed CRBM
0	0.14413	0.13433	0.12912	0.12287	0.1179
2	0.08904	0.07924	0.07404	0.06778	0.0588
4	0.07581	0.06600	0.06080	0.05454	0.0473
6	0.06873	0.05898	0.05373	0.04747	0.0375
8	0.06598	0.05618	0.05097	0.04471	0.0347
10	0.06439	0.05459	0.04939	0.04313	0.0337
12	0.06329	0.05349	0.04829	0.042035	0.0321
14	0.06218	0.05239	0.04718	0.040925	0.0309

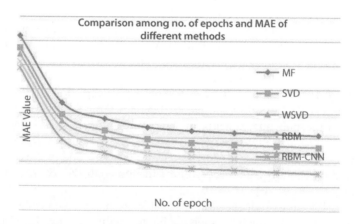

Figure 6.10 Comparison graph between MAE and no. of epochs.

cross domain recommendations. Therefore, this approach is used in business gain sales and revenues. In this chapter, we compare all existing methods with RBM and RBM-CNN in a movie recommender system that provides better accuracy. In the future, we will give more focus on algorithms which can be optimized and provide better accuracy than proposed method.

References

1. Isinkaye, F.O., Folajimi, Y.O., Ojokoh, B.A., Recommendation systems: Principles, methods and evaluation. *Egypt. Inform. J.*, 16, 3, 261–273, 2015.
2. Ortega, F., Hernando, A., Bobadilla, J., Kang, J.H., Recommending items to group of users using matrix factorization based collaborative filtering. *Inform. Sci.*, 345, 313–324, 2016.
3. Jooa, J., Bangb, S., Parka, G., Implementation of a recommendation system using association rules and collaborative filtering. *Procedia Comput. Sci.*, 91, 944–952, 2016.
4. Ponnam, L.T., Punyasamudram, S.D., Nallagulla, S.N., Yellamati, S., Movie recommender system using item based collaborative filtering technique, in: *2016 International Conference on Emerging Trends in Engineering, Technology and Science (ICETETS)*, IEEE, 1–5, 2016.
5. Sarwar, B.M., Karypis, G., Konstan, J.A., Riedl, J., Item-based collaborative filtering recommendation algorithms. *WWW*, 1, 285–295, 2001.
6. Hoseini, E., Hashemi, S., Hamzeh, SPCF: a stepwise partitioning for collaborative filtering to alleviate sparsity problems. *J. Inf. Sci.*, 38, 6, 578–592, 2012.
7. Yedder, H.B., Zakia, U., Ahmed, A., Trajković, L., Modeling prediction in recommender systems using restricted boltzmann machine, in: *2017 IEEE International Conference on Systems, Man, and Cybernetics (SMC)*, IEEE, pp. 2063–2068, 2017, October.
8. Cheng, H.T., Koc, L., Harmsen, J., Shaked, T., Chandra, T., Aradhye, H., Anderson, G., Corrado, G., Chai, W., Ispir, M., Anil, R., Wide & deep learning for recommender systems, in: *Proceedings of the 1st Workshop on Deep Learning for Recommender Systems*, ACM, pp. 7–10, 2016, September.
9. Ma, X., Lu, H., Gan, Z., Zeng, J., An explicit trust and distrust clustering based collaborative filtering recommendation approach. *Electron. Commer. R. A.*, 25, 29–39, 2017.
10. Riyaz, P.A. and Varghese, S.M., A scalable product recommendations using collaborative filtering in hadoop for bigdata. *Proc. Technol.*, 24, 1393–1399, 2016.
11. Canny, J., Collaborative filtering with privacy via factor analysis, in: *Proceedings of the 25th Annual International ACM SIGIR Conference on Research and Development in Information Retrieval*, ACM, 238–245, 2002, August.
12. Gope, J. and Jain, S.K., A survey on solving cold start problem in recommender systems, in: *2017 International Conference on Computing, Communication and Automation (ICCCA)*, IEEE, pp. 133–138, 2017, May.
13. Harper, F.M. and Konstan, J.A., The movielens datasets: History and context. *ACM TiiS*, 5, 4, 19, 2016.

14. Sahoo, A.K., Pradhan, C., Mishra, B.S.P., SVD based Privacy Preserving Recommendation Model using Optimized Hybrid Item-based Collaborative Filtering, in: *2019 International Conference on Communication and Signal Processing (ICCSP)*, IEEE, pp. 0294–0298, 2019, April.

15. Sahoo, A.K., Mallik, S., Pradhan, C., Mishra, B.S.P., Barik, R.K., Das, H., Intelligence-Based Health Recommendation System Using Big Data Analytics, in: *Big Data Analytics for Intelligent Healthcare Management*, pp. 227–246, Academic Press, USA, 2019.

16. Wei, J., He, J., Chen, K., Zhou, Y., Tang, Z., Collaborative filtering and deep learning based recommendation system for cold start items. *Expert Syst. Appl.*, 69, 29–39, 2017.

17. Li, T., Gao, C., Du, J., A NMF-based privacy-preserving recommendation algorithm, in: *2009 First International Conference on Information Science and Engineering*, IEEE, pp. 754–757, 2009, December.

18. Portugal, I., Alencar, P., Cowan, D., The use of machine learning algorithms in recommender systems: A systematic review. *Expert Syst. Appl.*, 97, 205–227, 2018.

19. Mu, R., A survey of recommender systems based on deep learning. *IEEE Access*, 6, 69009–69022, 2018.

20. Wu, J., Yang, L., Li, Z., Variable weighted BSVD-based privacy-preserving collaborative filtering, in: *2015 10th International Conference on Intelligent Systems and Knowledge Engineering (ISKE)*, IEEE, pp. 144–148, 2015, November.

21. Zhao, R., Yan, R., Chen, Z., Mao, K., Wang, P., Gao, R.X., Deep learning and its applications to machine health monitoring. *Mech. Syst. Signal Pr*, 115, 213–237, 2019.

22. Wu, H., Zhang, Z., Yue, K., Zhang, B., He, J., Sun, L., Dual-regularized matrix factorization with deep neural networks for recommender systems. *Knowl-Based Syst.*, 145, 46–58, 2018.

23. He, Y., Wang, C., Jiang, C., Correlated matrix factorization for recommendation with implicit feedback. *IEEE Trans. Knowl. Data Eng.*, 31, 3, 451–464, 2018.

24. Chen, J., Li, K., Rong, H., Bilal, K., Yang, N., Li, K., A disease diagnosis and treatment recommendation system based on big data mining and cloud computing. *Inform. Sci.*, 435, 124–149, 2018.

25. Jiang, L. and Yang, C.C., User recommendation in healthcare social media by assessing user similarity in heterogeneous network. *Artif. Intell. Med.*, 81, 63–77, 2017.

26. Belle, A., Thiagarajan, R., Soroushmehr, S.M., Navidi, F., Beard, D.A., Najarian, K., Big data analytics in healthcare. *BioMed Res. Int.*, Volume 2015, pg. 1-16, 2015.

27. Mishra, B.K., Sahoo, A.K., Pradhan, C., GPU based reduce approach for computing faculty performance evaluation process using classification technique in opinion mining. *IJDATS*, 10, 3, 208–222, 2018.

28. Lu, D. and Tang, J., Particle swarm optimisation algorithm for a time-delay system with piece-wise linearity. *IJAAC*, 11, 3, 290–297, 2017.
29. Mellouli, E.M., Alfidi, M., Boumhidi, I., Fuzzy sliding mode control for three-tank system based on linear matrix inequality. *IJAAC*, 12, 2, 237–250, 2018.
30. Benslimane, H., Boulkroune, A., Chekireb, H., Adaptive iterative learning control of nonlinearly parameterised strict feedback systems with input saturation. *IJAAC*, 12, 2, 251–270, 2018.

Machine Learning-Based Recommender System for Breast Cancer Prognosis

G. Kanimozhi, P. Shanmugavadivu* and M. Mary Shanthi Rani

Department of Computer Science and Applications, The Gandhigram Rural Institute (Deemed to be University), Gandhigram, Tamil Nadu, India

Abstract

The prognosis of the onset of cancer plays an inevitable role in saving the lives of the victims. The proposed "Machine Learning based Recommender System for Breast Cancer Prediction (MLRS-BC)" aims to provide an accurate recommendation for breast cancer prognosis through four distinct phases, namely: Data collection; Preprocessing; Training, Testing, Validation; and Prediction/Recommender. It is designed to predict the effect of risk factors associated with routine blood analysis in the Breast Cancer Coimbra Dataset (BCCD). The attributes of BCCD are age, body mass index, glucose, and insulin level in the blood, Homa, Leptin, Adiponectin, Resistin, and Monocyte Chemoattractant Protein-1 (MCP-1). The Root Mean Square Error (RMSE) and Mean Absolute Error (MAE) is used to evaluate the accuracy of the predictions. The MLRS-BC computes the error values for each attribute of BCCD. It recommends the best attribute having the least error rate as the pre-dominant attributes for breast cancer prognosis. It gains importance in automated breast cancer detection or classification, with a single optimal attribute, instead of engaging all the nine attributes of the dataset. MLRS-BC also recommends the best prediction algorithm for breast cancer detection. The outcomes of this research shall augment the quality of services in breast cancer care.

Keywords: Health recommender system, machine learning, breast cancer, attribute selection, BCCD, prediction algorithms, K-Fold cross-validation

Corresponding author: psvadivu67@gmail.com

Sachi Nandan Mohanty, Jyotir Moy Chatterjee, Sarika Jain, Ahmed A. Elngar and Priya Gupta (eds.) Recommender System with Machine Learning and Artificial Intelligence: Practical Tools and Applications in Medical, Agricultural and Other Industries, (121–140) © 2020 Scrivener Publishing LLC

7.1 Introduction

The exponential increase in the development of Recommender Systems (RS) for medicine and health care vouches for the need and importance in disease prognosis, diagnosis, and therapeutic choices as well as in the personalized-care system. Cancer is a terminal disease featured by abnormal and irregular cell growth in any part of the body, in the form of a tumour. The exponential growth of cancer victims and the availability of data/images across the world have triggered research in medicine, computer science, and allied disciplines [1]. Breast cancer is reported as one of the primary causes of female mortality. The recent statistics confirm that it is highly prevalent among younger age groups, which are higher than the global average. The National Institute of Cancer Prevention and Research (NICPR) has reported that this disease is about 14% of all types of cancer [2]. According to the Indian Council of Medical Research (ICMR), *"Around 1.5 lakh new breast cancer cases in India, of which, 70,000 succumb every year"* [3]. Early detection and diagnosis through periodic screening tests can provide ample chances for timely treatment and cure. Hence the researchers develop novel automated breast cancer recommender systems to attain higher accuracy in cancer predictions. Recent developments in recommender system models have motivated the researchers to explore its potential on breast cancer prediction in the light of Machine Learning (ML) and Deep Learning (DL) [4].

ML, a branch of Artificial Intelligence (AI), employs a variety of statistical, probabilistic, and optimization techniques for classification, clustering, and prediction [1]. In recent days, the RS is one of the most popular and effective applications built on ML and DL models. In the data-driven era, detection, classification, analysis, and prediction of any disease with a high degree of precision can be achieved with the support of ML prediction algorithms. It can recommend an item from a pool of alternatives. The recommendation of an item is made, based on many criteria such as user preferences, browsing patterns, personal details, professional/occupational profile, etc. It generally denotes any computer-based decision-making system which offers recommendations, as required [5]. A recommender system synonymously refers to a preferential filtering system or software called as an engine that can mimic the analytical and intellectual ability of an individual in decision making.

Recommender systems are active on-line information filtering systems that encompass a variety of distinct paradigms, which are shown in Figure 7.1.

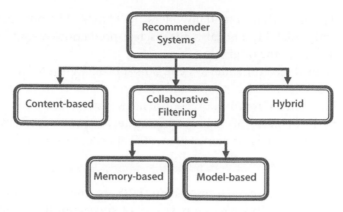

Figure 7.1 Hierarchy of recommender systems.

The common types of recommender systems are outlined in the following section.

- Content-Based (CB) Recommender System: This system works either explicitly or implicitly on the data that the user provides. A user profile is created based on this data, which will then be used to make recommendations for the user. In these systems, one needs to assess the similarity of any two distinct items based on the textual description for each item. As the user provides more inputs or takes actions on the recommendations, the engine becomes more and more accurate.
- Collaborative Filtering (CF) Recommender System: This system generally makes predictions and recommendations based on feedback information collected from the community of users, for a collection of items. It relies on the individual ratings of all users or based on usage patterns. It uses information about the user's past behavior and similar users to make suggestions. This system has two subcategories, namely memory-based algorithms and model-based algorithms.

  The memory-based algorithm uses all the available data to make predictions. It tries to find users who are similar to the active user and uses their preferences to predict ratings for the active user.

  The model-based algorithm uses the data to train a model that can later be used to make predictions for unrated data.

This approach potentially offers the benefits of both speed and scalability and also makes fast predictions using less data than the original.

- Hybrid recommender system: This approach aims to harness the potential of both CB and CF algorithms by incorporating both to improve a recommender system's accuracy and performance. The hybrid filtering technique is performed either by applying some CF in a CB approach or by utilizing some CB approach in CF [6].

The Health Recommendation System (HRS) is emerging as an effective health care system. This paves a new way of successful healthcare treatment based on patients' vital parameters. Besides, it improves the appropriate adoption and utilization of technology with the use of optimal information overload that helps to gather better insights for disease(s) prediction [7]. Due to its viability and validity, the HRS is deemed as an auxiliary decision-making tool in the prognosis and diagnosis of ailments and diseases.

This chapter titled "Machine Learning based Recommender System for Breast Cancer Prediction (MLRS-BC)" is designed for two-fold recommendation: the selection of optimal attributes from among the health dataset attributes and optimal machine learning model to be chosen for diagnosis or prediction.

7.2   Related Works

This section gives a bird's eye view on the prominent research work reported on ML-based breast cancer recommender systems using prediction algorithms. This literature review enables the researcher to understand the behaviour of those algorithms on the medical dataset. It may further help in exploring the new directions in this domain of research.

Aslan *et al.* proposed four ML models—Artificial Neural Networks (ANN), Extreme Learning Machine (ELM), Support Vector Machine (SVM), and K-Nearest Neighbors (KNN) for breast cancer diagnosis using routine blood analysis data named as Breast Cancer Coimbra Dataset (BCCD). The authors have experimented and validated their hyperparameter optimization-based algorithms on UCIrvine ML repository, which has 116 instances with 10 salient attributes. The dataset has a proper distribution of instances on non-cancerous and cancerous patients' data, and the results were analyzed. Among those algorithms, ELM produced an average classification accuracy of 80% [8].

Polat and Senturk proposed a novel hybrid method for breast cancer prediction using ML techniques. For their study, BCCD with 116 instances and 10 attributes were used. The Median Absolute Deviation (MAD) normalization, K-Means clustering-based feature weighting and, Adaptive Boosting Classifier was used to classify the breast cancer dataset. This hybrid method yielded an accuracy of 91.37% [9].

Austria *et al.* comparatively analyzed the performance criterion of different ML classifiers, namely Logistic Regression, SVM, Decision Tree, Naïve Bayes, Random Forest, Gradient Boosting Method (GBM), and KNN for the breast cancer classification and detection in BCCD. The results showed that GBM produced a higher accuracy of 74.14%. It is reported that among the patients' attributes, the Body Mass Index (BMI) has become the top predicted attribute followed by Glucose. They concluded that these two attributes formed a good pair of attributes for predicting breast cancer [10].

Kamath *et al.* presented a novel method for disease prediction and recommendation. The data was collected from the National Hospital Ambulance Medical Care Survey (NHAMCS), which consists of 37,000 instances and 430 attributes associated with 22 diseases. They used the CF method with Jaccard similarity measure to develop their recommendation system for suggesting related symptoms. The authors had compared the results of their SVM-based classifier with other classification algorithms. The accuracy obtained was 93.74% [11].

Marlin *et al.* proposed a CF recommender system for tailored health communications. The main aim of this work was to monitor the healthy behavior based on the messages sent to the individual patients and the explicit feedback on the past message selections. The results showed that most users had expressed positive opinions about the sent tailored messages. The correlation among the positive opinions was high. Furthermore, future rating prediction was performed by conducting a range of rating prediction experiments [12].

7.3   Methodology

7.3.1   Experimental Dataset

The numerical and categorical attributes of Breast Cancer Coimbra Dataset (BCCD) used for this analytical research study was obtained from the UCI

Online Machine Learning Repository [13]. Table 7.1 shows the description of BCCD attributes. It consists of 64 patients' records with breast cancer and 52 healthy records based on routine blood analysis. The targeted research analysis was carried out on the clinical features of the entire dataset of 116 instances. This repository was created in 2018 [14]. In this dataset, the numerical attributes are the independent parameters, and the categorical attribute is a dependent parameter.

High Body Mass Index (BMI) is a major risk factor for breast cancer. Also, the development of cancer is most likely when there is an increase in the levels of leptin, resisting, and a decrease of adiponectin secretion. In addition to that, women after menopause have a high risk of getting breast cancer through metabolic syndrome, specifically insulin resistance and abdominal fat. In order to identify the patients with sub-clinical insulin resistance, Homeostasis Model Assessment-Insulin Resistance (HOMA-IR) can be used. According to this dataset, the relationship between glucose, insulin, adiponectin, and resistance with BMI are the main factors for the development and progression of breast cancer [15].

Table 7.1 Clinical attributes of BCCD.

Attribute	Description	Units/Range
Age	Age of the patient in years	Range: 24–89
BMI	Body Mass Index of the patient	Units: kg/m^2 & Range: 18–38
Glucose	The glucose level of the patient	Units: mg/dl
Insulin	Insulin level of the patient	Units: µU/ml
HOMA	Homeostasis Model Assessment = [log ((If) × (Gf)) / 22.5]	–
Leptin	Leptin level of the patient	Units: ng/ml
Adiponectin	Adiponectin secretion level of the patient	Units: µg/ml
Resistin	Resistin level of the patient	Units: ng/ml
MCP-1	Monocyte Chemoattractant Protein-1	Units: pg/dl
Classification	Healthy controls (1), patients (2)	–

where If and Gf are insulin level and glucose level, respectively.

7.3.2   Feature Selection

Feature selection is the process of extracting the most relevant details having the best impact on the performance of computational models. Hence, this process plays a vital role while designing a model. It also helps in combating overfitting, which in turn may attribute to the improved accuracy and reduced training time. The correlation matrix with the heatmap feature selection technique is applied to this dataset. This method is observed to have the edge over the other feature selection techniques such as Univariate selection, and feature importance. A correlation matrix can be measured based on finding the degree of correlation among the independent attributes and the dependent attribute [10]. On the resultant correlation matrix, the heatmap is used to plot a correlated feature, which is illustrated in Figure 7.2.

By using this correlation matrix, the most related features: Age, BMI, Glucose, Insulin, and MCP.1 were selected to achieve high performance of prediction.

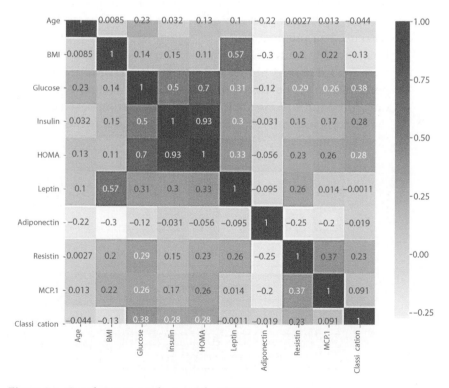

Figure 7.2 Correlation matrix heatmap for BCCD.

7.3.3　Functional Phases of MLRS-BC

The phases of MLRS-BC are depicted in Figure 7.3, and its workflow is shown in Figure 7.4. The functionalities of each phase [6] of MLRS-BC are described herein under:

- Data Collection Phase: This is the first phase that collects essential information about the patients and generates an experimental profile of the patient with relevant attributes. In this phase, the information collected is based on BCCD from the UCI ML repository, which has anthropometric data and health parameters of the patients [13].
- Preprocessing Phase: This phase accepts the dataset as input and extracts the best feature of the dataset. Then the result is passed for learning the data to obtain the patients features as output.
- Training, Testing, and Validation Phase: In this phase, the selected features are individually split into training and testing sets. The training set is used for learning, and the testing set is used for predictions.
- Prediction/Recommender Phase: Prediction algorithms were applied to the training and testing data, to measure the performance of the algorithms, based on the feature selection. The MLRS-BC recommends the best feature based on the performance metrics. This system also recommends the ideal ML model for prediction.

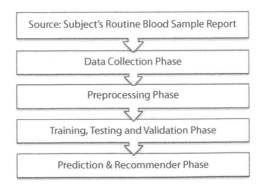

Figure 7.3 Phases of MLRS-BC.

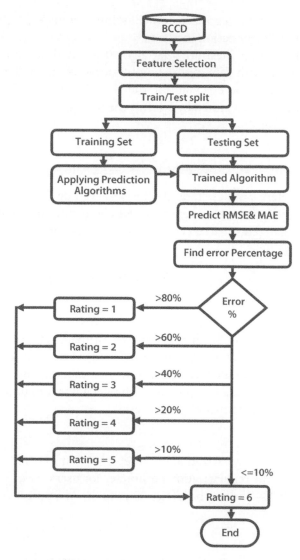

Figure 7.4 Flowchart of MLRS-BC.

7.3.4   Prediction Algorithms

The recommender system MLRS-BC is developed using *Surprise* package (2015), in Python, to develop prediction algorithms suitable for explicit ratings. There are eleven prediction algorithms in this package, of which three of them are explored for the analysis. In *Surprise,* the available pack of CF algorithms is categorized into Baseline Estimates, Neighborhood Models, Matrix Factorization methods.

Baseline Estimates: These are basic algorithms used to estimate the prediction accuracy, with minimum computational complexity [16]. In this algorithm, the baseline estimate for the overall rating is denoted by μ, unknown rating r_{ui} is denoted by b_{ui}, and the user and items are related, as shown in Equation 1.

$$b_{ui} = \mu + b_u + b_i \qquad (1)$$

The parameters b_u and b_i indicate the observed deviations of user u on item i respectively, from the average. These algorithms are applied to minimize the regularized squared error, as shown in Equation 2.

$$\sum_{r_{ui} \in R_{train}} \left(r_{ui} - \left(\mu + b_u + b_i\right)\right)^2 + \lambda\left(b_u^2 + b_i^2\right) \qquad (2)$$

BaselineOnly is a baseline model that can estimate in two different ways: using Stochastic Gradient Descent (SGD) and Alternating Least Squares (ALS), which are computed using the baseline function, 'bsl_options' with three parameters, during computation. The default values of each parameter are given within the pair of parentheses.

For ALS:

- reg_i–The regularization parameter for items (10).
- reg_u–The regularization parameter for users (15).
- n_epochs–The number of iterations of the ALS procedure (10).

For SGD:

- reg–The regularization parameter of the cost function that is optimized (0.02).
- learning_rate–The learning rate of SGD (0.005).
- n_epochs–The number of iterations of the SGD procedure (20).

Neighborhood models: These are directly derived algorithms from the nearest neighbor models. In this model, the actual number of neighbors aggregated to measure an estimation is necessarily lower than the centroid 'k' [17]. In this work, the KNNBasic algorithm is used for prediction analysis.

Parameters used are:

- k (int)—The (maximum) number of neighbors for aggregation (40).
- min_k (int)—The (minimum) number of neighbors for aggregation (1).
- sim_options (dict)—a representation for similarity measure.

Matrix Factorization Methods: These algorithms work by decomposing the user-item interaction matrix into a product of two lower dimensionality rectangular matrices [17]. Singular Valued Decomposition (SVD) is a matrix factorization technique that is used to reduce the number of features of a data set by reducing space dimensions from N to K where K < N. Parameters used are:

- n_factors—The number of factors (100).
- n_epochs—The number of iteration of SGD procedure (20).
- init_mean—Mean of the normal distribution for factor vectors initialization (0).

7.4   Results and Discussion

In this proposed MLRS-BC method, experiments were carried out using three prediction algorithms: *BaselineOnly*, *KNNBasic*, and *SVD*. These algorithms are the basic models in the respective categories, baseline estimates, neighborhood models, and matrix factorization methods. This recommender system projects the risk of breast cancer using these three prediction algorithms. It recommends the best prediction with reference to the metrics RMSE and MAE [17].

As the first step, the content of BCCD is loaded, and the data is preprocessed for feature selection and grouping. Then, the dataset (distributed over each column) is loaded in the *reader class* for error prediction.

Then the train/test split is performed on the dataset for recommendation and prediction based on RMSE, and MAE values calculated [17] by using Equations 3 and 4.

$$RMSE = \sqrt{\frac{1}{n}\sum_{i=1}^{n}(y_i - \hat{y}_i)^2} \tag{3}$$

$$MAE = \frac{1}{n} \sum_{i=1}^{n} | y_i - \hat{y}_i |^2 \qquad (4)$$

where y_i represents the targeted value, and $\hat{y}_i$ represents the predicted value.

Table 7.2 describes the RMSE and MAE obtained on the prediction algorithms with the BCCD dataset and the visualization of RMSE and MAE presented in Figure 7.5.

It is obvious from Table 7.2 that all the three algorithms produced a very minimum error of 0.02, 0.01, and 0.13 for the attribute insulin, and the next better attribute was BMI.

Table 7.3 describes the Best Prediction Error (BPE) and Worst Prediction Error (WPE) obtained for the experimented prediction algorithms. The BPE

Table 7.2 Comparison of RMSE and MAE for prediction algorithms.

Algorithms Attributes	BaselineOnly		KNNBasic		SVD	
	RMSE	MAE	RMSE	MAE	RMSE	MAE
Age	1.47	1.03	0.78	0.69	1.24	0.91
BMI	0.04	0.04	0.18	0.06	0.27	0.24
Glucose	0.91	0.8	1.06	0.93	1.42	1.05
Insulin	**0.02**	**0.02**	**0.01**	**0.01**	**0.19**	**0.13**
MCP.1	0.56	0.1	0.63	0.13	0.55	0.23

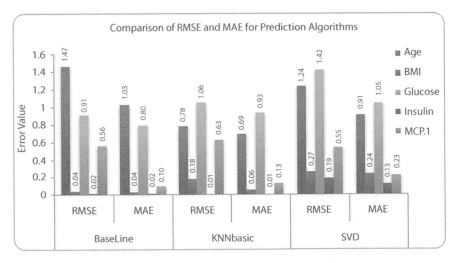

Figure 7.5 Comparison of RMSE and MAE for Prediction Algorithms.

Table 7.3 Comparison of BPE and WPE for prediction algorithms.

Algorithms / Attributes	BaselineOnly		KNNbasic		SVD	
	BPE	**WPE**	**BPE**	**WPE**	**BPE**	**WPE**
Age	**0.38**	**1.69**	0.41	0.97	0.53	1.29
BMI	**0.01**	0.06	0.02	0.13	0.16	**0.32**
Glucose	0.55	1.04	0.55	1.31	**0.54**	**1.55**
Insulin	**0.01**	0.03	**0.01**	0.01	0.08	**0.17**
MCP.1	0.12	0.21	**0.04**	0.21	0.12	**0.44**

is computed as an average of the best n/2 set of errors (i.e., the minimum error values), and the WPE is calculated as the statistical mean of the worst n/2 set of errors (i.e., the maximum errors values) on the testing set data, where n is the index number.

It is evident from Table 7.3 that BaselineOnly produced the BPE on the maximum number of attributes and SVD produced the WPE on the maximum number of attributes. The graphical representation of BPE and WPE is presented in Figure 7.6.

K-Fold cross-validation technique is used to improve the accuracy of classification by splitting the dataset randomly in an equal ratio for every fold. In this work, the data is split up into a set of 5 folds in the ratio 70:30, which is depicted in Figure 7.7.

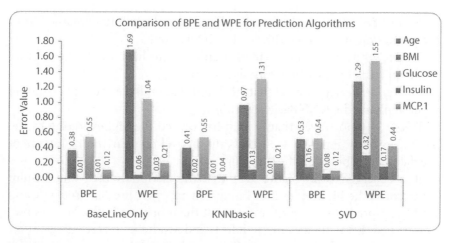

Figure 7.6 Comparison of BPE and WPE for prediction algorithms.

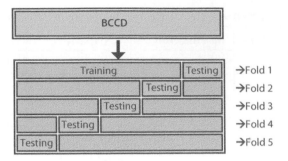

Figure 7.7 5-Fold Cross-Validation Technique.

Table 7.4 shows the RMSE and MAE values recorded by applying 5-fold cross-validation for each algorithm.

The highlighted values in Table 7.4 indicate the low error rate for the dataset attributes. The result revealed that the KNN Basic prediction algorithm has invariably produced a minimum error rate for all the attributes of the dataset. Furthermore, to make the recommendation, the influence of the attributes on each prediction algorithm is recorded in terms of rating, shown in Table 7.5. The 6-point rating scale (1–6) is evolved based on the error percentage computed using Equation 5. The rating is fixed as the maximum for the attribute with lease error and vice versa.

$$\textbf{Error } \% = \left(\frac{\text{Actual Value} - \text{Predicted Value}}{\text{Actual Value}} \right) * 100 \qquad (5)$$

Figures 7.8, 7.9, and 7.10 describe the ratings of attributes obtained from the prediction algorithms with the BCCD dataset.

Figure 7.8 demonstrates that BMI and Insulin have the highest rating while applying the BaselineOnly algorithm.

Figure 7.9 clearly showed that BMI and Insulin have the highest rating while applying the KNNBasic algorithm.

Figure 7.10 portrayed that Insulin has earned the highest rating by the SVD algorithm. Figure 7.11 depicts the overall comparison of ratings of the dataset attributes on the three algorithms.

It is observed from Figure 7.11 that the attributes BMI and Insulin have scored the highest level of ratings on applying the *BaselineOnly* and *KNNBasic* prediction algorithms against the other attributes. So, it is recommended that patients with high BMI and insulin levels are sufficient for preliminary classification and prediction of breast cancer.

Table 7.4 5-Fold cross-validation measures on prediction algorithms.

Attributes / Folds	Age		BMI		Glucose		Insulin		MCP.1	
	RMSE	MAE	RMSE	MAE	RMSE	MAE	RMSE	MAE	RMSE	MAE
BaselineOnly										
Fold1	0.76	0.68	0.36	0.13	0.67	0.61	0.01	**0.01**	0.03	0.02
Fold2	0.79	0.74	0.04	0.03	0.97	0.87	0.21	0.04	0.05	0.04
Fold3	0.75	0.67	0.04	0.03	0.72	0.67	0.01	**0.01**	0.63	0.13
Fold4	1.35	1.02	0.04	0.04	0.80	0.75	0.02	**0.01**	0.04	0.03
Fold5	1.30	0.83	0.04	0.03	1.51	1.10	0.01	**0.01**	0.04	0.03
KNNBasic										
Fold1	1.45	1.10	0.21	0.06	0.92	0.83	**0.01**	**0.01**	0.63	0.13
Fold2	0.76	0.62	**0.03**	**0.03**	0.88	0.81	**0.01**	**0.01**	**0.03**	**0.03**
Fold3	0.97	0.74	**0.03**	**0.03**	**0.63**	**0.55**	0.21	0.04	**0.03**	**0.03**
Fold4	**0.55**	0.62	0.21	0.06	0.87	0.78	**0.01**	**0.01**	**0.03**	**0.03**
Fold5	0.68	0.59	0.21	0.06	1.59	1.10	**0.01**	**0.01**	**0.03**	**0.03**

(*Continued*)

Table 7.4 5-Fold cross-validation measures on prediction algorithms. (*Continued*)

Attributes / Folds	Age		BMI		Glucose		Insulin		MCP.1	
	RMSE	MAE	RMSE	MAE	RMSE	MAE	RMSE	MAE	RMSE	MAE
SVD										
Fold1	0.97	0.76	0.25	0.19	0.86	0.80	0.09	0.09	0.62	0.24
Fold2	1.33	0.90	0.21	0.20	0.73	0.67	0.12	0.12	0.36	0.33
Fold3	0.69	**0.46**	0.23	0.18	0.93	0.80	0.14	0.13	0.38	0.33
Fold4	0.76	0.64	0.25	0.21	0.67	0.61	0.14	0.12	0.36	0.33
Fold5	1.10	0.86	0.20	0.18	1.59	1.20	0.20	0.11	0.34	0.31

Table 7.5 Rating scale formulation.

Error Percentage	Ratings
Below 10% (<=10%)	6 (Best rating)
Range from 11 to 20	5
Range from 21 to 40	4
Range from 41 to 60	3
Range from 61 to 80	2
Above 80%	1 (Worst rating)

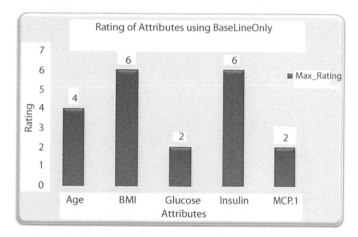

Figure 7.8 Rating of attributes using BaselineOnly.

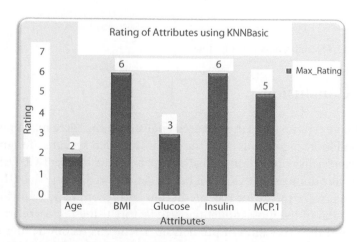

Figure 7.9 Rating of attributes using KNNBasic.

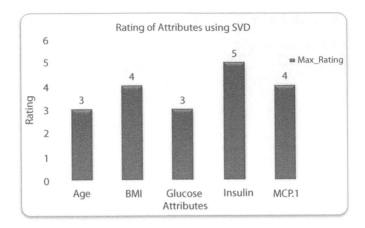

Figure 7.10 Rating of attributes using SVD.

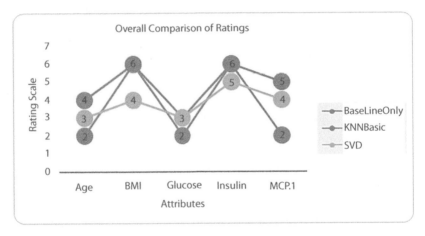

Figure 7.11 Overall comparison of ratings.

7.5   Conclusion

This chapter summarizes the research analysis on the three machine learning prediction algorithms and the recommender systems designed for breast cancer risk prediction using the experimental dataset BCCD. Several studies were done using BCCD for breast cancer prediction. The MLRS-BC depicts a novel strategy for risk prediction and recommendation based on the selection of the most influential risk factors using the correlation heat matrix and the error rates of prediction. Then, this recommender system assigns rating using a 6-point scale for the attributes. The experimental results reveal that perceptible improvement in the predictions and reliable attribute rating on the algorithms are obtained. These research outcomes would help to assess the risk of getting breast cancer with a single or a couple of attributes without compromising on accuracy. This mechanism can be ideally adopted for the datasets with numerous attributes too. This research work can further be augmented with the image dataset analysis to improve its robustness on breast cancer risk prediction.

Acknowledgment

The authors gratefully acknowledge the computing facilities used for experiments at the Advanced Image Processing Lab, funded under DST-FIST.

References

1. Cruz, J.A. and Wishart, D.S., Applications of machine learning in cancer prediction and prognosis. *Cancer Inform.*, 2, 59–77, 2006. 117693510600200030.
2. www.icmr.nic.in/sites/default/files/ICMR_News_1.pdf
3. https://timesofindia.indiatimes.com/city/hyderabad/high-cost-low-awareness-tied-to-rise-in-breast-cancer-cases/articleshow/67826472.cms
4. https://www.indiatoday.in/education-today/gk-current-affairs/story/cancer-rate-india-stats-cure-treatment-1386739-2018-11-12
5. Sahoo, A.K., Pradhan, C., Barik, R.K., Dubey, H., DeepReco: Deep Learning-Based Health Recommender System Using Collaborative Filtering. *Computation*, 7, 2, 25, 2019.
6. Sammut, C. and Webb, G.I., *Encyclopedia of machine learning and data mining.*, Springer Publishing Company, Incorporated, 2017.
7. Wiesner, M. and Pfeifer, D., Health recommender systems: concepts, requirements, technical basics, and challenges. *Int. J. Environ. Res. Public Health*, 11, 3, 2580–2607, 2014.
8. Aslan, M.F., Celik, Y., Sabanci, K., Durdu, A., Breast cancer diagnosis by different machine learning methods using blood analysis data. *Int. J. Intell. Syst. Appl. Eng.*, 6, 4, 289–293, 2018.
9. Polat, K. and Sentürk, U., A Novel ML Approach to Prediction of Breast Cancer: Combining of mad normalization, KMC based feature weighting, and AdaBoostM1 classifier, in: *2018 2nd International Symposium on Multidisciplinary Studies and Innovative Technologies (ISMSIT)*, IEEE, pp. 1–4, 2018, October.
10. Austria, Y.D., Jay-ar, P.L., Maria, L.B.S., Jr., Goh, J.E.E., Goh, M.L.I., Vicente, H.N., Comparison of Machine Learning Algorithms in Breast Cancer Prediction using the Coimbra Dataset. *Cancer*, 7, 10, 2019.

11. Kamath, A., Parab, A., Kerkar, N., Symptom Recommendation using Collaborative Filtering and Disease Prediction using Support Vector Machine. *Int. J. Comput. Appl.*, 179, 41, 14–18, 2018.

12. Marlin, B.M., Adams, R.J., Sadasivam, R., Houston, T.K., Towards collaborative filtering recommender systems for tailored health communications, in: *AMIA Annual Symposium Proceedings*, vol. 2013, American Medical Informatics Association, p. 1600, 2013.

13. http://archive.ics.uci.edu/ml/datasets/Breast+Cancer+Coimbra

14. Patrício, M., Pereira, J., Crisóstomo, J., Matafome, P., Gomes, M., Seiça, R., Caramelo,. F., Using resistin, glucose, age, and BMI to predict the presence of breast cancer. *BMC Cancer*, 18, 1, 29.11, 2018.

15. Crisóstomo, J., Matafome, P., Santos-Silva, D., Gomes, A.L., Gomes, M., Patrício, M., Seiça,. R., Hyperresistinemia and metabolic dysregulation: risky crosstalk in obese breast cancer. *Endocrine*, 53, 2, 433–442, 2016.

16. Koren, Y., Factor in the neighbours: Scalable and accurate collaborative filtering. *ACM TKDD*, 4, 1, 1, 2010.

17. Koren, Y., Factorization meets the neighbourhood: a multifaceted collaborative filtering model, in: *Proceedings of the 14th ACMSIGKDD International Conference on Knowledge Discovery and Data Mining*, ACM, pp. 426–434, 2008, August.

8

A Recommended System for Crop Disease Detection and Yield Prediction Using Machine Learning Approach

Pooja Akulwar

Department of Computer Science and Engineering, Sanjay Ghodawat University, Kolhapur, Maharashtra, India

Abstract

Agriculture is the mainstay of a rising economy in India. Traditionally farmers followed ancestral farming patterns and norms. However, a single farmer cannot be expected to take into account all innumerable factors that contribute to crop growth. A single misguided or imprudent decision by the farmer can have undesirable ramifications. With the advancements in various domains, intelligent agricultural system is needed for upliftment of Indian economy. The collaboration of recommender system with machine learning will lead to Intelligent Agriculture System that helps the farmer community in their decision making of farm management and agribusiness activities such as i) Predicting agriculture commodity market price before cultivation, ii) Determining best cultivars to plant iii) Determine optimum cultivation date v) Evaluate demand and supply risk vi) Investment Prioritizing. It also helps farmer to perform the activities like crop management including applications on yield prediction, disease detection, weed detection, crop quality, and growth prediction etc. This chapter describes the case study on "Crop Disease Detection and Yield prediction". The study includes identification of crop condition, disease detection, prediction about specific crop and recommendation using machine learning algorithms. It gives an idea about how recommender system is used in agriculture for disease detection and prediction.

Keywords: Agriculture, machine learning, recommender system, crop yield prediction, disease detection

Email: poojaakulwar13@gmail.com

Sachi Nandan Mohanty, Jyotir Moy Chatterjee, Sarika Jain, Ahmed A. Elngar and Priya Gupta (eds.) *Recommender System with Machine Learning and Artificial Intelligence: Practical Tools and Applications in Medical, Agricultural and Other Industries*, (141–164) © 2020 Scrivener Publishing LLC

8.1   Introduction

Agriculture is the fundamental source of food industry. It is one of the most oldest and important economic activities which is being practiced in the world wide since thousands of years. Its development has taken over the period of many years with the emergence of new technology, equipment, techniques of farming and domestication. Huge advancement and growth can be seen in this sector with the time period. This sector, not only witnessed the enormous growth but also gave rise to many other sectors with significant progress. Majority of the people are being involved in this occupation as it is the basic need of human beings survival. More than 50% of the land in the world has been devoted to agriculture. Agriculture sector accounts for 14% of Gross Domestic Product (GDP) of the Indian economy. About 70% of the population of India lives in rural areas and majority of them depend upon agriculture as their primary source of income. Agriculture not only helps people to survive but keeps economy on-going. It plays vital role in the economic development of India. Government of India has shown concern about the improvement of cultivator's knowledge of the soil, improvement of the fertility of the soil, irrigation facilities, fertilizer utilization, cattle-manure utilization, precise pesticides usage and grazing in forest area. Thus productivity has to be increased with the increase in population.

In agriculture planning to obtain maximum crop yield with restricted area of land is the largest task in an agro-based country like India. Yield rate of the crop can be increased with the help of indicators by investigating crop related problems. Crop selection will be more accurate and beneficial with minimum loss, whether unfavorable condition occurs [10]. Maximum crop yield can be obtained in favorable growing condition. Improving production rate of crop can be an important topic for research for the agro-meteorologists, for the development of economic growth of the country. The two main factors responsible for the yield rate of the crop is, first one is quality of seeds which can be improved by genetic development using hybridization technology and second one is the selection of crop based on the favorable and unfavorable conditions. The two techniques: statistical and machine learning both these techniques modelled. Many researchers had been tried to get an efficient and accurate model for crop yielding prediction, soil classification, crop classification, weather predictions [13], crop disease prediction classification of crops [5, 6]. Thus this new method called crop selection method (CSM) developed to increase in net yield rate of crops over seasons.

Crop production rate depends on the topography and geographic condition of the region (e.g. mountainous region, hilly area, river ground, depth regions), weather condition (e.g. humidity, temperature, rainfall, cloud) [14, 15], soil type (e.g. sandy, clay, peaty, saline, silty, loam soil), soil composition (e.g. PH value, nitrogen, phosphorous, magnesium, calcium, sulphur, potassium, organic carbon, copper, iron) and harvesting methods. Different prediction models are used for different parameters of different crops. Some of these prediction models are studied thoroughly through researches for the crop production. The prediction models are of two types: statistical model and machine learning. This chapter describes overall study on Machine learning concepts, algorithms, and methods. This also gives an overview of recommender system and how recommender system is used in agriculture for disease detection and prediction. The chapter also describes crop management activities such as crop yield prediction, disease detection, weed detection and crop quality. Lastly application of agriculture and recommender system is discussed.

8.2 Machine Learning

8.2.1 Overview

Machine learning is emerging technology day by day in different fields. But now-a-days agriculture is the sector where machine learning applications are in greater demand. Now the question arises what is machine learning? Actually it is nothing but machine that learns from experiences in order to perform specific task. It provides ability to learn. Huge real time data set is provided to the system. This data set contains set of attributes called as features. Learning uses these features for further analysis. The performance is measured with performance metric. As more data is added over a time, this performance metric is improved with experience. Various mathematical models are used to calculate performance of machine learning algorithm.

Machine learning tasks are broadly classified into supervised learning, unsupervised learning, reinforcement learning, Semi-supervised learning and learning models (classification, regression, clustering, and dimensionality reduction). Table 8.1 describes difference between supervised learning and unsupervised learning.

Table 8.1 Difference between supervised learning and unsupervised learning.

Factors	Supervised learning	Unsupervised learning
Input	Known and labeled data	Unknown data
Complexity	Very complex	Less Complex
Number of classes	Known	Unknown
Accuracy	Accurate and reliable	Moderately Accurate and reliable

1. *Supervised learning:*
   In supervised learning labeled dataset is used. Here the model is trained on labeled dataset. This dataset contains both input and output parameters. Supervised learning is learning where there is input data, output data and algorithm that maps to input and output. Learning means input and output is provided to machine and machine will develop its own logic for the given task. Some supervised learning algorithms are: Linear Regression, Nearest Neighbor, Guassian Naive Bayes, Decision Trees, Support Vector Machine (SVM), Random Forest, etc.

   The learning is called supervised learning because it is similar to a teacher who is acting as supervisor on entire learning process. The predictions on trained data are generated by learning algorithms. These predictions are corrected by the teacher and learning process is stopped when correct output is achieved [5, 6].
2. *Unsupervised learning:*
   Unsupervised learning is learning that contains only input data and no output data is present. This is applied where there is need to model data distribution inorder to get more and more data and there is no any supervisor (like teacher) to supervised the things. Algorithms themselves learn, discover and present structure in data. Here algorithm itself create data pattern. Some recommendation systems for marketing automation use this type of learning.
3. *Semi-supervised learning:*
   The supervised learning has disadvantage that it required labeled dataset. This process is very costly while dealing with large volume of data. Unsupervised learning also has disadvantage that the range of its application is limited. To solve these problems, semi supervised learning algorithms

concept was developed. This concept used both labeled data and unlabeled data so that it can work on any type of data. Mostly it contains small amount of labeled data and huge amount of unlabeled data.

8.2.2 Machine Learning Algorithms

There are various machine learning algorithms as described in Figure 8.1 below. These algorithms can be applied in any area to solve various problems.

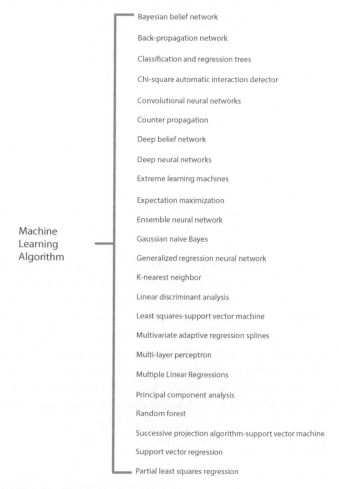

Bayesian belief network

Back-propagation network

Classification and regression trees

Chi-square automatic interaction detector

Convolutional neural networks

Counter propagation

Deep belief network

Deep neural networks

Extreme learning machines

Expectation maximization

Ensemble neural network

Machine Learning Algorithm

Gaussian naive Bayes

Generalized regression neural network

K-nearest neighbor

Linear discriminant analysis

Least squares-support vector machine

Multivariate adaptive regression splines

Multi-layer perceptron

Multiple Linear Regressions

Principal component analysis

Random forest

Successive projection algorithm-support vector machine

Support vector regression

Partial least squares regression

Figure 8.1 Machine learning algorithms [8, 9].

8.2.3   Machine Learning Methods

There are various Machine learning methods such as boosting techniques (RGF, GBDT, and Ada boost), Regression Tree (ID3, C4.5), Random Forest, SVM, K Nearest Neighbor, and ANN, etc.

8.2.3.1   *Artificial Neural Network*

Artificial Neural Network is a simple mathematical model of the brain. This is used to process nonlinear relationships between inputs and outputs in parallel form, for example human brain. So Artificial Neural Networks can be used in different variety of tasks one of the best use is classification. We can learn Artificial Neural Network speedily. The Information flows through a neural network in two different ways. Firstly when the model is learning or operating normally, the information from the dataset is given to the network through the input neurons, which then trigger the layers of hidden neurons, and then it is converted to the output neurons. So this is called as feed forward network. Each neuron receives inputs to its left, and then they are multiplied by the weights. So every neuron adds up all the inputs. If the sum is more than a certain threshold value then the neuron "fires". Whenever we use large datasets, the neural networks are more powerful at that time.

So in the basic structure of an Artificial Neural Network we can create 3 layers of "neurons"- The input layer, the hidden layer and the output layer as shown in Figure 8.2. The information flows from the input layer, from the hidden layer to the output layer. As each of the connections has a number associated with it, and it is called the connection weight. Also, each of the neurons has a number and a special formula associated with it called as threshold value. The neural network can be trained and then it can be provided with a set of inputs and outputs. Each neuron transforms the input and forwards it to the next layer and so on. The result is received on the output layer. Then the layer is compared to the outputs through special algorithms is used to produced outputs as close to each other as possible. As this process is repeated many times and here completes the training part. Whenever new inputs are provided to the network, we can get the actual outputs. So, the Artificial Neural Network can be used in predicting house prices and classifying objects and images.

8.2.3.2   *Support Vector Machines*

SVM stands for Support Vector Machine. It is a simple algorithm in machine learning. It belongs to the supervised learning category in

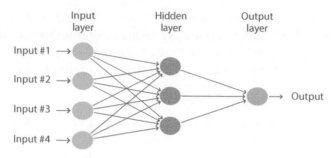

Figure 8.2 Simple Artificial Neural Network [11].

machine learning which is used for both regression and classification analysis but it is a discriminant classifier which is widely used as classification algorithm. It produces significant accuracy with less computation power. This algorithm is used to create a line or a hyper plane in order to separate the data into various classes. It takes the data as input and outputs a line that separates two classes. It is used in variety of applications such as face detection, classification of emails, news articles, web pages, handwriting recognition.

8.2.3.3   K-Nearest Neighbors (K-NN)

K-nearest Neighbor is supervised algorithm under machine learning. It is very easy to implement. It can give huge great classifiers. For classification and predictive problems, KNN is mostly used. It is also called as sample-based learning technique. For predictive target value, it uses all the past data. It uses distance function. There are various distance functions such as Euclidean, Manhattan, Makowski, etc. It computes distance between new input value (sample predictor) and all training set (sample predictor). After this smallest distance (k nearest distances) are selected. The sum of all the k neighbors is computed and target value is determined. This algorithm does not require training and any optimization method. This method is used for nonlinear and adaptable problems. KNN time and space complexity is very high because it uses all data samples while predicting target values. KNN can be used in agriculture efficiently.

8.2.3.4   Decision Tree Learning

In decision tree learning sampling of data is considered. Data is split into smaller sub sample space. The root of the tree contains entire sample data.

Other sample data is present into sub nodes. With the help of fork process, other nodes (children nodes) are created. After forking, during child creation data is split into smaller sub samples. This procedure is done recursively till last possibility. Data is split based upon some conditions provided by input attributes. The output value is assigned to those input values which exist between root and leaf node. The main aim is to combine multiple output values and allocate single output value to sample space. Size of node needs to be considered during splitting. For building decision tree, various algorithms such as CART, M5, M5 Prime, etc. are used. All these algorithms are similar but difference lie in impurity measures, leaf value assignment and prune rule.

8.2.3.5   Random Forest

A Random Forest algorithm is a supervised classification algorithm. It is an ensemble technique capable of performing both regression and classification tasks with the use of multiple decision trees and a technique called Bootstrap Aggregation, commonly known as bagging. It creates a forest by some way and makes it random. There are multiple decision trees. As per the name, it creates forest first and makes it randomly used as shown in Figure 8.3. The idea is to combine these trees and generate output instead of considering only individual tree. Applications of Random Forest algorithm are Banking, Medicine, Stock Market and E-commerce.

There are two stages in Random Forest algorithm, one is random forest creation, and the other is to predict classifier which was created in first stage. This works on various features such as binary, categorical and numerical.

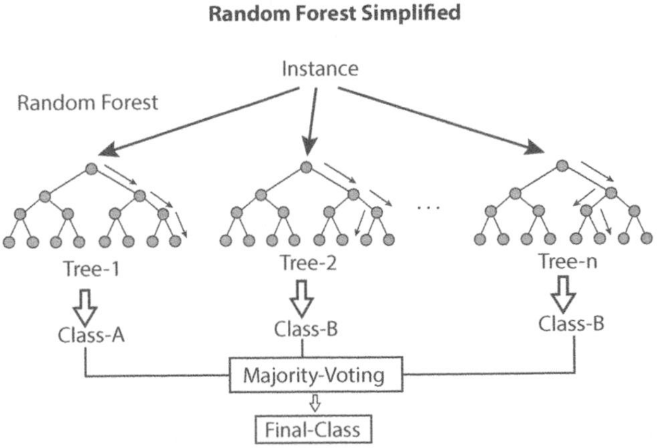

Figure 8.3 Simple random forest concept [11].

Very less processing work is required for this. The data does not need to be rescaled or transformed. Random forest improves on bagging because it correlates the trees with the introduction of splitting on a random subset of features. This means that at each split of the tree, the model considers only a small subset of features rather than all of the features of the model. That is, from the set of available features n, a subset of m features (m = square root of n) are selected at random. Bagging, or bootstrap aggregating, is where bagged trees are created by creating X number of decision trees that is trained on X bootstrapped training sets. The final predicted value is the average value of all our X decision trees. Bootstrapping is a sampling technique in which we randomly sample with replacement from the data set.

The predictive performance of Random Forest can compete with the best supervised learning algorithms. They provide a reliable feature importance estimate. Random forest handles outliers by essentially binning them. It is also indifferent to non-linear features. It is faster to train than decision trees because working is done only on a subset of features in this model, so it can easily work with hundreds of features. Prediction speed is significantly faster than training speed because generated forests can be saved for future uses.

8.2.3.6   Gradient Boosted Decision Tree (GBDT)

Gradient boosting is a machine learning technique for regression and classification problems, which produces a prediction model in the form of an ensemble of weak prediction models, typically decision trees. Like other boosting methods, GBDT also build the model according to some stages. Generalization will take place by optimizing differential loss function.

The Gradient Boosting Decision Tree (GBDT) is a popular machine learning algorithm. It has few effective implementations such as XGBoost and pGBRT. The Gradient boosting decision tree is a widely-used algorithm, due to its efficiency, accuracy, and interpretability. GBDT achieves state-of-the-art performances in many machine learning tasks, such as multi-class classification, click prediction, and learning to rank. Nowadays GBDT is facing new challenges, especially in the tradeoff between accuracy and efficiency. So the Conventional implementations of GBDT need for every feature to scan all the data instances and to estimate the information and gain of all the possible split points. Therefore, their computational complexities will be proportional to both the number of features and the number of instances. Handling of big data makes implementation very time consuming.

There are some techniques used in gradient boosting decision tree-Gradient-based One-Side Sampling (GOSS) and Exclusive Feature Bundling (EFB). GOSS keeps all the instances with large gradients and performs random sampling on the instances with small gradients. In order to compensate the influence to the data distribution, when computing the information gain, GOSS introduces a constant multiplier for the data instances with small gradients. While there is no native weight for data instance in GBDT, data instances with different gradients play different roles in the computation of information gain. Exclusive Feature Bundling (EFB) is usually real application, although there are a large number of features, the feature space is quite sparse, which provides us a possibility of designing a nearly lossless approach to reduce the number of effective features. As GBDT is an ensemble model of decision trees, which are trained in sequence. In each iteration, GBDT gives the decision trees by fitting the negative gradients. Specifically, in a sparse feature space, many features are exclusive, i.e., they rarely take nonzero values simultaneously e.g., one-hot word representation in text mining.

Gradient boosting algorithm uses gradient descent method to optimize the loss function. This algorithm is simple and can find the optimal split points; however, it is inefficient in both training speed and memory consumption. The main cost in GBDT is to learn the decision trees. The most time-consuming part in decision tree is to find the best split points.

8.2.3.7   *Regularized Greedy Forest (RGF)*

Regularized Greedy Forest (RGF) is a tree ensemble machine learning method that works directly with the underlying forest structure. Regularized greedy forest integrates mainly two ideas- one idea is to include tree-structured regularization into the learning formulation and the other idea is to use the fully-corrective regularized greedy algorithm. RGF does the change to existing forest and new forest is obtained which helps to minimize loss function. It also adjusts the weights of leaf to minimize loss function. Regularized greedy forest is nice algorithm that sits in between gradient boosting algorithm and random forest. The implementation can be done using different languages like Python, C, C++ etc. Regularized greedy forest algorithm builds decision forest through fully corrective regularized greedy search to underline the forest structure. It gives the higher accuracy and works faster. In RGF globally optimized decision tree is formed. In GBDT locally optimized decision tree is formed. As there is tree structure, RGF works by utilizing fully corrective regularized structure.

But GBDT does not consider full approach. It works on partially regularized tree structure.

8.3   Recommender System

8.3.1   Overview

In the world of internet and technology, data is growing tremendously with high speed. Contents are increasing along with number of users. Due to this enormous information, people face problem in finding right information at a specific time. People are in need of system that will give suggestion to them for their work. And this situation has made the evolution of concept of Recommender system. Recommender system guides users by providing recommendations about problem. It works on the concept of "most likely to be interesting" or "Relevant to need". These systems are widely used in many areas such as ecommerce websites, e-learning, e-library, e-government and e-business etc. Recommender system requires huge past data so that based upon the behavior and experience recommendations can be made.

Consider a recommender system that takes image as input. The general working of recommender system is shown in Figure 8.4. System will do image preprocessing that includes removal of noise and extraction of region of interest. Feature extraction will be followed after preprocessing. After features are extracted, machine learning algorithm is applied to and the results are predicted. The recommender system is used to provide the best recommendations.

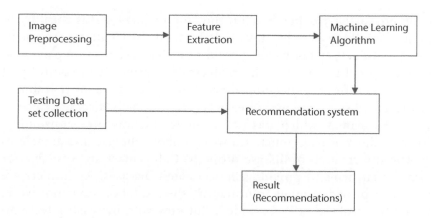

Figure 8.4 General overview of recommender system in agriculture [3].

Now these systems are used in agriculture sector too. Various recommendations are need to farmers at each and every step from sowing of seed till harvesting [7]. As farmers are mostly unaware of current updates in farming recommendation system helps them a lot. Recommendations regarding crop selection, disease identification and solution etc. can be generated and given to farmer. Consider the following scenario:

Scenario 1: Crop identification and recommender system

With the help of advanced technology, lot of improvement has been done in agriculture sector. When a farmer purchases a land for farming the most important question arises is which crop to be grown to have better production? If the selected crop is unsuitable for that land, then there will be less productivity. Generally, farmers are unaware about agriculture land requirements that is minerals needed, soil moisture and other soil requirements. The concept of precision agriculture solves this problem of farmer. In this characteristic of soil are identified and used for identifying the suitable crop for cultivation. Soil characteristics are soil type, texture, pH value, moisture, temperature and other environment conditions. Due to this risk of cultivating improper crop is avoided. Always farmer will cultivate proper crop that results in good crop yield and get enormous profit for particular land area. Here recommendation system helps in recommending the most suitable crop that yields in better productivity. Also, it prevents from crop loss making farmer to be financial stable.

Scenario 2: Disease detection and recommender system

Crop productivity depends upon the crop or plant status (healthy or unhealthy). If the plant has any kind of disease then it affects crop quality and production. For yielding good crop, disease detection plays vital role in agriculture. One of the problems for farmer is to control pest and diseases affecting that crop. Once the crop seeds are sown, it should be prevented from pest and disease [1]. Traditionally disease detection was done manual which was not accurate and was time consuming. Farmers did not have much knowledge about disease and unable to explain information of disease properly. Call centers are available for farmer that helps to provide solution about diseases. As farmers are unable to provide proper information, their solution does not work. Hence the problem still continued. But now with increasing technology, automatic disease detection is possible effortlessly. This disease detection can be done based upon images that are provided. Various applications have been developed to recognize and detect diseases that will lessen negative impact on harvest. After disease detection the solutions to overcome this disease must be provided. Hence recommendation system role is very important in this respect. Recommender system helps to provide the best solution to overcome this disease. But this solution is after detection disease.

Here the recommender system can work in two ways:

1. Before disease detection

Before disease detection results in precaution taken before the disease has occurred. Once the image preprocessing and feature extraction is done, the analysis or difference in features can predict the type of disease the crop will be affected from in future. If this information is known then precautions can be taken in advanced so that crop will remain unaffected and hence productivity will not be lessened.

2. After disease detection

Once the disease is detected, it must be cured properly to increase productivity. Recommender system helps by providing best solution to overcome diseases. This system analyzes the data such as symptoms, type of disease, medical treatment etc. based upon the available data, the system recommends the best possible solution to cure disease.

8.4   Crop Management

8.4.1   Yield Prediction

The most important topic in agriculture is yield prediction because yield prediction contributes to profit [5]. It includes activities such as yield mapping and estimation, pairing crop supply with demand and crop management. All these activities lead to increase production. One of the low costs and efficient machine learning application was developed that contributes in automatically counting coffee fruits on branch of a tree. The calculation of coffee fruits is classified into three types: fruits that are harvestable, fruits that are non-harvestable and fruits that are ignored from stage of maturation. This system also calculated the weight of coffee fruit and maturation percentage. This system aims to help the factory owner who wants to grow coffee by providing the best economic benefits and also plan. The machine learning application named a machine vision system was developed that automatically shake and catch cherries while harvesting process. This system does segmentation and detects the obstructed branches even though these branches are full of leaves and not visible clearly. This system aims to reduce labor work and manual handling of operation during harvesting.

One of the systems introduced was yield mapping system that identifies immature green citrus. This system aims to provide information of good citrus in citrus groove that will result in better profit and yield. This is very useful system for citrus growers. Based upon the Artificial Neural Network, a new model for calculating grassland biomass was developed. The study was also done on yield prediction. For study, wheat crop was considered and images were taken with the help of satellite. Using image processing crop growth characteristics were identified and data were fused to predict the result. Another application was developed to detect the tomatoes using images that were sensed remotely. These images were captured using Unmanned Aerial vehicle. Based on SVM, new rice development stage prediction model was developed. All the basic information that is required for processing was obtained from weather forecasting station in China. The study was done that focuses on helping farmers to overcome imbalances that happened in the market supply and demand. This may be due to quality of crop. A generalized method based on ENN application was developed for good agricultural yield prediction. The following table describes study about various crops along with their functionality, algorithms and results. Table 8.2 describes study about various crops along with their functionality, algorithms and results.

8.4.2   Disease Detection

Disease detection is very significant part in agriculture domain. If crop is affected by the disease it will lessen production resulting into profit decrement. Hence there is need to control pest and diseases in open farm and also in green house. To control pest and diseases, spraying pesticides is the most commonly used method. This method is costly and causes environmental hazards such as ground water contamination, problems to local wildlife, and other impact crop quality etc. excessive use of pesticides also decreases quality of crop and soil becomes barren. There is need to know exact quantity of adding pesticides as excess quantity causes side effects. To avoid this, machine learning applications can be used in agriculture that will identify disease automatically and provide the solution. The system was developed to automatically detect plant affected by fungus and also classify infected plant and non-infected plant. Another system was developed using image processing technique that classify parasites and detect thrips in the strawberry. This experiment was done in green house

Table 8.2 Summary of crops with their functionality and algorithm [8].

Crop	Functionality	Algorithm	Result
Coffee	Describes count of coffee fruit automatically	Support Vector Machine	Harvestable: Ripe/overripe: 82.54–87.83% visibility percentage Not harvestable: Unripe: 76.91–81.39% visibility percentage
Cherry	Detect cherry branches and foliage	Gaussian naïve Bayes	89.6% accuracy
Citrus	Detect immature green citrus	Support Vector Machine	80.4% accuracy
Grass	Calculate biomass in grassland	Artificial Neural Network	R2 = 0.85 RMSE = 11.07
Wheat	Predicted wheat yield	Artificial Neural Network	81.65% accuracy
Tomato	Detected tomatoes	Clustering	Recall: 0.6066 Precision: 0.9191
Rice	Predicted rice yield	Support Vector Machine	Middle-season rice: Tillering stage: RMSE (kg h^{-1} m^2) = 126.8 Heading stage: RMSE (kg h^{-1} m^2) = 96.4

environment. The system was presented to detect Bakanae disease in rice. The main aim was to detect pathogen into different rice. As these diseases are detected automatically, it saves time in identifying disease with naked eye. It also reduces manual work. Ultimately increase production with good quality yield.

Lot of studies has been done for disease detection on wheat crop. Wheat is given major importance among all crops. Hence to produce healthy wheat crop disease detection proved to be very essential and significant. A new system has been developed that classify healthy wheat and infected wheat due to nitrogen and yellow rust. The hyperspectral reflectance imaging technique is used to identify disease. The author described the system that accurately detect the disease and also provide solution about usage of fertilizers, Pesticides, fungicides etc. depending upon plant's requirement. Another study describes system that differentiate healthy wheat crop and infected wheat crop with Septoriatritici blotch (STB). Another research was done to develop system for identifying infected wheat by yellow color rust and healthy wheat. This was done using machine learning algorithm named SVM classifier along with data fusion technique. The similar kind of study was done using ANN models and considering spectral reflectance features. Development of such system is needed for accurate disease detection and providing solution earlier in order to produce better yield.

Mostly wheat is affected with diseases such as yellow rust, Septoriatritici blotch, fungus, etc. To detect yellow rust infected wheat, crop a real time system was developed which was handles remotely. This system uses Neural Network technique and data fusion technique. Data fusion also includes data obtained from hyper-spectral reflection and multi-spectral fluorescence image. The system was also developed to identify stress in plant and also nutrition deficiency under certain field conditions. This plant stress is caused by some disease. If plant has stress then there will be fewer yields. Finally, new system was designed that will identify and classify plant diseases using convolutional neural network (CNN). The images of plant leaves are taken as input to the system and image processing. After image preprocessing, features are extracted and CNN algorithm is applied to get desired output. The output will be either plant is infected by disease or healthy. Table 8.3 summarizes various crops and their functionality. It also describes the machine learning algorithm that is used in research along with predicted results.

8.4.3   Weed Detection

Weed is nothing but unwanted plant in cultivated area. If this weed is present in large amount then growth of required crop will be less and hence this will decrease productivity resulting into fewer profit. Therefore, weed detection and removal has obtained greater importance in field of agriculture. Most of the farmers consider this as major threat towards production of desired crop. As weeds are very difficult to identify and distinguish, there is need of accurate weed detection to increase productivity of crop. Various machine learning applications are developed to detect and distinguish weed from actual crops in coordination with sensors. These applications are low cost. Machine learning assist in the development of robots which will help in weed detection and removal that will lessen the requirement of herbicide. A system was presented that is used to identify weed named Silybummarianum using method counter propagation (CP)-ANN

Table 8.3 Summary of crops with their functionality and algorithm.

Crop	Functionality	Algorithm	Result
Silybummarianum	Disease detection and classification between healthy plant and plant infected by fungus Microbotyumsilybum	Artificial Neural Network	95.16% accuracy
Strawberry	Parasites are classified and insects/diseases are detected automatically	Support Vector Machine	MPE = 2.25%
Rice [2]	Detection of Disease (Bakanae, Fusarium)	Support Vector Machine	87.9% accuracy
Wheat	Disease detection (yellow rust Infected) and also nitrogen stressed	Artificial Neural Network/ XY-Fusion	Accuracy Nitrogen stressed: 99.63% Yellow rust: 99.83% Healthy: 97.27%
Wheat	Disease detection (Septoriatritici infected) and also water stressed	Support Vector Machine/ least squares-support vector machine	Inoculated treatment, with Septoriatritici 98.75% accuracy

(Continued)

Table 8.3 Summary of crops with their functionality and algorithm. (*Continued*)

Crop	Functionality	Algorithm	Result
Wheat [4]	Disease detection (yellow rust Infected)	Artificial Neural Network/ multi-layer perceptron	Accuracy Infected by Yellow rust: 99.4% Not infected: 98.9%
Wheat	Disease detection in wheat and classify infected wheat and healthy wheat	Artificial Neural Network/ self-organizing maps	Accuracy Infected by Yellow rust: 99.4% Not infected: 98.7%
Wheat	Identify healthy wheat and infected wheat by yellow rust or nitrogen stress	Artificial Neural Network/ self-organizing maps	Accuracy Infected by Yellow rust: 99.92% Nitrogen stressed: 100% Not infected: 99.39%

by capturing multispectral images. For recognition of the crop and weed, new methods based on machine learning techniques are developed. An active learning system was developed to recognize weed and plant named maize. The main aim is to automatically and accurately detect weed.

8.4.4   Crop Quality

Crop quality is very significant factor in agriculture sector that defines the profit for owner. For this accurate identification of crop quality along with its classification is must to judge production cost. Earlier this identification took place manually increasing the time and labor cost. But along with technological development various applications have been developed to accurately detect crop quality. Hence the error rate is minimized as compare to earlier giving exact profit to owner. A new system was designed to detect the botanical material inside cotton. This was done during harvesting period. The study was to improve crop quality and minimize damage to the fiber. Some of the detection system used hyperspectral reflectance imaging technique. The detection was made by capturing images of crop. Similar kind of application was developed by using various machine learning techniques to identify rice samples.

8.5   Application—Crop Disease Detection and Yield Prediction

For crop yield prediction Machine learning plays vital role. Many ML techniques are developed for yield prediction. The comparative studies are done by multiple researchers for defining most accurate technique. As very limited number of crops is evaluated, still exact decision is not achieved.

Production of crop depends upon some factors such as weather condition, soil condition, geographical region, soil composition and also harvesting method. Traditionally, monitoring techniques does not gather the crop conditions properly and prediction results were not yet optimized. Therefore, to overcome this problem, a system has been designed that identified type of crop, crop disease and predict crop yield in different conditions using machine learning techniques. The main aim was to detect disease and predict maximum production of crop using limited land resource.

The study has been done on agricultural land that cultivates strawberry and citrus crop. The dataset contains more than 1,000 strawberry images and citrus images. The image of crop was captured by using camera. Image undergoes preprocessing which includes removal of noise and extracting region of interest. Features such as color, position and size were extracted by feature extraction process. By using Convolution Neural Network (CNN) algorithm [12], the crop type is identified. CNN algorithm is used to classify the image by its features. After identifying the crop type, crop disease was detected. To calculate crop yield, there is need to remove this affected crop as it will contribute to bad production or affect production. Hence, good crop is selected and crop yield is predicted using machine learning algorithm (Figure 8.5).

In Figure 8.6, Anaconda 3.0 software is used in this system because the machine learning algorithms that we want to use have libraries written in python. The support for python is better than other languages when it comes to tensor flow as it has been around for some time now. Whereas for use of Opencv, Python or C Raspberry pi has good support. As shown in Figure 8.6 the different commands were used: first command is to activate the tensor flow environment. Second Command will set the path where the file is located. Third command will go to actual Keras library. Fourth command will execute actual image from dataset and gives the result.

By using above commands as shown in Figure 8.6, the system has detected the fruit and identified the disease. As shown in Figure 8.7, the system has detected the fruit i.e. strawberry and identified that strawberry has infected.

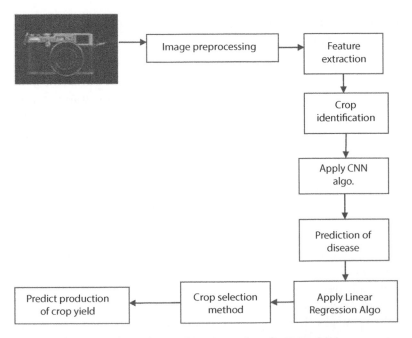

Figure 8.5 Architecture of crop disease detection and prediction system.

Then it gave which diseases strawberry has—whether it is suffering from Gray Mold (gm) or Rhizopus (Rz). First figure has detected gm disease 100%.and Rz disease 0% and the second figure detected Rz disease 100% and gm disease 0%.

Figure 8.6 Commands to run the model.

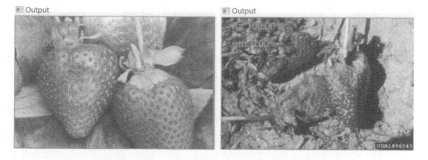

Figure 8.7 Fruit identification and disease detection in strawberry crop.

Figure 8.8 Identify and detect disease in citrus canker.

By using above commands as shown in Figure 8.6, the system has detected the fruit and identified the disease. As shown in Figure 8.8, the system has detected the fruit i.e. Citrus Canker and identified that Citrus Canker has infected. Then it gave how much Citrus Canker has infected. As shown in Figure 8.3, Blackspot is 31.29% detected.

References

1. Ebrahimi, M.A., Khoshtaghaza, M.H., Minaei, S., Jamshidi, B., Vision-based pest detection based on SVM classification method. *Comput. Electron. Agric.*, 137, 52–58, 2017.
2. Chung, C.L., Huang, K.J., Chen, S.Y., Lai, M.H., Chen, Y.C., Kuo, Y.F., Detecting Bakanae disease in rice seedlings by machine vision. *Comput. Electron. Agric.*, 121, 404–411, 2016.
3. Pantazi, X.E., Moshou, D., Oberti, R., West, J., Mouazen, A.M., Bochtis, D., Detection of biotic and abiotic stresses in crops by using hierarchical self-organizing classifiers. *Precis. Agric.*, 18, 383–393, 2017.
4. Moshou, D., Bravo, C., West, J., Wahlen, S., McCartney, A., Automatic detection of "yellow rust" in wheat using reflectance measurements and neural networks. *Comput. Electron. Agric.*, 44, 173–188, 2004.
5. Richardson, A., Signor, B.M., Lidbury, B.A., Badrick, T., Clinical chemistry in higher dimensions: Machine-learning and enhanced prediction from routine clinical chemistry data. *Clin. Biochem.*, 49, 1213–1220, 2016.
6. Wildenhain, J., Spitzer, M., Dolma, S., Jarvik, N., White, R., Roy, M., Griffiths, E., Bellows, D.S., Wright, G.D., Tyers, M., Prediction of Synergism from Chemical-Genetic Interactions by Machine Learning. *Cell Syst.*, 1, 383–395, 2015.
7. Kang, J., Schwartz, R., Flickinger, J., Beriwal, S., Machine learning approaches for predicting radiation therapy outcomes: A clinician's perspective. *Int. J. Radiat. Oncol. Biol. Phys.*, 93, 1127–1135, 2015.
8. Craven, B.D. and Islam, S.M.N., Ordinary least-squares regression SAGE. *Dict. Quant. Manag. Res.*, 224–228, 2011.
9. Friedman, J.H., Multivariate Adaptive Regression Splines. *Ann. Stat.*, 19, 1–67, 1991.
10. Alonso, J., Villa, A., Bahamonde, A., Improved estimation of bovine weight trajectories using Support Vector Machine Classification. *Comput. Electron. Agric.*, 110, 36–41, 2015.
11. Alonso, J., Castañón, Á.R., Bahamonde, A., Support Vector Regression to predict carcass weight in beef cattle in advance of the slaughter. *Comput. Electron. Agric.*, 2013.

12. Hansen, M.F., Smith, M.L., Smith, L.N., Salter, M.G., Baxter, E.M., Farish, M., Grieve, B., Towards on-farm pig face recognition using convolutional neural networks. *Comput. Ind.*, 98, 145–152, 2018.

13. Feng, Y., Peng, Y., Cui, N., Gong, D., Zhang, K., Modeling reference evapotranspiration using extreme learning machine and generalized regression neural network only with temperature data. *Comput. Electron. Agric.*, 136, 71–78, 2017.

14. Mohammadi, K., Shamshirband, S., Motamedi, S., Petković, D., Hashim, R., Gocic, M., Extreme learning machine based prediction of daily dew point temperature. *Comput. Electron. Agric.*, 117, 214–225, 2015.

Part 3
CONTENT-BASED RECOMMENDER SYSTEMS

## 9

Content-Based Recommender Systems

Poonam Bhatia Anand and Rajender Nath*

Department of Computer Science and Applications, Kurukshetra University,
Kurukshetra, India

Abstract

Recommender System guides the users to choose objects from variety of possible options in personalized manner. Broadly, there are two categories of recommender systems i.e. content based and collaborative filtering based. These systems suggest the items based on the interest of the customers in the past. They personalize the information by using relevant information. These systems are used in various domains like recommending movies, products to purchase, restaurants, places to visit, etc. This chapter deliberates the concepts of content-based recommender systems by including distinct features in their design and implementation. High level architecture and applications of these systems in various domains are also presented in this chapter.

Keywords: Content-based recommender system, item representation, profile cleaner, learning user profiles, probability method, Rocchio's algorithm, application of recommender system in agriculture and health sector

9.1 Introduction

The enormous amount of digital information generated by increasing number of users on internet have created the challenge of information overload. The information on the web is heterogeneous in nature and increasing day by day in dynamic manner. It becomes challenging, tedious and time-consuming for users to retrieve the exact information on time from web. Users need suggestions from the friends or experts who have knowledge

Corresponding author: rnath2k13@gmail.com

Sachi Nandan Mohanty, Jyotir Moy Chatterjee, Sarika Jain, Ahmed A. Elngar and Priya Gupta (eds.)
Recommender System with Machine Learning and Artificial Intelligence: Practical Tools and Applications in Medical, Agricultural and Other Industries, (167–196) © 2020 Scrivener Publishing LLC

about the item in such cases. This has increased the demand of recommender system. The aim of recommender systems is to aid users in finding relevant items. The preferences provided by the customers are taken as input in algorithms used for recommender systems and list of recommended items are generated as an output. These systems make predictions based on the past behavior of users and solve the problem of overloading of information by using the various approaches. The most prevalent used techniques are collaborative recommender system and content-based recommender systems which are also known as collaborative filtering and content-based filtering. Collaborative filtering needs only the information about the past preferences of the identical users. This approach identifies the users whose preferences are same as given the current users and recommend the items. Collaborative filtering works well when there is enough information of ratings. This system suffers from sparsity problem in case of insufficient information. To solve this problem content-based approach comes into picture which requires the complete information about the item rather the user preferences. They recommend the items according to the users liked in the past. Researchers also combined these two approaches into one known as hybrid approach of information filtering. In this chapter, content-based recommender system is studied.

In the next section, the background work with their existing work in this field in terms of their techniques, process, algorithms and applicability of this system in various domains are discussed. Semantic aware architecture of content-based recommender system along with the process of the recommendation is being described in the Section 9.3. The techniques for assimilating the user's profiles and representing the items are presented in Section 9.4. The applications of recommender systems in the field of healthcare and agriculture are discussed in Section 9.5. Various limitations and advantages of these systems are described in Section 9.6. Section 9.7 concludes the chapter.

9.2   Literature Review

The primary idea of content-based recommender systems is given in 1962 by [1]. The information was distributed by matching new information items with previous interests of users stored in user profiles. Also, these systems have found their roots in field of information retrieval in [18] and in information filtering research. Document encodings were developed in information retrieval by [2] on which content-based approaches relied.

Later, content-based techniques were applied in different domains to make personalized recommended systems by [9].

Initially, Researchers started work with representation of contents in content-based recommender system. Balabanovic and Shoham [12] recommended the web pages by representing the contents with 100 informative words by using Fab. Similarly, Pazzani *et al.* [9] represented the item with 128 informative words. The optimal number of words was used by [9] that was tested on many domains. The evaluation shown that this recommender system likely to exclusive important features with less than 50 keywords but with more than 300 words noise was introduced in the system. One of the most important measure for specifying weights of keyword was "Term Frequency/Inverse Document Frequency [TF-IDF]" that was used to identify most informative words in document by [3]. Even this weighing scheme was very effective but it was not able to deal with natural language issues. Textual content is full of noises and poorly informative words such as pronouns, articles etc. This problem was tackled by doing preprocessing methods such as removal of stop words, stemming and constituent of speech (POS) tagging borrowed from the field of Natural Language Processing. Porter Algorithm [Martin Porter, 1980] was introduced for stemmed representation of textual content. Keyword based representations was unable to capture the semantics of interest of users and item descriptions. These methods suffer from the problems of "POLYSEMY" and "SYNONYMY".

To tackle these problems, the concept of semantic analysis was used to introduce the semantics in content-based recommender system. Accessibility of a few open information bases as Wikipedia, DBpedia, freebase and so forth and semantic innovations have filled the advancement in the knowledge domain of content-based recommender systems. Semantic techniques have proposed for concept-based presentation of items and user profile instead of keyword-based representation. Word Sense Disambiguation (WSD) [Semeraro *et al.* 2007] was proposed for this purpose. Integration of semantic technologies and NLP resulted into semantic recommender system [49]. Later it became the most innovative field of research. For semantic technology two types of methods were used, i.e. top-down and bottom-up. The top-down approach was based on consolidating dictionaries, taxonomies and ontologies readable by machines. On the other hand, methods from the bottom up are able to induce the meanings of words by using unsupervised techniques to examine their utilization in broad corpus of textual documents [63].

With the development of semantic web [22], ontologies were risen up as strong discipline for domain knowledge representation domain knowledge in many fields. Therefore, many approaches have been introduced to utilize ontologies in recommender systems. Ontologies are utilized to depict explicit information and these are dealt as hierarchies of concept attributes and relations. Magini *et al.* [23] proposed a personal agent SiteIF for multilingual news website. MultiWordNet was used as knowledge base in their work. The user profile is built as semantic network. A web-based personalization system was proposed by [26] in which both user logs and semantics of web content were used to personalize the system. Domain specific taxonomy was used to semantically annotating the web pages for uniform and consistent library. Research topic ontology [27] was used to recommend the academic research papers in computer science. Correlation has been applied for matching between the topics in user profile and those inter-related with papers. The aforesaid process was followed by [31, 32] for recommending the news. Item descriptors are TF-IDF vectors in context of ontology, user profiles are portrayed in the similar context, and cosine similarity measure is used for matching the item and profiles which is different from the approaches used in [33, 34]. In these approaches, implicit communities of interest were built by clustering user space and items that enabled the recommendation by computing similarities among them. The position of concepts in three level ontology was used to find the similarity between user and item profile as done in [35]. Spreading activation algorithm was described in [36] in which ontology profiles are utilized to advise the interesting and unique items to the user. The same method was used in [64] where the advancement from small number of initial concepts to other related domain concepts allowed to provide the recommendation in better way and also to address the cold start problem.

As ontologies-based profiles was less ambiguous and these might be adopted for recommendation system because of using ontologies added the semantic dimension to items and user profiles and limited problems of content-based recommender systems. But it was very time consuming and laborious process to develop the ontologies for particular domains. Hence, Researchers used online resource aggregation of world knowledge of semantic-aware recommender systems.

The importance of knowledge have been recognized in Artificial Intelligence (AI) for solving the problem of ontologies by using structured and unstructured knowledge bases such as Wikipedia and Open Directory Project (ODP). Wikipedia emerged as most useful sources of information for many tasks used in [29, 37, 38, 65]. The main advantages of using

Wikipedia as a knowledge source in terms of free availability, wide coverage of resources, available in many languages and accuracy. To interpret the pages of Wikipedia and make them processed by machine, concept of Natural language understanding was used. Several authors [39, 41, 58] discussed the issue of information extraction and use in Wikipedia. Several techniques have been suggested in Wikipedia to pick out the most high-fidelity semantic features for representing items and for generation of new feature by using the encyclopedia knowledge. Wikify! [39] and Tagme [58] were the most used approaches for selecting the features. The important concepts for representing text was by extracting keywords and linking those concepts with Wikipedia pages by using WSD techniques in [39]. Tagme [58] implemented the disambiguation algorithms for augmenting the representation of text with hyperlinks to pages of Wikipedia. An approach named Explicit Semantic Analysis (ESA) was used in [41] that used knowledge from Wikipedia for generating new features for inspiring item representation. The conventional Bag of Words based retrieval models given in [37] have been enhanced by this technique. Use of Wikipedia in analysing contents was presented in [45] by using knowledge infusion process.

Previous work on ontology-based recommendation algorithms was based on limited domain ontologies, controlled vocabulary and taxonomies. Therefore, Linked Open Data (LOD) has opened the new possibilities for better recommending applications known as LOD based recommender system. The first approach that used LOD for building recommender system was [50] for collaborative recommender systems. Noia *et al.* in [59] implemented content-based recommender system that uses the data available within LOD datasets such as DBpedia [44], Freebase [40] and LinkedDB [42]. The use of LOD for content-based recommendation system was explored in [65]. This paradigm followed a semantic interpretation based on models of delivery and techniques for entity linking. Entity linking strategies were used to identify and map objects into LODs in free text. Recommendation strategies have been introduced in [72] to provide customized access to linked content. Noia [76] presented an overview on recommender systems along with usage of LOD.

Researchers worked on classification algorithms for learning the profiles to discriminate representations of highly rated documents from others. Rocchio's Algorithm was used to learn TF/IDF vector which was average of highly rated documents. Syskill & Webert [9] used Bayesian classifier to evaluate the probability of liked document. Winnow algorithm [Littlestone & Warmuth, 1994; Blum, Hellerstein & Littlestone, 1995] was designed to identify the relevant features when there were many possible attributes. This algorithm worked well with text classification as demonstrated by the [7].

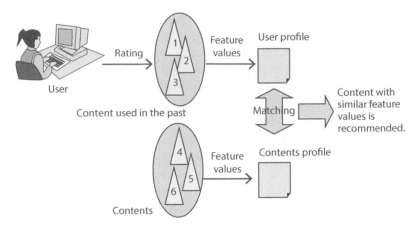

Figure 9.1 Content based recommender system.

9.3   Recommendation Process

Content based recommender systems analyze the descriptions of items and set of documents which are previously rated by the user to identify the items that are of user interests. They frame a model or outline the interests of users that are based on the features of the items rated by the users. The user profiles are matched with the contents profile and then the contents with similar features values are recommended to the users. Then, machine learning model is applied for making the recommendation based on user profile. This process is shown in Figure 9.1.

The detailed representation of these components along with their description are presented in the next section.

9.3.1   Architecture of Content-Based Recommender System

The architecture of semantic aware content based recommender system was proposed by [75]. An updated version of the same was presented by [87] which is shown in Figure 9.2.

The recommender process is performed using four components. These components are [54]:

- *Content Analyzer*: As the information available on web is in unstructured format, pre-treatment is done to draw out the relevant information. This component is responsible for representing the contents of items coming from the information

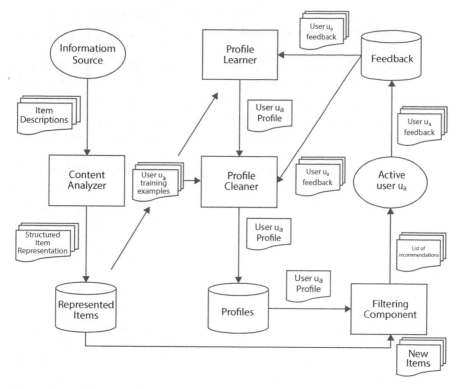

Figure 9.2 Architecture of content based recommender system [87].

source in suitable form for processing. Data items are analyzed using feature extraction techniques. This component's output is structured item description and stored in the repository of the representation item.

- *Profile Learner*: this component accumulates the descriptions of the active user preferences data for generalization purposes. Machine learning model is built to find the interests of user in past. User profile is the output of this components and sent for cleaning the incoherent items.
- *Profile Cleaner*: This component is intended to evaluate the profile and delete the incoherent objects before it is placed in the database profile.
- *Filtering Component*: This part, which compares the performance of the content analyzer and profile learner, performs the recommendation function. It resolves whether or not item is appropriate for the participating user by matching

the profile image with preferred items. Test of cosine similarity is used to assess similarity.

The user reflex action to the items are accumulated and stored in
feedback repository. These reactions are also called "annotations" [4].
The feedback given by users are used by the system to update the profile
of user. Users can define their interests without providing any feedback.
Two kinds of relevance feedback can be given, one infers the features
liked by users and other inferring the features not liked by the user [10].
The user's response can be adopted in two ways, first is explicit feedback in which the system demands the user to explicitly check out items
and second is implicit feedback in which active user requirement is not
required by the system. The feedback is deduced by analyzing the activities of the users.

The training set T_a for active user u_a must be defined to frame the profile of the active user u_a. T_a is set of ratings provided by the user on the
item representation. Representation of items are labeled with the ratings
provided by users. Then, Supervised learning algorithms is applied to
generate the profile of the users. Profile repository is used for storing the
user profiles. Filtering component compares the features in item representation with preferences stored in user profile and predicts about the
likeliness of the item by user. User profile must be updated and maintained with changing the interests of the user. At last, learning process is
repeated on another training set and generation of feedback is done based
on recommendations.

Some problems arise in the system by performing the steps without
profile cleaner component [87]. Suppose if the evaluation of the items is
done by another person from the account of the active user who have not
evaluated those items before then it will create noise in the profile of user.
The profile learners consider these incoherent items and make them part
of active user profile used by filtering component for recommendation.
Implementing incoherent objects will result in poor advice and impair
the system's reliability. Another problem arises in the case of ageing products in the user's profile when the successful user's interest shifts over age
but the older objects that do not reflect the user's latest tastes have been
positively assessed. The old objects will create noise until the machine
removes it. This would impact the advice process's reliability. If these two
problems exist together in the process, it will lead to a system in "magic
barrier state," i.e. a state where noise impacts the system and the reliability of the system cannot be further enhanced. These problems are being
solved in [87] by introducing one more component i.e. Profile Cleaner as

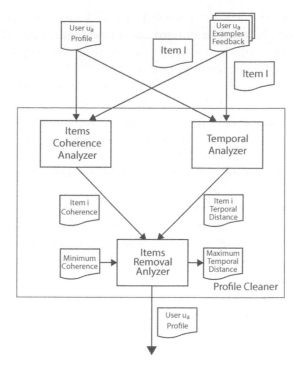

Figure 9.3 Architecture of profile cleaner [87].

shown in Figure 9.3. The organization of this component is described in next section.

9.3.2   Profile Cleaner Representation

As profile cleaner takes the user profile and item evaluated by the user as an input (as shown in Figure 9.2). The sub components of profile cleaner is shown in Figure 9.3 and is described as:

- *Items Coherence Analyzer*: Comparison of the organized representation of the items with the remaining of the user profile to determine the resemblance of the item with this element. Many methods used by [6, 8, 13, 16, 17] in the literature to determine the consistency of standardized representations including synsets. It is possible to apply any of these steps. The performance of the coherence function of this element is then used by another variable to assess the object should be omitted or not.

- *Temporal Analyzer*: It works in parallel with previous component. Evaluation of item considered with other items is done by this. Temporal distance will be the output which will use by next component.
- *Items Removal Analyzer*: the output of previous two components are managed by this component. The minimum value of coherence and maximum value of temporal distance are also taken as input. This determines whether or not to delete the object called from the user profile. Cleaned user profile u_a is the output of this module, which is free of incoherent and oldest objects.

After the incoherent items has been removed from user profile, the cleaned profiles are stored in the profile's repository. Then, the filtering component uses these cleaned profiles for recommendation process. In this way, profile cleaner solves the problems exist in early semantic aware recommender systems [75].

The techniques used for the representing the items and for leaning the user profiles are discussed in the next section.

9.4 Techniques Used for Item Representation and Learning User Profile

Content based recommender systems recommends the item based on matching the contents of item and profile of the user. Typically, these systems need two types of information i.e. textual description of items and describing user interests in terms of textual features. Recommendation step consists in matching characteristics of items with those describing interests of users [Loren Terveen, 2001, HCI in recommender system]. The result is relevance judgment that represents interests of users of items. The models for content-based recommendation system differs in way of representation of content, learning user profile and calculation of relevance score. The item representation and methods used to create profile are discussed in this section.

9.4.1 Representation of Content

Items are the contents that are represented by attributes. Attribute specifies the properties of the items such as actor name in movie recommendation applications, words in the document recommendation applications, etc. The content of each item is represented as set of terms that occur in the document. Items are characterized with attributes in structured manner [28]. Natural Language Processing (NLP) techniques came into picture when content-based recommender system has to represent textual contents. Item are outlined in terms of textual features that are obtained from web pages, emails, news articles etc. But, due to natural language ambiguity these features create lot of complications. Traditional keyword-based profile methods are based on string matching operation therefore these methods are unable to capture the semantics of user interests. To solve this problem, semantic based approaches was integrated with recommendation models in literature. In this combined approach, knowledge sources such as dictionaries, freebases and ontologies were adopted for defining the items and for profile representation. The basic model for representing the documents is described in next section.

9.4.2   Vector Space Model Based on Keywords

The mostly used semantic approach used for recommending the items is keyword space model with term frequency-inverse document frequency (TF-IDF). Vector space model is the image of text documents.

In n-dimensional space, each document is represented by vector where each dimension corresponds to a word from the total vocabulary of a given document array. A vector of term weight is given to every document where weight indicates the degree of link between document and term. Suppose $D = \{d_1, d_2, \ldots d_N\}$ denote the set of documents and $T = \{t_1, t_2, \ldots t_n\}$ is set of words in the document. These set of words are obtained by applying pre-processing techniques such as tokenization, removal of stop-words, and stemming [2]. Each document d_j is represented as a vector in a n-dimensional vector space, so $d_j = <w_{1j}, w_{2j}, \ldots, w_{nj}>$, where w_{kj} is the weight for term t_k in document d_j. The description of the text in the VSM poses two issues: weighing the words and calculating the consistency of the feature vector. TF-IDF (Term Frequency-Inverse Document Frequency) weighting, the most widely applied term weighting method, is based on empirical document observations for IDF, TF and normalization [3]:

- uncommon terms are no less important than common terms;
- Many instances of the word in a document are not less significant than one instance
- Long papers are not favored

In other words, terms that often appear in one text (TF = term frequency), but rarely in the rest of the principal (IDF = inverse-document-frequency), are more likely to be applicable to the document's topic. Therefore, the normalization of the resulting weight vectors stops longer records from having a better opportunity of recovery. The TF–IDF function is a good example of these assumptions:

$$TF - IDF(t_k, d_j) = TF(t_k, d_j).\log \frac{N}{n_k} \qquad (1)$$

Where N is the number of documents in the principal and n_k denotes the at least the number of documents in the collection in which the term t_k appears.

$$TF(t_k, d_j) = \frac{f_{k,j}}{max_z \ f_{z,i}} \qquad (2)$$

where the limit is determined at the $f_{z,j}$ frequencies of all t_z words in document d_j. In order to decrease the weights in the [0,1] interval and to represent the documents by vectors of same size, the weights obtained by Equation 1 are typically normalized by cosine normalization:

$$w_{k,j} = \frac{TFIDF(t_k, d_j)}{\sqrt{\sum_{s=1}^{|T|} TF - IDF(t_s, d_j)^2}} \qquad (3)$$

That enforces the presumption of normalization. As stated earlier, to decide the closeness between two records, a similarity measure is required. To define the proximity of two vectors, several similarity measures have been derived; among these values, cosine similarity is the most commonly employed:

$$sim(d_i, d_j) = \frac{\sum_k w_{ki}.w_{kj}}{\sqrt{\sum_k w_{ki}^2} \cdot \sqrt{\sum_k w_{kj}^2}} \qquad (4)$$

All profiles of users and objects are represented as weighted term vectors in content-based VSM-based recommender systems. Calculating the cosine similarity will produce projections of a user's interest in a particular item. The various keyword-based system is already reviewed in the literature survey.

9.4.3   Techniques for Learning Profiles of User

Machine learning strategies are well adapted to text categorization in the role of triggering content-based profiles [25]. An inductive process creates a classifier automatically by studying a set of documents that are marked with classes that belong to the classification function. Understanding user profiles question can be described as the process of categorizing binary text. Each document must be classified in terms of user preferences as interesting or not. The set of categories is therefore C = {c+, c−} where c+ is the positive class that the user likes and c− is the negative class that the user dislikes.

Naïve Bayes algorithm is presented in next section which is mostly used in content-based systems. Relevance feedback method is also used with Rocchio's formula and described in next section. These algorithms are able to define a function that represents the interests of the user. Documents are labelled by assigning the relevant score and infer the profiles automatically used in filtering process to rank the documents according to preferences of the user by using these techniques.

9.4.3.1   *Probabilistic Method*

Naïve Bayes is an inductive learning probabilistic method and belongs to the category of Bayesian classifiers. Based on the previously observed results, a probabilistic model is created. This model estimates that document d belonging to class c is a posteriori probability, $P(c)$. This estimate is supported on the probability of priori, $P(c)$, the likelihood of observing a document in category c, $P(d)$, the likelihood of observing document d given c, and $P(d)$, the likelihood of observing instance d.

$$P(c|d) = \frac{P(c)P(d|c)}{P(d)} \tag{5}$$

To classify the document d, the class with highest probability is chosen as:

$$c = argmax_{cj} \frac{P(c_j)P(d|c_j)}{P(d)}$$

(Pd) is generally removed as it is equal for all c_j. By observing the training data, value for $P(d|c)$ and $P(c)$ is projected. As estimation of $P(d|c)$ is problematic because the observed data is not enough to generate good probabilities. This problem is solved by using naïve Bayes algorithm by modifying the model through independence assumption i.e. all words in the observed document "d" are conditionally independent of each other. The probability of words in a document are calculated instead of whole document. Naïve Bayes algorithm worked well in classifying the text documents [7, 14]. In several content-based recommender systems such as Syskill & Webert [9, 11], NewsDude [19], Daily Learner [20], LIBRA [21] and ITR [43], the Naïve Bayes method has been used.

9.4.3.2   Rocchio's and Relevance Feedback Method

Relevance Feedback is the method taken from Information Retrieval which assist users to improve queries supported on the previous search results. It contains the feedback of users based on significance of retrieved documents as per need of information. Rocchio's formula uses this technique for recommendation. It allows users to rate the documents as per their needs. This collected information in form of feedback is used to incrementally polish the profile of user or to train learning algorithm that infers the user profile as classifier.

The method of Rocchio is used to make linear classifiers of the profile form. Data are defined by vectors in order to have identical vectors in the information file. Any part of such a vector in the study reflects a definition, i.e. a term. The TF–IDF approach is used to measure each word's weight. Training is done by transforming vectors of documents into vectors of models for each unit of class C. The similarity between model vectors and the corresponding document vector representing d is determined for each class in order to define a new document d as using cosine similarity measure, then d is assigned to the category whose document vector has the highest similarity value.

Rocchio's method computes the classifier $\rightarrow c_i = (w_{1i}, \ldots, w_{|T|i})$ for the category c_i (T is the set of distinct terms in training set known as vocabulary) by using the formula:

$$w_{ki} = \beta . \sum \{d_j \in POS_i\} \frac{w_{kj}}{|POS_i|} - \gamma . \sum \{d_j \in POS_i\} \frac{w_{kj}}{|NEG_i|} \qquad (6)$$

Where w_{kj} is the TF–IDF weight of the term t_k in document d_j, POS_i and NEG_i are set of positive and negative examples in training set for specific class c_j, To evaluate the relative importance of all positive and negative cases, two control parameters, β and γ are used. The similarity between each model vector c_i and document vector d_j is calculated to give a class c to document d_j and class c is determined with maximum similarity value. There is no theoretical justification for this strategy and there are assurances on quality [28].

Content-based recommendation system used this technique in YourNews [30], Fab [12] and NewsT [5].

9.4.3.3   Other Methods

The other training strategies such as Decision Tree, Decision rule classifiers and Nearest Neighbor algorithms were used in the recommendation system based on content. The following is a short description of these algorithms:

Decision trees are trees whose inner nodes are labeled with concepts, leaves are labeled with sections, and branches are marked on the weights the term has in the test document by the test These are trained by text data, i.e. repetitively partitioning training data into subgroups until such time as those subgroups only contain one-class example. Information gain or entropy criterion [15] was used to choose a term on which operation on the partition is applied. Syskill and Webert [9, 11] uses decision tree for learning the profiles.

Decision rule classifiers are exchangeable to decision trees as they worked in the same manner as the recursive approach to data partitioning. We tend to produce more lightweight classifiers than learners from the decision tree. Rule learning approaches aim to select the best one from any rule that classifies all practice examples correctly according to the minimum requirements.

Nearest Neighbor algorithms are also called lazy learners which essentially store memory training data and use similarity function to identify a new item by comparing it to stored items already. This decides the nearest neighbor or k-nearest neighbor products. The class labels of non-classified products are taken from the closest neighbor's class labels. Similarity function as objects are represented using vector space model is adopted as cosine similarity. These algorithms are effective but having inefficient classification time.

9.5   Applicability of Recommender System in Healthcare and Agriculture

Although recommender system has been applied in various domains like recommendation of news, products, movies, music, television programs, books, documents, websites, conferences, health sector etc. In this chapter, the recommendation system used in health care and agriculture sector has been discussed.

9.5.1   Recommendation System in Healthcare

The recommender system can be applied in health care for providing health resources to the consumers and for sharing the experiences related to patient conditions, symptoms and treatments as suggested by [46]. The challenges for using recommender system for health education in personalized manner was given by [47]. A system was presented by [48] in which Patients can rate the physicians based on their satisfaction which can help the patients to choose the doctor who is best suited according to their needs.

Most of the articles presented in literature have taken patients as end-users. Roitman *et al.* [51] worked on improvement of safety of patients by suggesting the appropriate information about interaction between dissimilar drugs to avoid health related risks. A recommender system named MED-StyleR was presented in [52]. This system was dedicated to support diabetes patient by improving care facility and improving the quality of life of patient. A system focused on suggesting the healthy recipes for patients was presented by [55]. Other recommendation system on changing lifestyle has been presented by [60] to improve the eating [77, 78], exercising and sleeping behaviour of patients. A short review on health recommender system was presented by [66] in which authors emphasized on reputation of health recommender systems. Wiesner and Pfeifer [73] differentiated between two scenarios of health recommender system by targeting patients and health professionals as end-users.

The research in healthcare system using content-based recommender system was performed by using health related ontology. An Application Programming Interface (API) for ontologies related to health sector was defined with their operations. One such example of this is Bio-ontology covering more than 600 ontologies related to health. The useful links for health-related videos on YouTube was recommended by [67]. The medical terms have been derived from the Medicine Plus API for the generic development organization for international health terminology. The institution developed a SNOMED-CT i.e. multilingual ontology of clinical healthcare. The algorithms were reused by introducing the Bio-Ontology API in [68]. This strategy is based on diabetes video to provide the content-based recommendation [69] for which the use of semantic technology has been explored. Several researches has been conducted using linguistic ontology methods to improve access and convergence of heterogeneous data from a number of sources [86, 89].

The network of health recommenders called HealthRecSys was implemented in terms of bio-ontology in which Medicine Plus links were created from text extracted from the metadata of selected YouTube videos [88].

Such systems suffered from the difficulties of mapping the appropriate terms to ontology, especially when video terms are extracted. One approach to this problem was use of NLP techniques in [53, 56, 57] in which syntactic, semantic and contextual analyses are combined together. These techniques have been used in [61, 79] for mining electronic health records [80].

Nithya *et al.* [90] identified the research on different tools and techniques for projecting machine learning. In this paper, application of machine learning throughout various fields is discussed by demonstrating the role of machine learning in the healthcare industry. In this field, a state-of-the-art health risk predicting study has been presented [94]. A comprehensive review of machine learning literature was carried out in prediction of health risks is presented in the paper.

Neloy *et al.* [96] suggested a content-based recommendation system that would use K-nearest, Apriori and Eclat neighbors as a network interface together with IBM cloud. The same work can be improved by incorporating additional data points and full health criteria to calculate the movement of the human body. In contrast to the machine learning method, an integrated system will be added to record a live reading from ICU devices.

Subramaniyaswamy [97] launched ProTrip, a health-centric tourist recommendation system based on hybrid recommendation approaches and smart recommendation models. This system was based on ontology-based model in which data on health and nutrition was distorted and the hybrid sorting process was used.

The incorporation of social media with the process and the introduction of user feedback was left as a future job.

9.5.2   Recommender System in Agriculture

The important tasks in the field of recommender system in agriculture is to increase the production of crops by considering climate conditions, soil fertility etc. In this domain, work on selecting the crop, maximizing the production, protection of crop has been covered in the literature.

Semantic web can be used to produce recommendations in agriculture in the agricultural database [24]. Simple "GO-ORGANIC" software achieved by customers or farmers by signing in with username and password. The result of the request was all things shown on the website and in the Android App [70]. Vijay [70] proposed a semantic web-based architecture for generating recommendations in agriculture using spatial data and agriculture knowledge bases. The recommendation to the farmers was sent to the farmers by domain experts based on the conditions of climate and geographical data. But the researchers implemented this system in partial manner and showed only initial results. The recommendation techniques existed in the research was not covered by the authors in their work. Genetic algorithms-based simulation software was used to maximize the crop yields in [74]. The various items have been accessed by the customers online in [81]. Various items could be found on the basis of interest of the customers. Mehdi [82] proposed the hybrid technique for recommendation by combining collaborative and content-based recommender systems. The system was used for recommending the agriculture products. A set of personalized record can be generated by combining the preferences of customers given in form of rating, tagging and using other metrices as presented in [83].

Researchers also worked on modern technique named precision agriculture in which problems faced by farmers by not choosing the right crop according to their soil was addressed. The research data based on characteristics of soil, types of soil, collection of crop yield data has been used by this technique. The right crop based on specific parameters has been recommended to the farmers which reduced the wrong choice on crop and increased the productivity. The paper [71] addressed the specifications and preparation necessary to develop the precision farming technology model. Researchers who applied the principles of Precision Agriculture (PA) to small, open farms at the individual farmer and plant level developed a template. Savla [83] explained the effect of pest on the crops and considered the amount of loss for the farmers. PCT-O was proposed to label the existence of the pest and removal mechanisms using chemicals or by other methods. A system called the eXtensible Crop Yield System (XCYPF) was established by Aakunuri [84] which mentioned the need for prediction of crop yield and its usefulness in national strategic agricultural policy. A tool has also been developed to aid people to predict crop yields for different crops with dependent and independent variables. The importance of selecting the crop and various factors such as rate of production, market price and government policies for deciding the crop selection was discussed in [85]. A crop selection method was proposed which solved the problem of selecting the crop and also improved the net yield rate of crop. Pudumalar *et al.* [91] addressed the problems faced by farmers because of insufficient choice of processed crops in the kind of soil accessible to them because of lack of knowledge. It was suggested that precision farming using data mining techniques recommend the right crop to farmers based on research data on their soil types, soil characteristics and crop yields. Raja *et al.* [92] made an attempt to estimate crop yield by comparing past data with the value a farmer can get from the crops. This recommended best plant choices for a farmer to respond to the farmers' demand for the usual social crisis. The proposed system also removed the instability in price of predicted price calculated by [62]. The price of production in agriculture was proposed by Grey Prediction system [62] that proposed the system which has given the best accuracy in the price forecast in agriculture production market. A recommendation framework for farmers [93] was suggested using past years' output level and agriculture-related environment data that helped the farmer select the right plant. Kuanr *et al.* [95] proposed recommender system for solving the problem of crop selection for farmers by considering the data of previous three months of temperature, humidity and rainfall. Different crop yield value was estimated based on past data and advised whether or not the farmer could cultivate that crop. Positive guidelines for fertilizers, pesticides and equipment's. The problem of encountering pest and diseases in crops has been addressed also in [98]. Recommendation system was used to solve this problem of farmers. The best suitable crop was predicted to the farmer with detection of pest and suggested the techniques for controlling the pest. For this reason, various algorithms such as Support Vector Machine (SVM), "Decision Tree" and "Logistic Regression" algorithms were implemented and SVM model gave better accuracy as compared to other algorithms. It has been left as a future work to develop this model with more soil characteristics and a bigger dataset. Kumar M.S. *et al.* [99] designed and developed recommender system model using Apriori algorithm to predict and suggest agricultural items use. Prediction and recommendation were done on basis on previous buying behavior of the customer and also their peer recommendation.

Researchers worked on recommendation system for selection of particular crop and also for protecting the crops from multiple pests such as insects, weeds and Plant Pathogens and the toxic effects by using ontologies and algorithms. Less research has been done in this field by using content-based approach of recommendation. The development of intelligent architecture and precision agriculture can be latest trend of research in this field so that better recommendation system could be provided to the farmers for their selection and protection of crops. The utilization of content-based approach in this field can provide the better recommendation to the farmers for their crops.

9.6 Pros and Cons of Content-Based Recommender System

As content-based recommender system was born from idea of collecting the contents of items for recommendation purposes. These systems tried to solve the problems of cold start for new users, sparsity, transparency occurred in collaborative recommender systems. Here are some advantages of adapting the content-based recommender systems [75]:

- *User Independence*: content-based recommender system builds their own profile based on the ratings provided by active users instead of collaborative systems which need ratings from other user to make recommendations.
- *Transparency:* As collaborative recommender systems are like the black boxes with only explanation of the unknown users with similar preferences. But, content-based systems explicitly list the description of the contents that is used for recommending the list of products. Therefore, there is more transparency in the content-based recommender system as compared to collaborative recommender systems.
- *Recommending New Items*: A content-based system that suggest products not previously inspected by any client that have not been impaired by the cold start issue in collaborative recommender systems.

However, content-based recommender system has removed the problems of collaborative systems but they suffer from many limitations as:

- *Limited Content Analysis*: Content-based approaches have a bound on the number and form of features shared with items which they propose manually or automatically. Also, the domain knowledge and ontologies for the particular domain are needed. If the analyzed contents don't contain enough information then content-based recommender system cannot provide the suitable suggestions.
- *Lack of Serendipity*: There is no essential method for finding something unexpected in Content based recommendation system. The items are suggested based on the high score while matching user profile, therefor the user recommends items similarly to previous rated items. This is also called over-specialization issue, which stresses the tendency for content-based systems to generate suggestions with a limited degree of creativity. A perfect content-based system is needed to find some novel unexpected recommendations.
- *Enough rating data*: A plenty of data of previous interests of the users is the backbone of content-based systems. These systems provide accurate recommendation only When there is enough data available. In the absence of sufficient data, the program will not be able to yield correct recommendations.

These are the pros and cons of content-based recommender systems which shows that research should be done on finding the unexpected recommendations and development of domain ontologies in constructive way. Also, there should be enough data for recommending the items in content-based systems. Therefore, for reliable recommendation data should be collected in meaningful and authentic manner.

9.7 Conclusion

In this chapter, content-based recommender system is described. The high-level architecture of content-based system is being discussed along with the process of recommendation. The techniques of representing the user contents and methods for learning the user profile is also described in this chapter. The related work in content-based recommender system is discussed along with their advantages and disadvantages. The utilization of recommender systems in healthcare and agriculture domain has been addressed along with their research trends in future.

References

1. Hensley, C.B., Savage, T.R., Sowarby, A.J., Resnick, A., Selective dissemination of information-a new approach to effective communication. *IRE Trans. Eng. Manage.*, 2, 55–65, 1962.
2. Salton, G. and McGill, M., *Introduction to Modern Information Retrieval*, McGraw-Hill, New York, 1983.
3. Salton, G., Automatic text processing: The transformation, analysis, and retrieval of reading: Addison-Wesley, 169, 1989.
4. Goldberg, D., Nichols, D., Oki, B., Terry, D., Using Collaborative Filtering to Weave an Information Tapestry. *Commun. ACM*, 35, 12, 61–70, 1992, URL http://www.xerox.com/PARC/dlbx/tapestry-papers/TN44.ps. Special Issue on Information Filtering.
5. Sheth, B. and Maes, P., Evolving agents for personalized information filtering, *Proceedings of 9th IEEE Conference on Artificial Intelligence for Applications*, Orlando, FL, USA, pp. 345–352, 1993.
6. Wu, Z. and Palmer, M., Verbs semantics and lexical selection, in: *Proceedings of the 32nd Annual Meeting on Association for Computational Linguistics, ACL '94*, Association for Computational Linguistics, Stroudsburg, PA, USA, pp. 133–138, 1994.
7. Lewis, D.D. and Ringuette, M., A Comparison of Two Learning Algorithms for Text Categorization, in: *Proc. of the Annual Symposium on Document Analysis and Information Retrieval*, Las Vegas, US, pp. 81–93, 1994.
8. Resnik, P., Using information content to evaluate semantic similarity in a taxonomy, in: *Proceedings of the 14th International Joint Conference on Artificial Intelligence—Volume 1, IJCAI'95*, Morgan Kaufmann Publishers Inc., San Francisco, CA, USA, pp. 448–453, 1995, URL http://dl.acm.org/citation.cfm?id=1625855.1625914.
9. Pazzani, M.J., Muramatsu, J., Billsus, D., Syskill and Webert: Identifying Interesting Web Sites, in: *Proceedings of the Thirteenth National Conference on Artificial Intelligence and the Eighth Innovative Applications of Artificial Intelligence Conference*, AAAI Press/MIT Press, Menlo Park, pp. 54–61, 1996.
10. Holte, R.C. and Yan, J.N.Y., Inferring What a User Is Not Interested, in: *Advances in Artificial Intelligence, Lecture Notes in Computer Science*, G.I. McCalla, (Ed.), vol. 1081, pp. 159–171, Springer, Berlin, Heidelberg, 1996.
11. Pazzani, M. and Billsus, D., Learning and Revising User Profiles: The Identification of Interesting Web Sites. *Mach. Learn.*, 27, 3, 313–331, 1997.
12. Balabanovic, M. and Shoham, Y., Fab: Content-based, Collaborative Recommendation. *Commun. ACM*, 40, 3, 66–72, 1997.
13. Jiang, J.J. and Conrath, D.W., Semantic similarity based on corpus statistics and lexical taxonomy, 1997, *arXiv preprint cmp-lg/9709008*.
14. Billsus, D. and Pazzani, M., Learning Probabilistic User Models, in: *Proc. of the Workshop on Machine Learning for User Modeling. Chia Laguna, IT*, 1997, http://www.dfki.de/~bauer/um-ws/.

15. Yang, Y. and Pedersen, J.O., A Comparative Study on Feature Selection in Text Categorization, in: *Proceedings of ICML-97, 14th International Conference on Machine Learning*, D.H. Fisher (Ed.), Morgan Kaufmann Publishers, San Francisco, US, Nashville, US, pp. 412–420, 1997, URL citeseer.ist.psu.edu/yang97comparative.html.

16. Lin, D., An Information-Theoretic Definition of Similarity. In *Proceedings of the Fifteenth International Conference on Machine Learning (ICML '98)*. Morgan Kaufmann Publishers Inc., San Francisco, CA, USA, 296–304, 1998.

17. Fellbaum, C. and Miller, G., Combining Local Context and Wordnet Similarity for Word Sense Identification, in: *WordNet: An Electronic Lexical Database*, MITP, pp. 265–283, 1998.

18. Baeza-Yates, R. and Ribeiro-Neto, B., *Modern Information Retrieval*, New York: ACM Press, vol. 463, 1999.

19. Billsus, D. and Pazzani, M.J., A Hybrid User Model for News Story Classification, in: *Proceedings of the Seventh International Conference on User Modeling*, Springer, Vienna, Banff, Canada, 1999.

20. Billsus, D. and Pazzani, M.J., User Modeling for Adaptive News Access. *User Model. User-Adapt.*, 10, 2–3, 147–180, 2000.

21. Mooney, R.J. and Roy, L., Content-Based Book Recommending Using Learning for Text Categorization, in: *Proceedings of the 5th ACM Conference on Digital Libraries*, ACM Press, New York, US, San Antonio, US, pp. 195–204, 2000.

22. Berners-Lee, T., Hendler, J., Lassila, O., The Semantic Web. *Sci. Am.*, 284, 5, 28–37, 2001.

23. Magnini, B. and Strapparava, C., Improving User Modelling with Content-Based Techniques, in: *User Modeling 2001. UM 2001. Lecture Notes in Computer Science*, Bauer M., Gmytrasiewicz P.J., Vassileva J. (eds), vol. 2019, Springer, Berlin, Heidelberg, 2001.

24. Berger, T., Agent-based spatial models applied to agriculture: A simulation tool for technology diffusion, resource use changes and policy analysis. *Agric. Econ.*, 25, 2–3, 245–260, 2001.

25. Sebastiani, F., Machine Learning in Automated Text Categorization. *ACM Comput. Surv.*, 34, 1, 1–47, 2002.

26. Eirinaki, M., Vazirgiannis, M., Varlamis, I., SEWeP: Using Site Semantics and a Taxonomy to enhance the Web Personalization Process, in: *Proceedings of the Ninth ACM SIGKDD International Conference on Knowledge Discovery and Data Mining*, ACM, Washington, DC, USA, pp. 99–108, 2003.

27. Middleton, S.E., Shadbolt, N.R., De Roure, D.C., Ontological User Profiling in Recommender Systems. *ACM Trans. Inf. Syst.*, 22, 1, 54–88, 2004.

28. Pazzani, M.J. and Billsus, D., Content-Based Recommendation Systems, in: *The Adaptive Web, Lecture Notes in Computer Science*, vol. 4321, Brusilovsky, P., Kobsa, A., Nejdl, W. (Eds.), pp. 325–341, Springer, Berlin, Heidelberg, 2007.

29. Banerjee, S., Ramanathan, K., Gupta, A., Clustering Short Texts Using Wikipedia, in: *Proc. of the 30th Annual International ACM SIGIR Conference on*

Research and Development in Information Retrieval, SIGIR '07, ACM, New York, NY, USA, pp. 787–788, 2007, http://doi.acm.org/10.1145/1277741.1277909.

30. Ahn, J.-W., Brusilovsky, P., Grady, J., He, D., Syn, S.Y., Open user profiles for adaptive news systems: Help or harm? In *Proceedings of the 16th international conference on World Wide Web (WWW '07)*. Association for Computing Machinery, New York, NY, USA, 11–20, 2007. DOI:https://doi.org/10.1145/1242572.1242575

31. Cantador, I., Bellogín, A., Castells, P., News@hand: A Semantic Web Approach to Recommending News, in: *Adaptive Hypermedia and Adaptive Web-Based Systems. AH 2008. Lecture Notes in Computer Science*, Nejdl W., Kay J., Pu P., Herder E. (eds), vol. 5149, Springer, Berlin, Heidelberg, 2008.

32. Cantador, I., Szomszor, M., Alani, H., Fernandez, M., Castells, P., Ontological User Profiles with Tagging History for Multi-Domain Recommendations, in: *Proceedings of the Collective Semantics: Collective Intelligence and the Semantic Web*, CISWeb2008, Tenerife, Spain, 2008.

33. Cantador, I., Bellogín, A., Castells, P., A Multilayer Ontology-based Hybrid Recommendation Model. *AI Commun.*, 21, 2, 203–210, 2008.

34. Cantador, I., Szomszor, M., Alani, H., Fernández, M., Castells, P., Enriching Ontological User Profiles with Tagging History for Multi-domain Recommendations, in: *Proc. of the 1st International Workshop on Collective Semantics: Collective Intelligence & the Semantic Web*, 2008. http://eprints.ecs.soton.ac.uk/15451/

35. Shoval, P., Maidel, V., Shapira, B., An Ontology-Content-based Filtering Method. *IJITA*, 15, 303–314, 2008.

36. Blanco-Fernandez, Y., Pazos-Arias, J.J., G.S., A., Ramos-Cabrer, M., Lopez-Nores, M., Providing Entertainment by Content-based Filtering and Semantic Reasoning in Intelligent Recommender Systems. *IEEE T. Consum. Electr.*, 54, 2, 727–735, 2008.

37. Egozi, O., Gabrilovich, E., Markovitch, S., Concept-Based Feature Generation and Selection for Information Retrieval, in: *Proceedings of the Twenty-Third AAAI Conference on Artificial Intelligence*, AAAI 2008, D. Fox, C.P. Gomes (eds.), AAAI Press, Chicago, Illinois, pp. 1132–1137, 2008.

38. Hu, J., Fang, L., Cao, Y., Zeng, H., Li, H., Yang, Q., Chen, Z., Enhancing text clustering by leveraging Wikipedia semantics. In *Proceedings of the 31st annual international ACM SIGIR conference on Research and development in information retrieval (SIGIR '08)*. Association for Computing Machinery, New York, NY, USA, 179–186, 2008. DOI:https://doi.org/10.1145/1390334.1390367.

39. Csomai, A. and Mihalcea, R., Linking Documents to Encyclopedic Knowledge. *IEEE Intell. Syst.*, 23, 5, 34–41, 2008.

40. Bollacker, K., Evans, C., Paritosh, P., Sturge, T., Taylor, J., Freebase: a collaboratively created graph database for structuring human knowledge, in: *SIGMOD '08*, pp. 1247–1250, ACM, Vancouver, BC, Canada, 2008.

41. Gabrilovich, E. and Markovitch, S., Wikipedia-based Semantic Interpretation for Natural Language Processing. *JAIR*, 34, 443–498, 2009.

42. Hassanzadeh, O. and Consens, M.P., Linked Movie Data Base, in: *LDOW*, datahub.io, 2009, April.

43. Semeraro, G., Basile, P., de Gemmis, M., Lops, P., User Profiles for Personalizing Digital Libraries, in: *Handbook of Research on Digital Libraries: Design, Development and Impact*, Y.L. Theng, S. Foo, D.G.H. Lian, J.C. Na (Eds.), pp. 149–158, IGI Global, 2009.

44. Bizer, C., Lehmann, J., Kobilarov, G., Auer, S., Becker, C., Cyganiak, R., Hellmann, S., Dbpedia- a crystallization point for the web of data. *Web Semant.*, 7, 154–165, September 2009.

45. Semeraro, G., Lops, P., Basile, P., Gemmis, M.d., Knowledge Infusion into Content based Recommender Systems, in: *Proc. of the 2009 ACM Conference on Recommender Systems*, RecSys 2009, L.D. Bergman, A. Tuzhilin, R.D. Burke, A. Felfernig, L. Schmidt-Thieme (Eds.), October 23-25, 2009, ACM, New York, NY, USA, pp. 301–304, 2009.

46. Swan, M., Emerging patient-driven health care models: An examination of health social networks, consumer personalized medicine and quantified self-tracking. *Int. J. Environ. Res. Public Health*, 6, 2, 492–525, 2009.

47. Fernandez-Luque, L., Karlsen, R., Vognild, L.K., Challenges and opportunities of using recommender systems for personalized health education, in: *MIE*, pp. 903–907, IOS Press, 2009.

48. Roitman, H., Messika, Y., Tsimerman, Y. and Maman, Y., Increasing patient safety using explanation-driven personalized content recommendation. In *Proceedings of the 1st ACM International Health Informatics Symposium (IHI'10)*. Association for Computing Machinery, New York, NY, USA, 430–434, 2010. DOI:https://doi.org/10.1145/1882992.1883057.

49. Jannach, D., Zanker, M., Felfernig, A., Friedrich, G., *Recommender systems: An introduction*, Cambridge University Press, 2010.

50. Heitmann, B. and Hayes, C., Using linked data to build open, collaborative recommender systems, in: *AAAI Spring Symposium: Linked Data Meets Artificial Intelligence*, The Association for the Advancement of Artificial Intelligence (AAAI) Press, 2010.

51. Roitman, H., Messika, Y., Tsimerman, Y., Maman, Y., Increasing patient safety using explanation-driven personalized content recommendation. In *Proceedings of the 1st ACM International Health Informatics Symposium (IHI '10)*. Association for Computing Machinery, New York, NY, USA, 430–434, 2010. DOI:https://doi.org/10.1145/1882992.1883057

52. Hammer, S., Kim, J., Andr, E., MED-StyleR: METABO diabetes-lifestyle recommender, in: *4th ACM Conference on Recommender Systems*, pp. 285–288, ACM Conference proceedings, Barcelona, Spain, 2010.

53. Alexander, C., Chris, F., Shalom, L., *The Handbook of Computational Linguistics and Natural Language Processing*, Wiley-Blackwell, USA, 2010.

54. Ricci, F., Rokach, L., Shapira, B., Introduction to recommender systems handbook, in: *Recommender systems handbook*, pp. 1–35, Springer, Boston, MA, 2011.

55. Pinxteren, Y., Gelijnse, G., Kamsteeg, P., Deriving a recipe similarity measure for recommending healthful meals, in: *16th Intl. Conference on Intelligent User Interfaces*, pp. 105–114, Conference Proceedings ACM, Palo Alto, CA, USA, 2011.

56. Nadkarni, P.M., Ohno-Machado, L., Chapman, W.W., Natural language processing: an introduction. *J. Am. Med. Inform. Assoc.*, 18, 5, 544–51, 2011.

57. Xu, H., Jiang, M., Oetjens, M., Bowton, E.A., Ramirez, A.H., Jeff, J.M. *et al.*, Facilitating pharmacogenetic studies using electronic health records and natural language processing: A case study of warfarin. *J. Am. Med. Inform. Assoc.*, 18, 387–91, 2011.

58. Ferragina, P. and Scaiella, U., Fast and Accurate Annotation of Short Texts with Wikipedia Pages. *IEEE Software*, 29, 1, 70–75, 2012.

59. Di Noia, T., Mirizzi, R., Ostuni, V.C., Romito, D., Zanker, M., Linked open data to support content-based recommender systems, in: *Proceedings of the 8th international conference on semantic systems*, ACM, Graz, Austria, pp. 1–8, 2012.

60. Farrell, R.G., Danis, C.M., Ramakrishnan, S., Kellogg, W.A., Intrapersonal retrospective recommendation: lifestyle change recommendations using stable patterns of personal behavior, in: *Proceedings of the First International Workshop on Recommendation Technologies for Lifestyle Change (LIFESTYLE 2012)*, ACM Conference, Dublin, Ireland, Citeseer, p. 24, 2012.

61. Jensen, P.B., Jensen, L.J., Brunak, S., Mining electronic health records: towards better research applications and clinical care. *Nat. Rev. Genet.*, 13, 395–405, 2012.

62. Zong, J. and Zhu, Q., Apply Grey Prediction in the Agriculture Production Price. *Fourth International Conference on Multimedia Information Networking and Security*, pp. 396–399, IEEE, Conference Article, 2012.

63. Mikolov, T., Le, Q.V., Sutskever, I., Exploiting Similarities among Languages for Machine Translation, 2013, CoRR abs/1309.4168.

64. Cena, F., Likavec, S., Osborne, F., Anisotropic Propagation of User Interests in Ontology based User Models. *Inf. Sci.*, 250, 40–60, 2013.

65. Narducci, F., Musto, C., Semeraro, G., Lops, P., de Gemmis, M., Exploiting Big Data for Enhanced Representations in Content-Based Recommender Systems, in: *Proc. of the 14th International Conference on E-Commerce and Web Technologies, EC-Web 2013, Lecture Notes in Business Information Processing*, vol. 152, C. Huemer, P. Lops (Eds.), pp. 182–193, Springer, Berlin, Heidelberg, 2013.

66. Sezgin, E. and Ozkan, S., A systematic literature review on health recommender systems, in: *E-Health and Bioengineering Conference (EHB)*, Iasi, 2013, IEEE, pp. 1–4, 2013.

67. Rivero-Rodriguez, A., Konstantinidis, S.T., Sanchez-Bocanegra, C.L., FernandezLuque, L., A health information recommender system: enriching YouTube health videos with MedlinePlus information by the use of SNOMEDCT

terms, in: *Proceedings of the 26th IEEE International Symposium on Computer-Based Medical Systems*, pp. 257–61, IEEE, Porto, Portugal, 2013.

68. Sánchez-Bocanegra, C.L., Rivero-Rodriguez, A., Fernández-Luque, L., Sevillano, J.L., Diavideos: A diabetes health video portal. *Stud. Health Technol. Inform.*, 2, 1, e6, 2013.

69. Gabarron, E., Fernandez-Luque, L., Armayones, M., Lau, A.Y., Identifying measures used for assessing quality of YouTube videos with patient health information: A review of current literature. *Interact. J. Med. Res.*, 2, 1, e6, 2013.

70. Vikas, K. *et al.*, Krishimantra: agricultural recommendation system, in: *Proceedings of the 3rd ACM Symposium on Computing for Development*, ACM, Bangalore, India 2013.

71. Babu, S., A software model for precision agriculture for small and marginal farmers, in: *2013 IEEE Global Humanitarian Technology Conference: South Asia Satellite (GHTC-SAS)*, IEEE, pp. 352–355, 2013.

72. Dojchinovski, M. and Vitvar, T., Personalised access to linked data, in: *EKAW*, Springer, Cham, vol. 8876, pp. 121–136, 2014.

73. Wiesner, M. and Pfeifer, D., Health recommender systems: concepts, requirements, technical basics and challenges. *Int. J. Environ. Res. Public Health*, 11, 3, 2580–2607, 2014.

74. Olakulehin, O.J. and Omidiora, E.O., A genetic algorithm approach to maximize crop yields and sustain soil fertility. *Net. J. Agric. Sci.*, 2, 3, 94–103, 2014.

75. De Gemmis, M., Lops, P., Musto, C., Narducci, F., Semeraro, G., Semantics-aware content-based recommender systems, in: *Recommender Systems Handbook*, pp. 119–159, Springer, Boston, MA, 2015.

76. Di Noia, T. and Ostuni, V.C., Recommender systems and linked open data, in: *Reasoning Web International Summer School*, pp. 88–113, Springer, Cham, 2015, July.

77. Rokicki, M., Herder, E., Demidova, E., Whats on my plate: Towards recommending recipe variations for diabetes patients. *Proc. of UMAP 15*, Conference Proceedings, 2015.

78. Elsweiler, D., Harvey, M., Ludwig, B., Said, A., Bringing the "healthy" into Food Recommenders. In *DMRS*, pp. 33–36, 2015.

79. Uzuner, O. and Stubbs, A., Practical applications for natural language processing in clinical research: The 2014 i2b2/UTHealth shared tasks. *J. Biomed. Inform.*, 58, S1–5, 2015.

80. Wang, Y., Luo, J., Hao, S., Xu, H., Shin, A.Y., Jin, B. *et al.*, NLP based congestive heart failure case finding: A prospective analysis on statewide electronic medical records. *Int. J. Med. Inf.*, 84, 1039–47, 2015.

81. Iorshase, A. and Charles, O.I., A well-built hybrid recommender system for agricultural products in Benue State of Nigeria. *J. Softw. Eng. Appl.*, 8, 11, 581, 2015.

82. Mehdi, E. *et al.*, Interaction design in a mobile food recommender system, in: *CEUR Workshop Proceedings*. CEUR-WS, 2015.

83. Savla, A., Dhawan, P., Bhadada, H., Israni, N., Mandholia, A., Bhardwaj, S., Survey of classification algorithms for formulating yield prediction accuracy in precision agriculture, *IEEE*, 1–7, March 2015.

84. Manjula, A. and Narsimha, G., XCYPF: A Flexible and Extensible Framework for Agricultural Crop Yield Prediction. *Conference on Intelligent Systems and Control (ISCO)*, IEEE, pp. 1–5, 2015.

85. Kumar, R., Singh, M.P., Kumar, P., Singh, J.P., Crop Selection Method to Maximize Crop Yield Rate using Machine Learning Technique. *International Conference on Smart Technologies and Management for Computing, Communication, Controls, Energy and Materials (ICSTM)*, IEEE, Conference Article, pp. 138–145, 2015.

86. Manogaran, G. and Lopez, D., Health data analytics using scalable logistic regression with stochastic gradient descent. *Int. J. Adv. Intell. Paradig.*, 9, 1–1544, 2016.

87. Boratto, L., Carta, S., Fenu, G., Saia, R., Semantics-aware content-based recommender systems: Design and architecture guidelines. *Neurocomputing*, 254, 79–85, 2017.

88. Bocanegra, C.L.S., Ramos, J.L.S., Rizo, C., Civit, A., Fernandez-Luque, L., HealthRecSys: A semantic content-based recommender system to complement health videos. *BMC Med. Inform. Decis.*, 17, 1, 63, 2017.

89. Manogaran, G., Thota, C., Lopez, D., Vijayakumar, V., Abbas, K.M., Sundarsekar, R., Big data knowledge system in healthcare, in: *Internet of things and big data technologies for next generation healthcare*, pp. 133–157, Springer International Publishing, New York, 2017.

90. Nithya, B. and Ilango, V., Predictive analytics in health care using machine learning tools and techniques, in: *2017 International Conference on Intelligent Computing and Control Systems (ICICCS)*, IEEE, 2017, https://doi.org/10.1109/ICCONS.2017.8250771.

91. Pudumalar, S., Ramanujam, E., Harine Rajashree, R., Kavya, C., Kiruthika, T., Nisha, J., Crop Recommendation System for Precision Agriculture. *IEEE International Conference on Advanced Computing*, Chennai, India, pp. 32–36, 2017.

92. Raja, S.K.S., Rishi, R., Sundaresan, E., Srijit, V., Demand based crop recommender system for farmers, in: *2017 IEEE Technological Innovations in ICT for Agriculture and Rural Development (TIAR)*, IEEE, Chennai, pp. 194–199, 2017, April.

93. Mokarrama, M.J. and Arefin, M.S., RSF: A recommendation system for farmers. *IEEE Region 10 Humanitarian Technology Conference (R10-HTC)*, Dhaka, pp. 843–850, 2017.

94. Shinde, S.A. and Rajeswari, P.R., Intelligent health risk prediction systems using machine learning: A review. *Int. J. Eng. Technol.*, 7, 1019, 2018, https://doi.org/10.14419/ijet.v7i3. 12654.

95. Kuanr, M., Rath, B.K., Mohanty, S.N., Crop Recommender System for the Farmers using Mamdani Fuzzy Inference Model. *IJET*, 7, 4.15, 277–280, 2018.

96. Neloy, A.A., Shafayat Oshman, M., Islam, M.M., Hossain, M.J., Zahir, Z.B., Content-Based Health Recommender System for ICU Patient, in: *Multidisciplinary Trends in Artificial Intelligence*, MIWAI 2019. Lecture Notes in Computer Science, vol. 11909, R. Chamchong and K. Wong (Eds.), Springer, Cham, 2019.

97. Subramaniyaswamy, V., Manogaran, G., Logesh, R., Vijayakumar, V., Chilamkurti, N., Malathi, D., Senthilselvan, N., An ontology-driven personalized food recommendation in IoT-based healthcare system. *J. Supercomput.*, 75, 6, 3184–3216, 2019.

98. Kumar, A., Sarkar, S., Pradhan, C., Recommendation System for Crop Identification and Pest Control Technique in Agriculture, in: *2019 International Conference on Communication and Signal Processing (ICCSP)*, IEEE, Chennai, India, pp. 0185–0189, 2019, April.

99. Kumar, M.S. and Balakrishnan, K., Development of a Model Recommender System for Agriculture Using Apriori Algorithm, in: *Cognitive Informatics and Soft Computing*, pp. 153–163, Springer, Singapore, 2019.

10

Content (Item)-Based Recommendation System

R. Balamurali

Dept. of Computer Science & Engineering, IcfaiTech, IFHE, Hyderabad, India

Abstract

The main idea behind Content-Based Recommendation System is to recommend an item to a customer similar to the previous items that are rated high by the same customer. Initially, we create an item profile based on the ratings provided by the user for the items he purchased, videos/movies watched, books (textual contents) read, music/songs heard etc.. The user profile captures information like frequently purchased products/brands, type of movies watched (with a specific actor/director/genre etc...), type of music listened (melody/beat etc...) and type of books read (comic/positive thinking etc...) by the particular user. The item profile will be represented as a Boolean vector based on the features of interest for a given user. The item profile will be created for all the items rated by a specific user. From, the item profile we infer the user profile. A simple way to create user profile is to take the average rating given by the user for a specific item. There are also several other ways of creating user profiles which we will discuss in this chapter in detail. Basically, the user profile captures the details of items which are likeable by a particular user. Once the user profile is created, given a new item that is not rated by the user which may be a product/movie/song/book etc...., it can be represented as a Boolean vector and this Boolean vector shall be compared with Boolean vector corresponding to the user profile using techniques like cosine similarity and if the cosine similarity is above a particular threshold the item may be recommended for the user. We shall discuss the various methods to recommend item based on contents in this chapter.

Keywords: Recommendation system, item profile, user profile, TF-IDF, gradient descent, induction tree algorithm

Email: balamurali@ifheindia.org

Sachi Nandan Mohanty, Jyotir Moy Chatterjee, Sarika Jain, Ahmed A. Elngar and Priya Gupta (eds.) Recommender System with Machine Learning and Artificial Intelligence: Practical Tools and Applications in Medical, Agricultural and Other Industries, (197–214) © 2020 Scrivener Publishing LLC

10.1   Introduction

The online commercial websites like Flipkart, Amazon, Snapdeal, Alibaba, eBay, Youtube, Facebook, etc. recommend products to the user based on the past behavioral history of the user. When a new product is made available to the online market, the product will be compared with the user's interest based on the user behavioral history. If, the product was found to be of user's interest, then the system will recommend the product to the user. This concept is called as the Content-Based Recommendation System. There are several ways available to do this mapping between the product feature and user's interest. This chapter discusses the various methods to achieve this.

Content-Based Recommendation System is all about recommending an item to a customer 'a' similar to the previous items rated highly by the same customer [1–5].

Examples:

1. An Amazon-registered user purchased 3 books on amazon on the topic—"Positive Thinking" and has provided very high review ratings for all the three books. Now, when a new book on "Positive Thinking" arrives at Amazon, it will be recommended for this particular user.
2. A user on Youtube keeps listening to topics on cooking from a specific Youtube channel. Now, when a new recipe was made available to the channel, it will be automatically recommended for the particular user.
3. Consider a user 'x' has updated his Facebook profile with the name of the organization he works for, with its full address. Now, another user 'y' from the same organization and not connected with user 'x' will be recommended/suggested as a friend for user 'x' by the recommendation system.

10.2   Phases of Content-Based Recommendation Generation

A typical Content-Based Recommendation system will have the following phases.

a. Feature extraction and selection: Feature extraction is the foremost operation done in Content-Based Recommendation system. This is the process of extracting the relevant features from the given dataset. The features may be classified as Extrinsic/direct features and implicit/indirect features. The extrinsic features are the one which are directly represented in the dataset like name of the actor, author, director, income, age etc. The intrinsic features are the ones which are derived from the extrinsic features like Noun and Noun Phrases, Term Frequency and Inter Document Frequency (TF-IDF), which is explained later in the chapter.

b. Feature Representation: The extracted feature should be represented in a particular format. Depending on the type of the data, different features will be represented in different formats. Typical representations are binary, continuous, categorical, etc.

c. User profile learning: Profile building is about automatically building the profile of a user based on the past behavior pattern of the user. This done based on the star rating given by the user, the products he purchased, the movies/videos he watched, etc.

d. Recommendation Generation: This phase represents the actual algorithm which is used to predict the user interest level for a particular product or when a new item is introduced in the store, the algorithm shall identify the preference score for all users for the particular item and recommend the item to the top 'M' users. The algorithm will also observe the user action and retrains itself, if required.

10.3   Content-Based Recommendation Using Cosine Similarity

This topic discusses on recommending items based on the cosine similarity. To achieve this, first we should build: Item profiles and user profiles. Item profile represents the set of features of an item purchased or rated high by a particular user. It can be represented as a boolean vector based on whether a feature exists or not. ('1'—feature exists and '0'—feature does not exist). The typical features of some of the products/items are shown in Table 10.1.

Similarly, build the item profile for each item purchased or rated by a particular user. User profiles are inferred or created from the item profile.

Table 10.1 Item/product vs features.

Sl. no.	Item product	Features
1.	Movie	Actor, director, composer, genre, etc.
2.	Articles	Scientific, Social, News, Spiritual, Comic, etc.
3.	Images	Meta data, tags, etc.
4.	Dresses	Color, brand, cost, size, design, etc.
5.	People	Set of friends, common Interests, etc.

Building User Profile

Consider a user who has rated 'n' items, the respective item profiles are represented as i_1, i_2, i_3....i_n. There are several ways to create the user profile from the item profile.

a. Simple Mean

Take all the items rated by the user and calculate the average of it. This is the simplest way to create the user profile (Table 10.2).

b. Weighted Mean

The weighted mean is calculated based on the below formula. This method takes into account the fact that the user likes certain item more than the other item and that is represented through the weight (Table 10.3).

Table 10.2 Simple mean.

Sl. no.	Item	Rating
1	Book	4
2	Book	3
3	Movie	3
4	Dress	2
Average		12/4 = 3

Table 10.3 Weighted mean.

Sl. no.	Item	Rating (Ri)	Weights (Wi)	RiWi
1	Book	4	0.8	3.2
2	Book	3	0.6	1.8
3	Movie	3	0.6	1.8
4	Dress	2	0.4	0.8
		ΣRi=12	ΣWi=2.4	7.6
Weighted Avg = ΣRiWi / ΣWi				3.17

$$WeightedAvg = \frac{\sum_{i=1}^{n} R_i W_i}{\sum_{i=1}^{n} W_i}$$

Ri = Rating of item 'i'.
Wi = Weight of item 'i'.

c. Normalized Ratings
This method normalizes the weight using the average rating of the user. Consider the item 'Book' and for keeping it simple, let's consider only one feature, say, 'Author'. Item profile can be represented as a Boolean vector with value '1' or '0' representing whether a particular author is present or not. Suppose, user 'x' has read 7 books from an online store—2 books authored by author 'A', 2 books authored by 'B' and 3 books authored by 'C'. From this, the weight of feature 'A' can be calculates as 2/7 = 0.28, the weight of feature 'B' is calculated as 2/7 = 0.28 and the weight of feature 'C' is calculated as 3/7 = 0.43. The star ratings given by the user for the 7 books are shown in Table 10.4.

The Normalized ratings are shown in Table 10.5.

Making Predictions/Recommendations
Assume a new product/item is introduced in the online store. To decide, whether this product should be recommended for user 'x' or not, first we will build the item profile. After building the item profile, take a random user profile and the item profile of the newly introduced item and figure out, what rating for that item, likely to be given by the respective user.

Table 10.4 Star ratings.

Sl. no.	Book Id	Author name	Ratings
1	B001	A	4
2	B002	A	3
3	B003	B	5
4	B004	B	3
5	B005	C	4
6	B006	C	5
7	B007	C	4
Users Average Rating			4

Table 10.5 Normalized ratings.

Author	Normalized rating	Profile weight	Positive/Negative
A	(4–4),(3–4)=(0, –1)	(0–1)/2 = –1/2	Mild Negative
B	(5-4),(3–4)=(1, –1)	(1–1)/2 = 0	Neither Positive nor Negative
C	(4–4),(5-4),(4-4)=(0,1,0)	(0+1+0)/3=1/3	Mild Positive

This is calculated by using the cosine similarity measure. Cos (theta) is used as the similarity measure. As theta becomes smaller cos (theta) becomes larger. As theta becomes larger cos (theta) becomes smaller. The cosine similarity measure is given as,

$$A.B = \|A\|\|B\|Cos\Theta$$
$$Similarity = Cos(\Theta) = \frac{A.B}{\|A\|\|B\|}$$

The parameters used in the above equations are explained in Table 10.6 Where, A and B are Vectors.

Table 10.6 TF-IDF parameters.

Sl. no.	Parameter	Meaning
1	f_{ij}	frequency of term (feature) 'i' in document (item) 'j'
2	n_i	number of docs that mention the term
3	N	Total number of documents

The cosine similarity will be calculated for all the newly introduced items in the online store for a particular user 'x' and those items with highest cosine similarity would be recommended.

Building Item profile for textual documents
The item profile for textual documents is calculated using a technique called TF-IDF (Term Frequency – Inverse Document Frequency). This technique will help us to pick the set of important words from the document [1].

$$TF_{ij} = \frac{f_{ij}}{Max_k f_{kj}}$$

Where,

$$IDF_i = Log\left(\frac{N}{n_i}\right)$$

IDF value will be low for more common words like 'the', 'a', 'is' 'was' etc.….

$$TF - IDFScore : W_{ij} = TF_{ij} \times IDF_i$$

Given a document, compute the TF-IDF score for every term in the document and then sort it based on TF-IDF score and then fix some threshold or pick the words with high TF-IDF score more than the threshold value and that will be your doc profile. In this case, it is a real valued vector as opposed to the Boolean vector.

10.4   Content-Based Recommendations Using Optimization Techniques

Let us discuss how to predict the missing values like star rating for a particular item would be given by a particular user. We shall discuss this with an example. Consider the star rating given for 6 books by 5 users as shown in the Table 10.7.

The above table represents the star ratings provided for 6 books B1, B2...B6 by 5 users User1, User2.... User5. The last 2 columns of Table 10.7, (X1 and X2) represents the degree of inclination of a given book towards X1 (self-help) or C2 (Drama). The field with '?', represents that we don't know the ratings of those fields. Let us discuss now, how to find the value of those fields using Content-Based Recommendation Systems.

Nu = Number of users. (Nu = 5)
Nb = Number of books. (Nb = 6)
X1 – Degree to which the book is inclined towards 'Self Help'.
X2 – Degree to which the book is inclined towards 'Drama'.

Each Book can be represented as a feature vector (X1->Self_Help, X2 -> Drama). We will add an extra feature which is the interceptor feature (X0 = 1). X0, X1 and X2 can take values between 0 and 1.

So, the **feature Vector** for

$$X^1 = \begin{array}{|c|} \hline 1 \\ \hline 0.8 \\ \hline 0.1 \\ \hline \end{array}$$

Table 10.7 Book ratings by users.

Books	User1	User2	User3	User4	User 5	Self Help (X1)	Drama (x2)
B1	4	4	0	0	?	0.8	0.1
B2	4	?	?	0	0	0.9	0.02
B3	?	5	0	?	4	0.89	0.3
B4	0	0	4	5	5	0.3	1.0
B5	0	0	4	?	5	0.2	0.8
B6	5	4	5	4	0	0.88	0.2

$$X^2 = \begin{array}{|c|} \hline 1 \\ \hline 0.9 \\ \hline 0.02 \\ \hline \end{array}$$

$$X^3 = \begin{array}{|c|} \hline 1 \\ \hline 0.89 \\ \hline 0.3 \\ \hline \end{array}$$

$$X^4 = \begin{array}{|c|} \hline 1 \\ \hline 0.3 \\ \hline 1.0 \\ \hline \end{array}$$

$$X^5 = \begin{array}{|c|} \hline 1 \\ \hline 0.2 \\ \hline 0.8 \\ \hline \end{array}$$

$$X^6 = \begin{array}{|c|} \hline 1 \\ \hline 0.88 \\ \hline 0.2 \\ \hline \end{array}$$

'**n**' represents the number of features, excluding the interceptor feature (Hence, **n** = 2). For each user '**j**', learn a parameter $\theta^j \in R^3$ (in general $R^{(n+1)}$). Predict '**j**' as the rating for book '**i**' with $(\theta^j)^T x^i$ stars. Every user will be associated with a different parameter vector. Let's say the parameter vector associated with **user1, user2, user3, user4 and user5 as** $\theta^1, \theta^2, \theta^3, \theta^4$ **and** θ^5 respectively.

Let's assume that some **unspecified learning algorithm** has learned the parameter vector 'θ^1' as

$$\theta^1 = \begin{array}{|c|} \hline 0 \\ \hline 4 \\ \hline 0.2 \\ \hline \end{array}$$

Which means that the user1 gives a weightage of '4' for 'Self Help' books and a weightage of '0.2' for 'Drama' oriented books. This can be considered as the **'user profile'** for **user1**. Parameter can take values between **0 and 5** (or the highest star rating available).

$$X^3 = \begin{array}{|c|} \hline 1 \\ \hline 0.89 \\ \hline 0.3 \\ \hline \end{array}$$

The prediction for B3 for user 1 will be

$$\begin{array}{|c|c|c|} \hline 0 & 4 & 0.2 \\ \hline \end{array} \quad \text{x} \quad \begin{array}{|c|} \hline 1 \\ \hline 0.89 \\ \hline 0.3 \\ \hline \end{array}$$

$$= (0 \times 1 + 4 \times 0.89 + 0.2 \times 0.3) = 5 \times 0.89 = \textbf{3.62 star rating.}$$

Exercises

1. Consider the parameter vector of $(\theta^2)^{\mathrm{T}}$ as (0, 5, 2), then predict the star ratings for B2 by user2.
2. Consider the parameter vector of $(\theta^3)^{\mathrm{T}}$ as (0, 4, 3), then predict the star ratings for B2 by user3.
3. Consider the parameter vector of $(\theta^4)^{\mathrm{T}}$ as (0, 3, 1), then predict the star ratings for B3 and B5 by user4.
4. Assume different parameter vector for $(\theta^5)^{\mathrm{T}}$ and predict the star ratings for B1 by user1 and observe how the ratings vary.

Assuming some small random value for the parameter 'θ', the actual 'θ' i.e. the parameter vector for user 'j' can be learned using the following equation [2].

$$Min(\theta^j) \frac{1}{2b^j} \sum_{i:r(i,j)=1} ((\theta^j)(X^i) - Y^{i,j}) + \frac{\lambda}{2b^j} \sum_{k=1}^{n} \left(\theta_k^{(j)}\right)^2$$

The various parameters used in the above equation is explained in Table 10.8.

In the above equation, the term $((\theta^j)(X^i) - Y^{i,j})$ represents subtracting actual 'Y' from the predicted 'Y'. The first part of the above equation is the **squared error term** and the second part of the above equation is the **regularization term**. The regularization term is included to ensure that the data performs better for the test data.

To learn θ^1, θ^2, θ^3,.......... $\theta^{(Nu)}$ (and by multiplying the above equation by b^j), we shall rewrite the above equations as shown below.

Optimization Algorithm

$$Min(\theta^1,\theta^2....\theta^{Nu})\frac{1}{2}\sum_{j=1}^{Nu}\sum_{i:r(i,j)=1}((\theta^j)(X^i)-Y^{i,j})+\frac{\lambda}{2}\sum_{j=1}^{Nu}\sum_{k=1}^{n}\left(\theta_k^{(j)}\right)^2$$

Gradient descent update

$$\theta_k^{(j)} = \theta_k^{(j)} - \alpha \sum_{i:r(i,j)=1}((\theta^{(j)})T_x^{(i)} - y^{(i,j)})x_k^{(i)}\,(for\ k=0)$$

$$\theta_k^{(j)} = \theta_k^{(j)} - \alpha\left(\sum_{i:r(i,j)=1}((\theta^{(j)})T_x^{(i)} - y^{(i,j)})x_k^{(i)} + \lambda\theta_k^{(j)}\right)(for\ k\neq0)$$

Using the above optimization algorithm, we shall predict the missing star ratings for a given product for a particular user. Based on the predicted star rating, the algorithm shall decide whether the product should be recommended or not.

Table 10.8 Parameter vector estimation.

Sl. No.	Parameter	Explanation
1.	r(i,j)	Will be '1', if user 'j' has rated book 'i'. (0 otherwise).
2.	$y^{(i,j)}$	Rating by user 'j' on book 'i' (if defined).
3.	θ^j	Parameter vector for user 'j'.
4.	b^j	No. of books rated by user j.
5.	x^i	Feature vector for book 'i'.

10.5   Content-Based Recommendation Using the Tree Induction Algorithm

A tree induction algorithm is a form of decision tree algorithm. The decision points of the tree are in a top-down recursive way. The tree is similar to the conventional if 'Yes' then do A, if 'No', then do B, etc. Using tree induction algorithm, we shall create a system that suggests user to buy products based on the users taste. Let's discuss this with an example:

Example: Induction Tree Algorithm (whether a user will purchase a 'Car' or not)

For Table 10.9, we can construct a tree using induction tree algorithm as shown in Figure 10.1.

Table 10.9 Chance of purchasing a car.

Age	Income	Family size (fs)	Travel distance (td)	Buys car
≤30	High	Big	High	Yes
≤30	Low	Big	High	No
≤30	Medium	Big	High	Yes
31 to 40	High	Average	Medium	Yes
31 to 40	Low	Average	Medium	No
31 to 40	Medium	Average	Medium	Yes
>40	High	Small	Low	Yes
>40	Medium	Small	Low	Yes
>40	Low	Small	Low	No
≤30	High	Average	Medium	Yes
≤30	Low	Average	Medium	No
≤30	Medium	Average	Medium	Yes
31 to 40	High	Small	Low	Yes
31 to 40	Low	Small	Low	No
31 to 40	Medium	Small	Low	Yes

Figure 10.1 Induction tree algorithm.

Each of the path of the tree says that whether it ends up in buying or not. This tree is constructed using decision tree induction algorithm. The decision tree algorithm helps us to partition the data in the appropriate way. Here the 'Income' is selected as the root of the tree. But, why only 'income'? and why not any other parameter. This is decided using the attribute selection measure. There are many attribute selection measures. Here, we will discuss one such measure. The information gain for each parameter is calculated using the below formula:

Expected Information (Entropy) needed to classify a tuple in the entire dataset (*D*):

$$info(D) = -\sum_{i=1}^{n} P_i log_2(P_i)$$

Information needed to classify/branch based on a specific attribute (*A*)

$$Info_A(D) = -\sum_{i=1}^{n} \frac{|D_i|}{|D|} \times I(D_i)$$

Information gained by branching on attribute *A*

$$Gain(D) = Info(D) - Info_A(D)$$

Let us say 'Pi' is the probability of buying the 'Car' is (10/15). Out of 15 tuples in Table 10.9, ten (10) tuples represent that the car is purchased. 'Ni' is the probability of not buying the 'Car' is (5/15). Out of 15 tuples in

Table 10.9, five (5) tuples represent that the car is not purchased. The whole dataset can be represented as, $D_i = \{P_i, N_i\}$.

Applying the above formula for the case whether the person will buy a computer or not:

Information of the entire data set

$$\text{Info (D)} = I (10, 5) = -(10/15) \log 2 (10/15)$$
$$- (5/15) \log 2 (5/15) = 0.918$$

a. Information Content for the attribute 'Age'

$$\text{Info}_{age} (D) = (6/15) I (4, 2) + (6/15) I (4, 2) + (3/15) I (2, 1) = 0.918$$

Here, the first $(6/15)$ I $(4, 2)$ represents that out of the 15 tuples 6 tuples corresponds the case where the age ≤30, out of which 4 tuples represents 'yes' and 2 tuples represents 'no' for the attribute 'Buys Car'. Similarly, the next $(6/15)$ I $(4, 2)$ represents that out of the 15 tuples 6 tuples corresponds to the case where the age is between 31 and 40, out of which 4 tuples represents 'yes' and 2 tuples represents 'no' for the attribute 'Buys Car'. The next, $(3/5)$ I $(2,1)$ represents that out of 15 tuples 3 tuples correspond to the case where the age is greater than 40, out of which 2 tuples represent 'yes' and 1 tuple represents 'no' for the attribute 'Buys Car' (shown in Table 10.10).

$$\textbf{Gain (age) = Info (D)} - \textbf{Info}_{age} \textbf{(D)} = 0.918 - 0.918 = 0.0$$

b. Information Content for the attribute 'Income'

$$\text{Info}_{income} (D) = (5/15) I (5, 0) + (5/15) I (0,5) + (5/15) I (5, 0) = 0$$

The information content calculation for income is shown in Table 10.11.

Table 10.10 Information content calculation for age.

Age	P_i	N_i	$I(P_i, N_i)$	Info_{age} (D)
≤30	4	2	0.918	(6/15)*0.918 = 0.367
31 to 40	4	2	0.918	(6/15)*0.918 = 0.367
>40	2	1	0.918	(3/15)*0.918 = 0.183
Info_{age} (D)				**0.918**

Table 10.11 Information content calculation for income.

Income	P_i	N_i	$I(P_i, N_i)$	$Info_{age}$ (D)
High	5	0	0	(5/15) * 0 = 0
Low	0	5	0	(5/15) * 0 = 0
Medium	5	0	0	(5/15) * 0 = 0
$Info_{age}$ (D)				**0.0**

$$\text{Gain (Income)} = 0.918 - 0 = 0.918$$

Similarly, Gain of Family Size, Travel Distance are calculated:

Gain (Family Size) = 0.0
Gain (Travel Distance) = 0.0

Python function to calculate the Info (D) is given below (Figure 10.2). The above function shown in Figure 10.2 can be called as:

```
Infor(10,5)
```

```
0.9182958340544896
```

The function shown in Figure 10.2, can be used to find **$Info_{income}$ (D)**, as shown below:

```
((5/15)*Infor(5,0)  +  (5/15)*Infor(0,5)  +  (5/15)*Infor(5,0))
```

```
0.0
```

```python
import math
def Infor(a,b):
    tot=a+b
    par1=a/tot
    par2=b/tot
    # print(par1,par2)
    if a!=0 and b!=0:
        sol=(-(par1)*math.log(par1,2))-(par2*math.log(par2,2))
    else:
        sol=0
    return(sol)
```

Figure 10.2 Python function to calculate Info (D).

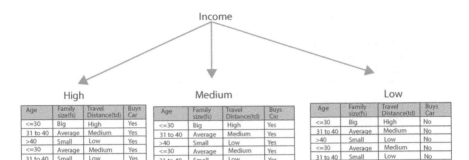

Figure 10.3 Induction tree for 'buying a car example'.

The parameter with the highest information gain will be considered as the root node. Income has the highest information gain, so we will consider '**Income**' as the root node for constructing the decision tree.

From Figure 10.3, we can see that the tree is completely partitioned. The branches 'High' and 'Medium' of the induction tree contains only tuples with value 'yes' for the, 'Buys Car' attribute. Similarly, the branch 'Low' of the tree contains only tuples with value 'no' for the 'Buys Car' attribute. If there, are mixed values of 'yes' and 'no' for the class attribute ('Buys Car') then, we should repeat the entire above process for that particular sub-table by calculating the Info(D), $\text{Info}_A(D)$. This process should be continued until the class/decision attribute holds all 'yes' or 'no' for the particular branch/sub branch.

10.6   Summary

This chapter described the various Content-Based Recommendation techniques. First, we discussed the several phases of Content-Based Recommendation systems. Followed by, the various techniques like Content-Based Recommendation using cosine similarity, Content-Based Recommendation using optimization techniques and Content-Based Recommendation using Induction Tree algorithm are discussed. In Content-Based Recommendation using cosine similarity technique, we build the item profile for every product and also we build the user profile for every user. The item profile and user profiles are represented as vectors. When a new item is introduced in the online store, an item profile will be created for that particular product (which is a vector). The cosine similarity will be calculated between the new item and all the users individually. The item will be recommended for the top 'M' users with highest cosine similarity value. The Content-Based Recommendation using optimization techniques is used basically to predict the rating for a particular product by a given user. To do this, we first identify the feature vector for every product and then we identify the parameter vector for every user. To predict the star ratings of a particular user for a specific product, we take the parameter vector of the respective user and transpose it, and then it will be multiplied with the feature vector of the specified product, the resultant value will be considered as the star ratings corresponding to that product for a given user. To, identify the feature vector initially we start with some random small values and using the optimization techniques, we shall arrive at the optimal feature vector. The Content-Based Recommendation using induction tree algorithm uses a tree called as the induction tree, which is similar to the 'if'/'else' construct. The induction tree algorithm helps us to estimate the node/attribute with high information content. The node with the high information content will be selected as the root node and the tree will be partitioned accordingly. This process continues for the sub trees also, until the tree is completely partitioned.

References

1. http://snap.stanford.edu/class/cs246-2015/slides/07-recsys1.pdf
2. https://www.coursera.org/lecture/machine-learning/content-based-recommendations-uG59z
3. https://nptel.ac.in/content/storage2/nptel_data3/html/mhrd/ict/text/110105083/lec52.pdf
4. Mooney, R.J., Content-Based Book Recommending Using Learning for Text Categorization. *Proceedings of SIGIR-99 Workshop on Recommender Systems: Algorithms and Evaluation*, Berkeley, CA, 1999.
5. Pazzani, M.J. and Billsus, D., Content-Based Recommendation Systems, in: *The Adaptive Web. Lecture Notes in Computer Science*, vol. 4321, Springer, Berlin, Heidelberg, 2007.

11

Content-Based Health Recommender Systems

Soumya Prakash Rana[1]*, Maitreyee Dey[1], Javier Prieto[2] and Sandra Dudley[1]

[1]Division of Electrical and Electronics Engineering, London South Bank University, London, United Kingdom
[2]Department of Computer Science and Automation Control, University of Salamanca, Salamanca, Spain

Abstract

The rapid growth of digital health information has elevated the application and egress of data analytics healthcare industry. One proposed solution, health recommender systems (HRS) have emerged for patient-oriented decision making to recommend better healthcare advice based on profile health records (PHR) and patient databases. The HRS can enhance healthcare systems and simultaneously manage patients suffering from a range of different diseases employing predictive analytics and recommending appropriate treatments. A content-based recommender system (CBRS) is a customized HRS approach that concentrates on the evaluation of a patient's history and 'learns', through machine learning (ML), to generate predictions. Additionally, CBRS intends to offer individualized and trusted information to the patient's regarding their health status. The CBRS is usually applied in case of medical document recommenders where patients give their preferences after receiving recommendations in the form of ratings where positively ranked items are recommended to the patient. The CBRS and associated popular ML algorithms are discussed in this chapter. Subsequently, the basic concepts, feature extraction methods, similarity measure, and ranking are presented and discussed. The privacy preservation phase is also discussed, particularly how data is protected, and intruders prohibited from altering valuable information. Finally, the challenges and open issues are deliberated.

*Corresponding author: ranas9@lsbu.ac.uk; soumyaprakash.rana@gmail.com

Sachi Nandan Mohanty, Jyotir Moy Chatterjee, Sarika Jain, Ahmed A. Elngar and Priya Gupta (eds.)
Recommender System with Machine Learning and Artificial Intelligence: Practical Tools and Applications in Medical, Agricultural and Other Industries, (215–236) © 2020 Scrivener Publishing LLC

11.1 Introduction

The increasing amount of digital and web-based information has propelled the development of recommender system (RS) technology [1] where one's data is transformed to predict their future interest (in some cases, what might be good for them) employing machine learning (ML) [2]. Primarily there are two entities in this setting; user and item. The person to whom the recommendation is made, referred to as the user and the recommended product is referred to as the item (beneficial advice or suggestion in some cases). The recommendation may be personalized or non-personalized. Personalized recommendation is made for a particular person whereas, non-personalized recommendation is generated following the trend of other persons. The RSs are classified into three groups depending on the application; collaborative recommender system, content-based recommender system, and knowledge-based recommender system. Content based recommender system (CBRS) is popular for personalized recommendations, where the user's own rating, preferences, personal data, and actions are enough to make appropriate recommendations for the them. This customized RS approach is useful when a new item enters the scenario and very few preferences are available for that item by the user themselves or only the user's information is applied to generate recommendations [3]. As the CBRS approach does not necessarily employ rating or preference correlations across all users it fits for user centric applications such as, health and well-being applications, is the focus of this chapter. The primary data source of CBRSs: (i) the description of the item, used as attributes, (ii) the information collected from the user profile i.e., implicit and explicit feedback. The implicit feedback are the user actions for an item whereas the explicit feedback is the rating and reviews of items given by the user in the past. It is noteworthy that the descriptions of item are employed as attribute or features, and the ratings utilized as labels to predict or recommend an item to the user with the help of ML methods (i.e., classification or regression) [3]. But, CBRS system face challenges when data or information are either unavailable or limited. This occurs when a new user or item enters in the process. This problem is known as cold-start problem in CBRS mechanisms. It indicates that the system has not yet gathered sufficient information which depends on the problem as well as the application scenario [4]. Recently, people engage heavily with the internet. Adults search for health-based information such as, symptoms of diseases, diagnosis procedures, treatment costs, etc. [5]. This content influenced to emerge a special kind of RS technology for improving quality of medical service and patient–physician relation, is known as health recommender system (HRS), was introduced by Ricci *et al.* [6]. The HRS provides suggestions based on individual health records, thus the basic principle and framework of CBRS is highly appropriate for this application.

This chapter provides a detailed analysis of HRSs employing the CBRS principles (described in Section 2), components (described in Section 3), medical data processing (described in Section 4), extraction of health attributes and attribute weighting (described in Sections 5, 6, and 7), learning the user profiles 8, evaluation of systems (described in Section 9), design principles of HRS (described in Section 10), conclusion and future research directions (described in Section 11).

11.2   Typical Health Recommender System Framework

Health recommender systems (HRS) are becoming an influential platform for health service and telemedicine providers. The HRS offers health related information to both health professionals and patients employing ML based decision making for patient's (user's) health. In view of the fact that medical prescriptions or suggestions by health professionals for a patient cannot depend on other patient's medical records, thus HRS provides suggestions only based on a user's own history, medical records, medical reports. Hence, HRSs need to employ the basic structure of CBRS and can also be known as, content-based health recommender system (CBHRS). Unlike the basic CBRS model, CBHRS has two data sources [5, 7, 8]:

(a) The medical information regarding patient health are available in the form of electronic medical record (EMR) or electronic health record (EHR) and collected from authorized health centers, hospitals, medical stores. These data sources are linked with each patient's personal health record (PHR) profile through secure network protocol. This PHR profile is used to obtain medical attributes or distinctive features regarding the patient's current health status.

(b) Secondly, the feedback (doctor's feedback) are used as labels for ML execution. Here is slight perceptual difference from a basic CBRS model. The basic CBRS model believes in user preferences and ratings i.e., implicit feedback. But explicit feedback is the doctor's suggestion for patient's health, are more relevant to this case and used as labels for automatic machine learning (aML) applications. Subsequently, it is also necessary to understand the types of medical recommendations (i.e., nutritional facts, exercise, diagnosis, and drugs-medicines) [9, 10] are being suggested by doctors in this context. The different types of explicit feedback are detailed in Section 7.

The ML is operated in two ways, (i) automatic recommendations are generated for patient's healthcare and healthy living, is known as automatic machine learning (aML), (ii) the doctors are ultimate experts for providing trustworthy feedback to their patients, thus the systems are capable to incorporate doctor's new suggestions and accommodates them in the system, this communication between doctor and the system is implemented employing ML and known as interactive machine learning (iML), and whole concept is known as human-in-loop (HiL) or doctor-in-loop (DiL). Along with the patient's information retrieval and automation, data security, privacy, and safety of technical systems also play a central role for successful implementation of CBHRS specially from a clinical point of view. The data security aspects of CBHRS has not been described in this chapter but demonstrated as design concern of CBHRS. This chapter only discusses the procedure for producing recommendations from health perspective.

11.3   Components of Content-Based Health Recommender System

Primarily, the components of CBHRS can be classified in three groups; (i) unstructured data processing, (ii) feature (distinctive attributes) extraction, feature selection, and feature weighting, (iii) health professional's feedback collection, (iii) learning user profiles (training phase) and health recommendation generation employing trained CBHRS models that would only be visible to the individual patients and doctors and further used to progress treatment, consultation purpose (depending upon health risk).

The schematic diagram of whole CBHRS is shown in Figure 11.1. There are several blocks included here to represent the generalized mechanism of the system. Two colors have been used in the diagram, light pink and green. The blocks with light pink color show the units

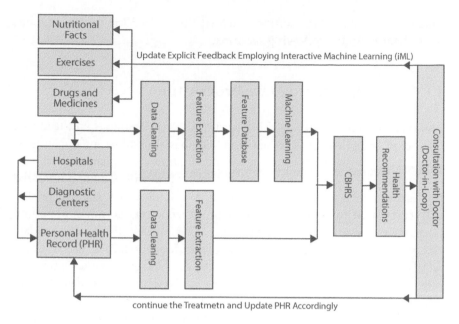

Figure 11.1 The flow chart of CBHRS system.

that use information from all existing patients to create medical database comprising historical medical records collected from authorized hospitals, diagnostic centers, pharmacists, well-being health applications. It is notable, that the patients don't need to log their own data and the medical data entry is performed either by trained medical staffs or automated network protocol system. Thus, the efficiency of creating the database plays significant role here because, mishandling of medical data would cause error, propagate through all over the system pipeline, and could destroy the patient's health. These archived data are further pre-processed and fed into ML algorithms to correlate medical facts e.g., disease, symptoms, health risks and their treatment process which is known as automatic machine learning (aML) application. The blocks colored with light green depend on individual data (known as medical content in this case). For example, when a new patient registers in CBHRS for seeking healthcare, the medically trained CBHRS starts predicting (or, recommending) medications, health tips depending upon his/her state of health which can be realized from PHR is being made at the time of patient registration. The recommendations are refined during the treatment with the assistance of registered doctors, the concept is known as doctor-in-loop (DiL) or human-in-loop (HiL) and implemented employing interactive machine learning (iML) setting. Each of these CBHRS components has been detailed in the following sections.

11.4 Unstructured Data Processing

The medical records such as, EMR and EHR of the patients and feedback of doctors are piled up from different web-based systems for implementing CBHRS. However, these valuable information are actually available in unstructured text format which are efficiently pre-processed and prepared for further processing [11]. Unlike other ML applications, the text feature extraction is the fundamental phase here, which is very common in natural language processing (NLP) domain [12]. This process also known as data cleaning, contains different algorithms such as, term-document matrix, stop-word deletion, stemming, phrase extraction, etc. However, feature extraction phase can be replaced by feature selection and weighting to escalate the prediction ability of CBHRS which is practiced in traditional CBRS where data are available in structured format and ready for processing (briefly described in Section 6). The popular data cleaning algorithms are discussed below:

(a) Term Document Matrix: It is a mathematical matrix that stores unique keywords appear in all available documents and makes dictionary to be used for further text feature extraction models e.g., bag of words (BoW) method [13, 14]. Table 11.1 shows an example of term document matrix where, rows contain related to medical conditions and columns represent number of times keywords appeared in each document.

(b) Stop Word Deletion: This process removes frequently occurring words of English dictionary which do not specify any meaningful information about patient's health or feedback

Table 11.1 An example of term document matrix created from medical records.

Terms	Documents					
	D_1	D_2	D_3	D_4	D_5	D_6
Fever	11	0	3	0	1	8
Cough	1	11	7	5	2	0
Sneeze	15	0	0	2	9	2

Table 11.2 An example of stemming process created from medical records.

Set of words	Unified concept
Sneeze, sneezing	Sneeze
Cough, coughing	Cough
Medication, medicine, pills	Medication

from doctor. These are part of English grammar such as, articles, parts of speech and considered as stop words and eliminated at the time of text processing [15, 16].

(c) Stemming: It combines the use of same words in different form such as, singular and plural of a word, different tenses of the same word, etc. [15, 17]. Table 11.2 shows an example of stemming process for text processing where; the first column contains different forms of same words and the second column indicates their stemmed versions or root form.

(d) Phrase Extraction: This method identifies the words that always appear together but mean something else as a whole. Different dictionaries are available and used to extract these phrases and its meaning to avoid the redundancy of language processing [15, 18].

11.5   Unsupervised Feature Extraction & Weighting

Commonly, health records are provided in textual format with different symbols also considered as text, and very few of them contain numerical form. Thus, the most important task is to find out appropriate and meaningful features (keywords) for generating fine recommendations, and mapping of the textual keywords to numerical vectors. This whole process is known as feature extraction in text processing [19]. The most popular and commonly employed text-based feature extraction methods of CBHRS are discussed below.

11.5.1   Bag of Words (BoW)

Creating a list of significant and discriminative keywords [20] which are chosen in such a way that can represent meaningful sentences and whole document can be transformed into the vector of keywords. The BoW employs the basic principle of term document matrix. The presence and absence of each keyword is denoted as 1 and 0, then the number of appearances of that word in the document is counted. The number of appearances is known as term frequency (TF). Subsequently, inverse document frequency (IDF) is used to highlight each word with a logarithmic calculation, where IDF of infrequent words obtain high value and frequent words receive low value. Finally, a TF–IDF value (i.e., TF × IDF) is measured against each unique keyword and generated the feature vector from the documents. For instance, Table 11.1 contains three different words from six different documents. In case of the word 'Fever' from document D_1, the TF and IDF can be determined as, TF = $11/(11 + 1 + 15) = 11/27 = 0.407$ and IDF = log $6/4 = 0.176$. Thus, the TF-IDF of word 'Fever' for document D_1 is $(0.407 \times 0.176) = 0.071$.

11.5.2   Word to Vector (Word2Vec)

This is also a popular text feature extraction algorithm in natural language processing (NLP) field. It extracts distinctive keywords from large text documents by organizing them with close proximity that share same contexts in the feature space [21, 22]. This is greatly employed where features must be extracted from analogical questions. Table 11.3 indicates an example of creating vector from text or sentence. A sentence has been taken to derive the feature vector where, a window size of 2 is considered to shift for each word and find its nearest words. In the right side, there two columns representing input and output. The highlighted words are considered as inputs whereas, all possible nearest words are considered as output. These input and output sets are employed as training set for implementing the ML.

11.5.3   Global Vectors for Word Representations (Glove)

Global vectors for word representations (Glove) are an advanced version of the word to vector algorithm. It constructs word co-occurrence matrix (WCM) with the keywords that have close proximity to each other [23]. Then, the statistics, i.e., probability is determined for them to appear in a document next to each other.

11.6   Supervised Feature Selection & Weighting

Many well-known CBRSs as well as CBHRSs exist comprising supervised feature selection [24] and weighting instead of unsupervised feature extraction approaches [25]. Supervised feature selection is applicable

Table 11.3 An example of creating vector from words.

Sentence									Input	Output
Have	plenty	of	rest	and	drink	lots	of	fluids	Have	plenty, of
Have	plenty	of	rest	and	drink	lots	of	fluids	plenty	Have, of, rest
Have	plenty	of	rest	and	drink	lots	of	fluids	of	Have, plenty, of, rest, and
..	..	..	..	..	..	..	..	..	..	..

when the data are available with proper structure and label information. This approach is common in conventional CBRS rather than customized CBHRS. Unlike the supervised approach, unsupervised feature extraction and weighting also entrusts high numeric values to uncorrelated and distinct attributes whereas, correlated and less important features are assigned with lower scores. The goal of both supervised and unsupervised feature selection/extraction is to determine highly informative features and reduce the size of feature vector space [26]. But supervised attribute selection and weighting have immense impact of feedback (i.e., implicit and explicit), whereas unsupervised feature extraction and weighting have no effect of feedback. The most popular supervised feature selection techniques are Gini index, entropy, x^2-statistic, and normalized deviation. Later, the weights of attributes are assigned by defining application specific weighting functions to control the sensitivity of the performance. Gini index is one of the most simple and popular text feature selection process of the literature and suits for the area specific applications where, textual descriptions are rated with binary or ordinal ratings [27]. These ratings are employed as categorical value for text descriptions. Entropy calculation is similar to Gini indexing and also based on ratings or ordinal numeric values. It determines score based on keyword's probabilistic occurrence in documents to create probabilistic interpretation of selected features [28]. The x^2-statistic utilizes contingency table approach by placing each word and its categorical value in the matrix arrangement to analyze the suitability of recommendation for users [29]. Another, supervised feature selection method is normalized deviation which addresses information loss problem due to sorting of ratings occurs in Gini index, entropy, and x^2-statistic calculation. Normalized deviation also employs the numeric rating values for feature selection process [30]. However, there are some other circumstances where, preferences are made by the users through another dependent variable rather than using numeric values. In conventional CBRS model these are handled by Fisher's discrimination index [11]. These cases are quite similar to health domain because doctors make suggestions to the patients by prescribing medication or therapy which also comes with textual form. This means, the texts are used to describe state of health dependent on the texts are employed in doctor's prescriptions.

Aforementioned supervised feature selection and weighting techniques have not been detailed much in this chapter because, these methods are not very common in CBHRS scenario but can be applied to observe the performance of the small CBHRS models.

11.7 Feedback Collection

The goal of CBHRS is to provide relevant medical advices to the patients employing artificial intelligence and ML techniques. Thus, the identification and integration of suitable medical advices to the system is the salient task while designing CBHRS. As mentioned before, the implicit feedback received from patients are not to the purpose here whereas, the explicit feedback acquired from doctors are more vital for patients as well as CBHRS [31]. Although, the scenario is opposite for traditional CBRS where user's choice needs to be known as a priori knowledge to generate recommendation for the users. Hence, the explicit opinions of doctors are collected and stored as a priori knowledge or label information for corresponding health conditions to provide medically aware responses. These feedbacks come from the doctor-patient conversation or web-based consultation where, the doctors meet their patients, actively listen to them, and patients must answer to the queries asked by the doctors. Thus, the extracted and interpreted medical knowledge [9, 10] can be classified into mainly three groups for labeling health records.

11.7.1 Medication & Therapy

Medication and therapy are the primary type of recommendations received by patients from their doctors at the time of medical appointments or in emergency cases. It contains different names of medicines and therapies (e.g., exercises, activities, etc.) appropriate to the patients' health and their healing process. Therefore, the feedback are directly stored as keywords and employed as labels against health conditions which are perceived from PHRs.

11.7.2 Healthy Diet Plan

Healthy diet plans are also the part of doctor's recommendations at the time health consultation. It can be healthy diet plans, some sequential routine activities, etc., and can be technically considered as series of keywords for data labeling.

11.7.3 Suggestions

Suggestions are given in written format (text based) to the patients. These are mostly different types of restrictions suggested by doctors in textual and descriptive form.

Such feedback are further integrated into the system to label medical records. After labeling the available stored data, CBHRSs are trained with these labeled medical information to leverage the learning phase.

11.8   Training & Health Recommendation Generation

The learning of different health problems and corresponding suggestions of doctors from stored or achieved EMRs, EHRs can be viewed as characteristic of CBHRS to acquire new knowledge from experiences (i.e., gain from more data and HCI mechanism). In this context, the ML provides the ability to the computer based CBHRS application for improving medical knowledge [32]. The ML algorithms mimic the natural learning potential of human and provide intelligence to the computer-based applications (CBHRS in this case). There are two types learning, rote learning and inference-based learning. The later helps to grow the ability for obtaining new declarative knowledge through observation and practical experiment whereas, the former implants the knowledge directly to the model and not popular in artificial intelligence (AI) field. The process of inferring knowledge is a systematic statistical process which can be further classified as instructive learning, analogical learning, and specimen-based learning.

The instructive learning represents the concept of feature or attribute extraction for ML implementation, which organizes the knowledge to perform decision making and the performance heavily depends upon this phase. This phase has been already described in Sections 5 and 6. The analogical learning is the process to derive rules based on the historical data, consequences, and known as rule-based ML (or rule-based classification). This is one kind of supervised method and performed with a priori knowledge (label information). The most popular ML technique is specimen based or example-based learning and employed to induce knowledge from data in hand. The specimen-based methods are mainly categorized in supervised, unsupervised, and reinforcement ML techniques. These methods derive functions that can represent and generalize the hidden knowledge from examples.

In the context of CBHRS, the analogical learning or rule-based ML and supervised ML (are considered as specimen or example-based learning) are mostly used. Thus, few of them from the literature have been discussed here. Its noteworthy that the explicit feedback of doctors are stored before as label information or ground truth to generate rules and form supervised classification function for producing health recommendations.

11.8.1   Analogy-Based ML in CBHRS

A rule-based health recommender system is proposed and named as computer-tailored health communication (CTHC) system by Sadasivam *et al.* [33]. The CTHC is integrated with rule-based machine learning engine which recommends health tips and motivational messages based on patient's PHR. Pattaraintakorn *et al.* presented hybrid health recommender system. This is a web-based health communication system which analyzes the patient records and medical history through rough sets and survival analysis, and final expert recommendations are generated by rule-based ML theory [34]. Espin *et al.* prototyped health recommender system to generate nutritional advice and diet plans for elderly persons [7]. Husain *et al.* proposed personalized therapeutic recommendation system. The system employs knowledge about different types of therapy and infers set of rules to create recommendation. The model has two phases rule-based and case-based for recommending relevant therapies for the patient's health [35]. Kim *et al.* designed rule based health recommender system for the aging society. The system generates customized diet plans for the aging patients suffering from coronary heart diseases [36].

11.8.2   Specimen-Based ML in CBHRS

As mentioned before, specimen-based or example-based ML is well known as supervised ML or classification, where researchers focus on statistical algorithms to predict outcomes which are known as recommendations in this case. Unlike other domains, ML is used here to predict medical advice for the patients, but also ML is implemented to improve interactive nature of the CBHRS alongside of prediction. The health recommendations are generated as a part of aML (described in Sections 2 and 3) whereas, the interactive nature is enhanced through iML or DiL process execution (described in Sections 2 and 3). The aML predicts medically aware recommendations depending on previously learned knowledge, however iML and DiL are different forms of human–computer interaction (HCI) that can accommodate new knowledge in the system for refining the recommendation outcomes. Thus, iML and DiL are also considered as a part of ML applications in CBHRSs. Hence, both the ML based CBHRS and interactive CBHRS from the literature are described here.

Cooperative ML algorithms are proposed by Holzinger, and Holzinger *et al.* [37, 38] to enhance CBHRS and keep human-in-loop (another form of iML) and DiL because the doctors are ultimate experts in case of HRS and are able to assess the recommendations generated by aML. Here, the doctors may want to consult with their registered patients to suggest different medications and therapies from auto generated advices based on their practical knowledge and experience [37, 38]. Yang *et al.* designed ecommerce based CBHRS which provides personalized health tips based on patient's emotional health condition. There are quite significant and practical attributes such as, study pressure, economic burden, social support, etc. applied to understand the depression level of patients employed to execute aML. Mainly two popular ML techniques are performed there, support vector machine (SVM) and decision tree (DT) to identify depression level and predict recommendations e.g., better management of finance, listening to music, talking to family and friends, following hobbies, etc. [39]. Bradley *et al.* [40], and Suchal *et al.* [41] modeled simple k-nearest neighbor (k-NN)-based approach instead of highly computationally complex ML algorithms to learn PHR profiles and feedback. Though, k-NN is known as lazy learning process but it doesn't need separate training phase and only uses straightforward similarity-based decision making procedure. The outcomes prove that k-NN algorithm outperforms in CBHRS context and can work efficiently. Bocanegra *et al.* prototyped probabilistic Naive Bayes classification approach to predict medical solutions based on their text based EMR, EHR stored in the database for better health care [42].

11.9   Evaluation of Content-Based Health Recommender System

Performance evaluation of any model is important and crucial to its success. Unlike any other field, standard statistical measures are also used to evaluate the performance of CBHRS. However, the measurements are nearly same to those which are used for information retrieval and ML based models such as, accuracy and error [43], precision and recall [44], F-measure [45], receiver operating characteristic (ROC) curve [46], root mean square error (RMSE) [47], etc. The accuracy indicates the amount of correctly recommended health suggestions and error indicates the incorrectly recommended health tips [43]. The amount of relevant suggestions that are correctly recommended out of all the recommended tips and the fraction of recommendations which are suggested from all relevant suggestions are known as precision and recall respectively [44]. Subsequently, F-measure depends upon the precision and recall measurements as it combines both precision and recall into a single measurement [45]. The ROC curve is the visualization of true positives against false positives that are identified employing sensitivity measurement [46]. ROC is also used to compare different CBHRS algorithms independent of their threshold value. The RMSE is determined to compare predicted recommendations over real recommendations. It calculates a squared error for all recommendations followed by the square root of the mean, which increase with wrong recommendations and decreases with accurate recommendations [47]. The working principle of HRS is slightly different from most of the information retrieval and ML based applications, thus the traditional performance metrics are not always satisfactory to provide performance overview. For instance, in case of content-based image retrieval (CBIR) process it is important to observe the number of relevant images appear in the first frame rather than focusing on all retrieved relevant images [48]. This scenario has effect on user's attention. Hence, recently there are three more metrics introduced such as, k-top recommendation, serendipity, and coverage to evaluate HRS performance in depth [15]. The k-top measures the amount of relevant recommendations is generated among first certain recommendations, serendipity checks whether the recommendation is new or old, and coverage measures whether all possible suggestions are recommended or not. The interface and interactive nature of the whole model is also significant to improve the HRS as well as CBHRS models along with the appropriate attribute selection and ML algorithm implementation. A better interactive and interfacing system always accommodate new knowledge into system, seeks attention of users (patients in this case), and gains trust for further use.

11.10   Design Criteria of CBHRS

There are no specific criteria to design successful HRS and none can ensure its success at the initial stage. It all depends upon the visualization of the application area and goals to be achieved. In case of CBHRS, the ultimate goal is health improvement and well-being of patients by providing mobile interface to exhibit patient's health condition and allow them to be informed the necessity to visit their physician according to their severity of health. This is the future of health care system, which is a virtual, internet-based medical platform that intends to bring the patients and doctors close. There are some issues need to be addressed by the designer and found the way for improving CBHRS model by the time such as, micro level and lucidity, participatory design, PHR data privacy, uncertainty and risk management, and DiL concept [15].

11.10.1 Micro-Level & Lucidity

The micro level property suggests that the health recommendations should be precise and specific for the patient's health. For example, when a registered user starts following CBHRS services, the patient should receive appropriate recommendations by the time according to their health state. The lucidity or transparency of the model indicates the fact that the working principle of the CBHRS model should be clear to the patients from the interface and information available in the interface.

11.10.2 Interactive Interface

The end goal of CBHRS is to predict relevant and better recommendations for patient's well-being. Hence, it should be always kept in mind, how to increase the engagement of patients with their CBHRS service through the interactive appearance of the systems [49]. In other words, the designer should put together different components in such a way that, the two-way communication between system and patient become more meaningful where patients find what they are looking for.

11.10.3 Data Protection

The CBHRS system is an electronic system framework where the data of medical authorities are stored and updated in order to run the system properly. The storage contains sensitive personal data. Hence, the data protection module should be designed securely as much as possible employing robust information technology (IT) and network system schemes. The system must contain encrypted and highly secure protocol to manage patient's data [50]. The typical algorithms like K-anonymity and l-diversity are used to securely handle the patient's data in existing systems. These methods can only trace back the data for a certain number of users which would not be enough for secure CBHRS implementation because the security of individual identity is more important here. In addition, the staffs should be trained and offered induction programs in regular basis and sign confidential agreement. All the stored and achieved data should be transferred and shared within the network via encrypted referral IT protocols.

11.10.4   Risk & Uncertainty Management

The risk management and uncertainty handling are also significant characteristics that need to be addressed here like any other long-term project for designing robust and efficient CBHRS [51]. This property must be taken care of cautiously throughout the life cycle of a system. This is somehow related to all the above-mentioned issues. The risk can occur from irrelevant recommendations, user's or patient's unawareness of system's working principle, miscommunication between patient and system, insecure data, etc. Therefore, these issues are called as known-risks of CBHRS whereas, some unknown-risks can also appear in the scene. The risks occur because of the uncertainty due to the gap between system visualization and operational management. This needs to be addressed with proactive planning and efficient operational management to successfully run CBHRS system.

11.10.5   Doctor-in-Loop (DiL)

This is the latest paradigm in data-driven and medically aware CBHRS. The CBHRS generates health recommendation based on patient's past history and gathered knowledge, and ML implementation (i.e., learning/classification, regressions) [37]. The recommendations may not relevant at some point or the health risk may not be managed by electronic CBHRS only. A consultation with doctor is more important rather than just producing health recommendations. Thus, the domain experts, doctors must be kept in loop while designing CBHRS. The patients may not always require consultation with their registered physicians, but the doctors can keep close eye to their patients and take decision about consultation or any other medical decision.

11.11   Conclusions and Future Research Directions

Recommender systems are used by the huge number of ecommerce systems to offer their users relevant and interesting products, service, etc. However, HRSs are different from other RS systems because, it has to give priority to the medical facts that are important for patient's health rather than what the patient prefers. This is a crucial task where medical advices are involved. In case of product-based RS, users are offered the similar products what they liked in past but, in case of medical field the patients supposed to follow the medical recommendations totally. Thus, irrelevant health recommendations are more inferior than irrelevant product suggestion. It would have effect on social health and could ruin the trust on HRS. This chapter describes the components, functionalities, design methodologies of CBHRS to provide an overall idea. Though, few sub-components are included in this chapter from HCI perception and feasibility point of view that might be included in future to the CBHRSs. The CBHRSs are improved a lot in recent years but it needs further research.

The CBHRS still in its infancy stage and should address several open research challenges to be self-dependent and mature ecommerce based medical service. There are six pivotal research challenges of CBHRS have been reported here that must be tackled by the field researchers in future. Firstly, the collaborative nature of CBHRS requires to be enhanced because, the performance relies on both medical and engineering knowledge. The system should be well informed about health knowledge and also interactive in real life with both patients and doctors. Second, human personality has effect on their health and well-being. Specifically, the health recovery depends on how obediently the patients follow medical advice and trust the advice. These psychological phenomena should be explored and integrated in CBHRS. Third, the financial matter needs to be handled carefully i.e., the price to use CBHRS should be fixed in a way so that everyone can use this service. It must be decided by efficient business model because, the goal of CBHRS is to provide better health care for everyone not to make profit for pharmaceutical industries. Fourth, the recommendations should be respectful to each community. For example, the nutritional food recommendations, therapies may vary depending upon the patient's community and this knowledge should be the part of CBHRS. Fifth, there is a difference in the way to deal psychological diseases from other diseases (e.g., cardiovascular, kidney, cold and cough, hypertension, gastrointestinal issues, etc.). Mostly, the doctors use observation, question–answers to identify patient's physical state. The researcher, and developers also must find the way to put this sense into CBHRS in future for making better CBHRS as well as improving social health and well-being. Sixth, very few CBHRSs have incorporated DiL mechanism hitherto however, the doctors are the only experts and decision makers in medical field. It may happen that, a CBHRS is unable to produce appropriate health recommendations because of cold start problem (insufficient data) [42] which can be handled by implementing DiL and iML. This will improve CBHRS performance as well as assist to create fast medical services and enable the service providers for offering better healthcare even in rural areas through remote access.

References

1. Subramaniyaswamy, V., Manogaran, G., Logesh, R., Vijayakumar, V., Chilamkurti, N., Malathi, D., Senthilselvan, N., An ontology-driven personalized food recommendation in IoT-based healthcare system. *J. Supercomput.*, 75, 6, 3184–3216, 2019.
2. Lampropoulos, Aristomenis, S., Tsihrintzis, G.A., *Machine learning paradigms. Applications in recommender systems*, Springer International Publishing, Switzerland, 2015.
3. Aggarwal, and Charu, C., *Recommender systems*, Springer, Cham, 2016.
4. Jannach, D., Zanker, M., Felfernig, A., Friedrich, G., *Recommender systems: an introduction*, Cambridge University Press, New York, 2010.
5. Wiesner, M. and Pfeifer, D., Health recommender systems: Concepts, requirements, technical basics and challenges. *Int. J. Environ. Res. Public Health*, 11, 3, 2580–2607, 2014.
6. Ricci, F., Rokach, L., Shapira, B., Introduction to recommender systems handbook, in: *Recommender systems handbook*, pp. 1–35, Springer, Boston, MA, 2011.
7. Espin, V., Hurtado, M.V., Noguera, M., Nutrition for Elder Care: A nutritional semantic recommender system for the elderly. *Expert Syst.*, 33, 2, 201–210, 2016.
8. Lim, T.P., Husain, W., Zakaria, N., Recommender system for personalised wellness therapy. *IJACSA*, 4, 54–60, 2013.
9. Davis, M.S., Variations in patients' compliance with doctors' advice: an empirical analysis of patterns of communication. *AJPH*, 58, 2, 274–288, 1968.
10. Boulton, M.G. and Williams, A., Health education in the general practice consultation: Doctors' advice on diet, alcohol and smoking. *Health Educ. J.*, 42, 2, 57–63, 1983.
11. Lops, P., De Gemmis, M., Semeraro, G., Content-based recommender systems: State of the art and trends, in: *Recommender systems hand-book*, pp. 73–105, Springer, Boston, MA, 2011.
12. Collobert, R., Weston, J., Bottou, L., Karlen, M., Kavukcuoglu, K., Kuksa, P., Natural language processing (almost) from scratch. *J. Mach. Learn. Res.*, 12, Aug, 2493–2537, 2011.
13. Musto, C., Enhanced vector space models for content-based recommender systems, in: *Proceedings of fourth ACM conference on recommender systems (RecSys'10)*, ACM, Barcelona, Spain, pp. 361–364, 2010.
14. Wang, D., Zhu, S., Li, T., Gong, Y., Multi-document summarization using sentence-based topic models, in: *Proceedings of the ACL-IJCNLP 2009 conference short papers*, Association for Computational Linguistics, Suntec, Singapore, pp. 297–300, 2009.
15. Valdez, A.C., Ziee, M., Verbert, K., Felfernig, A., Holzinger, A., Recommender systems for health informatics: state-of-the-art and future perspectives, in: *Machine Learning for Health Informatics*, pp. 391–414, Springer, Cham, 2016.

16. Guy, G.R., Hay, J., Walker, A., Phonological, lexical, and frequency factors in coronal stop deletion in early New Zealand English. *Lab. Phonol.*, 11, 53–54, 2008.

17. Jivani, A.G. *et al.*, A comparative study of stemming algorithms. *Int. J. Comp. Tech. Appl.*, 2, 6, 1930–1938, 2011.

18. Jacquemin, C. and Tzoukermann, E., NLP for term variant extraction: Synergy between morphology, lexicon, and syntax, in: *Natural language information retrieval*, pp. 25–74, Springer, Dordrecht, 1999.

19. Stavrianou, A., Brun, C., Silander, T., Roux, C., NLP based feature extraction for automated tweet classification, in: *Proceedings of the 1st ACM International Conference on Interactions between Data Mining and Natural Language Processing (DMNLP'14), Interactions between Data Mining and Natural Language Processing*, vol. 1202, p. 145, 2014.

20. Ristoski, P., Mencia, E.L., Paulheim, H., A hybrid multi strategy recommender system using linked open data, in: *Semantic Web Evaluation Challenge*, pp. 150–156, Springer, Cham, 2014.

21. Goldberg, Y. and Levy, O., word2vec Explained: Deriving Mikolov *et al.'s* negative-sampling word-embedding method. arXiv preprint arXiv:1402. 3722, 1–5, 2014.

22. Xiao, Y. and Shi, Q., Research and implementation of hybrid recommendation algorithm based on collaborative filtering and word2vec, in: *Proceedings of the 8th International Symposium on Computational Intelligence and Design (ISCID)*, vol. 2, pp. 172–175, IEEE, Hangzhou, China, 2015.

23. Achakulvisut, T., Acuna, D.E., Ruangrong, T., Kording, K., Science Concierge: A Fast Content-Based Recommendation System for Scientific Publications. *PLoS One*, 11, 7, e0158423, 2016.

24. Qu, W., Song, K.-S., Zhang, Y.-F., Feng, S., Wang, D.-L., Yu, G., A novel approach based on multi-view content analysis and semi-supervised enrichment for movie recommendation. *J. Comput. Sci. Technol.*, 28, 5, 776–787, 2013.

25. Rosati, J., Ristoski, P., Di Noia, T., de Leone, R., Paulheim, H., RDF graph embeddings for content-based recommender systems, in: *Proceedings of the 3rd Workshop on New Trends in Content-Based Recommender Systems (CBRecSys)*, vol. 1673, pp. 23–30, RWTH, Boston, MA, USA, 2016.

26. Dougherty, J., Kohavi, R., Sahami, M., Supervised and unsupervised discretization of continuous features, in: *Proceedings of the Twelfth International Conference on Machine Learning*, pp. 194–202, Tahoe City, California, 1995.

27. Rossetti, M., Stella, F., Zanker, M., Towards explaining latent factors with topic models in collaborative recommender systems, in: *Proceedings of the 24th International Workshop on Database and Expert Systems Applications (DEXA'13)*, pp. 162–167, IEEE, Prague, Czech Republic, Prague, Czech Republic, 2013.

28. Jin, X., Zhou, Y., Mobasher, B., A maximum entropy web recommendation system: Combining collaborative and content features, in: *Proceedings of the*

eleventh ACM SIGKDD international conference on Knowledge discovery in data mining (KDD '05), pp. 612–617, ACM, Chicago, Illinois, USA, 2005.

29. Hair, J.F., Jr., Babin, B.J., Krey, N., Covariance-based structural equation modelling in the Journal of Advertising: Review and recommendations. *J. Advert.*, 46, 1, 163–177, 2017.

30. Herlocker, J., Konstan, J.A., Riedl, J., An empirical analysis of design choices in neighborhood-based collaborative filtering algorithms. *Inform. Retrieval*, 5, 4, 287–310, 2002.

31. Deep, K.S., Griffith, C.H., Wilson, J.F., Communication and decision making about life-sustaining treatment: Examining the experiences of resident physicians and seriously-ill hospitalized patients. *J. Gen. Intern. Med.*, 23, 11, 1877–1882, 2008.

32. Pazzani, M.J. and Billsus, D., Content-based recommendation systems, in: *The Adaptive Web*, pp. 325–341, Springer-Verlag Berlin, Heidelberg, 2007.

33. Sadasivam, R.S., Cutrona, S.L., Kinney, R.L., Marlin, B.M., Mazor, K.M., Lemon, S.C., Houston, T.K., Collective intelligence recommender systems: Advancing computer tailoring for health behaviour change into the 21st century. *J. Med. Internet Res.*, 18, 3, e42, 2016.

34. Pattaraintakorn, P., Zaverucha, G.M., Cercone, N., Web based health recommender system using rough sets, survival analysis and rule-based expert systems, in: *Proceedings of 11th International Workshop on Rough Sets, Fuzzy Sets, Data Mining, and Granular-Soft Computing (RSFDGrC 2007)*, pp. 491–499, Toronto, Canada, 2007.

35. Husain, W. and Pheng, L.T., The development of personalized wellness therapy recommender system using hybrid case-based reasoning, in: *Proceedings of 2nd International Conference on Computer Technology and Development (ICCTD 2010)*, IEEE, pp. 85–89, Cairo, Egypt, 2010.

36. Kim, J.-H., Lee, J.-H., Park, J.-S., Lee, Y.-H., Rim, K.-W., Design of diet recommendation system for healthcare service based on user information, in: *Proceedings of Fourth International Conference on Computer Sciences and Convergence Information Technology (ICCIT 2009)*, pp. 516–518, IEEE, Seoul, Korea, 2009.

37. Holzinger, A., Interactive machine learning for health informatics: when do we need the human-in-the-loop? *Brain Inform.*, 3, 2, 119–131, 2016.

38. Holzinger, A., Valdez, A.C., Ziefle, M., Towards interactive recommender systems with the doctor-in-the-loop. *Mensch und Computer 2016 – Workshopband*, pp. 1–9, 2013.

39. Yang, S., Zhou, P., Duan, K., Shamim Hossain, M., Alhamid, M.F., emHealth: Towards emotion health through depression prediction and intelligent health recommender system. *Mobile Netw. Appl.*, 23, 2, 216–226, 2018.

40. Bradley, K., Rafter, R., Smyth, B., Case-based user profiling for content personalisation, in: *Proceedings of International Conference on Adaptive Hypermedia and Adaptive Web-Based Systems*, pp. 62–72, Trento, Italy, 2000.

41. Suchal, J. and Navrat, P., Full text search engine as scalable k-nearest neighbor recommendation system, in: *Proceedings of International Conference on Artificial Intelligence in Theory and Practice (IFIP AI)*, Brisbane, QLD, Australia, pp. 165–173, 2010.
42. Sanchez-Bocanegra, C.L., Sanchez-Laguna, F., Sevillano, J.L., Introduction on health recommender systems, in: *Data Mining in Clinical Medicine*, pp. 131–146, Springer, Humana Press, New York, NY, 2015.
43. Isinkaye, F.O., Folajimi, Y.O., Ojokoh, B.A., Recommendation systems: Principles, methods and evaluation. *Egypt. Inform. J.*, 16, 3, 261–273, 2015.
44. Basu, C., Hirsh, H., Cohen, W., Recommendation as Classification: Using Social and Content-Based Information in Recommendation, in: *Technical Report of the Association for the Advancement of Artificial Intelligence (AAAI)*, pp. 714–720, 1998.
45. Cremonesi, P., Garzotto, F., Negro, S., Papadopoulos, A.V., Turrin, R., Looking for good recommendations: A comparative evaluation of recommender systems, in: *Proceedings of Human-Computer Interaction (INTERACT 2011)*, pp. 152–168, Springer, Berlin, Heidelberg, 2011.
46. Melville, P., Mooney, R.J., Nagarajan, R., Content-boosted collaborative filtering for improved recommendations, in: *Proceedings of the 18th National Conference on Artificial Intelligence (AAAI-2002)*, vol. 23, pp. 187–192, 2002.
47. Ronen, R., Koenigstein, N., Ziklik, E., Nice, N., Selecting Content-based Features for Collaborative Filtering Recommenders, in: *Proceedings of the 7th ACM Conference on Recommender Systems (RecSys'13)*, ACM, New York, NY, USA, pp. 407–410, 2013.
48. Rana, S.P., Dey, M., Siarry, P., Boosting content based image retrieval performance through integration of parametric & nonparametric approaches. *J. Vis. Commun. Image R.*, 58, 205–219, 2019.
49. Steck, H., van Zwol, R., Johnson, C., Interactive Recommender Systems: Tutorial, in: *Proceedings of the 9th ACM Conference on Recommender Systems (RecSys '15)*, ACM, New York, NY, USA, pp. 359–360, 2015.
50. Wang, C., Zheng, Y., Jiang, J., Ren, K., Toward Privacy-Preserving Personalized Recommendation Services. *Engineering*, 4, 1, 21–28, 2018.
51. Lam, S. K. "Tony", Frankowski, D., Riedl, J., Do You Trust Your Recommendations? An Exploration of Security and Privacy Issues in Recommender Systems, in: *Emerging Trends in Information and Communication Security*, G. Muller (Ed.), pp. 14–29, Springer, Berlin Heidelberg, 2006.

12

Context-Based Social Media Recommendation System

R. Sujithra Kanmani* and B. Surendiran

*Department of Computer Science and Engineering, NIT Puducherry,
Karaikal, India*

Abstract

Context-based recommender system is the current trend incorporated in mobile devices. It provides the user their timely needs by considering the current location of the user in an effective manner. Location-based recommendation has three major services such as Geo-tagged media based services, Point location based services and Trajectory based services. In geo-tagged media-based services social media data such as photos, tags posted by the user are considered widely for providing recommendation. Geo-tagged data has an important role to play in Twitter, Instagram and Flickr dataset. Geo-tagged data has its wide range of applications in the field of Tourism, Smart traffic management, guidelines for roads, safety and health monitoring, etc. Thus the proposed work considers the context attributes along with the services provided by the social media for achieving better recommendation.

Keywords: Context, social media, geo-tagged, point location, trajectory, Flickr

12.1 Introduction

In recent times, travel-based recommendation is in ease with the use of smart phones. As there is abundance of information available, it is necessary to overcome the irrelevance issue. To provide solution to that problem location-based recommender system can be used. As it considers the geographical co-ordinates of the user and provides the recommendation

---

Corresponding author: sujithrakanmani@gmail.com

Sachi Nandan Mohanty, Jyotir Moy Chatterjee, Sarika Jain, Ahmed A. Elngar and Priya Gupta (eds.)
Recommender System with Machine Learning and Artificial Intelligence: Practical Tools and Applications in Medical, Agricultural and Other Industries, (237–250) © 2020 Scrivener Publishing LLC

based on the context attributes of the user such as spatial and temporal information. There are three major services provided by the Location-Based Recommendation System (LBRS) and they are as follows in the Figure 12.1.

Geo-tagged based services involves the usage of geo-tagged data which considers the spatial and temporal co-ordinates of the user. This data can be collected form twitter as it includes the posts, user tweets involving the current user's place. Since social networks consist of the history of activity of the user, it can be used to make recommendations based on their content and context for similar users. Supervised learning framework using spatial and temporal features of the user from geo-tagged data can be used for further finding the category of a place with the involvement of Foursquare dataset [1]. User preference based recommendation can also be provided with the usage of Flickr and other contextual data [2].

Point-based services involves the usage of temporal feature of the user by overcoming the sparsity problem [3]. As with the help of current point location the behavior of the user can be predicted and by collecting the region of the user, recommendation can be made by considering the place and area of interest. With the usage of Foursquare and Gowalla dataset users' past check-ins and supporting information can be got to expedite Point of Interest-based recommendation [4]. Consideration of temporal matching between users and Point of Interest provides better accuracy in recommendation [5].

Trajectory based services involves the usage of travel routes and movement history for recommendation. This type of service can be used in finding the correlation between the successive check-ins and helps in providing group recommendation.

Similar user preference is also very useful in making effective recommendations. Collaborative filtering can be implemented to solve the

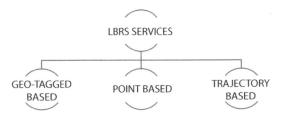

Figure 12.1 Location-Based Recommendation System (LBRS) services.

problem of information overload. Through offering useful tips to different users, it saves user time [6]. Collaborative filtering is one of the effective approaches in the recommendation system.

The similarity calculation is a very useful step done in case of recommender systems. The similarity calculation can be done upon item to user and user to item. After the computation of similarity the user or item having similar value of computation can be recommended with the items to the similar tasted user. The selection of similarity metric varies according to the need of the user. To find the linear correlation between two vectors Pearson correlation similarity measure is being used. Cosine similarity determines the relationship between two vectors using cosine angle calculation among these vector. Jaccard's similarity calculation also takes into account the number of items shared by two users rather than the ratings, meaning the more co-rated items, the more similar [12]. In Spearman Rank correlation nearest possible interesting locations are identified and recommended to the new users, depending on the geo-location of the user. It is achieved by measuring the Euclidean distance between the position coordinates using the k-Nearest Neighbor (k-NN). High cohort ratings consideration can also be made for providing better recommendation [7]. Thus the travel can be made smoother with the help of this recommendation technique.

The proposed work's contribution are listed as follows.

- Analyzing the presents location of the user collected from geo-tagged data
- User Attribute profiling is done by considering the important user attributes
- Providing similar user preference with the use of collaborative filtering
- Similarity computation is done for providing preference based results.
- Considering possible travel routes and recommending nearest location to the user with the use of Euclidean distance.

This proposed research can therefore be developed into a tourism-focused recommendation system, considering current location of the user obtained from Twitter data, identifying similar user preferences through cooperative filtering, measuring user similarities, considering possible routes and recommending the nearest POI. Section 2 deliberates the survey of related works. Section 3 which offers motivation and objectives of the work proposed.

Section 4 delivers the details about the work proposed. Section 5 discusses the implementation details. Section 6 deliberates the Performance measures. Section 7 discusses the evaluation results and the paper is concluded in Section 8 with the future work to be considered.

12.2   Literature Survey

Cai, Lee, & Lee [8] proposed a recommendation system by considering the semantic trajectory pattern of other user's sequences and preferences using Semantic trajectory pattern mining algorithm. This system uses Flickr dataset and helps in travel based recommendation.

Wang *et al.* [4] proposed a method on modelling users' past check-ins and supporting information to facilitate POI recommendation. It used Multinomial distribution technique for providing recommendation and it used Foursquare and Gowalla dataset.

Liao *et al.* [3] proposed a user-conscious topic choice POI recommendation framework is used to overcome data sparsity by mining time. Latent Dirichlet Allocation topic model and Higher Order Singular Value Decomposition algorithm was used in the real time dataset for recommendation.

Zhu *et al.* [9] proposed POI recommendation system supporting heterogeneous context information. It used Context Graph Attention (CGA) Model for providing recommendation. The evaluation was done on Foursquare and Gowalla dataset.

Sun *et al.* [2] seek to determine the probability of frequent users. The travel experience of the client in the target version is used to scope the POI of the applicant. The proposed method ranks the personalized need of the user by incorporating friend's choice, user desire, location attraction, and social suggestions. The framework suggested tackles the issue of cold start problem in a better way.

Logesh, Subramaniyaswamy, Vijayakumar, & Li [10] proposed an Activity and Behavior-induced Personalized Recommender System as a hybrid approach to forecast credible POI recommendations. This system is helpful in providing users list of POI places as recommendation.

Vakeel *et al.* [11] proposed a new approach to exploit location-based social networks (LBSNs) collected check-in data with the goal of optimizing POI recommendations through customized explanations. The proposed algorithm produces the motivation profile of a user and it addresses its applicability by analyzing a dataset derived from a common LBSN.

12.3   Motivation and Objectives

The main objective of the paper is to develop an effective recommendation system that can overcome various issues prevailing in the recommender systems. The proposed system uses the user's location coordinates as a guideline to resolve the information sparsity problem in supplying the user's POI. The proposed work also provides recommendation by considering the geo-tagged data which enables recommendation of innovative items that are unknown to new users. Similar user preferences are identified using collaborative filtering and hence varied recommendations are being provided. Similarity computation is being calculated so that the recommendation provided is fully of user preferred recommendation. Based on the closest neighborhood strategy, the POI accessible on the travel routes is recommended and coincidence is discussed.

12.3.1   Architecture

Considering the user's current location, similar user attributes, user interests, and nearest common locations on the travel routes, the proposed system is recommended. The proposed system's architecture is shown in Figure 12.2 as stated below.

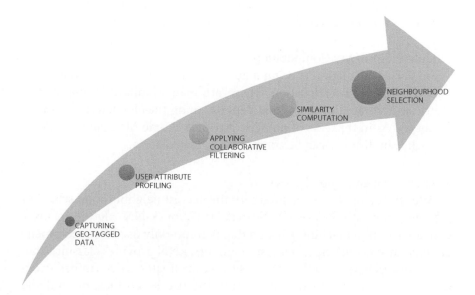

Figure 12.2 Proposed architecture.

12.3.2   Modules

Module 1: Capturing geo-tagged data

The current location of the user should be known in order to provide better advice to the client. This is done in such a way that it is possible to give advice by considering the available POI on the travel routes. The current location of the user is collected using geo-tagged information from twitter. Such data was obtained using the Twitter API. The latest geographic co-location will be given to geo-tagged data.

Module 2: User Attribute Profiling

After capturing the geo-tagged data user attributes like location co-ordinates, gender, mood etc. can be collected from the social media data. The user attribute profiling is done in this phase with the consideration of user data efficient recommendation can be provided.

Module 3: Applying Collaborative Filtering

Users with similar history of visits are marked and considered to be equivalent. This is achieved by finding the related users in the target user's position at different times. It is possible to collect the current position coordinates of the user from the geo-tagged information. The filtered similar users visit histories are made by using Collaborative Filtering technique. Prediction using these sequences makes it easier to identify POI and can therefore promote tourism by recommending it to the user.

Module 4: Similarity Computation

Similarity calculation is being made with the target user's current location and similar user location. There are many similarity computation metric and the application of that depends upon the characteristic of user attributes. As in this case of numeric attribute simple Manhattan distance or Euclidean distance can be considered for calculation.

Module 5: Neighborhood selection

After the computation of similarity the nearest neighborhood selection is being made with the use of k-Nearest Neighbor (k-NN) algorithm. kNN is an approach to machine learning that is commonly used for recommendations. By considering its closest neighbors, kNN provides classification. In our research, the length of the position coordinates is determined using the Euclidean equation by considering the user's geo-location and the nearest location is suggested using kNN classification results and the recommendation list is being suggested to the user.

12.3.3   Implementation Details

Using i3 processor with 4 GB RAM capability and Python language, the proposed system is implemented. It is possible to extract Twitter data, tweets and geo-location attributes using Tweepy. Tweepy is an open source library that allows Python to use its API to interact with Twitter. By knowing the geo-location, similar user's preferences are being provided by collaborative filtering. Therefore, improving the recommendation system is very useful as user preferences can be easily mined. The imported Python geopy library is used to collect and display the nearby POI on the travel routes. kNN is used to measure and indicate the nearest place. The Euclidean formula is used to calculate the distance between the coordinates of the position.

12.4   Performance Measures

In this paper, the accuracy can be considered as metrics for evaluating the system performance. The accuracy of the system is evaluated using the measures such as precision, recall and F-score as shown in the below Equations 1, 2 and 3.

12.5   Precision

It is the proportion of accurately prescribed things to add up to suggested things. It decides the portion of applicable things recovered out of all things recovered

$$Precision = \frac{Correctly recommended items}{Total recommended items} \qquad (1)$$

12.6   Recall

It is defined as the ration of properly recommended objects to recommended items of total use. It is a completeness index, which measures the proportion of relevant items from all relevant items.

$$Recall = \frac{Correctly recommended items}{Total useful recommended items} \qquad (2)$$

12.7   F- Measure

It is a single metric combination of Precision (P) and Recall (R). It is Precision's weighted Harmonic mean and recall.

$$F\text{-Measure} = \frac{2PR}{P+R} \tag{3}$$

12.8   Evaluation Results

The geo-tagged data can be collected from various social media and in this work we have collected the data from Twitter as shown below in the Figure 12.3.

It is being converted to csv from json format for further extraction and the user attribute profiling stage can be applied here by taking the selected user attributes in the geo-tagged data. In this work we are taking the user location attribute and by considering that the recommendation is being provided as shown in Table 12.1.

The user preference is being collected from their past histories and current location. It is being compared with the similar users available and the location preferences to be visited are listed. In this work nearby restaurants in the place of New Delhi from a particular user location are listed as shown in the below Figure 12.4.

The similarity computation among the location co-ordinates of the users can be calculated by means of numeric distance computation as shown in the below Figure 12.5.

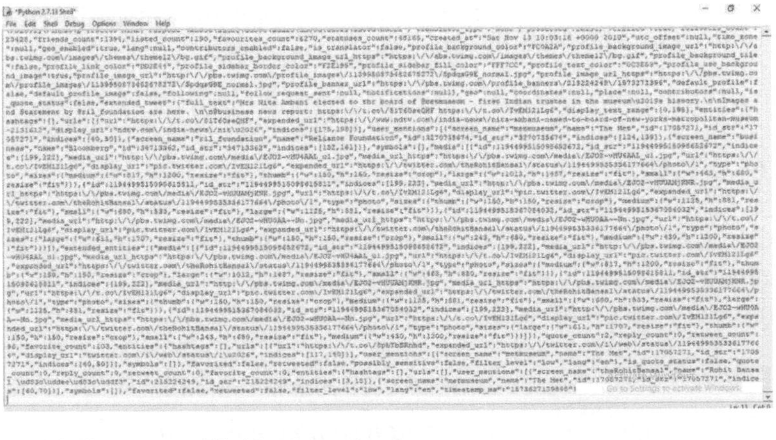

Figure 12.3 Extraction of Twitter streaming data.

Table 12.1 User profiling.

user_id	created_at	user_name	user_location	tweet_text	language
8.928E+44	Tue Aug 23 04:44:04 +0000 2017	ðŸ‡³ðŸ‡¬ Meister ðŸ‡³ðŸ‡¬	Metro Philadelphia	Five advanced Google Chrome hacks to level up your browsing—Popular Science https://t.co/E6l9ugydMO	en
8.964E+11	Tue Aug 10 06:23:06 +0000 2017	Musicâ	Worldwide	#dance #single Controlwerk—Expectations https://t.co/rRdR7i4sFh https://t.co/IdSnxOn4fj	fr
8.975E+23	Tue Aug 13 07:34:12 +0000 2017	diego martone	Lethbridge, Alberta	Aloysiusâ€™ forgotten Apple Password: Commission says use memory or deal with implications: https://t.co/8owKsRZdFZâ€¦ https://t.co/iaHVjyMGT8	en
8.983E+67	Wed Aug 26 02:44:10 +0000 2017	MAMIYï£¿	é•à´Žà¸à¸Šç¿	RT @dunkirkjp: ã„à¸ã¯ã€à¸ #ãƒ€ãƒ³ã±à¸ƒ«ã¯ã€à¸‚ã€â€°à¸ã ®è¸±à¸‡ºî°¼ ã€±à¸ã¡ºî°ï¼	ja

(*Continued*)

Table 12.1 User profiling. (*Continued*)

user_id	created_at	user_name	user_location	tweet_text	language
9.182E+13	Fri Sep 01 03:34:12 +0000 2017	Bonita applebum	Eliktitis	Rumor: 4K Apple TV in development with UHD iTunes movies https://t.co/ LQ0VJQz16B	en
9.454E+78	Mon Oct 24 05:44:13 +0000 2017	NINA	New Delhi, India	Dibuat menggunakan Photo Grid.	in
9.722E+17	Thu Dec 31 05:24:11 +0000 2017	é©¬æ ¥è¥¿å°ºä	Malaysia, Kuala Lumpur	RT @amuaznorman: Kepada penggemar Big Apple Malaysia ðŸ˜ https://t.co/JDwg3LE3W2	zh

```
Python 2.7.13 Shell
File  Edit  Shell  Debug  Options  Window  Help
Python 2.7.13 (v2.7.13:a06454b1afa1, Dec 17 2016, 20:42:59) [MSC v.1500 32 bit (Intel)] on win32
Type "copyright", "credits" or "license()" for more information.
>>>
================ RESTART: E:\project1\data\finalneraby.py ================
user_location
New Delhi, India

Warning (from warnings module):
  File "E:\project1\data\finalnerby.py", line 36
    radius=20000, types=[types.TYPE_FOOD])
DeprecationWarning: The query API is deprecated. Please use nearby_search.
Navandas Fine Dine Restaurant

(u'lat': Decimal('28.602606'), u'lng': Decimal('77.240848'))

Kalpak

(u'lat': Decimal('28.570293'), u'lng': Decimal('77.36223749999999'))

Kasturi Family Restaurant

(u'lat': Decimal('28.608871'), u'lng': Decimal('77.29251599999999'))

Tee Dee Tibetan Restaurant

(u'lat': Decimal('28.7019118'), u'lng': Decimal('77.23847399999999'))

Sakura Restaurant

(u'lat': Decimal('28.6327426'), u'lng': Decimal('77.2195969'))

New Kamal Restaurant

(u'lat': Decimal('28.5335862'), u'lng': Decimal('77.2313096'))

Hot Yak Restaurant

(u'lat': Decimal('28.7036934'), u'lng': Decimal('77.2287463'))

MOC The American Restaurant

(u'lat': Decimal('28.611117'), u'lng': Decimal('77.3357'))
```

Figure 12.4 Recommendation of POI to users.

Figure 12.5 Similarity computation among users.

After the computation of similarity the nearest neighborhood selection is being made with the use of k-Nearest Neighbor (k-NN) algorithm. K-NN is an approach to machine learning that is commonly used for recommendations and location is being suggested as shown in the below Figure 12.6.

12.9   Conclusion and Future Work

The proposed work discusses the services provided by the Location-based recommendation system and its usage in travel based recommendation. It provides recommendations regarding geo-tagged data, similar user

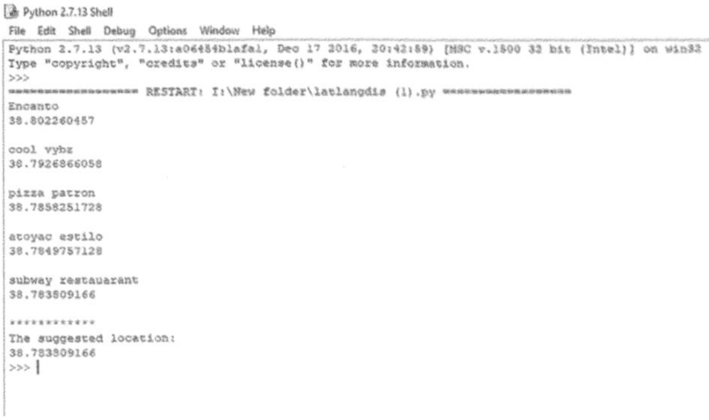

Figure 12.6 Neighborhood selection.

preferences, POI available on travel routes through collaborative filtering, similarity computing and selection of neighborhoods. The proposed system has been implemented and evaluation can be carried out using various performance measures such as precision, recall and F-score. Future work is to consider the recommendation of items that are common in different POIs and increase the selection of products so that more items from potential items are recommended.

References

1. Comito, C., Falcone, D., Talia, D., Mining human mobility patterns from social geo-tagged data. *Pervasive Mob. Comput.*, 33, 91–107, 2016. https://doi.org/10.1016/j.pmcj.2016.06.005.
2. Sun, X., Huang, Z., Peng, X., Chen, Y., Liu, Y., Building a model-based personalised recommendation approach for tourist attractions from geotagged social media data. *Int. J. Dig. Earth*, 12, 6, 661–678, 2019. https://doi.org/10.1080/17538947.2018.1471104.
3. Liao, G., Jiang, S., Zhou, Z., Wan, C., Liu, X., POI recommendation of location-based social networks using tensor factorization. *Proceedings—IEEE International Conference on Mobile Data Management*, 2018-June, pp. 116–124, 2018, https://doi.org/10.1109/MDM.2018.00028.
4. Wang, H., Ouyang, W., Shen, H., Cheng, X., ULE: Learning user and location embeddings for POI recommendation. *Proceedings—2018 IEEE 3rd International Conference on Data Science in Cyberspace*, pp. DSC 2018, 99–106, 2018, https://doi.org/10.1109/DSC.2018.00023.
5. Yao, Z., Exploiting human mobility patterns for point-of-interest recommendation. *WSDM 2018—Proceedings of the 11th ACM International Conference*

on Web Search and Data Mining, 2018-February, pp. 757–758, 2018, https://doi.org/10.1145/3159652.3170459.

6. Ravi, L., Subramaniyaswamy, V., Vijayakumar, V., Chen, S., Karmel, A., Devarajan, M., Hybrid Location-based Recommender System for Mobility and Travel Planning. *Mobile Netw. Appl.*, 24, 1226–1239, 2019. https://doi.org/10.1007/s11036-019-01260-4.

7. Dhanalakshmi, R. and Sinha, B.B., Hybrid Cohort Rating Prediction Technique to leverage Recommender System. *J. Sci. Ind. Res.* 78, 411–414, 2019.

8. Cai, G., Lee, K., Lee, I., Itinerary recommender system with semantic trajectory pattern mining from geo-tagged photos. *Expert Syst. Appl.*, 94, 32–40, 2018. https://doi.org/10.1016/j.eswa.2017.10.049.

9. Zhu, Q., Wang, S., Cheng, B., Sun, Q., Yang, F., Chang, R.N., Context-aware group recommendation for point-of-interests. *IEEE Access*, 6, 12129–12144, 2018. https://doi.org/10.1109/ACCESS.2018.2805701.

10. Logesh, R., Subramaniyaswamy, V., Vijayakumar, V., Li, X., Efficient User Profiling Based Intelligent Travel Recommender System for Individual and Group of Users. *Mobile Netw. Appl.*, 24, 3, 1018–1033, 2019. https://doi.org/10.1007/s11036-018-1059-2.

11. Vakeel, K.A. and Ray, S., Points of Interest Recommendations Based on Check-In Motivations. *Tour. Anal.*, 24, 2, 147–159, 2019.

12. Feng, J., Fengs, X., Zhang, N., An improved Collaborative filtering method based on similarity. *Plos One*, 13, 9, 1–18, 2018. https://doi.org/10.1371/journal.pone.0204003

## 13

Netflix Challenge—Improving Movie Recommendations

Vasu Goel

Computer Science and Engineering, SRM University, Delhi-NCR Campus, India

Abstract

This analysis is based on the challenge that Netflix offered to the data science community. The challenge was to improve Netflix's movie recommendation system by 10% [9]. The objective of this analysis is to train multiple machine learning models using inputs from one data set to predict movie ratings in another data set.

Keywords: Movie effect model, user effect model, residual mean square error (RMSE), naive approach, predicted rating, regularization

13.1 Introduction

The Netflix movie rating scheme uses a rating range from 0 to 5. The data set from which the two sets mentioned previously will be created can be found using the following link: http://files.grouplens.org/datasets/movielens/ml-10m.zip. Recommendation systems use ratings that users have given items to make specific recommendations [13]. Companies that sell many products to many customers and permit these customers to rate their products, like Amazon, are able to collect massive datasets that can be used to predict what rating a particular user will give a specific item. Items for which a high rating is predicted for a given user are then recommended to that user. Netflix uses a recommendation system to predict how many stars a user will give a specific movie. Based on the predictions, the movie with the highest predicted rating for a user is then recommended to the user. Although predicting ratings seems easy, there are many different biases in the movie ratings [7]. Many

---

Email: contact@vasugoel.com

Sachi Nandan Mohanty, Jyotir Moy Chatterjee, Sarika Jain, Ahmed A. Elngar and Priya Gupta (eds.) *Recommender System with Machine Learning and Artificial Intelligence: Practical Tools and Applications in Medical, Agricultural and Other Industries*, (251–268) © 2020 Scrivener Publishing LLC

users prefer different genres than others, some only rate the movies they liked and others only the movies they disliked. In addition, many movies get a great review most of the time. These biases can be taken into consideration using various machine learning models. The Netflix challenge used the typical error loss: they decided on a winner based on the residual mean squared error (RMSE) on a test set [3]. To provide satisfying results many different models were trained for this analysis (performed using R programming language) [6, 15] and the best model was chosen based on the RMSE on the validation set.

13.2   Data Preprocessing

a) Getting and Cleaning Data
First step in any data analysis project is to get the data. The Netflix data is not publicly available, but the GroupLens research lab generated their own database with over 20 million ratings for over 27,000 movies by more than 138,000 users. In this analysis, a smaller subset of about 10 million ratings was used. We can download the 10M version of MovieLens dataset [10] used in the analysis using this code:

```
# Note: this process could take a couple of minutes
if(!require(tidyverse))
        install.packages("tidyverse", repos = "http://
        cran.us.r-project.org")
if(!require(caret))
        install.packages("caret", repos = "http://cran.
        us.r-project.org")
if(!require(data.table))
        install.packages("data.table", repos = "http://
        cran.us.r-project.org")
# MovieLens 10M dataset:
# https://grouplens.org/datasets/movielens/10m/
# http://files.grouplens.org/datasets/movielens/ml-10m.zip
dl <- tempfile()
download.file("http://files.grouplens.org/datasets/
movielens/ml-10m.zip", dl)
ratings <- fread(text = gsub("::", "\t",
readLines(unzip(dl, "ml-10M100K/ratings.dat"))),
        col.names = c("userId", "movieId", "rating",
        "timestamp"))
```

```
movies <- str_split_fixed(readLines(unzip(dl,
"ml-10M100K/movies.dat")), "\\::", 3)
colnames(movies) <- c("movieId", "title", "genres")
movies <- as.data.frame(movies) %>% mutate(movieId =
as.numeric(levels(movieId))[movieId],
              title = as.character(title),
              genres = as.character(genres))
movielens <- left_join(ratings, movies, by = "movieId")
```

b) Create Train and Validation Sets

Use the following code to generate the datasets. The algorithm was developed using the *train* set. For a final test of the algorithm we predict movie ratings in the *validation* set as if they were unknown.

```
# Validation set will be 10% of MovieLens data
set.seed(1, sample.kind="Rounding")
# if using R 3.5 or earlier, use `set.seed(1)` instead
test_index <- createDataPartition(y = movielens$rating,
times = 1, p = 0.1, list = FALSE)
train <- movielens[-test_index,]
temp <- movielens[test_index,]
# Make sure userId and movieId in validation set are
also in train set
validation <- temp %>%
        semi_join(train, by = "movieId") %>%
        semi_join(train, by = "userId")
# Add rows removed from validation set back into train
set
removed <- anti_join(temp, validation)
train <- rbind(train, removed)
rm(dl, ratings, movies, test_index, temp, movielens,
removed)
```

13.3   MovieLens Data

MovieLens dataset initially had 10 million ratings (rows) with 6 variables (columns) which were partitioned into *train* and *validation* sets containing ~9M and ~1M ratings respectively.

We can see the sets are in tidy format:

```
train %>% as_tibble()
## # A tibble: 9,000,055 x 6
##  userId movieId rating timestamp title    genres
##  <int>  <dbl>  <dbl>   <int> <chr>         <chr>
## 1  1  122  5 838985046 Boomerang (1992)
Comedy|Romance
## 2  1  185  5 838983525 Net, The (1995)
Action|Crime|Thrill...
## 3  1  292  5 838983421 Outbreak (1995)
Action|Drama|Sci-Fi...
## 4  1  316  5 838983392 Stargate (1994)
Action|Adventure|Sc...
## 5  1  329  5 838983392 Star Trek: Generat...
Action|Adventure|Dr...
## 6  1  355  5 838984474 Flintstones, The (...
Children|Comedy|Fan...
## 7  1  356  5 838983653 Forrest Gump (1994)
Comedy|Drama|Romanc...
## 8  1  362  5 838984885 Jungle Book, The (...
Adventure|Children|...
## 9  1  364  5 838983707 Lion King, The (19...
Adventure|Animation...
## 10 1  370  5 838984596 Naked Gun 33 1/3: ...
Action|Comedy
## # ... with 9,000,045 more rows
validation %>% as_tibble()
## # A tibble: 999,999 x 6
##  userId movieId rating  timestamp title  genres
##  <int>  <dbl>  <dbl>   <int> <chr>         <chr>
## 1  1  231  5 838983392 Dumb & Dumber (1994)  Comedy
## 2  1  480  5 838983653 Jurassic Park (1993)
Action|Adventure...
## 3  1  586  5 838984068 Home Alone (1990)
Children|Comedy
## 4  2  151  3 868246450 Rob Roy (1995)
Action|Drama|Rom...
## 5  2  858  2 868245645 Godfather, The (1972)
Crime|Drama
```

```
## 6    2   1544   3 868245920 Lost World: Jurassic...
Action|Adventure...
## 7    3    590   3.5 1136075494 Dances with Wolves (...
Adventure|Drama|...
## 8    3   4995   4.5 1133571200 Beautiful Mind, A (2...
Drama|Mystery|Ro...
## 9    4    34   5 844416936 Babe (1995)  Children|Comedy|...
## 10   4    432   3 844417070 City Slickers II: Th...
Adventure|Comedy...
## # ... with 999,989 more rows
```

13.4   Data Exploration

Each row represents a rating given by one user to one movie. We can see the number of unique users that provided ratings and how many unique movies were rated in the *train* set:

```
train %>%
    summarize(n_users = n_distinct(userId),
    n_movies = n_distinct(movieId))
##    n_users    n_movies
## 1   69878      10677
```

If we multiply those two numbers we get a number much larger than 10M which means that not all users rated all movies. We can therefore think of this data as a sparse matrix with user u in rows and movie i in columns.

You can think of the task of a recommendation system as filling in those missing values. To see how sparse the matrix is, Figure 13.1 shows a matrix for a random sample of 100 movies and 100 users with yellow indicating a user/movie combination for which we have a rating.

```
users <- sample(unique(train$userId), 100)
train %>% filter(userId %in% users) %>%
    select(userId, movieId, rating) %>%
    mutate(rating = 1) %>%
    spread(movieId, rating) %>%
    select(sample(ncol(.), 100)) %>%
    as.matrix() %>% t(.) %>%
    image(1:100, 1:100,. , xlab="Movies", ylab="Users")
abline(h=0:100+0.5, v=0:100+0.5, col = "grey")
```

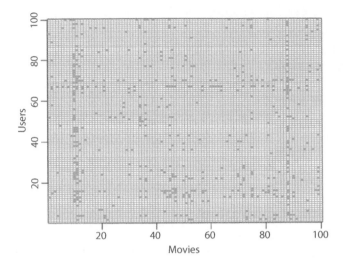

Figure 13.1 Matrix for a random sample of 100 movies and 100 users.

Note that if we are predicting the rating for movie i by user u, in principle, all other ratings related to movie i and by user u may be used as predictors, but different users rate different movies and a different number of movies. Furthermore, we may be able to use information from other movies that we have determined are similar to movie i or from users determined to be similar to user u. In essence, the entire matrix can be used as predictors for each cell [1].

13.5 Distributions

Let's look at some of the general properties of the data to better understand the challenges.

The first thing we notice is that some movies get rated more than others. Figure 13.2 shows this distribution.

```
train %>%
    dplyr::count(movieId) %>%
    ggplot(aes(n)) +
    geom_histogram(bins = 30, color = "black") +
    scale_x_log10() +
    ggtitle("Movies")
```

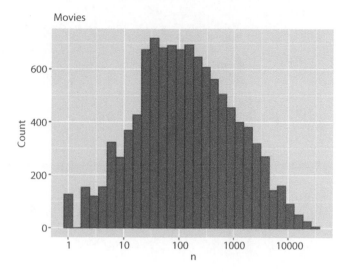

Figure 13.2 Distribution of movie ratings.

This should not surprise us given that there are blockbuster movies watched by millions and artsy, independent movies watched by just a few [5].

Our second observation is that some users are more active than others at rating movies. The distribution in Figure 13.3 confirms this trend.

```
train %>%
    dplyr::count(userId) %>%
    ggplot(aes(n)) +
    geom_histogram(bins = 30, color = "black") +
    scale_x_log10() +
    ggtitle("Users")
```

13.6   Data Analysis

Loss Function

We use residual mean squared error (*RMSE*) [2] as the metric to determine how good our algorithm performed. If we define $y_{u,i}$ as the rating for movie i by user u and denote out prediction with $\hat{y}_{u,i}$. The *RMSE* is then defined as:

$$RMSE = \sqrt{\frac{1}{N} \sum_{u,i} \left(\hat{y}_{u,i} - y_{u,i} \right)^2}$$

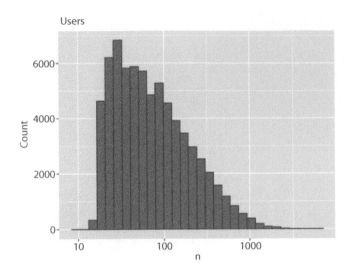

Figure 13.3 Distribution of users.

with N being the number of user/movie combinations and the sum occurring over all these combinations.

The *RMSE* can be interpreted similar to standard deviation: it is the typical error we make when predicting a movie rating [8]. If this number is larger than 1, it means our typical error is larger than one star, which is not good.

Let's write a function that computes the *RMSE* for vectors of ratings and their corresponding predictors:

```
RMSE <- function(true_ratings, predicted_ratings){
        sqrt(mean((true_ratings - predicted_ratings)^2))
}
```

a) First model: Naive approach
Let's start by building the simplest possible recommendation system: we predict the same rating for all movies regardless of user. What number should this prediction be? We can use a model-based approach [4] to answer this. A model that assumes the same rating for all movies and users with all the differences explained by random variation would look like this:

$$Y_{u,i} = \mu + \epsilon_{u,i}$$

with $\epsilon_{u,i}$ independent errors sampled from the same distribution centered at 0 and μ the "true" rating for all movies. We know that the estimate that minimizes the *RMSE* is the least squares estimate of μ and, in this case, is the average of all ratings:

```
mu_hat <- mean(train$rating)
mu_hat
## [1] 3.512465
```

If we predict all unknown ratings with $\hat{\mu}$ we obtain the following RMSE:

```
naive_rmse <- RMSE(validation$rating, mu_hat)
naive_rmse
## [1] 1.061202
```

As we go along, we will be comparing different approaches [14]. Let's start by creating a results table, Table 13.1 with this naive approach:

```
rmse_results <- data.frame(method = "Naive approach",
RMSE = naive_rmse)
rmse_results %>% knitr::kable()
```

b) Second model: Modeling movie effects
We know from experience that some movies are just generally rated higher than others. This intuition, that different movies are rated differently, is confirmed by data. We can augment our previous model by adding the term b_i to represent average ranking for movie i:

$$Y_{u,i} = \mu + b_i + \epsilon_{u,i}$$

These b_i are referred to as effects or bias [7], thus the b notation. We know that the least square estimate b_i is just the average of $Y_{u,i} - \hat{\mu}$ for each movie i. We can compute them as follows:

```
mu <- mean(train$rating)
movie_avgs <- train %>%
            group_by(movieId) %>%
            summarize(b_i = mean(rating - mu))
```

Table 13.1 RMSE with Naive approach.

Method	RMSE
Naive approach	1.0612018

We can see from Figure 13.4 that these estimates vary substantially:

```
movie_avgs %>% qplot(b_i, geom ="histogram", bins =
10, data = ., color = I("black"))
```

Table 13.2 shows how much our prediction improves once we use $\widehat{y}_{u,i} = \hat{\mu} + \widehat{b_l}$:

```
# calculate predictions considering movie effect
predicted_ratings <- mu + validation %>%
            left_join(movie_avgs, by='movieId') %>%
            pull(b_i)
# calculate rmse after modelling movie effect
model_1_rmse <- RMSE(predicted_ratings,
validation$rating)
rmse_results <- bind_rows(rmse_results,
            data_frame(method="Movie effect model",
                RMSE = model_1_rmse))
rmse_results %>% knitr::kable()
```

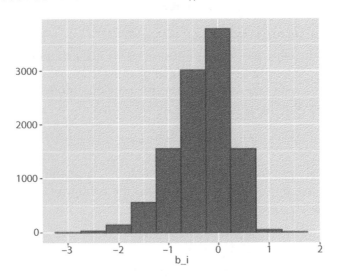

Figure 13.4 Movies Bias—Distribution of estimates b_i.

Table 13.2 RMSE with movie effects model.

Method	RMSE
Naive approach	1.0612018
Movie effects model	0.9439087

c) Third model: Modeling user effects

Let's compute the average rating for user u for those that have rated over 100 movies:

```
train %>% group_by(userId) %>%
       summarize(b_u = mean(rating)) %>%
       filter(n() >= 100) %>%
       ggplot(aes(b_u)) +
       geom_histogram(bins = 30, color = "black")
```

Notice in Figure 13.5 that there is substantial variability across users as well: some users are very cranky and others love every movie. This implies that a further improvement to our model may be:

$$Y_{u,i} = \mu + b_i + b_u + \epsilon_{u,i}$$

where b_u is a user-specific effect. Now if a cranky user (negative b_u) rates a great movie (positive b_i), the effects counter each other and we may be able to correctly predict that this user gave this great movie a 3 rather than a 5 [1]. We will compute an approximation by computing $\hat{\mu}$ and $\hat{b_i}$ and estimating $\hat{b_u}$ as the average of $y_{u,i} - \hat{\mu} - \hat{b_i}$:

```
user_avgs <- train %>%
       left_join(movie_avgs, by='movieId') %>%
       group_by(userId) %>%
       summarize(b_u = mean(rating - mu - b_i))
```

We can now perform inferences and see how much the RMSE improves in Table 13.3:

```
# calculate predictions considering user effects in
previous model
predicted_ratings <- validation %>%
       left_join(movie_avgs, by='movieId') %>%
       left_join(user_avgs, by='userId') %>%
       mutate(pred = mu + b_i + b_u) %>%
       pull(pred)
# calculate rmse after modelling user specific effect
in previous model
model_2_rmse <- RMSE(predicted_ratings,
validation$rating)
```

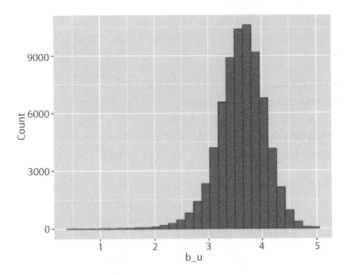

Figure 13.5 Users Bias—Distribution of estimates b_u.

```
rmse_results <- bind_rows(rmse_results,
      data_frame(method="Movie + User effects model",
          RMSE = model_2_rmse))
rmse_results %>% knitr::kable()
```

d) Fourth model: Regularizing movie and user effects

Regularization

The general idea behind regularization is to constrain the total variability of the effect sizes. Why does this help? Consider a case in which we have movie $i = 1$ with 100 user ratings and 4 movies $i = 2,3,4,5$ with just one user rating. We intend to fit the model:

$$Y_{u,i} = \mu + b_i + \varepsilon_{u,i}$$

Suppose we know the average rating is, say, $\mu = 3$. If we use least squares, the estimate for the first movie effect b_1 is the average of the 100 user ratings,

Table 13.3 RMSE with Movie + User effects model.

Method	RMSE
Naive approach	1.0612018
Movie effects model	0.9439087
Movie + User effects model	0.8653488

$1/100\sum_{i=1}^{100}\left(Y_{i,1}-\mu\right)$, which we expect to be a quite precise. However, the estimate for movies 2, 3, 4, and 5 will simply be the observed deviation from the average rating $\hat{b}_i = Y_{u,i} - \hat{\mu}$ which is an estimate based on just one number so it won't be precise at all [11]. Note these estimates make the error $Y_{u,i} - \mu + \hat{b}_i$ equal to 0 for $i = 2,3,4,5$, but this is a case of over-training. In fact, ignoring the one user and guessing that movies 2,3,4, and 5 are just average movies ($b_i = 0$) might provide a better prediction. The general idea of penalized regression is to control the total variability of the movie effects: $\sum_{i=1}^{5} b_i^2$. Specifically, instead of minimizing the least squares equation, we minimize an equation that adds a penalty:

$$\frac{1}{N}\sum_{u,i}\left(y_{u,i}-\mu-b_i\right)^2 + \lambda\sum_i b_i^2$$

The first term is just least squares and the second is a penalty that gets larger when many b_i are large. Using calculus, we can actually show that the values of b_i that minimize this equation are:

$$\hat{b}_i(\lambda) = \frac{1}{\lambda+n_i}\sum_{u=1}^{n_i}\left(Y_{u,i}-\hat{\mu}\right)$$

where n_i is the number of ratings made for movie i. This approach will have our desired effect: when our sample size n_i is very large, a case which will give us a stable estimate, then the penalty λ is effectively ignored since $n_i + \lambda \approx n_i$. However, when the n_i is small, then the estimate $\hat{b}_i(\lambda)$ is shrunken towards 0. The larger λ, the more we shrink.

Regularizing movie and user effects
We can use regularization for the estimate user effects [12] as well. We are minimizing:

$$\frac{1}{N}\sum_{u,i}\left(y_{u,i}-\mu-b_i-b_u\right)^2 + \lambda\left(\sum_i b_i^2 + \sum_u b_u^2\right)$$

Note that λ is a tuning parameter. We can use cross-validation to choose it. Figure 13.6 plots the optimal value of penalty term lambda, λ.

```
# choosing the penalty term lambda
lambdas <- seq(0, 10, 0.5)
rmses <- sapply(lambdas, function(l){
    mu <- mean(train$rating)
    b_i <- train %>%
    group_by(movieId) %>%
    summarize(b_i = sum(rating - mu)/(n()+1))
    b_u <- train %>%
    left_join(b_i, by="movieId") %>%
    group_by(userId) %>%
    summarize(b_u = sum(rating - b_i - mu)/(n()+1))
    predicted_ratings <-
      validation %>%
      left_join(b_i, by = "movieId") %>%
      left_join(b_u, by = "userId") %>%
      mutate(pred = mu + b_i + b_u) %>%
      pull(pred)
    return(RMSE(predicted_ratings, validation$rating))
})
qplot(lambdas, rmses)
```

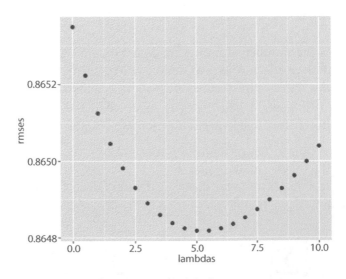

Figure 13.6 Optimal value of penalty term lambda, λ.

Table 13.4 RMSE with Regularized Movie + User effects model.

Method	RMSE
Naive approach	1.0612018
Movie effect model	0.9439087
Movie + User effects model	0.8653488
Regularized Movie + User effects model	0.8648177

For the full model, the optimal λ is:

```
lambda <- lambdas[which.min(rmses)]
lambda
## 5
```

So, $\lambda = 5$ is the penalty term that minimizes the RMSE, as shown in Table 13.4.

```
rmse_results <- bind_rows(rmse_results,data_
frame(method="Regularized Movie + User effect model",
RMSE = min(rmses)))
rmse_results %>% knitr::kable()
```

13.7   Results

We can inspect from Table 13.5, the RMSEs for the various models trained from naive approach (of predicting the mean rating regardless of the user) to regularized movie and user effects (by finding the optimal value of tuning parameter λ). The resultant RMSEs for various models discussed in this analysis are as follows:

Table 13.5 Results.

Method	RMSE
Naive approach	1.0612018
Movie effect model	0.9439087
Movie + User effects model	0.8653488
Regularized Movie + User effects model	0.8648177

As we see from the results each model is an improvement from the previous one with the last one having an RMSE lower than 0.8649. This is obviously a significant improvement from the first naive model. With the help of the last model our machine learning algorithm was able to predict movie ratings for the movies in validation set with an RMSE of about 0.8648201 i.e., we are within 0.8648201 of the "true" ratings.

13.8 Conclusion

The simplest model which predicts the same rating (mean rating) for all movies regardless of user gave an RMSE above 1. If RMSE is larger than 1, it means our typical error is larger than one star, which is not good. By taking into consideration the movie effect the RMSE went down to 0.9439087 which was a great improvement. RMSE further went down to 0.8653488 after modelling the user effect in the previous model. However, the lowest RMSE i.e., 0.8648201 was achieved by regularizing the movie and user effect, which penalized larger estimates of ratings from relatively small sample size of users.

Subsequently, regularizing the year and genres effects can further improve the residual mean squared error but regularizing the genres is computationally expensive since it requires separating multiple genres for many movies into separate observations for a given movie i having single genre in in each observation.

References

1. Bell, R.M. and Koren, Y., Lessons from the netflix prize challenge. *SiGKDD Explor.*, 9, 2, 75–79, 2007.
2. Chai, T. and Draxler, R.R., Root mean square error (RMSE) or mean absolute error (MAE)? *Geosci. Model. Dev.*, Discussions, 7, 1525–1534, 2014.
3. Chen, E., *Winning the netflix prize: A summary*, 2011, Retrieved from http://blog.echen.me/2011/10/24/winning-the-netflix-prize-a-summary.
4. Di Noia, T., Mirizzi, R., Ostuni, V.C., Romito, D., Exploiting the web of data in model-based recommender systems, in: *Proceedings of the sixth ACM conference on Recommender Systems*, pp. 253–256, 2012.
5. Feuerverger, A., He, Y., Khatri, S., Statistical significance of the Netflix challenge. *Stat. Sci.*, 27, 2, 202–231, 2012. Retrieved from www.jstor.org/stable/41714795.
6. Gorakala, S.K. and Usuelli, M., *Building a recommendation system with R.*, Packt Publishing Ltd, 2015.

7. Jannach, D., Lerche, L., Kamehkhosh, I., Jugovac, M., What recommenders recommend: an analysis of recommendation biases and possible counter-measures. *User Model. User Adap.*, 25, 5, 427–491, 2015.

8. Koren, Y., *The bellkor solution to the netflix grand prize*, 2009, Retrieved from https://www.netflixprize.com/assets/GrandPrize2009_BPC_BellKor.pdf.

9. Lohr, S., *Netflix awards $1 million prize and starts a new contest*, 2009, Retrieved from https://bits.blogs.nytimes.com/2009/09/21/netflix-awards-1-million-prize-and-starts-a-new-contest.

10. Miller, B.N., Albert, I., Lam, S.K., Konstan, J.A., Riedl, J., MovieLens unplugged: Experiences with an occasionally connected recommender system, in: *Proceedings of the 8th International Conference on Intelligent User Interfaces.*, ACM, pp. 263–266, 2003.

11. Park, K.W., Kim, B.H., Park, T.S., Zhang, B.T., Uncovering response biases in recommendation, in: *Workshops at the Twenty-Eighth AAAI Conference on Artificial Intelligence.*, AAAI Publications, 2014.

12. Rendle, S., Learning recommender systems with adaptive regularization, in: *Proceedings of the Fifth ACM International Conference on Web Search and Data Mining.*, ACM, pp. 133–142, 2012.

13. Resnick, P. and Varian, H.R., Recommender systems, in: *Commun. ACM*, vol. 40, pp. 56–59, Association for Computing Machinery, Inc, 1997.

14. Steck, H., Evaluation of recommendations: rating-prediction and ranking, in: *Proceedings of the 7th ACM conference on Recommender systems.*, ACM, pp. 213–220, 2013.

15. Team, R.C., *R: A language and environment for statistical computing.*, 2013, Retrieved from https://repo.bppt.go.id/cran/web/packages/dplR/vignettes/intro-dplR.pdf.

## 14

Product or Item-Based Recommender System

Jyoti Rani[1], Usha Mittal[2] and Geetika Gupta[1]*

[1]Department of Biotechnology, Thapar Institute of Engineering and Technology, Patiala, India
[2]Department of Computer Science and Engineering, Lovely Professional University, Phagwara, India

Abstract

Presently, most every tough task has been overtaken smoothly by machines in the name of intelligence/intellect/autonomous learning of computers from a given set of data. AI is being used on trial basis for a range of healthcare, entertainment, stock market and research purposes. It is widely used to make recommendations in different applications. Nowadays, users make their decisions by accessing the information on the internet. Before making any purchase, watch a movie, consult physicians, users check ratings about any particular event on internet. The item/product with high ratings is preferred by users. Even e-commerce sites have started taking feedback from customers after every transaction. Delivery service providers also demanding from customers to leave the rating after getting the product/service related to service. So, recommendation systems are becoming popular as it helps in increasing the sales of an organization. They provide recommendations based upon user's interest by considering previous purchase/interest from particular user or interested products or items by other users. The challenges in designing of these systems involved are lack of information, altering behavior and habits, etc.

In this chapter, different types of product/item-based recommendations systems as well as a food recommender system has been explained.

Keywords: Artificial intelligence, nutritional information, food sector

Corresponding author: geetika_12_gupta@yahoo.com

Sachi Nandan Mohanty, Jyotir Moy Chatterjee, Sarika Jain, Ahmed A. Elngar and Priya Gupta (eds.) *Recommender System with Machine Learning and Artificial Intelligence: Practical Tools and Applications in Medical, Agricultural and Other Industries*, (269–290) © 2020 Scrivener Publishing LLC

14.1   Introduction

Considering food the basic necessity of life either in human being or any other living form it's the mostly ignored need have been prevailing in the present busy hi-tech generation. As the life has become faster just like fast moving consuming goods, so the need has to be modified accordingly. Prioritizing the completion of work on time forced the food at the back end in terms of body need.

Because of massive amount of data is available related to food, maximum time is wasted in searching for appropriate food products. So, *"Where should we go for lunch?"* or *"What should we eat for dinner?"* are regular questions that comes to human's mind every day. Earlier recommender systems was used to make recommendations based upon preferences of the users like books, items, movie, or music, but now a days, they are extensively used in the food domain to resolve the above queries. Example, *"RecipeKey2"* is a food recommending system which extracts recipes depending upon item descriptions like cuisine, preparation time, meal type etc., food allergies and favorite ingredients chosen by users.

As the retrospective information available on internet is very high for a particular food, it becomes very hard for the person to extract beneficial information. Therefore, recommender systems have become an efficient tool for the extraction of the relevant facts and return it in a productive way. Recommender systems estimate the user's preference for unranked things and make new recommendations to users and enhance the scope of the system.

These days, due to changing life-style and eating habits, people are suffering from many chronic diseases like obesity, diabetes [35]. A person may take care of him/her-self by consuming suitable nutritional and balanced diet [23]. Thus, food recommending software are acting as powerful tools to help the people nourish themselves with healthy food [12]. In this way, these act as a learner for user's or consumers' preferred ingredients and food styles, as well as recommends healthy food by considering one's health problems, nutritional needs, and previous eating behaviors.

Incomplete balanced diet and food consumption habits are the major reasons of minor and major diseases. As, a person is not aware about major reasons of deficiency or excess of different primary nutrients, like vitamins, proteins, calcium and how to balance them in daily diet.

Many research outcomes [31, 39] had given various food recommendation systems. These systems can be characterized as:

(a) Food recommender systems [31, 21],
(b) Diet plan recommender systems,
(c) Menu recommender system [33],
(d) Recipe recommender system [39],
(e) Health recommender systems [13, 26].

All the given systems have given suggestions to either some particular disease or to balance the diet. For example, in [31], a food recommender system is given for the diabetic patients. The system suggests several foodstuffs for diabetic patients irrespective of diabetes level that may fluctuate frequently. Also, the authors in [21] do not take into account the nutritional information that is very important for a balanced diet.

14.2 Various Techniques to Design Food Recommendation System

In some researches, authors [6, 8] defined the recommending system as given in the following definition:

"Any system that guides a user in a personalized way to interesting or useful objects in a large space of possible options or that produces such objects as output".

These systems are mainly used for suggesting products or services like mobile phones, digital cameras, movies, financial services, books and products which best meet the interest of the users'. Nowadays, the food recommending systems are playing a crucial role to aid users to handle with the huge volume of data associated with foods and recipes. Various methods have been suggested by different researchers have discussed are as follows.

14.2.1 Collaborative Filtering Recommender Systems

CF is the most popular technique in which intelligence/interest of the crowd (large group of people) is used for recommending items. A rated dataset id used for considering the others interest. Then, nearest neighbor algorithm is applied which returns the results that are comparable to given input [9]. To implement CF based systems various approaches are used like: item-based [34], user-based [3], matrix factorization, and model-based approaches [24].

14.2.2   Content-Based Recommender Systems (CB)

Here, the recommendations are made by exploiting information of available items like ingredients and nutrition's and user profiles. CB based systems make recommendations with recorded content, like books [28], articles, and web-pages [30]. Machine learning algorithms [27] and information Retrieval [4] are the two main approaches used for development of these systems.

14.2.3   Knowledge-Based Recommender Systems

Knowledge-based systems (KBS) systems were designed to address the issues of classical approaches like ramp-up problems [6]. These types of systems are mainly used where availability of rated data is scarce like apartments and financial services or where user defines his/her own requirements explicitly (e.g., "the color of the car should be white"). To implement knowledge based recommendation systems, two main approaches are used i.e. constraint-based recommendation [15] and case-based recommendation [5]. Critiquing-based recommendation is an alternative of case-based system that is widely used to make recommendation of particular things, and it produces users' opinion in terms of reviews/critiques so that system accuracy [14] can be enhanced. For the implementation of KB systems following steps are followed:

- *Requirement specification*: To specify the requirements, users must interact with recommender systems.
- *Repair of inconsistent requirements*: In case, if a recommender fails to provide a possible solution, it must suggest a set of corrective measures that should propose alternatives/options to user requirements [16].
- *Result presentation*: For a single input, a multiple recommendations can be generated by the same system. System should present them in a rank wise order [18].
- *Explanation*: For every recommendation, system should provide a brief explanation to understand the relevance of a particular item [17].

14.2.4   Hybrid Recommender Systems

Hybrid recommender systems (HRS) are designed by using two or more than two different techniques so that limitations of one technique can overcome by using the approach. Author [32] describes *"A hybrid system combining techniques A and B tries to use the advantages of A to fix the disadvantages of B"*. For example, collaborative filtering method performs worse when a *new-item* is given as input. While CB approach provides a valid result as it makes recommendation for new things depending upon existing description. Author [7] proposed many hybrid approaches by merging both collaborative filtering and content based, including, *switching, mixed, weighted, cascade, feature augmentation, feature combination* and *meta-level*.

14.2.5   Context Aware Approaches

Various exploratory data analysis has proved that context to a specific food is important in food recommendation. Thus gender, hobbies, location, food availability, and time are identified as important variables. Importance of every variable can be understood by identifying what is actually lacking with respect to context like color of the food with respect to cooking duration and effect of that on the nutritional content of that specified food.

14.2.6   Group-Based Methods

Normally people eat and go for dinner in a group. Usually these activities are done together with friends, families or colleagues as food has a social role too. According to the psychology, the food choices made by a user is influenced by the society to one belongs. If the food recommendation system in such social context is addressed by human group recommendation system will be a boon for online purchasing. In such systems, a list of items is produced, for a group of people rather than for an individual user. Despite the pervasiveness of shared food consumption experiences, group based food recommender systems research has been limited.

14.2.7   Different Types of Food Recommender Systems

As presented in [29] two kinds of food recommending systems are widely used. Earlier, first type (type 1) systems were mainly used to recommend healthier recipes or food items. The type 2 recommender system recommends items which are acknowledged by nutritionist. Type 3 makes recommendations by considering both type 1 and type 2 criteria to make a balance between the user liking and healthy life style. Above defined systems are mainly intended for particular users.

Type 1: Based on user preferences
To implement these systems, the first step is to learn and characterize the user taste. Many researchers have proposed various food recommendation systems based upon user preferences [10, 20, 36], and/or combine with other approaches to enhance the accuracy of system [11, 25].

Here, a simple food recommending system was presented [10] which made recommendations for single user. In this, TF–IDF (Term Frequency–Inverse Document Frequency) filtering method was used to create user profile and to calculate similarity between a food and profile of user. As a knowledge base, healthy and standard food database taken from the United States Department of Agriculture 3 (USDA) is used. Food items are rated by each user as relevant or not relevant. Final recommendation is made by computing the similarity value. If the computed value is greater than a fixed threshold, then food item is suggested, else it will be ignored.

Author [20] proposed an approach which uses a CB algorithm to provide the recommendation by exploiting relevant data of matching ingredients present in this recipe. The recommendation procedure follows the following steps:

a) Divide an unranked target recipe *(rt)* into its ingredients.
b) Allocate the ranking score for every ingredient in the target recipe *(rt)*.
c) Calculate the ranking score of the user *(ua)* for the target recipe *(rt)* (i.e., *pred(ua, rt)*) based on the average of ranking scores of all ingredients $ingr_1$, ..., $ingr_j$ included in this recipe.
d) High predicted ranking score things will be recommended to user.

Type 2: Based on nutritional needs of users
Due to bad eating habits and imbalanced nutritional food, people are suffered from obesity and other dietary-related diseases like hypertension, diabetes etc. Nutritionists or dieticians suggests regular exercises and give diet plans to their patients as a treatment and preventive measures.

Thus, Nutritionists become burdened with too many patients to manually advice personalized diet plan for every user. In this situation, food recommending systems can act as a smart nutrition consultation system.

Consider an example where recommendation system provides recommendations based upon users health problems as well as nutritional needs. Suppose a user enters his personal information like age: 54, gender: female, occupation: office work, physical activities: walking (15 minutes per day), disease: cardiovascular. Based on this information, recommender system performs the following steps:

a) An energy table is referred to find the total calories (in *kcal*) a user needs in a day. The total calories required to every person are computed as per age, gender, medical history and PAL (Physical Activity Level) value.

   In the above example, user works in an office and does very less physical activity (only 15 minutes per day for walking). By referring energy table according to age, gender, medical history and physical activity assume, calories requirement for user is 2,300 kcal.

b) Filter foods with the total calories ≤2,300 *kcal/day*.

c) Filtered foods must be ranked in the increasing order of fat as user suffered from heart disease; so less oily food will be recommended to him.

Type 3: Based upon preferences of users and nutrition's requirements of users

If recommendation system considers only one parameter i.e. either user preference or nutritional needs, the system may provide sub-optimal results. For example, if system considers only preferences given by user, then bad ingestion behaviour would be encouraged. On the other hand, if only requirement of nutrition's are referred then users will not be attracted towards the designed. Thus, taking together, nutritional needs and preferences of users will give the best solution as users get more interesting results.

Consider an example in which system provides recommendations by considering both preferences of users and nutrition's requirements. Suppose user enters personal information as follows: *Age*: 54, *Gender*: female, *Occupation*: office work, worker, *Physical activity*: walking (15 min per day), disease: cardiovascular, *Favorite ingredients*: potato. The proposed model makes recommendations considering both elements preferred by the user and user-related information as follows:

a. Finding the total calories a user needs by referring to the energy table. As the user works in office and is a sedentary worker (only 15 min per day for walking), so calories requirement for user is 2,300 kcal.
b. Extracting food which contains less than or equal to 2,200 kcal of calories, and consider favorite ingredient *"potato"*.
c. Rank the extracted food in the increasing order of fat as user has vascular disease.

Author [12] suggested two ways to balance users' preferences and nutritional needs to incorporate nutritional aspects into consideration.

- *The first approach* balances between the food liked by user and healthy foods. To implement such models, following steps are followed:
  1. A prediction algorithm is used which recommends favorite recipes with computed probability greater than a predefined threshold.
  2. For each recipe extracted by model calories and fat per gram present in it is calculated.
  3. Foods with minimum fat or calories per gram will be recommended to user.
- *In the second approach*, rather than recommending individual foods, complete diet plans are proposed to user, which are generated.

14.3 Implementation of Food Recommender System Using Content-Based Approach

Food domain can be defined as a set of foods in which each food contains a set of ingredients. Content-based approaches make recommendations by searching related items. On the basis of a graded food, the system finds the related items with the same ingredient. For example, if a user likes salmon then system might recommend foods having salmon like sushi. The recommender system implemented in the following section is represented by vectors. Flow diagram of the proposed model is given in Figure 14.1.

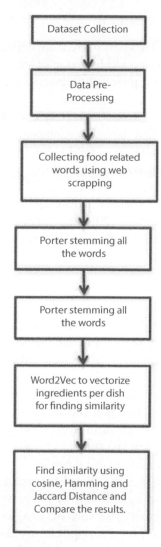

Figure 14.1 Flow chart of proposed method.

14.3.1   Item Profile Representation

In CB systems, features and attributes are used to describe the items. Different similarity metrics are used to compute the similarity between the feature vectors such as Euclidian or cosine similarity. Though, human decision of matching two things often gives different weights to different features. Other than this, document frequency is also commonly used criteria.

14.3.2   Information Retrieval

Information retrieval (IR) is a data search and collection technology which includes crawling, processing and indexing of content, and questioning for content. Web crawling is the process by which information is collected from the web, so that ranking can be performed. It supports a search engine. The aim of crawling is to quickly and efficiently collect as much suitable web pages as possible, along with the link structure that interconnects them.

Due to the high complexity of food domain, several challenges arise while making recommendations. For making suitable suggestions, maximum number of food items/ingredients need to be collected. As foods/ingredients are typically associated with each other in a recipe instead of being consumed independently [20], recipes dataset needs to collect. From the recipes datasets, food/ingredient words are extracted and all unnecessary words are discarded.

14.3.3   Word2vec

Machines are not good in dealing with raw data. In fact, it's almost impossible for machines to deal with any other data except for numerical data. So, representing text in the form of vectors is the most important step in all NLP processes.

Word2vec embedding's the most popular method introduced to the NLP community in 2013. This embedding's proved to be state-of-the-art for tasks such as word analogies and word similarities. Word2vec embedding's also able to accomplish tasks such as King—man, woman ~= Queen, which is considered an almost magical result.

There are two alternatives of a word2vec model II—Continuous Bag of Words and Skip-Gram model. In this implementation, Bag of Words model is used. In a document, the word occurrence is represented by bag-of-words model and widely used in applications like natural language processing (NLP) and information retrieval (IR). The model deals checks the presence of word without looking at the context. It consists of two things: a vocabulary of known words and a measure of the presence of known words. Features from the text can be extracted to model learning applications.

14.3.4   How are word2vec Embedding's Obtained?

A word2vec model is a simple neural network (NN) model with a single hidden layer. The task of this model is to estimate the nearby words for each and every word in a sentence. However, our objective has nothing to with this task. All we want are the weights learned by the hidden layer of the model once the model is trained. These weights can then be used as the word embeddings. Let me give you an example to understand how a word2vec model works. Consider the sentence below:

"Quantum computing researcher's teleport data inside a diamond."

Let's say the word "teleport" is our input word. It has a context window of size 2. This means we are considering only the 2 adjacent words on either side of the input word as the nearby words.

Note: The size of the context window is not fixed; it can be changed as per our requirement.

Now, the task is to pick the nearby words (words in the context window) one-by-one and find the probability of every word in the vocabulary of being the selected nearby word.

14.3.5 Obtaining word2vec Embeddings

Now, let's say we have a bunch of sentences and we extract training samples from them in the same manner. We will end up with training data of considerable size. Suppose the number of unique words in this dataset is 5,000 and we wish to create word vectors of size 100 each. Then, with respect to the word2vec architecture given in Figure 14.2:

- V = 5000 (size of vocabulary)
- N = 100 (number of hidden units or length of word embeddings)

The inputs would be the one-hot-encoded vectors and the output layer would give the probability of being the nearby word for every word in the

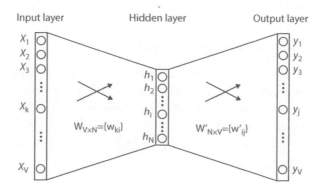

Figure 14.2 word2vec Model.

vocabulary. Once this model is trained, we can easily extract the learned weight matrix $W_{V \times N}$ and use it to extract the word vectors.

14.3.6   Dataset

For the implementation of recommender system, dataset has been collected from "eightportions.com". It contains approximately 125,000 recipes which are collected by web scrapping various web sites. A recipe is defined in a systematic system using different components like title of the recipe, a list of ingredients and measurements, directions for preparation, and a photo of the resultant dish.

This dataset is mainly used for machine learning algorithms as each recipe comprises many components, each of which provides additional information about the recipe.

14.3.6.1   Data Preprocessing

Data preprocessing is used to clean the data and converted into the input format. As dataset contains information of complete recipes, so a lot of unnecessary words are present. A list of stop words like 'for, of, you' etc. has been created and based upon stop lists useless words are removed from dataset.

14.3.7   Web Scrapping For Food List

As we have lot of unnecessary words in the recipe like cups, tablespoons, number etc. Thus, these words must be removed and only words related to foods needs to be retained. For this, knowledge of food words is mandatory. So, a list of food words has been created by using web scrapping from various websites.

14.3.7.1   Porter Stemming All Words

Porter stemming is a method for eliminating suffixes from words in English. Eliminating suffixes automatically is an operation which is especially useful in the information retrieval. Thus by using this, each word is converted into root word.

14.3.7.2   Filtering Our Ingredients

After stemming all words into the root words, all the recipes are filtered to get only food words.

14.3.7.3   *Final Data Frame with Dishes and Their Ingredients*

Final data frame with dishes and their ingredients have been created using word2vec method.

14.3.7.3.1   Similarity Metrics

Results are computed using three different matrices: Cosine Similarity, Hamming Distance and Jaccard Distance.

14.3.7.3.2   Cosine Similarity

Cosine similarity: It computes the similarity between user and item. This method is best when we have high dimensional features especially in information retrieval and text mining. The range of this is between −1 and 1 and there are two approaches:

- Top-n approach: In this, best 'n' suggestions are selected and here n is decided by user.
- Rating scale approach: In this a threshold is set and all the recommendations above threshold are recommended.

The cosine of two non-zero vectors can be computed by using the Euclidean dot product formula:

$$A.B = ||A||.||B||\cos\theta \qquad \text{(i)}$$

Thus, cosine similarity, $\cos(\theta)$ is computed for given two vectors of attributes, A and B, is as follows

$$Similarity = Cos\theta = \frac{A.B}{||A||\,||B||} \qquad \text{(ii)}$$

14.3.7.4   *Hamming Distance*

Hamming distance is computed by matching two binary strings of equal length. It is the number of bit positions in which the two bits are different. It is mainly used for detection and correction of errors during the transmission of data over computer networks. It is also using for measuring similarity in coding theory.

14.3.7.5 Jaccard Distance

This metric is performed to check for similarity between two items. It compares item vectors with each other and rejects the most similar item. This is only useful when vectors contain binary values. If any ratings or rankings having multiple values then this method is not applicable.

The Jaccard index, also called as Intersection over Union (IoU).

Figures 14.3, 14.4 and 14.5 show the results computed using hamming distance, Jaccard distance and cosine similarity respectively.

14.4 Results

Input Data: Potato
Results of Hamming Distance:

```
Enter your favourite ingridients : onion

  ingredients                                           title
0                          Tagliatelle (Flat Egg Noodles)
1                                             Whale Steaks
2                                               Brave Bull
3           Smoked Salmon with Egg Salad and Green beans
```

Figure 14.3 Hamming distance output.

Results of Jaccard Distance:

```
Enter your favourite ingridients : onion

              ingredients                      title
0   shrimp,pearl,onion,garlic    Shrimp and Onion Kebabs
1     slice,onion,oil,peanut                  Onion Oil
2  paprika,powder,onion,sugar  Neely's Barbecue Seasoning
3       salt,onion,pearl,red    Grilled Red Pearl Onions
```

Figure 14.4 Jaccard distance output.

Results of Cosine Similarity

```
Enter your favourite ingridients : onion

/usr/local/lib/python3.6/dist-packages/scipy/spatial/distar
  dist = 1.0 - uv / np.sqrt(uu * vv)
              ingredients                      title
0   shrimp,pearl,onion,garlic    Shrimp and Onion Kebabs
1     slice,onion,oil,peanut                  Onion Oil
2  paprika,powder,onion,sugar  Neely's Barbecue Seasoning
3       salt,onion,pearl,red    Grilled Red Pearl Onions
```

Figure 14.5 Cosine similarity output.

14.5   Observations

From the experimental results, it can be concluded that hamming distance does not show any semantic similarity between input and output ingredients. Cosine similarity shows the semantic similarity but results are much better with Jaccard distance.

14.6   Future Perspective of Recommender Systems

The present study on the framework of the food recommender system plays an important role in terms of helping people to select a diet which matches their health conditions and interests. In order to develop food recommendation system, these research studies utilize the information about the user recipes and the profiles. It has been identified that the excellence of recommendations is greatly influenced by the capability and precision of nutritional and user information of food. However, on this concern, the modern study has not generated so much detailed information or outcome. But as per the postulates of some researchers [1, 40] that suggests food recommendations in perspective with health issues but suggestions on the subject of altering eating behaviors were still missing which are essential for the maintenance of healthy lifestyle. To generate the more trust of the users in the recommendations systems and to encourage the users to follow good eating habits explanations could be beneficial but the incorporation of explanations or detailed information has not received much attention from the researchers [18]. Moreover, food recommendation research rather than focusing on group scenarios focuses on the scenarios of the single user. Till now, research on group scenarios food recommender system in healthy food domain is very restricted. In the research [20] suggested a variety of aggregation techniques for creating food recommendations for user groups. However, still there exist some open concerns which need to be taken into consideration along with the scope of the future work for e.g.: development of group based food recommender system. Here, some research challenges of food recommender systems and their potential solutions are discussed.

14.6.1   User Information Challenges

14.6.1.1   *User Nutrition Information Uncertainty*

To provide efficient results, program must have nutritional needs, food item ratings/recipes and users,' previous meal information [29]. Maximum data can be collected through regular interactions with the users. Though, nutritional intake is recorded by using some mechanism but in reality, recording users' nutritional intake cannot avoid faults as users usually forget to or give false information regarding the foods they have eaten [19]. However, many researchers have proposed many systems to address these issues, such as FOODLOG [2], they are unable to provide precise data on the foods consumed, even though they can estimate the amount of nutritional balance from various type of food in a meal.

14.6.1.2   User Rating Data Collection

Food recommendation systems require user preferences information for the recommendation food items [29, 41]. It is possible to collect this information by requesting users to rank recipes/food. Though, it is not appropriate, if the system asks users to rank too many items. Therefore, it is big challenge that how to collect enough user ratings without taking much user time.

14.6.2   Recommendation Algorithms Challenges

Any algorithm requires the following information to calculate nutritional recommendations for user [29].

14.6.2.1   User Information Such as Likes/Dislikes Food or Nutritional Needs

when the food recommending system is first in other areas, it has faced the cold-start issue [29]. This issue can be resolved by considering knowledge about previous meals to measure similarities and then suggest new recipes to users [41], though this approach needs a great effort from the user and diminishes the incentive for device use.

14.6.2.2   Recipe Databases

Author [32] described about two issues: number of recipes should the program contain? The amount of recipes collected should be sufficiently large to satisfy multiple users, tastes and modify the suggested recipes while reducing the time consumption to make suggestions. This is a difficult issue when the system attempts to balance the response time of the system and variety of recommendations.

Ge *et. al.*, [22] point out that long response times are the reasons of the user dissatisfaction that further limits the systems continued use. How to collect correct recipes nutritional information? Author [29] reported that with the same food item we can receive different nutritional values from it if we use different ways to cook it.

Furthermore, it is very hard to confirm that whether collected nutritional tables for food items are accurate, as it sometimes returns different values for the same food times on comparing different nutritional value table. For example, in "a salad recipe," the nutritional value of celery differs from the nutritional value of itself "in a fried recipe," as cooking at high temperatures causes celery to lose a large amount of essential oil. This means that in the "fried recipe" the quantity of essential celery oil may be less than in the "salad recipe."

14.6.2.3   A Set of Constraints or Rules

The quality of recommendations will be enhanced by more constraints and rules in the recommendation process.For example, Food menus with less fat and salt should be recommended with a user who has heart disease. In addition, the contradictions between the constraints or rules that prevent the recommendation algorithms from finding a solution are very important to identify. Nevertheless, testing constraints/rules in the database with the large database (e.g., thousands of foods/recipes) has negative effects on system performance. Therefore, food recommendation systems must take into account restrictions about the availability of ingredients in households in order to help consumers to save money and avoid the actions of food waste. The problem here is how to recommend food that serves consumers' health and nutritional needs, as well as take advantage of the ingredients already in the refrigerator. Recommendation systems appear to require a lot of effort from consumers in this situation as consumers need to document the use of all ingredients on a regular basis and this can discourage consumers from using the program permanently.

14.6.3   Challenges Concerning Changing Eating Behavior of Consumers

Presently, due to inappropriate eating habits, many people suffer from health problems [37]. For example, in relation with their level of physical activity, most people eat too much food and eventually become obese. While others limit extreme intake of nutrition, this leads to malnutrition.

Therefore, recognizing the eating habits of consumers and persuading them to alter eating patterns in positive ways is one of the main functions of food recommender systems. This is a huge challenge for food recommendation system; however, as eating activity is influenced by many factors. In order to inspire consumers to follow healthy diet, food recommendation systems should incorporate health psychology theory. Using one simple change at a specific time, the first approach can be used until consumer behaviour becomes usual [32]. Further approach can be applied for food recommender system is to compare the ideal nutrient. Consumers can find the optimal diet structure from reputable data based on age and physical activity level (e.g., USDA, DACH) and then analyze the food they eat with what is prescribed in [37]. The comparison approach is also proposed to provide consumers with potential dietary changes in paper proposed [27].

14.6.4   Challenges Regarding Explanations and Visualizations

Visualizations and explanations have a vital role in recommendation systems as consumers' confidence increases in the outcome of decisions [38]. Explanations are even more important in the healthy food domain as they not only increase confidence in recommenders but also encourage consumers to eat healthy foods and improve their eating habits. For the purpose of this, it makes sense that food recommendation systems explanations explain how adequacy results are obtained [11]. In addition, a specific explanation of food items such as a nutritional value table for a recipe must be involved in a manner that focuses the health of a particular consumer food.

14.7   Conclusion

Food recommender system plays a vital role in both individual's life and society. Food recommender systems for nutritional researchers have suggested various approaches of integrating nutrition like nutritional components in algorithm, meal plans, and nudging etc., yet all these methods are not clear and none of them is proved best method to consider.

In this chapter, on the basis of addressing, various kinds of food recommendation systems are discussed. In many food recommendation systems, commonly used recommendation techniques such as collaborative filtering recommendation, content based recommendation, and constraint based recommendation are used. In addition, hybrid methods are also used for the improvement of the performance of the recommender.

While seen in different contexts, all food recommendation systems generally play a vital role in providing food products or items that meet the preferences of the consumers' and appropriate nutritional needs as well as persuading them to follow healthy eating habits.

Acknowledgements

The authors are grateful to Mr. Sambhal Shikhar, student of Lovely Professional University, Phagwara, India who helped us in the implementation of the project.

References

1. Aberg, J., Dealing with Malnutrition: A Meal Planning System for Elderly, in: *AAAI Spring Symposium: Argumentation for Consumers of Healthcare*, pp. 1–7, 2006.
2. Aizawa, K., De Silva, G.C., Ogawa, M., Sato, Y., Food log by snapping and processing images, in: *2010 16th International Conference on Virtual Systems and Multimedia*, IEEE, pp. 71–74, 2010.
3. Asanov, D., *Algorithms and methods in recommender systems*, Berlin Institute of Technology, Berlin, Germany, 2011.
4. Balabanović, M. and Shoham, Y., Fab: content-based, collaborative recommendation. *Commun. ACM*, 40, 3, 66–72, 1997.
5. Bridge, D., Göker, M.H., McGinty, L., Smyth, B., Case-based recommender systems. *Knowl. Eng. Rev.*, 20, 3, 315–320, 2005.
6. Burke, R., Knowledge-based recommender systems, in: *Encyclopedia of library and information systems*, vol. 69, Marcel Dekker (Ed.), pp. 180–200, 2000.
7. Burke, R., Hybrid recommender systems: Survey and experiments. *User Model. User-ADAP*, 12, 4, 331–370, 2002.
8. Burke, R., Felfernig, A., Göker, M.H., Recommender systems: An overview. *AI Mag.*, 32, 3, 13–18, 2011.
9. Ekstrand, M.D., Riedl, J.T., Konstan, J.A., Collaborative filtering recommender systems. *Found. Trends' Hum.–Comput. Interact.*, 4, 2, 81–173, 2011.
10. El-Dosuky, M.A., Rashad, M.Z., Hamza, T.T., El-Bassiouny, A.H., Food recommendation using ontology and heuristics, in: *International Conference on Advanced Machine Learning Technologies and Applications*, Springer, Berlin, Heidelberg, pp. 423–429, 2012.
11. Elahi, M., Ge, M., Ricci, F., Fernández-Tobías, I., Berkovsky, S., David, M., Interaction design in a mobile food recommender system, in: *CEUR Workshop Proceedings*, CEUR-WS, 2015.

12. Elsweiler, D., Harvey, M., Ludwig, B., Said, A., Bringing the "healthy" into Food Recommenders, in: *DMRS*, pp. 33–36, 2015.

13. Evert, A.B., Boucher, J.L., Cypress, M., Dunbar, S.A., Franz, M.J., Mayer-Davis, E.J., Yancy, W.S., Nutrition therapy recommendations for the management of adults with diabetes. *Diabetes Care*, 37, Supplement 1, S120–S143, 2014.

14. Felfernig, A., Biases in decision making, in: *Proceedings of the First International Workshop on Decision Making and Recommender systems (DMRS2014), Bolzano, Italy, September 18–19, 2014*, vol. 1278, CEUR Proceedings, pp. 32–37, 2014.

15. Felfernig, A. and Burke, R., Constraint-based recommender systems: technologies and research issues, in: *Proceedings of the 10th International Conference on Electronic Commerce*, ACM, p. 3, 2008.

16. Felfernig, A., Friedrich, G., Jannach, D., Zanker, M., Developing constraint-based recommenders, in: *Recommender systems handbook*, pp. 187–215, Springer, Boston, MA, 2011.

17. Felfernig, A., Zehentner, C., Ninaus, G., Grabner, H., Maalej, W., Pagano, D., Reinfrank, F., Group decision support for requirements negotiation, in: *International Conference on User Modeling, Adaptation, and Personalization*, pp. 105–116, Springer, Berlin, Heidelberg, 2011.

18. Felfernig, A., Hotz, L., Bagley, C., Tiihonen, J., *Knowledge-based configuration: From research to business cases*, Elsevier, Newnes, 2014.

19. Felfernig, A., Stettinger, M., Ninaus, G., Jeran, M., Reiterer, S., Falkner, A.A., Tiihonen, J., Towards Open Configuration, in: *Configuration Workshop*, pp. 89–94, 2014.

20. Freyne, J. and Berkovsky, S., Intelligent food planning: personalized recipe recommendation, in: *Proceedings of the 15th International Conference on Intelligent User Interfaces*, ACM, pp. 321–324, 2010.

21. Ge, M., Elahi, M., Fernaández-Tobías, I., Ricci, F., Massimo, D., Using tags and latent factors in a food recommender system, in: *Proceedings of the 5th International Conference on Digital Health 2015*, ACM, pp. 105–112, 2015.

22. Hoxmeier, J.A. and DiCesare, C., System response time and user satisfaction: An experimental study of browser-based applications. *AMCIS. 2000 Proc.*, 347, 140–145, 2000.

23. Knowler, W.C., Barrett-Connor, E., Fowler, S.E., Hamman, R.F., Lachin, J.M., Walker, E.A., Nathan, D.M., Reduction in the incidence of type 2 diabetes with lifestyle intervention or metformin. *N. Engl. J. Med.*, 346, 6, 393–403, 2002.

24. Koren, Y., Bell, R., Volinsky, C., Matrix factorization techniques for recommender systems. *Comput.*, 8, 30–37, 2009.

25. Kuo, F.F., Li, C.T., Shan, M.K., Lee, S.Y., Intelligent menu planning: Recommending set of recipes by ingredients, in: *Proceedings of the ACM*

Multimedia 2012 Workshop on Multimedia for Cooking and Eating Activities, pp. 1–6, ACM, 2012.

26. LeFevre, M.L., Behavioral counseling to promote a healthful diet and physical activity for cardiovascular disease prevention in adults with cardiovascular risk factors: US Preventive Services Task Force Recommendation Statement. *Ann. Intern. Med.*, 161, 8, 587–593, 2014.

27. Mankoff, J., Hsieh, G., Hung, H.C., Lee, S., Nitao, E., Using low-cost sensing to support nutritional awareness, in: *International Conference on Ubiquitous Computing*, Springer, Berlin, Heidelberg, pp. 371–378, 2002.

28. Mooney, R.J. and Roy, L., Content-based book recommending using learning for text categorization, in: *Proceedings of the Fifth ACM Conference on Digital Libraries*, ACM, pp. 195–204, 2000.

29. Mika, S., Challenges for nutrition recommender systems, in: *Proceedings of the 2nd Workshop on Context Aware Intel. Assistance, Berlin, Germany*, pp. 25–33, 2011.

30. Pazzani, M.J., Muramatsu, J., Billsus, D., Syskill & Webert: Identifying interesting web sites, in: *AAAI/IAAI*, vol. 1, pp. 54–61, 1996.

31. Phanich, M., Pholkul, P., Phimoltares, S., Food recommendation system using clustering analysis for diabetic patients, in: *2010 International Conference on Information Science and Applications*, IEEE, pp. 1–8, 2010.

32. Ricci, F., Rokach, L., Shapira, B., Introduction to recommender systems handbook, in: *Recommender systems handbook*, pp. 1–35, Springer, Boston, MA, 2011.

33. Runo, M., FooDroid: a food recommendation app for university canteens. Unpublished semester thesis, Swiss Federal Institute of Theology, Zurich, 2011.

34. Sarwar, B.M., Karypis, G., Konstan, J.A., Riedl, J., Item-based collaborative filtering recommendation algorithms. *Www*, 1, 285–295, 2001.

35. Robertson, A., Tirado, C., Lobstein, T., Knai, C., Jensen, J., Ferro-Luzzi, A., James, W., *Food and Health in Europe: A New Basis for Action* (European Series No 96), WHO, 2004.

36. Svensson, M., Laaksolahti, J., Höök, K., Waern, A., A recipe based on-line food store, in: *Proceedings of the 5th International Conference on Intelligent User Interfaces*, ACM, pp. 260–263, 2000.

37. Snooks, M.K., *Health psychology: Biological, psychological, and sociocultural perspectives*, Jones & Bartlett Publishers, 2009.

38. Tintarev, N. and Masthoff, J., A survey of explanations in recommender systems, in: *2007 IEEE 23rd International Conference on Data Engineering Workshop*, IEEE, pp. 801–810, 2007.

39. Teng, C.Y., Lin, Y.R., Adamic, L.A., Recipe recommendation using ingredient networks, in: *Proceedings of the 4th Annual ACM Web Science Conference*, ACM, pp. 298–307, 2012.

40. Ueta, T., Iwakami, M., Ito, T., A recipe recommendation system based on automatic nutrition information extraction, in: *International Conference on Knowledge Science, Engineering and Management*, Springer, Berlin, Heidelberg, pp. 79–90, 2011.

41. Van Pinxteren, Y., Geleijnse, G., Kamsteeg, P., Deriving a recipe similarity measure for recommending healthful meals, in: *Proceedings of the 16th International Conference on Intelligent User Interfaces*, ACM, pp. 105–114, 2011.

Part 4

BLOCKCHAIN & IoT-BASED RECOMMENDER SYSTEMS

A Trust-Based Recommender System Built on IoT Blockchain Network With Cognitive Framework

S. Porkodi and D. Kesavaraja*

Dr. SivanthiAditanar College of Engineering, Tiruchendur, Tamilnadu, India

Abstract

In this era of technology, some of the major innovative revolutions includes Blockchain, Internet of Things and Cognitive systems. Whereas, the combination of these technologies can develop a new technology with high capacity and high potential. IoT includes sensors and actuators which is connected via internet where the objects can interact and communicate. It makes the device smart by yielding useful information from gathered raw data which are monitored and controlled remotely. Blockchain is a tamper resistant distributed ledger where all transactions of blocks are recorded with timestamp. Blockchain is also a decentralized network with properties including anonymity and integrity, which have the capacity to give security to data transferred over IoT. Cognitive system repeatedly learns by interacting with environment, situations, people and gathered data. It improves its capability via learning and understanding the way of thinking ability of humans thus generating a way to produce a recommendation system for users. So, existing combinations of these technologies are analyzed and a framework for blockchain based cognitive IoT is proposed. A recommender system is built, where trust is the key in decision making process. The proposed recommender is with additional benefits, more secure and high potential compared to the existing systems.

Keywords: Blockchain, cognitive system, Internet of Things, trust-based recommender system

Corresponding author: dkesavraj@gmail.com

Sachi Nandan Mohanty, Jyotir Moy Chatterjee, Sarika Jain, Ahmed A. Elngar and Priya Gupta (eds.)
Recommender System with Machine Learning and Artificial Intelligence: Practical Tools and Applications in Medical, Agricultural and Other Industries, (293–312) © 2020 Scrivener Publishing LLC

15.1   Introduction

15.1.1   Today and Tomorrow

In today's world there is a lot of revolution in technologies that will change the path in which the world is developing. The technologies in the digital revolution include Internet of things, Blockchain, Cognitive Systems, Artificial Intelligence and much more. In future there are also more technologies to be merged or supporting one another which leads to a creation of a new technology with high potential.

15.1.2   Vision

The vision is to see what are all the innovations and developments these technologies can bring in to the world which can be adopted by government and business to develop and yield a greater benefits from it. Many startups can develop business based on these technologies to sustain in the future.

In order to easily understand Internet of Things, Blockchain, Cognitive Systems consider all these technologies to be interconnected processes. Where Internet of things acts as the nervous system, which is used to sense with millions of devices interconnected all throughout the world collecting every new data. Cognitive system acts as the decision making system of the brain, it analyses the data and make decisions. Blockchain acts as the memory which is secure and keeps record of each and every data transaction. The detailed description of these three technologies are as given in the upcoming sections.

15.1.3   Internet of Things

The basic concept for the Internet of things were started to discuss very early around 1982 and solutions were proposed around 1999 [20]. Internet of things is basically the interconnection among any number of devices across the world. Anything such as computers, phones, mechanical machines, digital devices, things and objects also living beings can be interconnected with each other where the data and information can be transferred over internet as shown in Figure 15.1.

Things includes anything from smart lights to satellite control system but these things consist of different type of actuators (such as electric

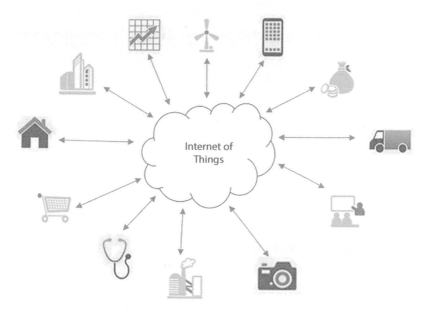

Figure 15.1 Examples of IoT things.

motor, comb driver, hydraulic cylinder, etc.) or sensor (such as light sensor, heartbeat sensor, motion sensor, temperature sensor, etc.) to collect data and act according to the given condition. The IoT devices not only collect data but also compute the resources and also acts as a communication medium [1, 2, 5, 13, and 36].

15.1.4 Blockchain

A Blockchain consists of blocks which is a continuously growing list of the records or transaction blocks. For the privacy and security of the blocks, cryptography is been used. Peer to peer type of network technology is used in order to get a distributive ledger of the blockchain. The Blockchain's high potential is understood when the crypto currency called as bitcoin came into the use. The bitcoin is mined, managed and rotated by the network users of bitcoin and there is no central authority in it. The transaction of the digital currency bitcoin is done through internet in the system that is decentralized by using the blockchain public ledger. A sample Bitcoin transaction is shown in Figure 15.2. Blockchain is also tamper resistant where each block transaction is recorded along with a timestamp. The properties of the blockchain includes integrity and anonymity which helps to manage the security of the data in the network [6, 9, 25, 28, 37 and 44].

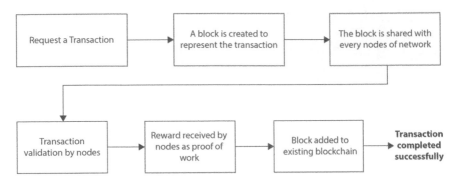

Figure 15.2 Blockchain transaction.

15.1.5   Cognitive Systems

Cognitive systems can interact with anything in the environment (such as people, situation, and data) and continuously learns from it. The cognitive system develops and improves its learning and reasoning capability [32]. These system are built mainly with the idea of resembling the human brain which learns from the data, belief, idea, assumption, information and the society around to get the best possible answer in any situation. That can be expressed as the capability of reacting to a situation in the society [24, 29, 33, 39 and 40].

15.1.6   Application

Many applications can be obtained by merging these three technologies. Some of the application includes

Smart health care recommender system: The patient's health condition data can be continuously obtained through the sensors of the IoT, then the blockchain is used to keep the data safe and securely transfer it over internet, where the cognitive system can use the data, analyze it to recommend some help to the patient in the case of the patient doesn't know what to do in certain emergency health condition state.

Smart support in bank: The users can use bitcoin to pay the banks, the transaction can be secured by using blockchain. All these data are collected in the cognitive system and analyzed. When a user needs any help the system can answer from analyzing the data and learning from it without any staff support.

Smart news recommender system: The user data can be collected via smart phones and can be transferred securely over blockchain network, where the data can be analyzed in the cognitive system and promotes the news and media stories to the user automatically even before the user searches for the news. This can change personally according to the user needs.

Smart traffic control and recommendation system: The traffic details are collected from the IoT devices in the vehicles and are safely transferred through blockchain network. Where the data can be analyzed. When there arises an accident or any other emergency situation it can be automatically recommended to the vehicles that needs to take a diversion or some necessary measures.

Smart Shopping: The shopping application in the mobile can collect all the user likes, dislikes, needs and all other data and transfer safely using blockchain. Then the data is been analyzed in the cognitive system and recommend the items according to the user need.

15.2   Technologies and its Combinations

The combination of two or more technologies can pave a way to the creation of a more useful and powerful new technology. Now the possible combinations of the above three technologies such as Internet of Things, Blockchain, Cognitive Systems as in Figure 15.3 can be analyzed.

15.2.1   IoT–Blockchain

The combination of Internet of Things and Blockchain gives a high secured Internet of Things. In this combination of systems, the data is collected form the IoT devices are transferred through blockchain network which

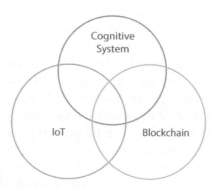

Figure 15.3 Combination of technologies.

gives more security to the data, cost can be reduced. Blockchain has a good integration while combining with IoT also it adapts and makes the transaction fast [3, 7, and 16].

15.2.2   IoT–Cognitive System

The combination of Internet of Things and Cognitive System gives an efficient management system in low cost to the internet of things. This new version is termed as Cognitive IoT, it makes the system to be more efficient and gives more productivity. As the Internet of things act dynamically and are distributed across the world it's a high challenge for developers to develop a correct cognitive system [14, 17, 19, 21, 22, 31, 34, 38 and 42].

15.2.3   Blockchain–Cognitive System

The combination of Blockchain and Cognitive System gives the solution to overcome the challenge of managing transaction and smart contracts as the blockchain is basically a distributive technology, also increases the security of the system and manage trust in decision making. These are the very challenging task in blockchain which can be solved easily by using cognitive system [23 and 30].

15.2.4   IoT–Blockchain–Cognitive System

Day by day the number of IoT devices is increasing. As there are huge number of devices, the will be huge number of transactions every day. There is a need in the evolving the applications based on IoT. The blockchain provides Internet of Things with micro payment function among the IoT devices by using smart contracts and crypto currency. So by combining these two technologies will be a great evolution in terms of data security. Now the combine technology of Internet of Things and Blockchain should have a proper and efficient management system to handle things which should also be smart so cognitive systems are designed.

The combination of these three technologies such as Internet of Things, Blockchain and Cognitive system could give rise to a new efficient technology in the field of computer science which can provide benefits from all these three technologies. The only drawback of this system to work and find a way to overcome in the near future is that, the fully distributive computation is not supported by this system. This type of computation is mostly required in the crypto currency like bitcoin. In this chapter, a trust based recommender system built on IoT Blockchain network with Cognitive framework is proposed. The combination of the framework is novel and thus the proposed work is novel.

15.3   Crypto Currencies With IoT–Case Studies

Crypto currencies are digital or virtual money which can be represented in the form of coins or tokens. Some type of crypto currency can be converted into physical money by using credit cards where as some type of crypto currency are not. These digital money can be safely transacted through blockchain system. There are nearly 1600 crypto currencies in use, which has been using different platforms. The new platforms are been created as there are some issues while using the digital currencies. There are many crypto currency platforms which uses Internet of Things some of them are studied in the Table 15.1.

15.4   Trust-Based Recommender System

A trust based recommender system built on IoT blockchain network with cognitive framework is proposed. The proposed system's structure is shown in Figure 15.4. It has three different layers they are, requirement, cognitive process, things management. Internet of things devices and blockchain technology are combined in the layer of things management. This combination has the properties of being dynamic, distributive, works on large scale of data, which leads to lot of management problem. These bigger problems could not be solved with solved with the usage of manual power or solutions that are not smart. In the proposed work, all these management problems are solved by using cognitive system in the layer of things management [14, 41 and 42].

15.4.1   Requirement

The behavior and goal are expressed in cognitive specification language (CSL) in the requirement layer. Configuration file is created using this language. Then configuration files are distributed among people who is managing the configuration of Internet of Things. If the goal is changes in the

Table 15.1 Study on crypto currencies employed in IoT.

Crypto currency platform	Goals
Bitcoin	It is the first and well known digital currency, which is decentralized with no admin or central bank. The coins can be shared among users with peer to peer network without any other intermediates.
IoTA	It is the 4th most exchanged digital currency in the world. IoTA was mainly developed to allow paradigm shift in the Internet of Things with the establishment of leger of everything. In short, IoTA is an open platform to use all the available resources to be used as service for trade, where each and every industries and companies can find and develop various business to business model.
Ethereum	It is an open, decentralized, distributive blockchain platform with the feature of smart contract for transaction. Ether is the digital currency used in this platform.
ICON	It is an independent decentralized network, where any people can have connection with any blockchain to easily interact and use their crypto currency. Even the isolated communities can be connected and services can be utilized and shared via network.
Stellar	It is an open source, decentralized payment network for converting crypto currency to physical money. Thus it has the connection with people, payment system and bank without any profit.
Ripple	It is a distributive, open source gross settlement payment protocol system, which acts in the real time. It is mainly used for exchanging currency, best way to send money internationally.
Dentacoin	It is a blockchain system mainly developed as a solution to global dental industry. An infrastructure is developed to maintain the security of patient's data. The patients can pay through dentacoin to the dentist.

(Continued)

Table 15.1 Study on crypto currencies employed in IoT. (*Continued*)

Crypto currency platform	Goals
Golem	It is a decentralized system with peer to peer network, which is designed to share computing power. It also provides cloud service in a very low cost to open source developers to bring up new innovations.
MONERO	It is an open source, decentralized crypto currency. It maintains security and privacy also no one can see the record of the transactions which remains untraceable.

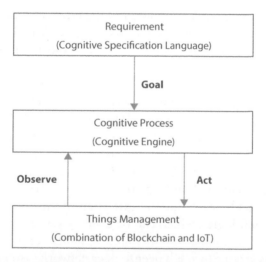

Figure 15.4 Structure of IoT blockchain network on cognitive framework.

layer of requirement then it leads to the change of optimizing function which is in layer of cognitive process. The system goals can be feed in by command lines, voice command or any other type of interaction between system and user. Some elements such as, sensors, actuators, smart contract, service and payment can determine the features of goals. These elements are used in command to adjust the system configuration to bring out the perfect output for the user. These commands also can be taken in from outside the framework. As Internet of things have distributive nature to share configuration file, some algorithms are suggested.

Fully distributed: The latest version of configuration file is downloaded by a thing periodically from the neighbor thing in the fully distributed algorithm.

Semi centralized: In the semi centralized algorithm, the in-charge is given to multiple servers at the same time to manage configuration file which is present in Internet of Things.

Centralized: In the centralized algorithm, one well known server is responsible to store the latest version of configuration file.

The technology of the blockchain could also be used in managing configuration file even with much more high security.

15.4.2 Things Management

The necessary information is gathered in the layer of things management which is been sent to layer of cognitive process. This layer has several elements as shown in Figure 15.5 to operate and manage. They are as follows:

Blockchain: The blockchain maintains the necessary information within one or more blockchains. Any type of blockchain (such as banking [27], health care [8] or insurance [12]) can be used. Blockchain consist of three sub units. They are, micro service blockchain, smart contract blockchain, blockchain for things. The micro service information which is utilized in the system are been listed out in the micro service blockchain. The information regarding smart contacts are been listed out in the smart contract blockchain. The extension of this unit can be done by blockchain of ontologies, which can be used by system.

Peer to peer communication: Data exchange and communication between things is done through peer to peer network system. The management issue of the blockchain for things is supported by this unit.

Smart contract: Required functions are provided by this unit for the usage of smart contract, which is been defined in system. Blockchain unit

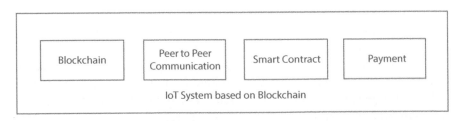

Figure 15.5 Layer of things management.

stores all the codes in the blockchain respective to its smart contracts. To obtain the system's goal, cognitive system adjust and use the smart contract accordingly. The smart contract has the ability to do operations on actuators of system.

Payment: This unit is in the cooperation with all the other units present in things management as well as the cognitive process for the payment process to be successful. The information regarding the users wallet and the type of digital crypto currency that is used by the users are also managed by this unit. So, this unit must have the ability to contact with platform of each and every variety of crypto currency digital coin [16, 35 and 43].

15.4.3   Cognitive Process

The system goals are listed out in requirement layer of the system. The cognitive process layer have cognitive engine that is used to observe information about the system and then to manage the system, appropriate algorithm is been executed. There are different types of engine which are designed to handle different type of works in the system. Some of the goals for which the engines are been designed are listed below,

- To find the system goals where the configuration file is interpreted by using machine learning algorithm. This algorithm is used to extract the exact goals of the system.
- To manage the complexities that arises during the payment process. As there are lots of smart contracts implemented onto the system.
- To manage the complexities of handling smart contracts.
- To detect the unauthorized intrusions.
- To handle the usage of memory and knowledge.
- To manage the blockchain and peer to peer communication network.

The information gathered from the IoT devices and things are shared within all types of engines listed above. Humans cannot resist harmful actions caused by cognitive engines so a cognitive engine must be required to design as a safe engine. In the cognitive process implementation, many decision making process are involved. Some of the decision making process are listed below,

- Decision to determine what engine must be designed based on cognitive engine goals.
- Decision to select smart contract, which is in use of cognitive engine.
- Decision to select blockchain technology for IoT things based on the cognitive engine goals.
- Decision to select machine learning method appropriately based on the cognitive engine characteristics. Artificial intelligence which uses distributed information in blockchain is very much suitable for a dynamic and distributed cognitive engine types.

To adapt the distributed nature in Internet of Tings, the implementation of cognitive engine shall be done by any one of the methods given below,

Fully distributed: Every device and things of IoT has their own separate cognitive engine.

Semi centralized: The implementation of the cognitive engines are done on multiple servers.

Centralized: The implementation of the cognitive engine is done on only one server.

15.5   Recommender System Platform

A trust based recommender system algorithm is built on IoT blockchain network with cognitive frame work is proposed for shopping center. The description of the system that is given by user should be used to design a system. The description of a shopping center is given below,

- Based on the user's purchase history, items should be recommended.
- To compute any discount or offer, check the user's healthcare profile.
- To do any payment, Bitcoin wallet is used.
- A recommender service which can be called as Service_ Recommendation is used.

These commands are given to cognitive engine and also the functions that are required to process the work are issued. The cognitive engine algorithm is given below,

Cognitive Engine Algorithm
Inputs:
 Commands of user;
 Sensor information of user;
Notations:
 Smart_Contract_1   //based upon shopping history
 Smart_Contract_2   //based upon health care
 Service_Recommendation//collaborative filtering to do recommenda-
 tion. This service has to be bought by user themself
Begin
 Get user commands;
 Convert user commands to system goals;
 Acquire smart contracts based on system goals;   //Get Smart_
                                                   Contract_1 and
                                                   Smart_Contract_2
                                                   from blockchain
 Gather and Store sensor information into blockchain;
 Call Service_Recommendation;   //Service_Recommendation
                                 shows the recommendation list,
                                 the information about Service_
                                 Recommendation can be found in
                                 blockchain
 Compute offer/discount based on Smart_Contract_1 and Smart_Contract_2;
 Calculate Total Payment Cost;
 Pay using digital wallet;   //Digital wallet is a bitcoin wallet
End

In the above proposed algorithm, whenever a user first enter into the shopping center, the information about that user are been sensed with sensors and is stored into blockchain. As soon as the user's command is received from the user, cognitive engines and respective services are been called in order to interpret commands in turn to draw the system goals for user. From the extracted goals, smart contracts and the respective recommended services are called. Then the system recommends appropriate items to customer. Then the user purchase the recommended product, the discounts are computed based on the smart contracts of the system. Finally, the payment can be processed by using user's bitcoin wallet, which changes the value of the wallet after payment process is done.

The proposed chapter is compared with existing features of other works as shown in Table 15.2.

Table 15.2 Comparison of recommendation systems.

Reference no.	System model	Internet of Things	Blockchain	Cognitive systems
26	Towards Automated IoT Service Recommendation	Yes	Not Found	Not Found
10	Multi-Agent Recommendation System in Internet of Things	Yes	Not Found	Not Found
18	Towards Incorporating Context Awareness to Recommender System in Internet of Things	Yes	Not Found	Not Found
15	Information and Environment: IoT-Powered Recommender System	Yes	Not Found	Not Found
4	Efficient CRan Random Access for IoT Devices: Learning Links via Recommendation System	Yes	Not Found	Not Found
11	Collaborative Filtering on the Blockchain: A Secure Recommender System for E-Commerce	Not Found	Yes	Yes
14	A Framework for Cognitive Recommender Systems in the Internet of Things	Yes	Not Found	Yes
–	Proposed Work	Yes	Yes	Yes

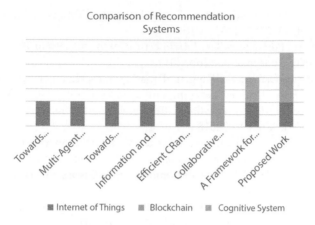

Figure 15.6 Comparison of recommendation systems.

In Figure 15.6 comparison of recommendation systems shows that proposed method is the novel one with a combination of Internet of Things, Blockchain and Cognitive Systems.

15.6   Conclusion and Future Directions

In this chapter, a trust based recommender system built on IoT blockchain network with cognitive framework is proposed. In the layer of cognitive process, the cognitive engine observes status of all the IoT things from layer of things management. After that cognitive engines acts upon actuators and sensors to triggers the correct smart contracts list. Peer to peer network communication protocol is used in payment process for any type of crypto currencies. An example system for shopping center is also studied and applied. The proposed chapter is also compared with existing features of other works. This recommender system work is found to be novel according to the research on other works. In the future, Web of Things technology can be used in the proposed chapter.

References

1. Al-Fuqaha, A., Guizani, M., Mohammadi, M., Aledhari, M., Ayyash, M., Internet of Things: A Survey on Enabling Technologies, protocols and Applications. *IEEE Commun Surv. Tut.*, 17, 4, 2347–2376, 2015.

2. Atzori, L., Iera, A., Morabito, G., The Internet of Things: A Survey. *Comput. Netw.*, 54, 15, 2787–2805, 2010.

3. Atzori, M., *Blockchain-Based Architecture for the Internet of Things: A Survey*, University College of London, 2017.

4. Bursalioglu, O.Y., Li, Z., Wang, C., Papadopoulos, H., Efficient CRan Random Access for IoT Devices: Learning Links via Recommendation System. Paper published at *IEEE International Conference on Communication Workshop*, Kansas City, Mo, USA, 2018.

5. Choudhary, G. and Jain, A.K., Internet of Things: A Survey on Architecture, Technologies, Protocol and Challenges. Paper presented at *International conference on Recent Advances and Innovation in Engineering (ICRAIE)*, Jaipur, India, pp. 1–8, 2016.

6. Christidis, K. and Devetsikiotis, M., Blockchains and Smart Contracts for the Internet of Things. *IEEE Access*, 4, 2292–2303, 2016.

7. Conoscenti, M., Vetro, A., De Martin, J.C., Blockchain for the Internet of Things: A Systematic Literature Review. Paper presented at *IEEE 13th International Conference in Computer Systems and Applications (AICCSA)*, Agadir, Morocco, pp. 1–6, 2016.

8. Daniel, J., Sargolzaei, A., Abdelghani, M., Sargolzaei, S., Amaba, B., Blockchain Technology, Cognitive Computing and Healthcare Innovations. *J. Adv. Info. Technol.*, 8, 194–198, 2017.

9. Engelhardt, M.A., Hitching Healthcare to the Chain: An Introduction to Blockchain Technology in the Healthcare Sector. *Technol. Innov. Manag. Rev.*, 7, 10, 22–34, 2017.

10. Forestiero, A., Multi-Agent Recommendation System in Internet of Things. Cluster, Cloud and Grid Computing (CCGRID). Paper presented at *17th IEEE/ACM International Symposium*, Madrid, Spain, pp. 772–775, 2017.

11. Frey, R., Worner, D., Ilic, A., Collaborative Filtering on the Blockchain: A Secure Recommender System for E-Commerce. Paper presented at *22nd Americas Conference on Information System (AMCIS)*, San Diego, CA, USA, 2016.

12. Gantait, A., Patra, J., Mukherjee, A., *Implementing Blockchain for Cognitive IoT Applications*, IBM Developer Works, IBM Corporation, 2017, Retrieved from developer.ibm.com website: Https://Www.Ibm.Com/Developerworks/Cloud/Library/Cl-BlockchainFor-Cognitive-Iot-Apps-Trs/.

13. Gazis, V., Gortz, M., Huber, M., Leonardi, A., Mathioudakis, K., Wiesmaier, A. *et al.*, A Survey of Technologies for the Internet of Things. Paper presented at *International Conference in Wireless Communication and Mobile Computing (IWCMC)*, Dubrovnik,Croatia, pp. 1090–1095, 2015.

14. Gholizadeh Hamlabadi, K., Saghiri, A.M., Vahdati, M., Dehghan Takhtfooladi, M., Meybodi, M.R., A Framework for Cognitive Recommender Systems in the Internet of Things (IoT). Paper Presented at *IEEE 4th International Conference on Knowledge-Based Engineering and Innovation (Kbei)*, Tehran, Iran, 2017.

15. Hahn, J., Information and Environment: IoT-Powered Recommender System. Proceedings of the ASIS&T 2018 Annual Meeting. pp. 151–160, 2018. Arxiv Preprint Arxiv: 1801.06552.

16. Huh, S., Cho, S., Kim, S., Managing IoT Devices Using Blockchain Platform. Paper presented at *19th International Conference in Advanced Communication Technology (ICACT)*, Bongpyeong, South Korea, pp. 464–467, 2017.

17. Jiang, Y., Xie, W., Wang, F., Li, N., An Implementation of Cognitive Management Framework for the Internet of Things System. Paper presented at *2nd International Conference in Information Technology and Electronic Commerce (ICITEC)*, Seoul, South Korea, pp. 103–106, 2014.

18. Kaur, P.D., Towards Incorporating Context Awareness to Recommender System in Internet of Things. Paper presented at *1st International Conference on Smart System, Innovation and Computing*, Jaipur, India, pp. 771–780, 2018.

19. Kelaidonis, D., Somov, A., Foteinos, V., Poulios, G., Stavroulaki, V., Vlacheas, P. *et al.*, Virtualization and Cognitive Management of Real World Objects in the Internet of Things, in: *IEEE International Conference on Green Computation and Communication (Greencom)*, Besancon, France, pp. 187–194, 2012.

20. Kevin, A., That "Internet of Things" Thing: In the Real World Things Matter More than Ideas. RFID journal. 2009. Retrieved from Rfid Journal website: https://www.rfidjournal.com/articles/view?4986.

21. Khan, A.A., Rehmani, M.H., Rachedi, A., Cognitive-Radio-Based Internet of Things: Application, Architechture, Spectrum Related Functionalities and Future Research directions. *IEEE Wirel. Comm.*, 24, 3, 17–25, 2017.

22. Khan, A.A., Rehmani, M.H., Rachedi, A., When Cognitive Radio Meets the Internet of Things? Paper presented at *Conference on 12th International Wireless Communication and Mobile Computing (IWCMC 2016)*, Paphos, Cyprus, pp. 469–474, 2016.

23. Kotobi, K. and Bilen, S.G., Blockchain-Enabled Spectrum Access in Cognitive Radio Networks. Paper presented at *Wireless Telecommunication Symposium (WTS)*, Chicago, Il, USA, pp. 1–6, 2017.

24. Mitola, J. and Maguire, G.Q., Cognitive Radio: Making Software Radios More Personal. *IEEE Pers. Commun.*, 6, 4, 1318, 1999.

25. Nakamoto, S., *Bitcoin: A Peer-To-Peer Electronic Cash System*, Bitcoin. Retrieved from: https://bitcoin.org/bitcoin.pdf, 2008.

26. Noirie, L., Le Pallec, M., Ammar, N., Towards Automated IoT Service Recommendation. Paper presented at *20th Conference in Innovations in Clouds, Internet and Network*, Paris, France, pp. 103–106, 2017.

27. Peters, G.W. and Panayi, E., *Understanding Modern Banking Ledgers through Blockchain Technologies: Future of Transaction Processing and Smart Contracts on the Internet of Money. In Banking Beyond Banks and Money: A Guide to Banking Services in the Twenty-First Century*, pp. 239–278, Springer, 2016. ISBN: 978-3-319-42446-0

28. Pilkington, M., *Blockchain Technology: Principles and Applications. Research Handbook on Digital transformation*, O.F. Xavier, Z. Majlinda, E. Edward (Eds.), Edward Elgar Publishing, Cheltenham, UK, p. 225, 2016.

29. Pourpeighambar, B., Dehghan, M., Sabaei, M., Multi-Agent Learning Based Routing for Delay Minimization in Cognitive Radio Network. *J. Netw. Comput. Appl.*, 84, C, 82–92, 2017.

30. Raju, S., Boddepalli, S., Gampa, S., Yan, Q., Deogun, J.S., Identity Management Using Blockchain for Cogitive Cellular Networks. Paper presented at *IEEE International Conference on Communications (ICC)*, Paris, France, 2017.

31. Riahi, A., Natalizio, E., Challal, Y.; Mitton, N., Iera, A., A Systemic and Cognitive Approch for IoT Security. Paper presented at *International Conference in Computing, Networking and Communication (ICNC)*, Conference On, Honolulu, HI, USA, pp. 183–188, 2014.

32. Sangaiah, A.K., Thangavelu, A., Sundara, V.M., *Cognitive Computing for Big Data Systems over IoT*, Springer, Switzerland, 2018, Gewerbestrasse 11, 6330 Cham.

33. Saghiri, A.M. and Meybodi, M.R., An Approach for Designing Cognitive Engines in Cognitive Peer-To-Peer Network. *J. Netw. Comput. Appl.*, 70, C, 17–40, 2016.

34. Shah, M.A., Zhang, S., Maple, C., Cognitive Radio Network for Internet of Things: Application, Challenge and Future. Paper presented at *19th International Conference in Automation and Computing (ICAC)*, London, UK, pp. 1–6, 2013.

35. Siever, B. and Rogers, M.P., An IoTA of IoT, in: *Proceedings of ACM Sigcse Technical Symposium on Computer Science Education*, Seattle, WA, USA, p. 742, 2017.

36. Singh, D., Tripathi, G., Jara, A.J., A Survey of Internet-of-Things: Future Vision, Architecture, Challenge and Service. *IEEE World Forum on Internet of Things*, Seoul, South Korea, pp. 287–292, 2014.

37. Swan, M., *Blockchain: Blueprint for A New Economy*, O'reilly Media, Inc, Sebastopol, CA, USA, 2015.

38. Tervonen, J., Isoherranen, V., Heikkila, M., A Review of the Cognitive Capabilities and Data Analysis Issues of the Future Industrial Internet-of-Things. Paper presented at *6th IEEE International Conference on Cognitive Infocommunication (Coginfocom)*, Gyor, Hungary, pp. 127–132, 2015.

39. Thomas, R.W., Friend, D.H., Dasilva, L.A., Mackenzie, A.B., Cognitive Network: Adaption and Learning to Achieve End-To-End Performance Objective. *IEEE Commun. Mag.*, 48, 51–57, 2006.

40. Thomas, R.W., Friend, D.H., Dasilva, L.A., Mackenzie, A.B., *Cognitive Networks. Cognitive Radio, Software Defined Radio and Adaptive Wireless System*, H. Arslan (Ed.), Springer, Ed Dordrecht. The Netherlands, 2007.

41. Thomas, R.W., Friend, D.H., Dasilva, L.A., Mackenzie, A.B., *Cognitive Radio, Software Defined Radio and Adaptive Wireless System. Chapter Cognitive Networks*, Springer, Dordrecht, 2007.

42. Wu, Q., Ding, G., Xu, Y., Feng, S., Du, Z., Wang, J. *et al.*, Cognitive Internet of Things: A New Paradigm Beyond Connection. *IEEE Internet Things*, 1, 129–143, 2014.
43. Zhang, Y. and Wen, J., An IoT Electric Business Model Based on the Protocol of Bitcoin. Paper presented at *18th International Conference in Intelligence in Next Generation Networks (ICIN)*, Paris, France, pp. 184–191, 2015.
44. Zyskind, G. and Nathan, O., Decentralizing Privacy: using Blockchain to Protocol Personal Data. Paper presented at *IEEE Security and Privacy Workshops (SPW)*, San Jose, CA, USA, pp. 180–184, 2015.

16

Development of a Recommender System HealthMudra Using Blockchain for Prevention of Diabetes

Rashmi Bhardwaj[1]* and Debabrata Datta[2]

[1]*University School of Basic & Applied Sciences, Nonlinear Dynamics Research Lab, Guru Gobind Singh Indraprastha University, Delhi, India*
[2]*Radiological Physics & Advisory Division, Bhabha Atomic Research Centre, CT & CRS Building, Anushaktinagar, Mumbai, India*

Abstract

HealthMudra is an algorithm coined as recommender system designed to generate protocol to prevent diabetes, most challenging disease in healthcare sector. HealthMudra is based on block chain technology embedded with suitable machine learning algorithms and optimization process. Recommendations are used by filtering. Prevention of diabetes be possible by reducing symptoms as prescribed by doctors. Information available to reduce symptoms of diabetes originated from large number of doctors can be stored in decentralized database named as Blockchain. Usage of blockchain helps patients to become true owners of their medical history. Similar to schema, patients can sign off transactions using their unique identification code in form of local keys and authorized access to history of data to users or researchers in field of machine learning/artificial intelligence and medical practitioners. HealthMudra being dynamical unstructured database has an incentive system that tracks all sorts of lifestyles of patient. HealthMudra provides risk assessment methodology on basis of epidemiological study on diabetes affected patients. The outcome of queries or retrievals entered into blockchain. Information sharing is available in HealthMudra. Uploading, storing, sharing and assessing risk related to health issues on diabetes are store in successive blocks and blockchain is useful to discuss the perspectives of HealthMudra.

Keywords: Recommender system, healthmudra, blockchain, machine learning, artificial intelligence, hashing

*Corresponding author: rashmib@ipu.ac.in

Sachi Nandan Mohanty, Jyotir Moy Chatterjee, Sarika Jain, Ahmed A. Elngar and Priya Gupta (eds.)
Recommender System with Machine Learning and Artificial Intelligence: Practical Tools and Applications in Medical, Agricultural and Other Industries, (313–328) © 2020 Scrivener Publishing LLC

16.1   Introduction

Diabetes is a disease in which the capability of human body is substantially lost to maintain blood glucose (alternate name as blood sugar) at the permissible and safe level. Three types of diabetes can develop in human body, such as Type-I, Type-II and gestational. An alternate name of Type-I is juvenile diabetes. Signature of Type-I diabetes exhibits when production of insulin in our body stops. Therefore, people having diabetes of Type-I are dependent on insulin which is to be injected into their body every day to stay in good health. The body still makes insulin with Type-II diabetes. However, even with normal response to insulin that the body produces is absolutely nil for persons having Type-II diabetes. As per National Institute of Diabetes, diseases occurring in kidney and digestive systems are the most common forms of diabetes. Women during their pregnancy are prone to gestational diabetes and their bodies exhibit less sensitivity to insulin during the period of pregnancy. However, all women do not show the symptoms of gestational diabetes but the issue gets resolved usually after giving birth. Occurrence of cystic fibrosis-related diabetes and monogenic are not common types. Doctors provide the knowledge for borderline diabetic cases subject to the blood glucose (BG) level is in the range of 100–125 mg/dL. Normal level of BG falls in the range lying between 70 and 99 mg/dL. It is known that fasting BG level of a diabetic person should be greater than 126 mg/dL. The level of BG for borderline cases is higher than usual but the level does not alarm them as diabetic. However, borderline people always are at risk of developing Type-II diabetes, even though they do not usually exhibit all the symptoms of diabetes. The patient records collected and stored in medical industry is sparse, that is to say keeping records of a large number of patients suffering from diabetes in a central database is a challenging task. Therefore, to retrieve this kind of sparse information we need to have a decentralized database technology. Blockchain technology has been developed for this purpose.

As per the literature provided by the Encyclopedia of Machine Learning, the definition of a recommender system is as follows: "The goal of a recommender system is to generate meaningful recommendations to a collection of users for items or products that might interest them". In general, a blockchain is a public ledger of information collected through a wide network placed on top of the internet. Machine learning algorithm such as convolution neural network (CNN), percentile bootstrap, aggregate data and boosting with optimization algorithm using BAT are implemented in HealthMudra. CNN is a variation of multilayer perceptron implemented in HealthMudra as a collaborative filter to segregate the profile of an individual patient to recommend the correct blockchain to get the information towards benefit of diabetics. BAT algorithm is a self-optimizing algorithm which performs the optimization for searching the information across the network. Architecture of the recorded information gives a ground-breaking potential to blockchain. So, one can say that blockchain generates a decentralized and immutable storage system of data which can be accessed anytime, from anywhere in the world. Scientifically, blockchain is defined as a system in which bitcoin is the main format for transaction of a record and this is maintained across several computers linked in a network known as peer-to-peer (P2P). A P2P network is interconnected and decentralized network in which sharing of tasks among all participants in an equal weightage [1]. The main utility of blockchain under the platform of HealthMudra is the possibility of exchanging electronic information across the participants in a distributed network without any support and requirement of reliable third party (RTP). Basically, popularity of blockchain technology as a distributed ledger system gained very fast [1].

Literature study [1] proves that transactions for exchanging electronic information either among persons or vendors are relied on a RTP, like bank, mediator, etc. Reliability of RTP is one main hurdle. So, the motivation behind blockchain technology is to overcome the limitations associated with the reliability of RTP. Diabetic patients will be benefited by the blockchain technology due to its easy access on the internet. The said technology will help on-the-spot diagnosis of the patient's medical condition and will facilitate prompt treatment without wasting precious time. The implementations of blockchain oriented crypto currencies (Bitcoin) framed the generation of this type of technology (Generation number I) is also referred to as blockchain 1.0 [2]. We propose HealthMudra that uses blockchain technology to improve prevention for every aspect of diabetes, heart disease and obesity.

A large number of data pertaining to the disease with other information related to health effect is generated by diabetic patients. In the context of healthcare, data among cross institutions are not shareable due to complexity as wells as confidentiality in nature. As a consequence, during treatment of the patient, availability of data to health care provider is poor. In this context, development takes place for second generation of blockchain technology [2]. The properties of the system are intelligent and they are basically attributed by number system. They have ownership controlled by a platform based on blockchain where the computer codes represent intelligent resources and all these software have the capability to encode the rules required to manage intelligent properties including controls of management system. Examples of blockchain are crypto currencies include

Ethereum [3], Ethereum Classic [4], NEO [5] and QTUM [6]. Advancement of data science may improve blockchain further. Consequently, blockchain can be thought of as a utility for fulfilling all demands at user end [7, 8].

Applications in different industries with various case studies are found elsewhere [8]. These applications are practiced to identify the address of a patient, to resolve disputes, to manage contracts, managing supply chain, maintaining insurance and healthcare, etc. [7, 9]. In view of the progress of blockchain technology, information system pertaining to healthcare issues has become landmarked. Performance of blockchain can be assessed by a number of identified useful events. Research community members and practitioners in the field may have to find out several applications for blockchain in the healthcare industry, especially to prevent other non-communicable diseases such as asthma and many more.

The current chapter presents a brief review focused towards the issues of blockchain technology in the field of sharing information on healthcare, specifically diabetes. Important and interesting reviews are found elsewhere in [10, 14]. Objectives and methodology of our approach is different. Angraal et al. [10] in their review, presents few examples pertaining to blockchain application in healthcare. For example, identities of patients of citizens of Estonia are validated by executing Guard time firm that operates a blockchain-based healthcare platform. In a similar way, a cluster of blockchain based examples for solving healthcare issues can be found elsewhere in [11]. The companies involved for this task are categorized under different events of healthcare. Prescription for detection of drug fraud, patient oriented management of records pertaining to medical and study of the dental related issues are few examples of those categories. Mettler [12] reported blockchain driven applications, research in the domain of medical, research in the pharmaceutical industry (drug delivery and drug management) and research in the domain of public health management. Ku et al. [13] published the net benefit of blockchain over traditional databases by a comparison with later for healthcare applications. They also explained about the improvement for management of medical information, enhancement of processes to claim insurance, improvement of clinical research and advancement of data ledgers of healthcare.

Finally, review of Roman-Belmonte et al. [14] highlighted the coverage of the many important applications and utilities of blockchain which are available in various branches of medicine. All these tasks contain the tools representing data analytics of healthcare with legal medicine, biomedical research, digital medical records, meaningful usage and expenditure related issues for services in medical sector and so on.

Recommendation systems are developed to reduce the information overloaded problem. HealthMudra falls into this category and hence justify as a recommender system. Here information is overloaded through several blockchain which is discussed through blockchain architecture. The objective of this work is to deliver a scheme to share health care data using blockchain technology. The scheme includes data sharing, concerns pertaining to privacy and patients of diabetes as the main node to govern their data. The in-depth formation the HealthMudra facilitates a knowledge base for diabetic patient to decide the appropriate procedures to enhance their health. Various habits such as doing exercise, eating proper food, increasing daily activity and adjusting very good mental health are available in the structure of HealthMudra. These events are reflected in biomarkers immediately and all the activities associated with those events are monitored closely using the HealthMudra system.

Evolutionary improvement leads to a reduction of medical costs and the same produced by the people who provide insurance. A substantial knowledge will be gained by patients seeking to minimize the cost of their medical bill. Subsequently the knowledge gained will help them to make the best alternates suitable for minimizing the signatures of diabetes, and all these issues are entangled later in their biomarkers.

Technological based various outcome of HealthMudra will continue to gain attraction. Progress of a small company dealing with this kind of information may help to handle the serious problem encountered with the disease. The remaining portion of this chapter is arranged in the following way. Section 2, describes a brief architecture of blockchain. Section 3, describes the role of HealthMudra to prevent diabetic. Section 4, presents blockchain technology solutions. Section 5, presents the conclusions.

16.2   Architecture of Blockchain

Architecture of blockchain starts with conceptual definition of blockchain and proceeds further to present its various categories. In the context of architecture of blockchain, we can say that blockchain can be of centralized, decentralized and distributed ledger. Distributed ledger is further subdivided into public (global) and private (local). All these architectures are shown in Figure 16.1.

Instead of copying the digital information, the blockchain technique allows them to be distributed in a ledger system which provides data security, transparency and trust. Architecture of blockchain as shown in Figure 16.2 is always different from database.

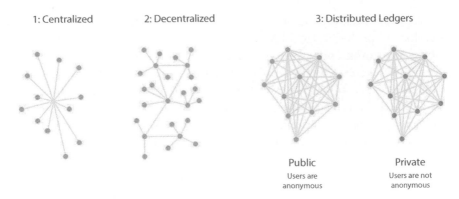

Figure 16.1 Architecture of blockchain.

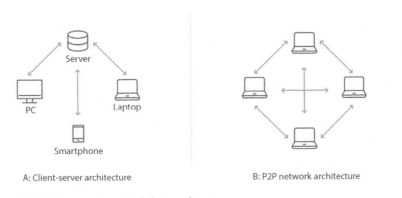

Figure 16.2 Database versus Blockchain architecture.

16.2.1 Definition of Blockchain

In short, a decentralized, distributed ledger (may be public and private) containing various types of transactions arranged into a P2P network is defined as blockchain. We can also say that blockchain is organized as a linearly linked list of blocks (alternately, chain of blocks), each of these blocks performs a specific task in an ordered manner and each of these tasks is linked in the form of a chain to generate meaningful information.

16.2.2 Structure of Blockchain

A set of proposals collected as authenticated transactions received during a few minutes (e.g. 10 min) is said to be a block. An authenticated transaction proposal is defined as a proposal satisfying the necessary requirements for validation. Two very important data structures present in blockchain are:

(a) linked list and (b) pointers. Basically, pointers represent the address of a variable and points to the location of another variable which contains another piece of information. Linked lists represent a sequence of block and each such block holds a piece of data and linked to the next block by a pointer. A pointer (address variable) can be of various types such as near, far and huge. The complete structure known as hashing is shown in Figure 16.3. The modality of authentication ensures that the transaction invoked is able to be defended with logic or justification. For example, the procedure starts with an authenticated user. It is known that once a transaction gets permission of its authenticity, we say that the transaction is valid. Therefore, authenticated transactions are said to be validated transactions. So, throughout the chapter, we will use authenticated transaction instead of valid transaction.

Consensus algorithm which decides the order to append the authenticated blocks to the database system is the working function. In the network of blockchain, some distinct nodes maintain their specialty and they are main resource to execute the consensus algorithms. These special pieces of lists are said to be dataminers. These miners play the role of transactions process and their place in the blockchain. The said method is known as data mining. Once the proposal of a transaction is accepted by a data decision maker, it checks the validity of the transaction. Authenticated transactions are only included into a block. The foreign chunk of authenticated transactions is appended (or chained) to the last block after a certain time period or block period, thus create a chain of blocks. The chain of these blocks (a chunk of records) is labeled as blockchain (B-Chain). The B-chain is always occurs as an exact copy of the same over the distribution of all nodes (e.g. a chunk of data and a pointer for its connectivity with the next one) in the network. Each such replicate has an identical ledger (database) for every transaction in the network.

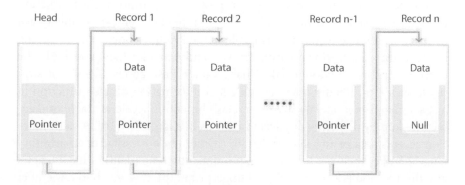

Figure 16.3 Data structure of Blockchain (Hashing).

The chaining algorithm of blocks to build the structure of B-chain is similar to a self-referential data structure but it is associated with a large number of learning algorithm. We can first consider the different types of B-chain. The implementation event of B-chain (e.g. HealthMudra) says that in the network any node can join without any security check and in the similar way, they can give their consent to take part in the data processing task (that is, participation in chaining of the validated new blocks with the existing ones). Participating for joining of any node in the network as data processor without authorization or accessing permission and implementing the same process into a system is said to be a public or permission less B-chain. In contrast, authorized permitted B-chain is one in which members are required to authorize and should have permission to access before their participation and joining in the network. Only certain piece of information representing nodes are allowed to take part in the data processing task (data analytics) in permitted B-chain. The structure of permitted B-chain networks implies that they are generally smaller in size, speedier in data traffic and secured in data handling compared to that available in the global B-chain networks.

A permitted B-chain can be identified further either as a static or a consortium B-chain (CB-C). The difference between static and CB-C depends on the number of data chunks to be permitted by data miners. In CB-C, two or more pieces of information keeping their validity are permitted to take part in the process of data mining. Obviously, authenticated or empowered users can be members of the grid in CB-C. Hence, the CB-C has the advantages of redistribution along with enhanced security and inherent privacy in the private B-chain. Information pertaining to the various categories of B-chain (global, local and consortium) can be found elsewhere in [15]. It is worth to consider the procedure representing the linking of blocks to construct the B-chain. The linking of data (chunk of information) is carried out by hash function, which is known as a cryptographic primitive. Hash function plays major role in this mechanism. As per reference, we can define a hash function as a procedure which is implemented to have one to one mapping between the data having an arbitrary size and data of a fixed size [16]. The outcome of this function is called hash values, hash codes, digests, or simply hashes [16]. Readers can get the detail information of hash function in any standard book on data structure. Hash functions accelerate table or database lookup by detecting duplicated records in a large file [16]. A hash function accepts data of an arbitrary length (it could be a message of an arbitrary length) and crunches it into a corresponding outcome (data) of fixed length, and this method is known as digital fingerprint [16]. It is worth to remember that collision resistant is a property of hash function, i.e., no two different digital fingerprints will produce the same hash output [16]. Basis of chaining of new "chunk of information [CI] (block)" follows the property as directed by hash function. In order to link a new CI to the B-chain, the new block header (BH) is appended with hash output of the previous BH. Thus, the tail node CI of B-chain contains the fingerprint of the transactions of the previous CI. Figure 16.1 represents the schematic diagram of chaining of CIs.

Now, from Figure 16.4, it can be stated that architecture of B-chain can be constructed by hash function. Now, in a similar manner records pertaining health information of diabetic patient are chained rather structured. In view of this, patient will be aware of the preventive tips and will be cautioned about the short falls of diabetic disease. It can be seen from Figure 16.1, little bit of change in transactions in a block results an enormous change in corresponding hash output resulting a breaking the chain to the next linked blocks of the B-chain. So, a modification (deletion, insertion, search and sort operations) of the contents of a block in the B-chain in the network can be identified very easily (task is alternatively known as detection). This certifies that insertion of a transaction into a block once done and chained to the B-chain, the same transaction cannot be modified. Thus, information on the B-chain is said to be immutable. Operation of retrieving a record after its creation or prohibition of any kind of modification is called as immutability. We can say that immutability is one of the important properties of B-chain. Because of this property, after creation of a record, the same record cannot be changed or recaptured. In order to refurbish the said chain, a new record must have to be created. Hence, B-chain can be named as "append-only" ledger. Transactions are time

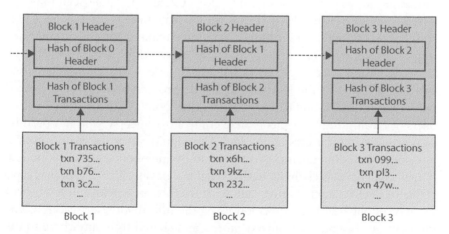

Figure 16.4 A schema showing the chain of blocks to form a blockchain [17].

stamped and this is ensured by the process of chaining CIs to the B-chain. Audit on transactions made by a person can be framed as a triplet {"the person who did", "what he did", and "when he has done"}.

16.3   Role of HealthMudra in Diabetic

With a view to a long list of diseases occurred in patients prevention of diabetes is one of the important tasks in the field of medical industry for survivability. Many more people are the candidate of this disease due to change in dietary habits and change in lifestyle patterns. It is evident that there exists a rapid growth of the public costs spent to prevent the disease. Anything should be stopped at route itself. Our proposed algorithm known as HealthMudra, uses an admixture of incentives and technology for influencing the choice of people. Prevention of diabetes can be possible to maintain by using HealthMudra based B-chain attempts to prevent incidence of diabetes. Symptoms of current patients also can be brought down to a very minimal figure by HealthMudra. B-chain being an innovative technology creates a highly reliable method (cryptography) to store and exchange information. Advantage of HealthMudra is that it has the capability to reduce the effects of diabetes. Literature study evidenced that estimation of one quarter adults in America suffers from diabetes by 2050 [17]. Expenditure for curing diabetes of any individual is substantially high. In addition, individuals suffering from diabetes believe that they may prone to other diseases ranging from cardiovascular to blood related problems [17]. All these issues alarm frequent usage of the health care system. Indirectly it addresses more expenditures as well as more insurance bill. However, an innovative technological based solution is available in HealthMudra which keeps track all of a person's lifestyle choices. On the basis of continual making good selections, they implement various signatures such as heart rate, weight, sugar level, etc. (all these signatures are collectively called as biomarker) in a knowledge based system execute over the HealthMudra. The progressive outcome is stored on the HealthMudra and this is one of the key points of the innovation. The users of HealthMudra have complete control over people who has permission or login id for accessing the fact. This signifies that the main resource personnel including doctors, insurers, family members and the individual patients will have accessibility in that reliable database. The patient may have rights to decide about sharing data with friends, an employer, the government or public health organization using the information for research. The data can be always synchronized, stored and shared from anywhere in the world but at the same time it is well secured due to B-chain technology.

The graph of the HealthMudra system provides a robust base for the patient to make the appropriate choice to improve their health. These involve activities like exercising, eating healthy and appropriate foods, increase of daily activity and better psychological health. In HealthMudra system, these varieties are immediately attributed as biomarkers and each of these activities is monitored closely. Time based improvement may lead to a depletion of medical costs along with the reduction of the costs generated by the insurer as financial expenditure. Patients seeking to minimize their medical expenditures would be sagacious to practice the healthy possibilities that decrease the symptoms of diabetes and all are echoed in their biomarkers. Ground-breaking solutions with advanced technology of HealthMudra are continuing to gain momentum. Rapid increase in urban population as a proportion of total population, sluggish style of living and overexertion due to technology-driven isolation are just some of the factors which generally pumps an increase in chronic diseases like diabetes, cancer, and heart attack [18]. Literature study reports that patients suffering from diabetes, in China and India alone are 114 million and 69 million respectively [18]. It is also evidence that 415 million people suffer diabetes globally and the number 415 million is expected further to rise in future [18]. The number of diabetologists at the same time is very low, expenditure on healthcare is increasing exponentially and expectations of patients from healthcare providers are changing rapidly [18]. All these factors are triggering tech administrators to understand the unique intricacies of business and clinical workflows across the healthcare value aided chain [18]. Health tech administrators are putting their effort to improve the accessibility of patient-healthcare worker's interaction by Artificial Intelligence (AI), telemedicine, virtual care and voice user interface. A physician's clinical practice can be more scalable by these advanced technologies [18].

However, as of today, two key components are still missing in the innovations in technology oriented healthcare systems. First component signifies that personalized reward programs for patients adhering to their care plan cannot be created by the present method of solutions. For example, the individual is not readily motivated and rewarded properly to reduce time spent on social media apps even if they are asked by a therapist to do the same. Second component addresses the fact that patients are not the sole responsible of their health records because the information pertaining to their health resides on the corresponding repository in many places such as (1) in hospital EMR systems, (2) in primary care physician files, (3) in pharmacy systems, etc. Patients or individuals either should be able to access their health data or should be able to share their health data anonymously with innovators similar to AI scientists and medical researchers. These issues can be resolved by blockchain. Usage of HealthMudra blockchain can guide to improve the health data management of diabetes. In future, the blockchain technology will be implemented in existing small-scale diabetes health care system to explore its real-world benefits and challenges.

16.4   Blockchain Technology Solutions

Technology solution of blockchain based healthcare data is nothing but to device the storage platform in which data for diabetic patients can be kept permanently. Such a device can be labeled as electronic device medical record (EDMR). Patients can opt in to share this device. Methodology of tokenization similar to the operation of bank's teller counter can be adopted to extract the clinical protocols of individuals and plan for caring patients. The financial matters pertaining to payment is designed in the framework of coins. Patient's wallet scan be filled with these coins and at the same time business can be marked to trade corresponding valuation. Direct use of tokens can fulfill the necessary costs of healthcare. Finally, tokens are accepted by insurers and also by insurance for hospitals. Method of tokenization to deal with health outcomes of each individual can facilitate patients to spend their tokens at any locations wherever need is there. HealthMudra-based blockchain will allow patients to own their data. Patients can access their own data to other parties. They can also come out of transactions by using their network based accessible keys. Access level, time period, and deletion of information related to personal data such as {Name, Name of Father, Name of Mother, Age, Address, Working experience, phone, and email}. Once the system authenticates the accessibility of data of an individual, he/she can pay their financial cost by these tokens. The system will work as an ecosystem and predator-prey model is the backbone of this techniques. If patients are ready to share their diabetic condition (health information) they can be paid and huge volume of healthcare data can be distributed among medical researchers to derive further innovations such as to discover medicines perfectly. In view of this, a better understanding of disease will take place among participants. Decision for donating certain portion of the amount earned by patients to hospitals and insurers can be made by patients so that the amount earned can be helpful as an aided fund to treat indigent patients. Needy population segments in the present society will be benefitted by this crowd sourcing care subsidy programs. A protocol implemented in computer and designed to digitally facilitate, verify, or enforce the negotiation, is said to be a smart contract [16]. Third parties do not have any role behind the performance of credible transactions allowed by smart contracts. Irreversibility is the characteristics property of these transactions due to which it is possible to track them. Blockchain technology is the platform to formulate smart contracts [16]. These contracts are completely auditable and transparent. Code can be viewed by anyone. Rules pertaining to business to disburse tokens can easily understand. Reduction of healthcare cost will be possible by storing patient health records on blockchain if enabled. Lending more transparency to share patient data is also carried out by the storage mechanism. In summary, blockchain provides most sophisticated technological solutions for preventing disease like diabetic.

16.4.1   Predictive Models of Health Data Analysis

Data analysis for diabetic patients to estimate various confounding factors can be carried out by logistic regression—a prime component of HealthMudra. Generally, logistic regression based predictive model estimates odds ratio to find the probability of causation. Support vector regression classifies the data into two clusters such as cases for benign clusters and cases borderline groups. Harnessing the power of advanced machine learning techniques by blockchain can realize the importance of predictive healthcare data analytics. The research can be winged further in the area of biomedical and biotechnology to improve supply of medicines in precise form. Usage of the HealthMudra based blockchain case also provides a comprehensive roadmap of diagnostic pathways for prevention of diabetics.

16.5   Conclusions

The main objective of recommender system HealthMudra is to explore the utilization of blockchain in various sector of healthcare. HealthMudra reduce the overload of distributed information. CNN has been applied as a learner for activating the exact blockchain to retrieve the information and validating by BAT algorithm. Healthcare related issues have been identified with the help of a review of relevant databases pertaining to medical industry. It is possible to isolate those problems which can be solved in a better way by using other techniques. Applications of blockchain in many directions pertaining to science, social science, engineering and medical are proposed in literatures. But, a few of these prototype versions are functional. So, it is very important to realize the implementations of blockchain in healthcare industry and also into the other health related identified domains such as supply of medicines, maintenance of blood banks, etc. Learning theory with database technology via blockchain in the domain of healthcare will help the practitioners to fulfill research gaps and also will enrich knowledge for making decisions with uncertain information. Databases constructed using fuzzy set theory, rough set theory and neutrosophic set theory and a learner to fie the appropriate database through blockchain may be an important research domain in near future. So, it is mandatory to look at the challenges and drawbacks of the blockchain applications. Based on networked database management system, prototype applications developed till date, limitations associated with healthcare-related problems can be reduced. In order to improve further, HealthMudra blockchain technology can be modified. Non-financial related events will be considered in future version of HealthMudra.

References

1. Nakamoto, S., *Bitcoin: A Peer-to-Peer Electronic Cash System*, 2008, Available online: www.bitcoin.org (accessed on 12 March 2019).
2. Swan, M., *Blockchain: Blueprint for a New Economy*, O'Reilly Media, Inc., Sebastopol, CA, USA, 2015.
3. Ethereum Project, 2019. Available online: https://www.ethereum.org/ (accessed on 12 March 2019).
4. Ethereum, *Classic—A Smarter Blockchain that Takes Digital Assets Further 2018*, 2019, Available online: https://ethereumclassic.org/ (accessed on 12 March 2019).
5. NEO Smart Economy 2018, 2019. Available online: https://neo.org/(accessed on 12 March 2019).
6. Qtum, 2018. Available online: https://qtum.org/en (accessed on 12 March 2019).
7. Burniske, C., Vaughn, E., Cahana, A., Shelton, J., *How Blockchain Technology Can Enhance Electronic Health Record Operability;*, Ark Invest, New York, NY, USA, 2016.
8. Jovanovic, B. and Rousseau, P.L., General Purpose Technologies, in: *Handbook of Economic Growth*, Elsevier, New York, NY, USA, 2005.
9. Androulaki, E., Barger, A., Bortnikov, V., Cachin, C., Christidis, K., De Caro, A., Enyeart, D., Ferris, C., Laventman, G., Manevich, Y. *et al.*, Hyperledger Fabric: A Distributed Operating System for Permissioned Blockchains, in: *Proceedings of the Thirteenth EuroSys Conference; EuroSys '18*, Association for Computing Machinery, New York, NY, USA, vol. 30, pp. 1–30:15, 2018.

10. Angraal, S., Krumholz, H.M., Schulz, W.L., Blockchain Technology Applications in Health Care, in: *Circ. Cardiovasc. Qual. Outcomes*, vol. 10, p. e003800, 2017.

11. Engelhardt, M.A., Hitching Healthcare to the Chain: An Introduction to Blockchain Technology in the Healthcare Sector. *Technol. Innov. Manag. Rev.*, 7, 22, 2017.

12. Mettler, M., Blockchain Technology in Healthcare the Revolution Starts Here, in: *Proceedings of the 2016 IEEE 18th International Conference on E-Health Networking, Applications and Services (Healthcom)*, Munich, Germany, 14–17 September 2016, pp. 520–522, 2016.

13. Kuo, T.T., Kim, H.E., Ohno-Machado, L., Blockchain Distributed Ledger Technologies for Biomedical and Health Care Applications. *J. Am. Med. Inform. Assoc.*, 24, 1211, 2017.

14. Roman-Belmonte, J.M., De la Corte-Rodriguez, H., Rodriguez-Merchan, E.C.C., la Corte-Rodriguez, H., Carlos Rodriguez-Merchan, E., How Blockchain Technology Can Change Medicine. *Postgrad. Med.*, 130, 420, 2018.

15. Alhadhrami, Z., Alghfeli, S., Alghfeli, M., Abedlla, J.A., Shuaib, K., Introducing Blockchains for Healthcare, in: *Proceedings of the 2017 International Conference on Electrical and Computing Technologies and Applications (ICECTA)*, Ras Al Khaimah, UAE, 19–21 November 2017, pp. 1–4, 2017.

16. https://en.wikipedia.org, 2001.

17. www.mdpi.com, 1996.

18. www.datascience.com

Part 5
HEALTHCARE RECOMMENDER SYSTEMS

Case Study 1: Health Care Recommender Systems

Usha Mittal[1], Nancy Singla[2] and Geetika Gupta[3]*

[1]Department of Computer Science and Engineering, Lovely Professional University, Phagwara, India
[2]Department of Pharmacology, University Institute of Pharmaceutical Sciences and Research, BFUHS, Faridkot, India
[3]Department of Biotechnology, Thapar Institute of Engineering and Technology, Patiala, India

Abstract

Healthcare is prominent area of medical domain which needs to analyse large number of patient's data to go into the deep insights and judge the health condition based upon life style, social activities and physical health records. The best way to cope with disease is to detect their symptoms as soon as possible. The health recommender system (HRS) becomes an indispensable tool in making decision in healthcare sector that maximizes the effectiveness and quality of medical services. The main objective of HRS is to assure the availability of valuable information at the right time by establishing information quality, authentication, privacy concerns and trustworthiness. Prediction made by HRS should not only be accurate but also help one to define appropriate treatment, precautions to be made, risk to individual as well present that risk in a secured and personalized manner with respect to illness and undesirable outcomes of treatments.

In this chapter, various health care recommender systems, different technologies to design recommender system are explained as well as a case study is given for recommending system for Parkinson's disease using machine learning and artificial intelligence.

Keywords: Lifestyle, healthcare, self-diagnostic, Parkinson's disease

*Corresponding author: geetika_12_gupta@yahoo.com

Sachi Nandan Mohanty, Jyotir Moy Chatterjee, Sarika Jain, Ahmed A. Elngar and Priya Gupta (eds.) *Recommender System with Machine Learning and Artificial Intelligence: Practical Tools and Applications in Medical, Agricultural and Other Industries*, (331–350) © 2020 Scrivener Publishing LLC

17.1 Introduction

In every field the technologies give rise to innovations and developments. Due to the availability of big data on the network, Recommender System (RS) acquired significant to receive filtered data after cleansing and mining. Effective information can be retrieved by throwing ways of filtering such as: collaborative filtering, content based filtering and Hybrid filtering. These are the fundamental types with these the emerging filtering methods are also thereof such as a Mobile recommender system, knowledge based recommender system and many more [32].

a) Collaborative filtering: Collecting and analyzing activity and behavior data, users and predicting what users are likely to do about their similarities to other users [1].
b) Content-based filtering: Examination of past data and present user expectations and prediction based on item characteristics
c) Hybrid recommender systems: Combination of content-based skills with a cooperative method or integration of methods into a single model
d) Knowledge-based recommender systems: Collecting customer awareness and building a recommendation strategy by reasoning on what items would meet user needs
e) Mobile Recommender Systems: Besides traditional approaches, mobile RS contains regional information and makes context-sensitive recommendations [2, 29].

17.1.1 Health Care Recommender System

Health recommender system (HRS) belongs to recommender system (RS). As the hospitals have a huge number of data about their patients and their health parameters and thus it is necessary for health professionals to use this information effectively. HRS is a decision-making system, it provides health care information to both patients and health professionals and this information can be used for diagnostic assistance as well as personal health advising. Drives from patient's current health status, current medications, prehistory, symptoms and past treatment, HRS individuals with similar parameters can be categorized such as current status of patient's health, prehistory, current modes of treatment, past treatments and symptoms. The medicines suitable for the same group of patients are suggested by recommender system. With the help of recommender system, the physician will be able to take a better-informed decision to treat a patient. The aim is to demonstrate the already available treatments for the health care providers to improve the selection of medicine process and select a suitable medication for the patients [33].

For the successful development of a health recommender system, many of the methods and procedures should be used to ensure the development of this system. To make is specific and intricate the Health area and Recommender system have to face many challenges. Firstly, For HRS no proper task definition available, which items have to recommend the main aim depends on that. In a health scenario several things are imaginable. For instance, recommender system on a mobile device could suggest physical activities that suit the present user situation to improve their health. Patients suffering with arthritis and obesity can get benefit from physical activity recommendations that drop not any extra strain on inflamed joints. Furthermore, various cancer therapies can be proposed to both patients as well as a doctor with the help of this system. To get the optimal therapies and alternatives this system integrates many properties which include additional medication, as other illness, family situation and job requirement. It could imagine the extent, experience and possible side effects of multiple treatments, thus increasing patient awareness of their situation. The recommendation program could be a communication tool used by both doctor and patient to help make choices that are difficult. The primary procedures can be taken from recommendation systems research in both scenarios, but they serve extremely different objectives and therefore change the requirements to the recommendation system [3].

17.1.2   Parkinson's Disease: Causes and Symptoms

In pars compacta of substantia nigra, the loss of dopaminergic neurons leads to Parkinson's disease. Still the reason behind the death of neurons is not known. It results in the downfall of dopamine level in the striatal region of the brain. Imbalance between the neurotransmitters is the crucial factor that gives rise to motor symptoms such as hyperkinesia and tremor [4, 5]. Furthermore, non motor symptoms takes place in Patients suffering with PD for instance, mood disorders, imbalance, and sleep, learning impairment, urinary and gastrointestinal dysfunction. Clinical practitioners could benefit with a number of non motor signs to identify the stage of illness [6].

With the progression of PD to control movements become difficult. Patients suffering with the disease bearing symptoms such as gait abnormality and occurrence of tremors vary stage to stage. With the help of Gait analysis, which is made of the gait cycle PD can be diagnosed. From physionet data base the raw force data was filtered with the help of Chebyshev 2 Type high pass filters with minimum frequency 0.8 Hz to diminish noises which were due to modification in the subject's body with another factor measurement. The data obtained after filtration helped to get several gait features with the pulse duration measuring techniques and peak detection. The number of threshold values obtained from the detection of gait algorithm was tuned to different subjects. Various mobile features which include the heel and toe forces were obtained with a peak detection algorithm. Various temporal features were obtained which includes swing and stance phases, and stride time with the development of the pulse duration algorithm. The most common symptom of PD is Tremors, occurs due to involuntary movement of body parts. Firstly, the tremors appear in specific body parts such as leg, arm or one side of the body, furthermore it can pass on both body sides. The cardinal sign of PD is resting tremor 92.7% of an average accuracy is obtained for the diagnosis of PD with Gait analysis and Severity of PD can be known by the tremor analysis [7].

17.1.3   Parkinson's Disease: Treatment and Surgical Approaches

Measurement of disease stages and quantitative, repeatable, reliability of severity are the key requirements for a better treatment and Monitoring of PD. During the last 50 years of PD study, empirical, subjective ratings have been controlled by human interpretation of the appearance of signs and symptoms of illness at medical visits. More recently, "wearable," sensor-based, standardized, purpose and easy-to-use systems have been developed to measure PD signs over extended periods for large numbers of participants. This technology has the capability to significantly recover PD diagnosis and management as well as clinical studies conduct. Though, the large-scale, high-dimensional nature of the data collected by, these wearable sensors needs to be sophisticated signal processing and machine-learning algorithms to transform it into scientifically appropriate algorithms and data of clinical significance. These procedures that "read" from data have shown amazing success in predicting complex problems that require human expertise to date, but they are forced to evaluate and submit without a basic knowledge of their underlying logic [8].

For the treatment of Parkinson's disease (PD) the established therapy is deep brain stimulation (DBS). Time intensive management after surgery is required to maintain balance between the coupled stimulation and medication treatment. Clinical Decision support system (CDSS) depends on the machine learning algorithms can help in treatment optimization with large and complex parameters [9].

17.2   Review of Literature

To decrease the Parkinson disorder progression rate between the individuals, it is important to be detected in the initial stages of the commencement of the Parkinson disease. Different researchers have been made to discover the basic cause and several researchers have reached to the heights by proposing a system that differentiates the healthy individuals from those with any Neurodegenerative disorders (ND'S) with techniques by machine learning. In the past decades, a large number of the preprocessing, classification techniques and feature selection have been implemented. In this chapter, we have categorized the prediction of the Parkinson's disorder into three parts i.e.

a) Preprocessing techniques
b) Classification methods
c) Different computational methodology

a) Preprocessing techniques
Yadav *et al.* [10] reported three methods i.e. Decision stump, Logistic Regression and Sequential Minimization Optimization using data mining techniques. The findings inferred, supporting vector machine model with 76% accuracy, sensitivity 0.97 while statistical model specificity has done well with 0.62 compared with two other models.

Bonato *et al.* [11] suggested evidence that data mining and artificial intelligentsia could help to recognize the severity of motor fluctuations in PD patients. They collected data using ACC (accelerometer) and EMG (electromyography) signals that were recorded during the performance of standardized motor assessment tasks.

In another research, Sonu *et al.* [12] implemented a JavaScript program to record the patient's voice and later used Praat to convert that accepts input into a.wav file and using a script xvii give way a voice report. Decision tree yielded the best results among the algorithm applied with 100% accuracy without feature selection and 94% with feature selection.

b) Classification methods

Challa *et al.* [13] discussed the importance of non-motor systems that many physicians over motor systems have neglected. In this study four machine learning techniques were used i.e. The prediction is performed by Multilayer Perceptron, Bayes Net, RF and Boosted Logistic Regression and Sleep behavior distortion, olfactory loss and the Rapid Eye Movement (REM) were also considered. Among which, with an accuracy of 97.159 % was Boosted logistic regression and 98.9 % was area under the ROC curve is considered as a better method.

Agarwal *et al.* [14] reported extreme learning machines for the prediction of PD. They performed a comparative analysis using ELM and concluded that, unlike traditional Neural Network, elms do not need iterative variation of hidden neurons. So the simple architecture makes elm a method of prediction that is reliable than others.

Dinesh and He [15] found that a fundamental frequency among all voice recording apps is the best feature for predicting Parkinson's disease and they also tested different methods of machine learning, including Boosted Decision Tree, Decision Jungle, Locally Deep SVM, Logistic Regression, Neural Networks and SVM on Microsoft Azure Machine Learning Studio in which Two-class Boosted decision trees is the best as ensemble technique.

Fiscon *et al.* [16] diagnose brain abnormalities using EEG Electroencephalography. To support medical doctors, they have given an automatic classification of patients from the EEG biomedical signals involved in Alzheimer's disease and MCI. The researchers used time-frequency transforms to preprocess and then used machine learning to apply classification.

Rodrigues *et al.* [17] uses K-mean to obtain temporary events (EEG) to improve the diagnosis of PD. They achieved the EEG energy variation sequence that is found in AD patients more frequently than in any healthy individual.

Novoa-Del-Toro *et al.* [18] found there was a volume reduction in Alzheimer's disease in some areas of the brain. Some regions, such as precuneus, begin to show changes when tested by MRI (Magnetic Resonance Imaging). So in their research, using machine learning methods, they used precuneus as a biomarker to recognize defects in the brain.

Johnstone *et al.* [19] took the plasma proteome dataset from ADNI (Neuroimaging Initiative for Alzheimer's disease). Combinatorial optimization like selection of features was applied. The MCI patient and the AD patient were therefore distinguished depending on whether APOE was included or whether there were some other considerations. Finally, by generating the signature longitudinal, they get an accuracy of 90%.

Rathore and Kumar [30] primarily used regression techniques in various machine learning techniques. The error rates are determined after comparing the ML techniques i.e. AAE and ARE. To confirm the results, K fold validation is applied. Finally, the Kruskal–Wallis test and Dunn's multiple comparison test are used to perform comparative analyses of techniques. Tiwari [20] proposed minimum duplicity maximum relevance feature selection procedure to select the most important feature that can predict Parkinson's disease on its own. He found that the random forest received the overall accuracy of 90.3% which is better than all other methods focused on machine learning such as rotational forest, bagging, supporting vector machines, random subspace, etc.

Manmoshina *et al.* [21] used deep learning to reflect his work because he says it is different from traditional learning features. With multiple hidden layers, he uses deep learning to provide meaningful and higher abstraction levels. He illustrates the three-step approach. (i) Started by preprocessing raw data to overcome major problems such as missing values, data quality and outliers. (ii) The second step is to apply unattended deep learning to produce a higher level of input data abstraction. (iii) Lastly, supervised method of learning is used to predict the target value and model evaluation. Using unsupervised learning before supervised learning helped the author achieve the high predictive value accuracy as all ML techniques depend on the representation and extraction of features.

c) Different computational methodology
Bioinformatics is evolving day by day in the diagnosis of neurodegenerative disorder, and many scientists are now drawn to this branch of science as bioinformatics examines the biological aspects of individuals such as nutrition, health, and the environment. One of the most popular disorders is neurological disorders, which has shown considerable growth in recent years. Therefore, after analyzing all the diseases, we found that multiple researchers used different technologies to differentiate the ND patient from the stable/healthy one. Big data processing, virtual reality, recognition of facials and feelings, recognition of handwriting and artificial intelligence are the technologies used.

17.2.1   Machine Learning Algorithms for Parkinson's Data

For accurate diagnosis and early detection of Parkinson's data Nalls *et al.* [22] used the longitudinal data available from Parkinson's Progression Markers Initiative (PPMI) data. For researchers and clinical practice, this research has the ability to be of great advantage. Their work aimed at creating an accurate system for the diagnosis of Parkinson's disease. The study has shown on Parkinson's Progression Marker Initiative (PPMI) dataset with 367 PD patients and phenotypic imaging data and 165 controls without neurological disease. The model for the classification of logistic regression had an olfactory role, genetic risk, family history of Parkinson's disease, age, and sex as key features. The study sample had 825 subjects 8 with Parkinson's disease and 261 controls with specific selection methods and models from five separate cohorts. The data were collected from the Disease Biomarkers Program (PDBP), the Parkinson Associated Risk Study (PARS), 23andMe, the PD Longitudinal and Biomarker Study (LABS-PD), and the Disease Research Center of Excellence (Penn-Udall) of Morris K Udall Parkinson. The model also used patients who had imaging scans without dopaminergic deficit (SWEDD) evidence to investigate. Four out of 17 SWEDD participants identified in this model as having Parkinson's disease turned into Parkinson's disease within one year. This model offered a potential new way to separate Parkinson's disease patients from controls. This research has future scope to also recognize individuals with prodromal or preclinical Parkinson's disease in probable cohorts that could contribute to the biomarkers identification.

The work also needs to be expanded to image files with a high-precision classification system. Dinov *et al.* [23] studied the LONI Pipeline in detail. The LONI pipeline is a graphical environment for advanced data analysis of neuroimaging. The LONI pipeline allows neuroimaging analysis to be constructed, validated and implemented. LONI has a computer tool library that allows automated conversion of data format. LONI Pipeline performs better for graphical analysis than the other workflow architectures. LONI is a distributed environment for Grid computing. The critical features of the LONI environment are efficient tool integration, protocol validation, and new algorithms for neuro-images. It is straightforward and intuitive to incorporate existing data and computational tools within the LONI Pipeline environment. Based on the database infrastructure, the LONI Pipeline has several forms of application submissions. The LONI pipeline is compact, effective, distributed and independent in terms of computation. In pipeline data-analysis workflows, the individual binary processes 9 do not affect the performance of the LONI pipeline. Advanced computational algorithms with brain structure and function quantitatively mapped. LONI has developed sophisticated computer algorithms with quantitative mapping of brain structure and function. This work has focused on Alzheimer's evidence and can be applied to neuroimages of Parkinson's disease.

Chen *et al.* [24] studied another effective and efficient algorithm for the diagnosis of Parkinson's disease (PD) was Fuzzy k-nearest neighbor (FKNN). The proposed system based on FKNN is contrasted with the approaches based on support vector machines (SVM). The main component analysis was used to further improve the diagnostic accuracy for PD detection. Experimental results have shown that the KNN-based system in the literature dramatically beats SVM-based methods and other approaches. A 10-fold FKNN cross-validation technique had 96.07% accuracy. Promisingly, the system proposed could serve as a powerful diagnostic tool for PD.

Ramentol *et al.* [25] reported unbalanced data are the most common problem in classification. This phenomenon is important because the data is imbalanced in practice. Many techniques have been developed in supervised learning to handle the unbalanced training sets. These methods have been categorized into two large groups: algorithm-level ones and data-level ones. Data level groups focused balancing the training sets by either removing samples in the larger class or building new samples for the smaller class, also known as under sampling and oversampling. In the study for the preprocessing of imbalanced data-sets, a hybrid method was proposed.

Several machine learning algorithms such as C4.5, k-Means, Apriori, EM, PageRank, AdaBoost, kNN, Naive Bayes, and CART have been applied to the data set of different Parkinson. These are the top 10 algorithms of data mining identified by the IEEE International Data Mining Conference (ICDM) [26]. As the most powerful and influential analytical models, the data mining research community values these top 10 algorithms. These 10 algorithms cover classification, clustering, statistical learning, association analysis, and linking mining.

The quality of the top 10 data mining algorithms on Parkinson data should be reviewed. An automatic machine learning technique is designed to detect Parkinson's disease by analyzing a person's speech/voice [31]. In the analysis, the fuzzy C-means clustering algorithm was used to classify the disease of Parkinson which had precision of 68.04%, 45.83% specificity and 75.34% sensitivity. The research was expanded with the implementation of the boosting algorithms and the main data reduction element analysis. In order to calculate the ranking, the researchers also researched and performed the function significance analysis. UPDRS (Unified Parkinson Disease Rating Scale) were influential in correctly diagnosing the Parkinson. Further improvements were made using five different classification paradigms using a wrapper feature selection scheme that can predict each of the class variables in the range of 72–92 with an estimated accuracy [6]. A SVM and k-Nearest Neighbor (k-NN) were also proposed. PD patients were monitored at regular intervals to record their voice. In the machine 11 learning algorithms, age, gender, voice recordings have been taken at baseline, after three months, and after six months are used as features. Support Vector Machine detected significant deterioration in patients' UPDRS score. The random forest selection and support vector machine feature selection process increased the accuracy of discriminating PD from healthy controls. Only ten features of dysphonia led to 99% classification accuracy. For a large dataset, they also suggested a nonlinear signal approach.

In order to determine Parkinson's, many researchers worked on a subset of data. In the papers above, the data considered for analysis were limited to only one subset of data such as voice dataset and gait dataset. In the Progression Markers Initiative (PPMI) of Parkinson, complex, heterogeneous and incomplete data from multiple sources have been cleaned, curated, harmonized and various classification algorithms for machine learning were implemented in the Parkinson's Progression Markers Initiative (PPMI) [28]. The study focuses not only on neighbors nearest to Fuzzy K, but also on other classification techniques. This research paper compares PPMI dataset techniques for model-based and model-free classification and indicated that the cognitive scores of PD (Parkinson's disease), HC (Healthy Control) groups were significantly different. Classification significantly improved when re-equilibrated data were used.

17.2.2 Visualization

After knowing the different types of research contained in data from Parkinson, attempting to understand the latest studies using big data techniques in other diseases could also help Parkinson implement these well-proven ideas. Ovarian cancer diagnosis is very complicated and costly [34]. Once examined, the data collected from the medical device had a specific pattern. Clinicians found it difficult to analyze the medical data in MATLAB. The tool was found very convenient when data mining model was built and the output was visually published by clinicians. The research paper focuses on the application of various Big Data 12 methodologies for earlier ovarian cancer diagnosis. The aim of the research paper was to develop a software tool that helps discover ovarian cancer in the early biomarker. Data was collected from Luminex equipment for researching and developing customized software tool that produces a tremendous amount of complex medical data. Luminex computer data has been curated, operational regression has been applied. In the form of a histogram, scatter plot, ROC curve, the output was presented. On the output data from the Luminex machine, logistic regression algorithm was run. The custom visualization software resulted in a reduced lead time for analysing the Luminex machine result.

Existing systems of visual analysis enable users to explore data trends [27]. Results of the study suggest that interactive displays and related views provide great insights into events. Study visual analytics help to understand the connections between different attributes such as individuals, activities, and locations. Analysts use visual analytics to work on their interesting events; drill down into the data and make visualization-based hypotheses. The visualization of spatiotemporal information was used to classify hotspots (high incidence of events). Analysts would like to predict the future. Spatiotemporal and numerical analytical views of data are related through predictive visual analytics. Such visual analytics tools allowed analysts to conduct a hypothesis test and prepare resources to address the threats expected.

This work would address the limitations of different methods of classification and examine PPMI data in a systematic manner. This study's key contributions include An approach to cleaning and curating the data set

- Adding a wide range of attributes
- Preprocessing and imputation of the sparse data set
- Applying the methodology of dimension reduction such as the main element analysis
- Use the limited key components to conduct supervised algorithms for machine learning
- Visualization of highly correlated characteristics in each main component.

17.3 Recommender System for Parkinson's Disease (PD)

As Parkinson's disease (PD) is a progressive illness, it can be detected by observing the following symptoms:

Following motor symptoms can be seen in a patient due to the loss of dopamine:

- Tremor (shaking)
- Muscle stiffness (rigidity)
- Slowness of movement
- Impaired balance

Other symptoms may also occur like:

- Small handwriting
- Soft speech
- Stooped posture
- Reduced facial expression
- Muscle Pain

Other than the motor signs, there are some *non-motor* symptoms which include:

- Sleep disturbance
- Constipation
- Fatigue
- Bladder urgency and frequency
- Memory problems
- Dizziness on standing
- Depression: feeling sad, having less energy or losing interest in activities

17.3.1   How Will One Know When Parkinson's has Progressed?

Although everyone is different, by observing some symptoms, person can analyse that PD is progressing. One may find that person is doing his daily activities slowly and facing trouble in performing these activities like walking, brushing, etc. The effect of tremor is increasing and visible on other parts as well. Signs may be worse one day and not the next. Patience may notice that he needs to take his medicines regularly.

17.3.2   Dataset for Parkinson's Disease (PD)

The dataset contains many biomedical voice measurements from 31 people, out of which 23 were suffered from Parkinson's disease (PD). The primary objective of the dataset is to differentiate persons suffering from Parkinson's disease (PD) and healthy persons. Dataset consists of 24 features.

17.3.3   Feature Selection

It is the process of selecting features (manually or automatically) which contributes most to prediction or classification. Features with high correlation denote redundancy in the dataset. In the dataset, Jitter (%) and Jitter (Abs) features are designed from pitch period sequences and measure the average absolute temporal differences in these periods. As there is high correlation, only one feature will make more contribution for the classification. Therefore, a systematic examination has been done on all features. From the features having high correlation i.e. correlation coefficient more than 95%, one of the feature has been removed and final feature vector is constructed. Out of 24 features, 11 features are extracted to perform classification.

17.3.4   Classification

Classification is the task of finding the target of given data points. It is a supervised learning method in which algorithm is trained using training data and then trained model is used to categorize new data. There are different methods available for classification like perceptron, logistic regression, SVM, decision tree etc. Here, four models are used and their results are compared.

17.3.4.1   Logistic Regression

It is a predictive analysis method and uses the theory of probability. It accepts any real number as input and maps it into between 0 and 1. Output of the function is S-shaped curve. To make the predictions, sigmoid activation function is used.

$$Sigmoid\ function\ f(X) = \frac{1}{1+e^{-X}}$$

17.3.4.2   K Nearest Neighbor (KNN)

It is a supervised learning algorithm that is used for both classification and regression tasks. It is simplest and easy to implement. It works on the similarity concept i.e. that similar entities occur in close proximity.

17.3.4.3   Support Vector Machine (SVM)

It is a classifier described by a separating hyper-plane. It returns an optimal hyper-plane which divides unseen data by learning from training data.

17.3.4.4   Decision Tree

It is a non-parametric supervised algorithm widely used for classifying data. The aim is to build a model that finds the value of a target by considering decision rules learnt from the training data.

17.3.5   Train and Test Data

Complete dataset consists of 195 records. Dataset is divided into two parts i.e. training data and testing data, in the ratio 70:30.

Evaluation of classifier: All the models are trained and tested on same dataset. Trained models are evaluated on test data and accuracy is computed. Table 17.1 shows the comparison of different models in terms of accuracy.

17.3.6   Recommender System

After detecting whether a person is suffered from PD or not. Based upon symptoms, food and medications are recommended to patients. Table 17.2 shows recommended diagnosis based upon symptoms. Table 17.3 shows recommended medications for Parkinson's disease. Table 17.4 shows recommendations for non-motor signs of Parkinson's disease.

Some common recommendation made to PD patient:

1. Levodopa is the best pharmacologic usage for PD symptoms, particularly for rigidity and bradykinesia.

Table 17.1 Comparison of different classifiers.

Classifier	Accuracy
Logistic Regression	67.7%
KNN	74.5%
SVM	69.4%
Decision Tree	81.3%

Table 17.2 Differential diagnosis of Parkinson's.

Symptoms	Diagnosis
Difficulty with tasks, rigidity, tremor	Idiopathic Parkinson's disease
Rigidity, Tremor, bradykinesia	Drug-induced parkinsonism
Fixed deficits from previous events	Vascular parkinsonism
Change in mental status, Ataxic gait	Normal-pressure hydrocephalus
Vertical gaze paralysis (or slowed vertical saccadic movements); resting tremor, normal olfaction ,marked postural instability; nuchal dystonia;	Progressive supranuclear palsy
Resting tremor (rare), transient response to levodopa (25% of patients)	Multiple system atrophy
Sensory disorders, dystonia, Apraxia, positive Babinski test, aphasia, myoclonus,	Corticobasal degeneration
Visuospatial abilities, episodes of syncope, impaired attention and increased falls.	Dementia with Lewy bodies

2. Dopamine agonists effectively treat early Parkinson's disease.
3. Motor difficulties in patients with advanced PD can be cured by taking a monoamine oxidase-B inhibitor, dopamine agonist, or catechol-O-methyltransferase.
4. Subthalamic nucleus can be stimulated in deep brain to improve Parkinson's disease symptoms.
5. In diet, patient should consume fava beans, omega -3s, anti-oxidants like tree nuts, blueberries, cranberries, tomatoes, eggplant, spinach, etc.
6. Patient should avoid dairy products and foods high in saturated fat.

17.4   Future Perspectives

Nowadays, people access information on internet before taking decisions almost in every field like education, entertainment, e-commerce,

Table 17.3 FDA-approved medications for Parkinson's disease.

Symptoms	Medication
Constipation, dry mouth, hypotension, dry eyes, urinary retention, cognitive weakening.	Benztropine (Cogentin), trihexyphenidyl (Artane)
Nausea, somnolence, dyskinesia, hypotension, hallucinations	levodopa (Sinemet)
Diarrhea; bright orange urine	Entacapone (Comtan)
Diarrhea; rare liver failure	Tolcapone (Tasmar)
Nausea, headache, dizziness	Bromocriptine (Parlodel)
Somnolence; pulmonary fibrosis; hallucinations; nausea; lung, and retroperitoneum; edema; retroperitoneal	Pergolide (Permax)
Nausea, hallucinations, sleep disturbance, hypotension, edema,	Pramipexole (Mirapex), Ropinirole (Requip)
Nausea, insomnia	Selegiline (Eldepryl)
Weight loss, dry mouth, hypotension	Rasagaline (Azilect)
Nausea, hypotension, edema, confusion	Amantadine (Symmetrel)

etc. Also, popularity of recommender system is increasing in health care sector. But data security, privacy and believe in safe technical system plays vital role in medical domain and these aspects dominate acceptance of these systems. By using complete domain knowledge, expert evaluations and online doctor-in-the loop, as integral part of recommender system, these constraints can be mitigated.

17.5 Conclusions

Health care recommendations systems help users to understand the type of illness and based upon it suggest some medications, therapies, and precautions to be taken. Therefore, people before consulting to doctor, refer the information on internet about the disease, and searches for a suitable expert in the area. In this chapter, various techniques for health care recommender system are discussed with their advantages

Table 17.4 Management of non-motor symptoms of Parkinson's disease.

Symptoms	Management strategies
Cognitive impairment	Diagnose dehydration, infection, metabolic disorders; reduce antiparkinsonian dosage; reduce or stopanticholinergics, dopamine agonists, selegiline (Eldepryl), amantadine (Symmetrel), and; use a cholinesterase inhibitor.
Constipation	Patients should increase fiber and fluid intake; physical activity should be increased; stop anticholinergics; and use lactulose, stool softeners, enemas, mild laxatives as needed.
Depression	Start counseling; use drug treatment with selective serotonin reuptake inhibitors or tricyclic antidepressants.
Orthostatic hypotension	Stop antihypertensive dose; patients should rise slowly from a prone position; the head of the patient's bed should be elevated, and; considermidodrine (Proamatine) or fludrocortisone (Florinef).
Delirium or psychosis, hallucinations	Reduce or stop dopamine agonists, anticholinergics, decrease levodopa, amantadine, and selegiline; quetiapine (Seroquel); consider low-dose clozapine (Clozaril)
Sleep disturbance	Discontinue dopamine agonists, sleep attacks and daytime somnolence Nighttime awakenings due to bradykinesia; mention a bedtime dosage of long-acting carbidopa/levodopa (Sinemet), a dopamine agonist, adjuvant entacapone (Comtan). Reduce or stop night time usage of antiparkinsonian medicines; consider clonazepam (Klonopin), rapid eye movement sleep behavior disorder
Urinary urgency	Minimize intake of evening fluid; mention tolterodine (Detrol LA) or oxybutynin (Ditropan); mention urology evaluation to patient, if needed.

and disadvantages. A case study on Parkinson's is given which detects disease based upon some speech signal and gives recommendations by considering symptoms.

References

1. Fernandez-Luque, L., Karlsen, R., Vognild, L.K., Challenges and opportunities of using recommender systems for personalized health education, in: *MIE*, pp. 903–907, 2009, August.
2. Ricci, F., Rokach, L., Shapira, B., Introduction to recommender systems handbook, in: *Recommender systems handbook*, pp. 1–35, Springer, Boston, MA, 2011.
3. Valdez, A.C., Ziefle, M., Verbert, K., Felfernig, A., Holzinger, A., Recommender systems for health informatics: state-of-the-art and future perspectives, in: *Machine Learning for Health Informatics*, pp. 391–414, Springer, Cham, 2016.
4. Berardelli, A., Rothwell, J.C., Thompson, P.D., Hallett, M., Pathophysiology of bradykinesia in Parkinson's disease. *Brain*, 124, 11, 2131–2146, 2001.
5. Turner, R.S., Grafton, S.T., McIntosh, A.R., DeLong, M.R., Hoffman, J.M., The functional anatomy of parkinsonian bradykinesia. *Neuroimage*, 19, 1, 163–179, 2003.
6. Armañanzas, R., Bielza, C., Chaudhuri, K.R., Martinez-Martin, P., Larrañaga, P., Unveiling relevant non-motor Parkinson's disease severity symptoms using a machine learning approach. *Artif. Intell. Med.*, 58, 3, 195–202, 2013.
7. Abdulhay, E., Arunkumar, N., Narasimhan, K., Vellaiappan, E., Venkatraman, V., Gait and tremor investigation using machine learning techniques for the diagnosis of Parkinson disease. *Future Gener. Comput. Sy.*, 83, 366–373, 2018.
8. Kubota, K.J., Chen, J.A., Little, M.A., Machine learning for large-scale wearable sensor data in Parkinson's disease: Concepts, promises, pitfalls, and futures. *Mov. Disord.*, 31, 9, 1314–1326, 2016.
9. Shamir, R.R., Dolber, T., Noecker, A.M., Walter, B.L., McIntyre, C.C., Machine learning approach to optimizing combined stimulation and medication therapies for Parkinson's disease. *Brain Stimul.*, 8, 6, 1025–1032, 2015.
10. Yadav, G., Kumar, Y., Sahoo, G., Predication of Parkinson's disease using data mining methods: A comparative analysis of tree, statistical and support vector machine classifiers, in: *2012 National Conference on Computing and Communication Systems*, IEEE, pp. 1–8, 2012, November.
11. Bonato, P., Sherrill, D.M., Standaert, D.G., Salles, S.S., Akay, M., Data mining techniques to detect motor fluctuations in Parkinson's disease, in: *The 26th Annual International Conference of the IEEE Engineering in Medicine and Biology Society*, vol. 2, IEEE, pp. 4766–4769, 2004, September.

12. Sonu, S.R., Prakash, V., Ranjan, R., Saritha, K., Prediction of Parkinson's disease using data mining, in: *2017 International Conference on Energy, Communication, Data Analytics and Soft Computing (ICECDS)*, IEEE, pp. 1082–1085, 2017, August.

13. Challa, K.N.R., Pagolu, V.S., Panda, G., Majhi, B., An improved approach for prediction of Parkinson's disease using machine learning techniques, in: *2016 International Conference on Signal Processing, Communication, Power and Embedded System (SCOPES)*, IEEE, pp. 1446–1451, 2016, October.

14. Agarwal, A., Chandrayan, S., Sahu, S.S., Prediction of Parkinson's disease using speech signal with extreme learning machine, in: *2016 International Conference on Electrical, Electronics, and Optimization Techniques (ICEEOT)*, IEEE, pp. 3776–3779, 2016, March.

15. Dinesh, A. and He, J., Using machine learning to diagnose Parkinson's disease from voice recordings, in: *2017 IEEE MIT Undergraduate Research Technology Conference (URTC)*, IEEE, pp. 1–4, 2017, November.

16. Fiscon, G., Weitschek, E., Felici, G., Bertolazzi, P., De Salvo, S., Bramanti, P., De Cola, M.C., Alzheimer's disease patients classification through EEG signals processing, in: *2014 IEEE Symposium on Computational Intelligence and Data Mining (CIDM)*, IEEE, pp. 105–112, 2014, December.

17. Rodrigues, P.M., Freitas, D., Teixeir, J.P., Alzheimer electroencephalogram temporal events detection by K-means. *Proc. Technol.*, 5, 859–864, 2012.

18. Novoa-Del-Toro, E.M., Acosta-Mesa, H.G., Fernández-Ruiz, J., Cruz-Ramírez, N., Applied machine learning to identify Alzheimer's disease through the analysis of magnetic resonance imaging, in: *2015 International Conference on Computational Science and Computational Intelligence (CSCI)*, IEEE, pp. 577–582, 2015, December.

19. Johnstone, D., Milward, E.A., Berretta, R., Moscato, P., Alzheimer's Disease Neuroimaging Initiative, Multivariate protein signatures of pre-clinical Alzheimer's disease in the Alzheimer's disease neuroimaging initiative (ADNI) plasma proteome dataset. *PLoS One*, 7, 4, e34341, 2012.

20. Tiwari, A.K., Machine learning based approaches for prediction of Parkinson disease. *Mach. Learn. Appl.*, 3, 2, 33–39, 2016.

21. Mamoshina, P., Vieira, A., Putin, E., Zhavoronkov, A., Applications of deep learning in biomedicine. *Mol. Pharm.*, 13, 5, 1445–1454, 2016.

22. Nalls, M.A., McLean, C.Y., Rick, J., Eberly, S., Hutten, S.J., Gwinn, K., Hardy, J., Diagnosis of Parkinson's disease on the basis of clinical and genetic classification: a population-based modelling study. *Lancet Neurol.*, 14, 10, 1002–1009, 2015.

23. Dinov, I., Van Horn, J., Lozev, K., Magsipoc, R., Petrosyan, P., Liu, Z., Toga, A.W., Efficient, distributed and interactive neuroimaging data analysis using the LONI pipeline. *Front. Neuroinf.*, 3, 22, 2009.

24. Chen, H.L., Huang, C.C., Yu, X.G., Xu, X., Sun, X., Wang, G., Wang, S.J., An efficient diagnosis system for detection of Parkinson's disease using fuzzy k-nearest neighbor approach. *Expert Syst. Appl.*, 40, 1, 263–271, 2013.

25. Ramentol, E., Caballero, Y., Bello, R., Herrera, F., SMOTE-RSB*: a hybrid preprocessing approach based on oversampling and undersampling for high imbalanced data-sets using SMOTE and rough sets theory. *Knowl. Inf. Syst.*, 33, 2, 245–265, 2012.

26. Wu, X., Kumar, V., Quinlan, J.R., Ghosh, J., Yang, Q., Motoda, H., Zhou, Z.H., Top 10 algorithms in data mining. *Knowl. Inf. Syst.*, 14, 1, 1–37, 2008.

27. Maciejewski, R., Hafen, R., Rudolph, S., Larew, S.G., Mitchell, M.A., Cleveland, W.S., Ebert, D.S., Forecasting hotspots—A predictive analytics approach. *IEEE T. Vis. Comput. Gr.*, 17, 4, 440–453, 2010.

28. Dinov, I.D., Heavner, B., Tang, M., Glusman, G., Chard, K., Darcy, M., Foster, I., Predictive big data analytics: a study of Parkinson's disease using large, complex, heterogeneous, incongruent, multi-source and incomplete observations. *PLoS One*, 11, 8, e0157077, 2016.

29. Mika, S., Challenges for nutrition recommender systems, in: *Proceedings of the 2nd Workshop on Context Aware Intel. Assistance, Berlin, Germany*, pp. 25–33, 2011, October.

30. Rathore, S.S. and Kumar, S., An empirical study of some software fault prediction techniques for the number of faults prediction. *Soft Comput.*, 21, 24, 7417–7434, 2017.

31. Rustempasic, I. and Can, M., Diagnosis of parkinson's disease using fuzzy c-means clustering and pattern recognition. *Southeast Eur. J. Soft Comput.*, 2, 1, 42–49, 2013.

32. Sezgin, E. and Özkan, S., A systematic literature review on Health Recommender Systems, in: *2013 E-Health and Bioengineering Conference (EHB)*, IEEE, pp. 1–4, 2013, November.

33. Stark, B., Knahl, C., Aydin, M., Elish, K., A Literature Review on Medicine Recommender Systems. *IJACSA*, 10, 8, 6–13, 2019.

34. Cheong, K.S., Song, H.J., Park, C.Y., Kim, J.D., Kim, Y.S., Biomarker discovery and data visualization tool for ovarian cancer screening. *IJBSBT*, 6, 2, 169–178, 2014.

Temporal Change Analysis-Based Recommender System for Alzheimer Disease Classification

S. Naganandhini, P. Shanmugavadivu* and M. Mary Shanthi Rani

Department of Computer Science and Applications, The Gandhigram Rural Institute (Deemed to be University), Gandhigram, Tamil Nadu, India

Abstract

The development of recommender systems gathered momentum due its relevance and application in providing personalized recommendation on a product or a service for customer relations management. It has proliferated into medicine and its allied domains for the recommendations on disease prediction/detection, medicine, treatment and on other medical services. This chapter describes about a new composite and comprehensive recommender system named Temporal Change Analysis-based Recommender System for Alzheimer Disease Classification (TCA-RS-AD) using deep learning model. Its performance is evaluated on the dataset with T1-weighted MRI clinical temporal data of OASIS and the results were recorded in terms of Precision, Recall, F1-Score and Accuracy, Hamming Loss, Cohen's Kappa Coefficient, and Matthews Correlation Coefficient. The improved accuracy of this recommendation model endorses its suitability for its application in the classification of AD.

Keywords: Deep learning models, confusion matrix, Matthews correlation coefficient, hamming loss, Cohen's Kappa, OASIS dataset

---

**Corresponding author*: psvadivu67@gmail.com

Sachi Nandan Mohanty, Jyotir Moy Chatterjee, Sarika Jain, Ahmed A. Elngar and Priya Gupta (eds.) *Recommender System with Machine Learning and Artificial Intelligence: Practical Tools and Applications in Medical, Agricultural and Other Industries*, (351–372) © 2020 Scrivener Publishing LLC

18.1   Introduction

The semi-automated brain image analysis aims to discover or diagnose the Alzheimer's disease due to brain disorders. The prognosis of AD is essential for providing timely treatments to the patients at an early stage. The Magnetic Resonance Imaging (MRI) Clinical Data is a comprehensive dataset that contains high-resolution and high contrast images for the gray and white matter of the brain. The novelty of Machine Learning (ML) classification techniques have been vastly explored for many applications in medical diagnosis [1]. The prediction capabilities of machine learning methods are ideal for many clinical applications. These methods find application in neuroimaging research for early detection and diagnosis of AD. Deep learning is an offshoot of machine learning. Deep Neural Networks (DNN) is a type of neural network with more than two layers. The TCA-RS-AD is designed to have multiple hidden layers.

The most common approaches to create a recommender framework are content-based and collaborative filtering. Content-based approach requires a good amount of information about the functionality of the objects, rather than using experiences and suggestions from users. Collaborative filtering is the process of filtering or evaluating items using the opinions of other people.

This chapter presents a new prediction and recommender scheme termed as, "Temporal Change Analysis based Recommender System for Alzheimer Disease Classification (TCA-RS-AD)". This system uses MRI clinical temporal data for experimental analysis and validation. The proposed model is designed to classify and predict the early stage of AD.

18.2   Related Work

Zhe Wang et al. [2] developed a new method named as Resting-State fMRI based Network Connectivity Analysis (RS-fMRINC) using feature vector-based classification method. This model could detect AD and Mild Cognitive Impairment (MCI).

Naganandhini et al. [3] developed a new method for detecting various stages of AD using ML algorithms. This model is designed to perform feature extraction and classification using the association between the data attributes.

Sajna et al. [4] developed a new method for two-stage Convolutional Neural Network (CNN) model for prediction and early diagnosis of the AD. In the first stage, image patches were taken as input to learn inherent associations between local image patches and target landmarks. In the second stage, the entire image is considered as input in order to detect AD.

Lebedev *et al.* [5] developed a new method for Computed Aided Diagnosis (CAD) of AD. The Random Forest Classifier was trained using different structural MRI measure constraints to improve the performance of detection and prediction of AD.

Jyoti Islam *et al.* [6] designed a new method for AD diagnosis using an ensemble of deep CNN models. Their model used the clinical dataset to identify the different stages of AD for early diagnosis.

Xia-an Bi *et al.* [7] developed the random neural network cluster, composed of multiple neural networks to improve the performance of feature selection and classification. Sixty-one subjects comprising of 25 AD and 36 Healthy Control were acquired from the Alzheimer's Disease Neuroimaging Initiative (ADNI) dataset to validate their method.

Abnaya Kumar *et al.* [8] developed a deep learning-based health recommender system using collaborative filtering. This method was designed for the implementation of an effective health recommender engine. This model was evaluated with Mean Absolute Error (MAE).

Raid Lafta *et al.* [9] developed an intelligent recommender system based on short-term risk prediction for heart disease. This system offers a solution to reduce the time and cost factor involved in taking frequent medical test for medical intervention. The experimental results showed that the proposed system yields satisfactory accuracy in recommendations.

Sivapalan *et al.* [10] devised a new recommender system for classification, regression, and time series analysis using various types of classification models, namely decision tree induction, Bayesian classification, Neural Networks, Support Vector Machine (SVM), and association.

18.3   Mechanism of TCA-RS-AD

The TCA-RS-AD method involves three phases: preprocessing, prediction, and recommendation. In the preprocessing phase, the clinical data is read and subjected to data imputation, transformations, and grouping. In the prediction phase, the training dataset is trained by tuning the hyperparameters to predict the different stages of AD. In the recommendation phase, recommendation is performed by using rating scale based on accuracy.

18.4   Experimental Dataset

The TCA-RS_AD algorithm is tested on the magnetic resonance imaging (MRI) dataset comprising of normal and stages of AD chosen from OASIS Longitudinal Neuroimaging [11] are used. The vital attributes are as follows: Sex, Hand, Educ, SES, CDR, eTIV, nWBV, Group, Visit, MR Delay. The performance of TCA-RS-AD was experimented on the OASIS dataset with 448 data, 112 data are of Mild AD, 112 data are Moderate AD, 112 data are Non-Demented, and 112 data are Very Mild AD-affected.

Table 18.1 shows the demographics characteristics in clinical data and Table 18.2 depicts the clinical information of the datasets.

The TCA-RS-AD used data imputation, one-hot encoding and normalization to prepare the dataset for training. One hot encoding is the most widespread and commonly used approach and it works very well unless

Table 18.1 Demographic characteristics.

Descriptor	Explanation	Datatype
M/F	Gender	Categorical
Hand	Handedness (actually all subjects were right-handed, so this item can be omitted)	Categorical
Age	Age in years	Numerical
EDUC	Years of education	Numerical
SES	Socio-economic status as assessed by the Hollings head Index of Social position and classified into categories from 1 (highest rank) to 5 (lowest status)	Numerical

Table 18.2 Clinical information of OASIS dataset.

Descriptor	Explanation
MMSE	Mini-Mental State Examination Score; Range: 0 (Worst) to 30 (Best)
CDR	Clinical Dementia Rating (0: No dementia; 0.5: Very Mild AD; 1: Mild AD; 2: Moderate AD)

the categorical variable large in number. This coding creates new (binary) columns, indicating the presence of each possible value from the original data. The most commonly used coding system is one-hot coding. It compares every level to a specified reference point of the categorical variable. The coding with dichotomous values 0 and 1 is suitably used to code gender and hand as shown in Figure 18.1.

The dataset used in this work is a time series data that provides insight into the perceivable changes useful for the early detection or prediction of any disorder or ailment. Table 18.3 shows the sample time series data in OASIS dataset. The visit attribute helps to harness the information for AD classification based on the count of patients' visit for diagnosis.

The schematic description of TCA-RS-AD is given in Figure 18.2, that explains the stages of computation for AD recommendation.

MRI ID	Gender	Hand
OASIS_MR_01	M	R
OASIS_MR_02	F	L
OASIS_MR_03	M	R
OASIS_MR_04	F	L

MRI ID	Gender	Hand
OASIS_MR_01	0	0
OASIS_MR_02	1	1
OASIS_MR_03	0	0
OASIS_MR_04	1	1

Figure 18.1 Illustration of one-hot encoding for categorical data.

Table 18.3 Sample time series OASIS dataset.

Subject ID	MRI ID	Visit	CDR	Group
OAS2_0048	OAS2_0048_MR5	5	1	Mild AD
OAS2_0048	OAS2_0048_MR4	4	1	Mild AD
OAS2_0048	OAS2_0048_MR3	3	1	Mild AD
OAS2_0048	OAS2_0048_MR2	2	1	Mild AD
OAS2_0048	OAS2_0048_MR1	1	1	Mild AD
OAS2_0007	OAS2_0007_MR4	4	1	Mild AD
OAS2_0007	OAS2_0007_MR3	3	1	Mild AD
OAS2_0007	OAS2_0007_MR2	2	0.5	Very Mild AD
OAS2_0007	OAS2_0007_MR2	1	0.5	Very Mild AD

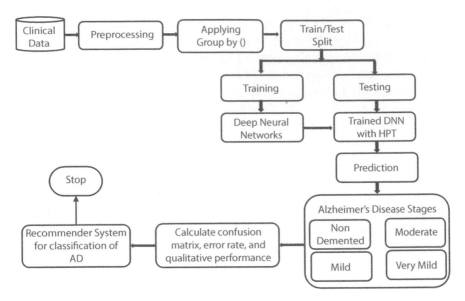

Figure 18.2 Flowchart of TCA-RS-AD.

Algorithmic Description of TCA-RS-AD

Input: Clinical Data
Output: Classification and Recommendation on AD stages

Begin
Phase I: Preprocessing
Step 1: Read the Clinical Data
Step 2: Preprocess Clinical Data using
      A. Data Imputation
      B. Transformation
      C. Collaborative Filtering using groupby()
Step 3: Partition the dataset for training and testing
Phase II: Training & Prediction
Step 4: Train the Deep Neural Network model with hyperparameters tuning
Step 5: Test the model with Test dataset
Step 8: Predict AD stages
Step 9: Measuring the model performance by calculating Confusion Matrix, Cohen's Kappa, MCC, Hamming Loss and Accuracy, Mean Absolute Error, MSE, BAS, Median Absolute Error in Training and Testing Data.
Step 10: Measure accuracy rating and error rating
Step 11: Make recommendations
End

In order to compute group analysis for making recommendations on AD detection, the proposed method used groupby() function on the visit attribute thus performed collaborative filtering for collection of items. The resultant aggregation of data is illustrated in Table 18.4. This table showed the sample grouped data based on visit attribute on the OASIS dataset. The train/test split for DNN is then applied to such grouped data.

18.5   Neural Network

The Neural Network (NN) is a ML algorithm that is built on the concept of biological neural network and its functions. The NN consists of discrete elements called neurons. Figure 18.3 depicts the basic NN structure and its elements.

After splitting into train/test set, the proposed method uses three types of layers for training the data:dense layer, activation layer and dropout layer. The input size of the first dense layer is 168. It is representing the number of one-hot encoded input features. Since all the inputs from the

Table 18.4 Sample time series data using *groupby()* function.

Visit	Subject ID	CDR	Group
1	OAS2_0048	1	Mild AD
	OAS2_0007	0.5	Very Mild AD
2	OAS2_0007	0.5	Very Mild AD
	OAS2_0058	0.5	Very Mild AD
	OAS2_0048	1	Mild AD
3	OAS2_0048	1	Mild AD
	OAS2_0007	1	Mild AD
4	OAS2_0007	1	Mild AD
	OAS2_0048	1	Mild AD
5	OAS2_0048	1	Mild AD
	OAS2_0017	0	Non Demented
	OAS2_0073	0	Non Demented
	OAS2_0127	0.5	Very Mild AD

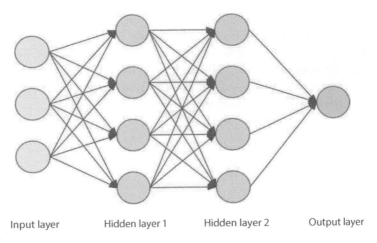

Input layer   Hidden layer 1   Hidden layer 2   Output layer

Figure 18.3 Basic neural network model.

dataset are categorical, one-hot encoding scheme was used to transform those inputs to numeric and vector type. The essential elements of a DNN are described herein under:

1. Dense Layer: It is the input layer. The first dense layer is connected to every output by weight. So, there are n_{inputs} * $n_{outputs}$ *weights.*
2. Activation Layer (ReLU): The dense layer is followed by a non-linear activation function namely ReLU (Rectified Linear Unit) that performs non-linear operation, as shown in Eqn.(1).

$$f(x) = max\ (0,x) \qquad (1)$$

The ReLU activation function performs non-linearity in the DNN model.
3. Dropout: This layer is used to avoid overfitting in the DNN model. In this method, a dropout of 0.8 is used.
4. Fully-Connected Layer: The final output layer is typically a fully connected neural network layer. The dense layer and ReLU are repeated from a network with a known Deep neural network.
5. The proposed optimal DNN uses fully connected layer with SoftMax, which is a non-linear activation function used for multiclass classification.

The model summary of the TCA-RS-AD is given in Table 18.5, where in Layer type, Output Shape and Param# denote the functionality of the layer, dimension of the output and the number of trained parameters respectively.

The hyperparameters tuning is performed on the TCA-RS-AD model to improve the performance accuracy. The hyperparameters used for tuning is listed in Table 18.6.

The performance metrics [12–15] used in this study are described in Table 18.7. The efficiency of classification is measured using Precision, Recall, F1-Score, Hamming Loss, Cohen's Kappa Coefficient, Matthews Correlation Coefficient (MCC), Mean Absolute Error (MAE), Mean Square Error (MSE), Balanced Accuracy Score (BAS), Median Absolute Error (M_dAE).

The above mentioned metrics were applied to both DNN model and DNN with hyperparameter tuning model called TCA-RS-AD. The computational potential of DNN and TCA-RS-AD was experimented on the OASIS dataset and the obtained results are furnished in Table 18.8.

It is apparent from Table 18.8 that the DNN model produced the Support value for the Very Mild AD detection. Its performance was relatively moderate for Non-demented and Mild AD. It is also worth noting that this model has failed to handle Moderate AD class. It could be observed that this model exhibits inconsistent Precision, Recall, F1-Score, and Support in classifying Mild and Moderate AD as well as the testing

Table 18.5 Model summary of the TCA-RS-AD.

Layer type	Output shape	Param #
Dense_1 (Dense)	(None, 64)	768
Dense_2 (Dense)	(None, 64)	4160
Dropout_1(Dropout)	(None, 64)	0
Dense_3 (Dense)	(None, 50)	3250
Dense_4 (Dense)	(None, 100)	5100
Dropout_2 (Dropout)	(None, 100)	0
Dense_5 (Dense)	(None, 4)	404
Total Params: 13,682		
Trainable Params: 13,682		
Non-Trainable Params: 0		

Table 18.6 Hyperparameters for TCA-RS-AD.

Hyper parameters	Default value
Epochs	1,500
Batch Size	16
Optimizer	Adam
Learning Rate	0.001
First Moment	0.09
Loss Function	Categorical_Cross_entropy
Last Moment	0.999

accuracy is low. These measures are graphically depicted in Figure 18.4. This disadvantage offers scope to modify the basic DNN into TCA-RS-AD, to obtain enhanced accuracy on all the classes of data. A support value of zero for Moderate AD indicates a shallow performance of the model. It is apparent that the classification accuracy of DNN on AD classification is not promising. As a part of improving the performance of the model, data imputation and hyper parameter tuning were applied to the OASIS data.

DNN and TCA-RS-AD are Excellent for Moderate AD classification, while DNN alone is excellent for both non-demented and Very Mild AD. DNN and TCA-RS-AD exhibit excellent performance for demented and non-demented classes in terms of Recall and F1-Score metrics. Also, on the classification of Moderate AD, except TCA-RS-AD, these classifiers uniformly exhibit scant or poor performance. It is evident TCA-RS-ADthat consistently outperforms its counterparts, in the classification of Mild AD, Very Mild AD, Moderate AD, Non-DementedwhileDNN and TCA-RS-AD are observed to perform far below average. It can also be inferred from the results presented in Table 6 that TCA-RS-AD outperforms the rest of the classifiers. It is believed that the excellent performance of TCA-RS-AD may be attribute to the process of boosting in TCA-RS-AD that ideally helps to minimize overfitting, bias, and variance.

The prediction accuracy for Non-Demented and Very Mild AD have increased approximately by 8%. Moreover, its overall accuracy increased to 96.42% against that of DNN which was 81.25%. This performance augmentation of about 15% is attributed to the data imputation and fine tuning of the hyperparameters. This improvement is endorsed by the Support values shown in Figure 18.5. The accuracy of the classification in both

Table 18.7 Description of performance metrics.

S. no.	Metric	Formula	Notational definitions	Remarks
1	Precision	$\dfrac{TP}{(TP+FP)}$	TP: True Positive FP: False Positive	Measure of Correctness. High value denotes higher accuracy and vice-versa.
2	Recall	$\dfrac{TP}{(TP+FN)}$	FN: False Negative	Measure of prediction accuracy.
3	F1-Score	$\dfrac{(1+\beta)^2 * Recall * Precision}{\beta^2 * Recall * Precision}$	F1 score can be interpreted as a weighted and average of the precision and recall	The F1 score best value is 1 and worst score is 0
4	Hamming Loss (HL)	$\dfrac{1}{NL}\displaystyle\sum_{i=1}^{L}\sum_{j=1}^{N} Y_{i,j} \oplus X_{i,j}$	Fraction of labels that are incorrectly predicted	It's always between 0 and 1, lower being better.

(Continued)

Table 18.7 Description of performance metrics. (*Continued*)

S. no.	Metric	Formula	Notational definitions	Remarks
5	Cohen's Kappa Coefficient	$\dfrac{P_o - P_c}{1 - P_c} = 1 - \dfrac{1 - P_o}{1 - P_c}$	The level of agreement between two annotators on a classification problem.	The number between −1 and 1. The maximum value means complete agreement zero or lower means change agreement.
6	Matthews Correlation Coefficient	$\dfrac{TP*TN - FP*FN}{\sqrt{(TP+FP)*(TP+FN)*(TN+FP)*(TN+FN)}}$	The MCC is essence a correlation coefficient value	The coefficient of +1 represents a perfect prediction, 0 an average random prediction and −1 an inverse prediction.
7	Mean Absolute Error	$\dfrac{\sum_{i=1}^{n} |y_i - x_i|}{n} = \dfrac{\sum_{i=1}^{n} |e_i|}{n}$	Calculating the loss function	Output is non-negative floating point. The best value is 0.0
8	Mean Square Error	$\dfrac{1}{n}\sum_{i=1}^{n}(y_i - y_i^{\char`\^})^2$	Calculating the loss function	The best value is 0.0

(*Continued*)

Table 18.7 Description of performance metrics. (*Continued*)

S. no.	Metric	Formula	Notational definitions	Remarks
9	Balanced Accuracy Score	$\dfrac{(Sensitivity + Specificity)}{2}$	Multiclass classification problems to deal with imbalanced dataset	Random performance would score is 0 and perfect performance score 1.
10	Median Absolute Error	$\displaystyle\sum_{i=1}^{j} f_i \geq \dfrac{n+1}{2}$	Calculating the loss function of positive floating-point value	The best value is 0.0

Table 18.8 Performance analysis of DNN and TCA-RS-AD model.

Group	Precision		Recall		F1-Score		Support	
	DNN	TCA-RS-AD	DNN	TCA-RS-AD	DNN	TCA-RS-AD	DNN	TCA-RS-AD
Non-Demented	0.53	1.00	0.62	0.81	0.57	0.90	13	15
Moderate AD	0.00	0.00	0.00	0.01	0.00	0.01	0	1
Very Mild AD	0.96	0.99	0.90	1.00	0.93	0.99	61	69
Mild AD	0.74	0.90	0.76	096	0.75	0.93	37	27
Classification Model Report								
Macro Avg	0.56	0.96	0.54	0.93	0.56	0.94	112	112
Weighted Avg	0.83	097	0.81	0.96	0.82	0.96	112	112
Accuracy (DNN): 0.8125 (81.25%)					Accuracy (TCA-RS-AD): 0.9642 (96.42%)			

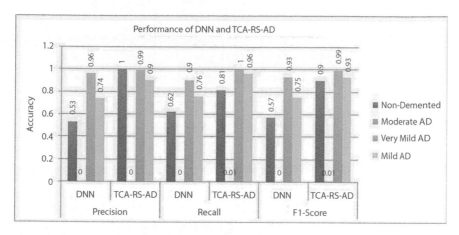

Figure 18.4 Performance of DNN and TCA-RS-AD.

training and testing samples were recorded, by varying the epochs, batch sizes, and the optimizers.

In addition to the accuracy metrics, the merits of the proposed model are demonstrated by the error rate metrics namely MAE, MSE, BAS and M_dAE listed in Table 18.9. These observations confirmed that the error rate is significantly minimized and accuracy is maximized in AD detection.

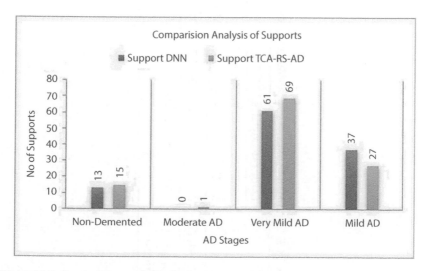

Figure 18.5 Comparison analysis of support on DNN and TCA-RS-AD.

Table 18.9 Comparison analysis of error rate metrics.

Model	Error rate metrics				Accuracy		
	MAE	MSE	M_dAE	HL	Cohen's Kappa	MCC	BAS
DNN Model	0.392	1.0357	0.1	0.142857	0.743744	0.76485	0.5645
TCA-RS-AD Model	0.0893	0.2500	0.0	0.035714	0.933363	0.93440	0.9251

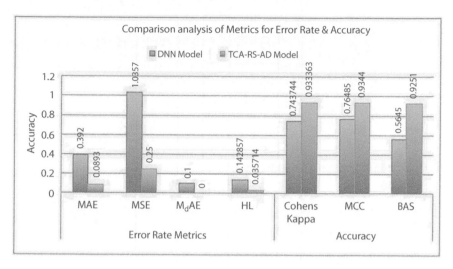

Figure 18.6 Comparison analysis of Metrics for Error Rate & Accuracy.

Figure 18.6 shows the comparative analysis of the recorded error and accuracy metrics for both models. It clearly illustrates the superiority of TCA-RS-AD in AD detection over DNN.

Based on the performance measures of TCA-RS-AD, the degree of recommendation on AD classification is given a 6-point scale [Excellent, High, Moderate, Low, Poor and Scant] and the respective performance mapping is given below:

S: Scant performance if value achieved is 0–9%;
P: Poor performance if value achieved is 10–29%;
L: Low performance if value achieved is 30–49%;
M: Moderate performance if value achieved is 50–69%;
H: High performance if value achieved is 70–89%;
E: Excellent performance if value achieved is 90–100%

Table 18.10 summarizes the performance rating of DNN and TCA-RS-AD for the three prominent metrics namely precision, recall and F1-Score, in terms of the 6-point Recommender scale. It is observed that the TCA-RS-AD exhibits its novelty and robustness in the prediction of very mild and Mild AD which is a vital factor for the early detection of AD. In all other classes except Moderate AD, the TCA-RS-AD is confirmed to recommend better than the basic DNN. These observations vouch its merits and applicability over its counterpart. These inferences are pictorially depicted in Figure 18.7, for precision, recall and F1-Score.

Table 18.10 Performance summary of the classifiers.

Metric / Classifier	Precision				Recall				F1-Score			
	VM	M	MAD	ND	VM	M	MAD	ND	VM	M	MAD	ND
DNN	E	H	S	M	E	H	S	M	E	H	S	M
TCA-RS-AD	E	E	S	E	E	E	S	H	E	E	S	E
AD Stages	VM: Very Mild AD; M: Mild AD; ND: Non-Demented; MAD: Moderate AD											
Recommender Scale	Excellent: E; High: H; Moderate: M; Low: L; Poor: P; Scant: S											

The Figure 18.8 revealed the overall rating comparison of Error ratings for DNN and TCA-RS-AD models. This showed that the error rating of TCA-RS-AD is highest when compared to DNN model.

From the above results, it is recommended that the proposed TCA-RS-AD Model works better for the detection of AD.

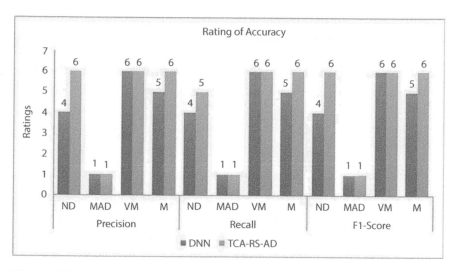

Figure 18.7 Accuracy rating for DNN and TCS-RS-AD.

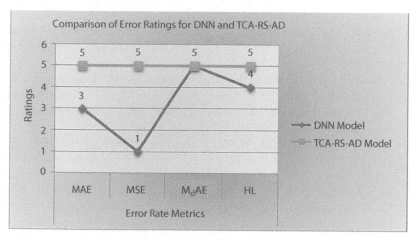

Figure 18.8 Comparison of error ratings for DNN and TCA-RS-Ad Models.

18.6 Conclusion

The Temporal Change Analysis based Recommender System for Alzheimer Disease Classification (TCA-RS-AD) works on the principle of deep learning. This intelligent model exhibits its potential in the classification of Alzheimer's disease and provides recommendation on a 6-point scale using the accuracy of classification. The performance of this system is exceptionally good in the time-series based early stage prediction of AD, as evidenced by its results. The results of this model may serve as a supplementary tool for AD detection for clinical trials. This model is designed to be computationally light and hence it can be effortlessly deployed in edge devices.

References

1. Ashby-Mitchell, K., Burns, R., Shaw, J., Anstey, K.J., Proportion of dementia in Australia explained by common modifiable risk factors. *Alzheimer's Res. Ther.*, 9, 1, 11, 2017.
2. Arnold, L., Rebecchi, S., Chevallier, S., Paugam-Moisy, H., An Introduction to Deep Learning. *ESANN 2011 Proceedings, European Symposium on Artificial Neural Networks, Computational Intelligence, and Machine Learning*, Bruges, Belgium, vol. 27, pp. 477–488, 2011.
3. Naganandhini, S., Shanmugavadivu, P., Asaithambi, A., MansoorRoomi, M.M., Alzheimer's Disease Classification Using Machine Learning Algorithms, in: *Advances in Computerized Analysis in Clinical and Medical Imaging*, Taylors and Francis, CRC Press, pp. 1–18, 2019.
4. Sajna, T. and Anish Kumar, B., Land Mark Detection and Alzheimer's Disease Prediction Using Two-Stage CNN and Landmark Features. *IJAECS*, 5, 6, ISSN: 2393-2835, 72–75, 2018.
5. Lebedev, A.V., Westman, E., Van Westen, G.J.P., Kramberger, M.G., Lundervold, A., Aarsland, D., Vellas, B., Random Forest ensembles for detection and prediction of Alzheimer's disease with a good between-cohort robustness. *NeuroImage: Clin.*, 6, 115–125, 2014.
6. Islam, J. and Zhang, Y., Brain MRI analysis for Alzheimer's disease diagnosis using an ensemble system of deep convolutional neural networks. *Brain Inf.*, 5, 2, 2–7, 2018.
7. Bi, X.A., Jiang, Q., Sun, Q., Shu, Q., Liu, Y., Analysis of Alzheimer's disease based on the random neural network cluster in fMRI. *Front. Neuroinf.*, 12, 60, 2018.

8. Sahoo, A.K., Pradhan, C., Barik, R.K., Dubey, H., DeepReco: Deep Learning Based Health Recommender System Using Collaborative Filtering. *Computation*, 7, 2, 1–18, 2019.

9. Lafta, R., Zhang, J., Tao, X., Li, Y., Tseng, V.S., An intelligent recommender system based on short-term risk prediction for heart disease patients. *2015 IEEE/WIC/ACM International Conference on Web Intelligence and Intelligent Agent Technology (WI-IAT)*, vol. 3, pp. 102–105, 2015.

10. Schafer, J.B., Konstan, J., Riedl, J., Recommender systems in e-commerce, in: *Proceedings of the 1st ACM conference on Electronic commerce*, pp. 158–166, ACM, 1999. https://doi.org/10.1145/336992.337035

11. OASIS, Longitudinal: Principal Investigators: Marcus, D., Buckner, R., Csernansky, J., Morris, J., P50 AG05681, P01 AG03991, P01 AG026276, R01 AG021910, P20 MH071616, U24 RR021382.

12. Precision and Recall, https://en.wikipedia.org/wiki/Precision_and_recall. Accessed: 2019-01-04.

13. F1 Score, https://en.wikipedia.org/wiki/F1-Score. Accessed: 2019-01-04.

14. MCC, https://en.wikipedia.org/wiki/Matthews_correlation_coefficient. Accessed: 2019-03-05.

15. MAE, https://en.wikipedia.org/wiki/Mean_absolute_error. Accessed: 2019-03-12.

Regularization of Graphs: Sentiment Classification

R.S.M. Lakshmi Patibandla

Assistant Professor, Department of IT, Vignan's Foundation for Science, Technology and Research, AP, India

Abstract

Recommender systems of deep learning have been comprehensively reconnoitred in topical years. Conversely, the enormous quantity of simulations anticipated apiece year stances an immense experiment for composed researchers and specialists in mimicking the outcomes for auxiliary assessments. While a slice of documents delivers source code, they embraced altered software design or dissimilar deep learning packages, which also elevations the bar in acquisitive the designs. Erudition representations of image to seizure fine-grained semantics have been an exciting and imperative task assisting various requests such as image search and clustering. In this paper, first part contains introduction of neural networks, second part consists of neural structured learning, third consists of some models of neural networks, fourth contains the results of comparison between base model and graph regularization are made based on supervision ratio and then concluded.

Keywords: Graph, dataset, accuracy

19.1 Introduction

The task of recommender systems is to produce a list of recommendation results that match user preferences given their past behavior. Collaborative filtering (CF) is a conjoint hit her to prevailing methodology, spawn's consumer recommendations by the captivating benefit of the collective wisdom from all users. Numerous collaborative filtering established recommendation processes have been publicized to work healthy through

Email: patibandla.lakshmi@gmail.com

Sachi Nandan Mohanty, Jyotir Moy Chatterjee, Sarika Jain, Ahmed A. Elngar and Priya Gupta (eds.) *Recommender System with Machine Learning and Artificial Intelligence: Practical Tools and Applications in Medical, Agricultural and Other Industries*, (373–386) © 2020 Scrivener Publishing LLC

several provinces and existed recycled in voluminous real life solicitations. The essential indication of model-based CF systems is to absorb squat dimensional depictions of consumers and things as of whichever unequivocal consumer association such as rankings or inherent opinion.

Machine Learning taking place displays is an essential in addition to pervasive task by solicitations vacillating since instruction scheme to companionship endorsement in societal nets. The major contest now this purview to catch an approach towards epitomize, or else scramble, diagram erection so as to the situation be able to definitely subjugated by machine learning simulations. Conventionally, Machine Learning methodologies defined heuristics to excerpt structures scrambling essential indication nearby a graph such as degree statistics or kernel purposes. Though, current existences have grasped a swell in slants that spontaneously acquire to scramble graph erection addicted to low-dimensional embeddings, spending performances established continuously Deep Learning then non-linear dimensionality decline. At this point delivers an intangible appraisal of basic expansions herein region of illustration education on charts, containing Matrix Factorization-based systems, Random-walk based systems, and Graph Convolutional Networks.

A session of Artificial Neural Networks wherever associates among modules usage a rapt chart laterally a progressive structure in Recurrent Neural Network. This tolerates it to parade progressive energetic behavior. Disparate Feedforward Neural Networks, RNNs must exploit their interior retention headed for practice a series of responses. This creates them related to errands such as unsegmented, allied speech or handwriting recognition.

Thru the advancement in communication expertise like the World Wide Web, a massive amount of societies starting entirely on extractions through the world taking chunks in societal nets and precise with their excitements or sentiments on an eclectic series of issues. Nowadays it is an ominous requisite to digest the statistics shaped by societies beyond the societal nets and grasp the intuitions as of them. Moreover, in the research of NLP, it has to turn into a theme of colossal awareness. As it is necessary to create shrewd recommending systems, antedating the outcomes of partisan votes, the response of societies has been sympathetic on open occasions and schedules.

19.2 Neural Structured Learning

NSL is a new erudition exemplar to train neural networks by leveraging structured gestures along with feature responses. A structure can be explicit as symbolized by a graph or implicit as induced by adversarial disquiet, Figure 19.1 describes the NSL framework.

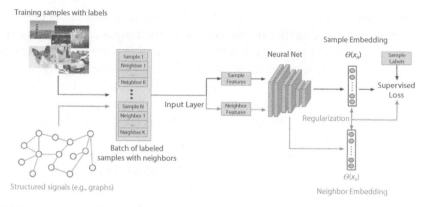

Figure 19.1 NSL framework.

Structured signals are commonly used to represent relations of similarity among samples that may be labeled or unlabeled. Therefore, leveraging these signals during neural network training harnesses both labeled and unlabeled data, which can improve model accuracy, particularly as soon as the expanse of labeled data is relatively trivial. Additionally, models trained with samples that are generated by adding adversarial perturbation are robust against malicious attacks, which are designed to mislead a model's prediction or classification.

NSL generalizes to Neural Graph Learning as well as Adversarial Learning. The NSL framework in Tensor Flow provides the following easy-to-use APIs and tools for developers to train models with structured signals: Keras APIs to enable training with graphs (explicit structure) and adversarial excitements (implicit structure). TF ops and functions to enable training with structure when using lower-level Tensor Flow APIs. Tools to build graphs and construct graph inputs for training.

19.3   Some Neural Network Models

LSTM is the CNN model is merely adept of supervision a solitary image, renovating it as of input pixels into an internal matrix or vector depiction. Essential to review this task through various imageries and consent the LSTM to shape up core formal and apprise weightiness expending BPTT crossways a structure of the core vector illustrations of input images. The CNN might be stable in the situation with a surviving pre-trained classical resembling VGG for feature extraction from images. CNN may perhaps not be expert and may hope to train it by back-propagating fault from the LSTM crossways various input images to the CNN model. In both of these cases, abstractly close by is a single CNN model and a series of LSTM models, one to each interval period. CNN model is applied to per capita input image and permit on the output of each input image toward the LSTM as a distinct period. By draping the intact CNN involvement exemplary in a Time Distributed layer. This layer triumphs the chosen effect of smearing a similar layer or layers of numerous epochs. In this case, relating it various spells to numerous input phases and in fit as long as a structure of "image elucidations" or "image structures" to the LSTM model to exertion.

BiLSTMs are supported exclusively supportive in the instances everywhere the perspective of the response is required. It is suitable for workings alike classification on sentiments. In unidirectional LSTM evidence tides as of the backward to forward. On the conflicting in Bi-directional LSTM statistics not solitary drifts forward but also forward to backward with two hidden states. In future Bi-LSTMs cognize the perspective well. BiLSTMs existed recycled towards worsen the piece of input data practical to the net. This results to the erection of both RNN with LSTM and BiLSTM. Essentially, BRNN monitors such a manner wherever the neurons of a typical RNN are ruined into bidirectional techniques. One is for backward shapes or negative spell track, and alternative on behalf of positive time direction or forward states. The inputs of the converse path shapes are not allied to these two shapes' outcomes. The edifice or BiLSTM is presented in Figure 19.2. As a result of exploiting dual time advices, input data since the earlier in addition to imminent of the contemporary time frame will be able to recycle, although usual RNN entails the adjournments for comprising forthcoming data [18].

Feedforward Neural Networks remain better recognized as per Multi-layered Network of Neurons. These networks of simulations exist termed Feedforward for evidence merely explorations Forward in the Neural Network, over the input nodes formerly concluded the hidden layers and lastly over the output nodes (Figure 19.3).

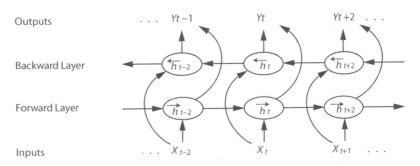

Figure 19.2 Bidirectional LSTM.

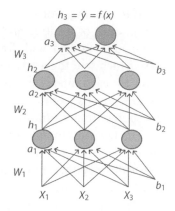

Figure 19.3 FNN model.

Customary replicas such as McCulloch Pitts, Perceptron and Sigmoid models of neuron capability are inadequate to linear purposes, to switch the intricate non-linear verdict margin among input and the output.

Graph regularization is a specific technique under the broader paradigm of Neural Graph Learning (Bui *et al.*, 2018). The core idea is to train neural network models with a graph-regularized objective, harnessing both labeled and unlabeled data exhausting the Multi-layered Network of Neurons. Here, it explores the use of graph regularization to classify documents that form a natural (organic) graph. The general recipe for creating a graph-regularized model using the Neural Structured Learning (NSL) framework is to generate training data from the input graph and sample features. Nodes in the graph resemble to samples also edges in the graph correspond to the similarity between pairs of samples. The resulting training data will contain neighbor features in addition to the original node features. Create a neural network as a base model using the Keras sequential, functional, or subclass API. Wrap the base model with the Graph Regularization wrapper class, which is provided by the NSL framework, to create a new graph Keras model. This new model will include a graph regularization loss as the regularization term in its training objective and train and evaluate the graph Keras model.

19.4   Experimental Results

Experimentation is conducted using Tensorflow2.0 in the Google colaboratory on the IMDB dataset. This dataset comprises a copy of movie analyses of 50,000 as of the database IMDB. These are split obsessed by half for training and another half for testing. Both sets are poised, implication they enclose an equivalent amount of positive and negative assessments. The above-said dataset emanates bundled with Tensor Flow. Its devices already existed pre-processed such that the analyses have been adapted to edifices of integers, wherever for each integer epitomizes a precise term in a thesaurus. The highest 10,000 utmost commonly stirring disputes in the training data. The erratic disputes are superfluous to preserve the extent of the vocabulary practicable. The Dataset emanates pre-processed: for apiece illustration is an array of integers signifying the disputes of the movie analysis. Apiece tag is an integer value of either 0 or 1, wherever 0 is a destructive analysis, and 1 is a constructive analysis. This work categorizes movie analyses as constructive or destructive exhausting the text of the analysis with binary classification, an indispensable then extensively pertinent mild of problems on machine learning.

The use of graph regularization in this work is shown by building a graph from the given input. The general technique for building a graph-regularized model using the Neural Structured Learning (NSL) framework when the input does not contain an explicit graph is as follows:

- Create embeddings for each text sample in the input. This can be done using pre-trained models such as word2vec, Swivel, BERT, etc.
- Build a graph based on these embeddings over through a resemblance metric for instance the 'L2' expanse, 'cosine' distance, etc. Nodes in the graph resemble to samples and also edges in the graph correspond to the similarity between pairs of samples.
- Generate training data from the above-synthesized graph and sample features. The resulting training data will contain neighbor features in addition to the original node features.
- Create a neural network as a base model using the Keras sequential, functional, or subclass API.
- Wrap the base model with the Graph Regularization wrapper class, which is provided by the NSL framework, to create a new graph Keras model. This new model will include a graph regularization loss as the regularization term in its training objective.
- Train and evaluate the graph Keras model.

Graph construction comprises forming embeddings for text samples and then consuming a parallel utility to associate the embeddings.

First, form trial embeddings, custom anxious Swivel embeddings to form embeddings in the TF train. For example, the layout for each sample in the input and the ensuing embeddings will be stored in the TF Record layout laterally through a surplus feature that epitomizes the ID of each sample. This is imperative and consents us contest sample embeddings with analogous nodes in the graph far ahead. Then shape a graph, have the sample embeddings, will practice them to form a resemblance graph, nodes in this graph will match to trials and edges in this graph will resemble to match amongst pairs of nodes.

Neural Structured Learning affords a graph building tool that forms a graph built on sample embeddings. It customizes cosine similarity as the similarity measure to relate embeddings and shape edges amid them. It moreover consents us to postulate a similarity threshold, which can be recycled to thrust aside divergent edges from the ultimate graph. In this example, using 0.99 as the similarity threshold, ends up with a graph that has 445,327 bi-directional edges.

Augment training data with graph neighbors, have the sample features and the fused graph can spawn the amplified training data for Neural Structured Learning. The NSL framework affords a tool that can trust the graph and the sample structures to yield the ultimate training data for graph regularization. The resultant training data will comprise inventive sample features along with features of their analogous neighbors.

19.4.1   Base Model

This model is now ready to build a base model without graph regularization. To build this model, we can either use embeddings that were used in building the graph or can learn new embeddings jointly along with the classification task? Hyper parameters will use an instance of HParams to include various hyper parameters and constants used for training and evaluation. The following are the parameters momentarily designate each of them.

- num_classes: There are 2 classes—positive and negative.
- max_seq_length: This is the maximum number of words considered from each movie review in this example.
- vocab_size: This is the size of the vocabulary considered for this example.
- distance_type: This is the distance metric used to regularize the sample with its neighbors.

- graph_regularization_multiplier: This controls the relative weight of the graph regularization tenure in the whole loss function.
- num_neighbors: The number of neighbors used for graph regularization. This value has to be less than or equal to the – max_nbrs command line value used above when you ran the pack_nbrs utility.
- num_fc_units: The numeral units now the fully connected level of the Neural Network.
- train_epochs: Number of training epochs.
- batch_size: Batch size used for training and evaluation.
- eval_steps: The number of batches to process before deeming evaluation is complete. If set to None, all instances in the test set are evaluated.

The analyses, the arrays of integers, requisite to be renewed to tensors earlier actuality nurtured obsessed by the neural network to prepare the data. This restoration can be ended a pair of techniques Translate the collections into vectors of 0s and 1s signifying word occurrences, analogous to a one-hot coding. Suppose, the sequence [3, five] would prove to be a 10,000-dimensional vector that's all zeros excluding in aid of catalogues three and 5, that ar ones. Formerly, mark this the primary layer in our internet, a Dense layer, that may grip floating-point vector knowledge. This technique is memory complete, yet, lacking a num_words * num_reviews size matrix. Otherwise, will swab the arrays therefore all of them have the equal length, then build Associate in Nursing number tensor of form max_length * num_reviews. will use Associate in Nursing entrenching level adept of supervising this form because the 1st layer in our internet. In this, norm the succeeding methodology. Meantime the reviews of films would like be the equal length, spirit use the pad_sequence operate outlined below the lengths to standardize. A Neural Network is formed via amassing covers, this entails 2 foremost field resolutions:

- How to use several layers within the model?
- In what way several hidden units to custom for every level?

Here, a computer file resides of a group of word-indices. The tags to predict stay either zero or one. The layers area unit effectively collected chronologically to form the classifier:

The first layer is an input layer that takes the integer-encoded words. The following layer is an entrenching layer, that take the integer-encoded words and gazes up and regarding the entrenching vector for each word-index. These vectors area unit erudite because the exemplary trains. The vectors enhance a dimension to the yield array. The following proportions area unit batch, series, entrenching. Next, a two-way LSTM layer takes a fixed-length yield vector for each illustration. This fixed-length yield vector is tweeted over a fully-connected dense layer with hidden units of sixty-four. The last layer is densely coupled via a solitary output knob. With the Sigmoid activation performs, this price could be a float between zero and one, demonstrating a clear stage, or buoyancy level.

The higher than aforesaid exemplary devours twin transformation or "hidden" layers, amongst the input and output, and excluding the Embedding layer. The amount of outputs like units, nodes, or neurons is that the side of the figurative galaxy for that layer. In alternative words, the expanse of sovereignty the system is indorsed whereas scholarship an indoor depiction. If a model has a lot of hidden units, and/or a lot of layers, then Infobahn will learn a lot of multifarious depictions. Conversely, it varieties Infobahn any computationally exclusive and would possibly cause scholarship annoying patterns, that mend enactment on coaching information however not on the check information i.e.; overfitting. An exemplary desires a loss perform and an optimizer for coaching. Since this can be a binary classification drawback and also the model yields a clear stage, a single-unit layer with a sigmoid activation, use the binary cross entropy loss perform. As soon as training, need to plaid the accuracy of the model on data it hasn't grasped earlier. After that construct a validation set by set separately a portion of the inventive training data. In this, takings coarsely 10% of the primary training samples (10% of 25,000) as labeled data for training and the remaining as validation data. Since the initial train/test split was 50/50 (25,000 samples each), the effective train/validation/test split we now have is 5/45/50. The 'train_dataset' has previously been

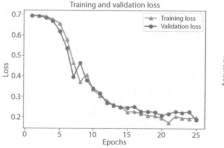
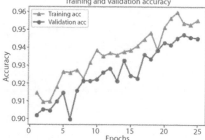

Figure 19.4 Loss & accuracy of base model.

batched and shuffled. Now, train the model in mini-batches. Whereas training, monitor the model's loss and accuracy on the validation set. Note that the training loss declines with apiece epoch and the training accuracy escalations thru to apiece epoch. This is estimated as soon as consuming a gradient descent optimization, it must minimalize the chosen extent on each recapitulation, Figure 19.4.

19.4.2 Graph Regularization

Now ready to try graph regularization using the base model that built above and use the Graph Regularization wrapper class provided by the Neural Structured Learning framework to wrap the base (bi-LSTM) model to include graph regularization. The rest of the steps for training and evaluating the graph-regularized model are similar to that of the base model. To assess the incremental benefit of graph regularization, create a new base model instance. This is because a model has already been trained for a few iterations, and reusing this trained model to create a graph regularized model will not be a fair comparison for the model. Around six entries: one for each censored metric—loss, graph loss, as well as accuracy—during training and validation. Use these to plot the training, graph, and validation losses for comparison, as well as the training and validation accuracy. Note that the graph loss is only computed during training; so its value will be 0 during validation Figure 19.5.

Semi-supervised learning and more specifically, graph regularization in the context, can be powerful when the amount of training data is small. The lack of training data is compensated by leveraging similarity among the training samples, which is not possible in traditional supervised

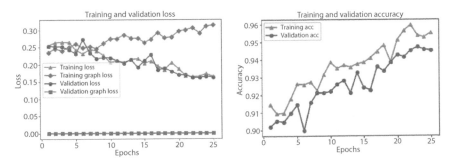

Figure 19.5 Loss & accuracy of graph regularization.

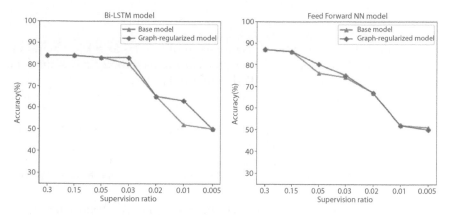

Figure 19.6 Loss & accuracy of BiLSTM model.

learning. Define the supervision ratio as the ratio of training samples to the total number of samples which includes training, validation, and test samples. In this, a supervision ratio of 0.05 (i.e., 5% of the labeled data) for training both the base model as well as the graph-regularized model, Figure 19.6.

It can be observed that as the supervision ratio decreases, model accuracy also decreases. This is true for both the base model and for the graph-regularized model, regardless of the model architecture used. However, notice that the graph-regularized model performs better than the base model for both the architectures. In particular, for the Bi-LSTM model, when the supervision ratio is 0.01, the accuracy of the graph-regularized model is ~20% higher than that of the base model. This is primarily because of semi-supervised learning for the graph-regularized model, where structural similarity among training samples is used in addition to the training samples themselves.

19.5   Conclusion

This work demonstrated the use of graph regularization using the Neural Structured Learning (NSL) framework even when the input does not contain an explicit graph. Here, I considered the task of sentiment classification of IMDB movie reviews for which synthesized a similarity graph based on review embeddings. In future, this may be applied different parameters on different datasets.

References

1. Ahmed, A., Shervashidze, N., Narayanamurthy, S., Josifovski, V., Smola, A.J., *Distributed large scale natural graph factorization*, Proceedings of the 22nd international conference on World Wide Web, 2013.

2. Angles, R. and Gutierrez, C., Survey of graph database models. *ACM Comput. Surv.*, 40, 1, 1, 2008.

3. Benson, A.R., Gleich, D.F., Leskovec, J., Higher-order organization of complex networks. *Science*, 353, 6295, 163–166, 2016.

4. Bhagat, S., Cormode, G., Muthukrishnan, S., Node classification in social networks, in: *Social Network Data Analytics*, pp. 115–148, https://arxiv.org/abs/1101.3291, 2011.

5. Bronstein, M.M., Bruna, J., LeCun, Y., Szlam, A., Vandergheynst, P., Geometric deep learning: Going beyond Euclidean data. *IEEE Signal. Process Mag.*, 34, 4, 18–42, 2017.

6. Chang, S., Han, W., Tang, J., Qi, G., Aggarwal, C.C., Huang, T.S., Heterogeneous network embedding via deep architectures, in: *KDD*, Sydney, NSW, Australia, 1–10. http://dx.doi.org/10.1145/2783258.2783296, 2015.

7. Chen, H., Perozzi, B., Hu, Y., Skiena, S., Harp:Hierarchical representation learning for networks. arXiv preprint arXiv:1706.07845, 2017.

8. Cho, K., Van Merriënboer, B., Gulcehre, C., Bahdanau, D., Bougares, F., Schwenk, H., Bengio, Y., Learning phrase representations using rnn encoder-decoder for statistical machine translation, in: *EMNLP*, https://arxiv.org/abs/1406.1078, 2014.

9. Chung, F.R.K., *Spectral Graph Theory*. Number 92, American Mathematical Soc, UK ed. Edition, 1997.

10. Dai, H., Dai, B., Song, L., Discriminative embeddings of latent variable models for structured data, in: *ICML*, https://arxiv.org/pdf/1603.05629.pdf, 2016.

11. Defferrard, M., Bresson, P., Vandergheynst, X., Convolutional neural networks on graphs with fast localized spectral filtering, in: *NIPS*, In: *NIPS 30th Conference on Neural Information Processing Systems*, Barcelona, Spain, 2016.

12. Dong, Y., Chawla, N.V., Swami, A., metapath2vec: Scalable representation learning for heterogeneous networks, in: *KDD*, Halifax, NS, Canada, 135–144, http://dx.doi.org/10.1145/3097983.3098036, 2017.

13. Ester, M., Kriegel, H., Sander, J., Xu, X. *et al.*, A density-based algorithm for discovering clusters in large spatial databases with noise, in: *KDD*, -96 *Proceedings*, 226–231, 1996.

14. Fortunato, S., Community detection in graphs. *Phys. Rep.*, 486, 3, 75–174, MIT Press. 2010.

15. Getoor, L. and Taskar, B., *Introduction to Statistical Relational Learning*, MIT press, 2007.

16. Gori, M., Monfardini, G., Scarselli, F., A new model for learning in graph domains, in: *IEEE International Joint Conference on Neural Networks*, Montreal, Que., 2.7(19), pp. 729–734, 2005.

17. Goyal, P. and Ferrara, E., *Graph embedding techniques, applications, and performance: A survey*, https://arxiv.org/abs/1705.02801, 2017.

18. Grover, A. and Leskovec, J., node2vec: Scalable feature learning for networks, in: *KDD*, San Francisco, CA, USA, 1–10, 2016.

19. Hamilton, W.L., Ying, R., Leskovec, J., *Inductive representation learning on large graphs*, 31st Conference on Neural Information Processing Systems (NIPS 2017), Long Beach, CA, USA, 4, 1–19, 2017.

20. Henderson, K., Gallagher, B., Eliassi-Rad, T., Tong, H., Basu, S., Akoglu, L., Koutra, D., Faloutsos, C., Li, L., Rolx: structural role extraction & mining in large graphs, in: *KDD*, Beijing, China, 1–9, 2012.

21. Hintonand, G. and Salakhutdinov, R., Reducing the dimensionality of data with neural networks. *Science*, 313, 5786, 504–507, 2006.

22. Hochreiter, S. and Schmidhuber, J., Long short-term memory. *Neural Comput.*, 9, 8, 1735–1780, 1997.

23. Hoff, P., Raftery, A.E., Handcock, M.S., Latent space approaches to social network analysis. *JASA*, 97, 460, 1090–1098, 2002.

24. Kearnes, S., McCloskey, K., Berndl, M., Pande, V., Riley, P., Molecular graph convolutions: moving beyond fingerprints. *J. Comp. Aided Mol. Des.*, 30, 8, 595–608, 2016.

25. Kipf, T.N. and Welling, M., Semi-supervised classification with graph convolutional networks, in: *ICLR*, 4, 1–14, 2016.

26. Kipf, T.N. and Welling, M., Variational graph auto-encoders, in: *NIPS Workshop on Bayesian Deep Learning*, 1, 1–3, 2016.

27. Kruskal, J.B., Multidimensional scaling by optimizing goodness of fit to a nonmetric hypothesis. *Psychometrika*, 29, 1, 1–27, 1964.

28. Lee, J.A. and Verleysen, M., *Nonlinear dimensionality reduction*, Springer Science & Business Media, New York, 2007.

29. Li, Y., Tarlow, D., Brockschmidt, M., Zemel, R., Gated graph sequence neural networks, in: *ICLR*, 4, 1–20, 2015.

30. Liben-Nowell, D. and Kleinberg, J., The link-prediction problem for social networks. *J. Assoc. Inf. Sci. Tech.*, 58, 7, 1019–1031, 2007.

31. Lu, Q. and Getoor, L., Link-based classification, in: *ICML*, vol. 3, pp. 496–503, 2003.

32. Murphy, K., Weiss, Y., Jordan, M., Loopy belief propagation for approximate inference: An empirical study, in: *UAI*, 1–9, 1999.

33. Nickel, M., Murphy, K., Tresp, V., Gabrilovich, E., A review of relational machine learning for knowledge graphs. *P. IEEE*, 104, 1, 11–33, 2016.

34. Niepert, M., Ahmed, M., Kutzkov, K., Learning convolutional neural networks for graphs, in: *ICML, Proceedings of the 33rd International Conference on Machine Learning*, New York, NY, USA, 2016. JMLR: W&CP , 48, 1–10, 2016.

35. Ou, M., Cui, P., Pei, J., Zhang, Z., Zhu, W., Asymmetric transitivity preserving graph embedding, in: *KDD, 2016*, pp. 1–10, San Francisco, CA, USA, 2016.
36. Paranjape, A., Benson, A.R., Leskovec, J., Motifs in temporal networks, in: *WSDM 2017*, vol. 1, pp. 1–10, Cambridge, United Kingdom, 2017.
37. Perozzi, B., Al-Rfou, R., Skiena, S., Deepwalk: Online learning of social representations, in: *KDD*, 14, 2, 1–10, 2014.

TSARS: A Tree-Similarity Algorithm-Based Agricultural Recommender System

**Madhusree Kuanr[1]*, Puspanjali Mohapatra[1]
and Sasmita Subhadarsinee Choudhury[2]**

*[1]Department of Computer Science, IIIT, Bhubaneswar, India
[2]MCKV Institute of Engineering, Howrah, India*

Abstract

In the advancement of world wide web, people are getting more closer to online applications for fulfilling their most of the requirements. In the meantime, they have minimal free time to spend in the process of selection. Therefore, the need to take assistance of the recommender systems to resolve this issue is growing and recommender systems successfully providing users with personalized recommendations on various items to make the task of the users easier. This study aims at developing a recommender system based on tree data structure for farmers. The proposed system (TSARS) recommends seeds, fertilizers, pesticides and instruments based on farming and farmers' location preferences when buying seeds online. It uses tree data structure to store the information of the database users. To find similar users for the active query user, a preorder traversal is used. The performance of TSARS is measured by different parameters like precision, accuracy and positive predictive value (PPV). The results revealed that better recommendation is provided by TSARS compared to traditional recommender systems.

Keywords: Recommendation system, collaborative filtering, tree data structure, precision, accuracy and positive predictive value (PPV)

*Corresponding author: madhu.kuanr@gmail.com

Sachi Nandan Mohanty, Jyotir Moy Chatterjee, Sarika Jain, Ahmed A. Elngar and Priya Gupta (eds.) *Recommender System with Machine Learning and Artificial Intelligence: Practical Tools and Applications in Medical, Agricultural and Other Industries*, (387–400) © 2020 Scrivener Publishing LLC

20.1   Introduction

In the era of internet, intranet and E-commerce system, large quantity of information is available that we hardly deal with. People are getting more inclined to the web applications for fulfilling their requirements as they are providing more options for selecting a particular product. But at the same time, it is very difficult for the user to select an appropriate item according to their need from the large pool of items. So, the web applications must be responsible to provide good recommender systems which can help the user in this regard. Recommender systems are the subclass of information filtering system which helps the users to take right decision to choose a particular item from a large catalogue of items by accurately considering the interest and preference of the user. It helps users in various domains like e-commerce, health, agriculture, finance, social networks, education and sports for making appropriate decisions Figure 20.1 and Figure 20.2 depict the basic concept of recommender System and types of recommender system respectively. Agriculture is the backbone of Indian economy, still it suffers from a heaping number of disasters such as climate change, unpredictable monsoon or lack of it, droughts, floods, migration of farmers towards the cities in search of better-paying jobs, and more. For motivation and profitable farming, it requires efficient recommender system to suggest

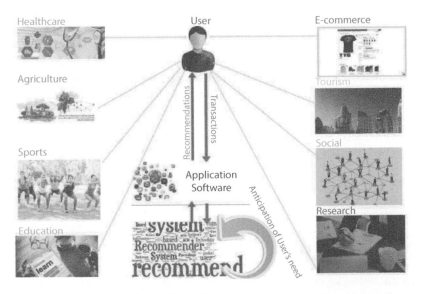

Figure 20.1 Basic concept of a recommender system.

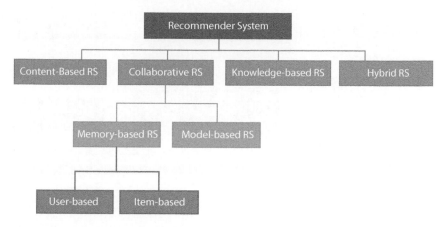

Figure 20.2 Types of recommender system.

that farmers take suitable decisions to help them protect themselves from bearing losses in their farming, which in turn affects the country's social and economic growth. Machine learning plays a vital role in recommender system as it increases efficiency of recommender systems by filtering out the more accurate information from the large set of information present in the database. Machine learning can learn various factors such as digitally soil checking and crop mapping, weather, fertilizers, disease detection and pest management and adaptation to climate change etc. and accordingly it recommends the either seeds, fertilizers, pests or instruments to be used based on requirements. Machine learning algorithms in recommender system are broadly classified into two categories—collaborative and content-based.

Collaborative recommender system recommends those items to the user which is liked by the people of the similar taste in the past. It tries to discover the peers to a given query user and tries to recommend the items which are liked by the peers in the past. Various measures like similarity and correlation are used to find the peers to a given query user. Collaborative algorithm can be categorized into memory based and model-based algorithms. Memory based algorithms are basically based on the rating predictions of the items by considering the past items liked by the peers [1] [2]. Memory based algorithms may not always be fast and scalable which can be replaced by model-based algorithms. In model-based algorithms, a model is designed based on the past information and used for recommendation purposes. The content-based recommender systems recommend the items by finding the items which are similar to the items which are liked by the query user in the past. The content-based approach is based on the concept of information retrieval and information filtering. Various measures like TF–IDF (term

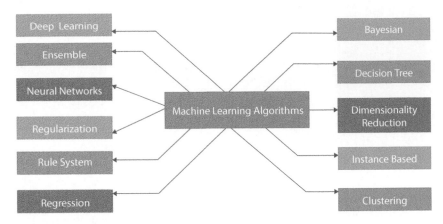

Figure 20.3 Machine learning algorithms.

frequency–inverse document frequency) can be used for content-based approaches. Machine learning algorithms are classifed into various sub categories as shown in Figure 20.3. Though recommending relevant products to users according to their interests, effective recommender systems can be devloped using different techniques to increase the capability of those systems. Different researchers have found that Bayesian algorithms and Decision tree algorithms are commonly used in recommender systems due to their low complexity. The other two varieties of the recommender systems are hybrid, knowledge-based and Demographic recommender system. Hybrid recommender incorporate collaborative and content-based recommender systems functions. Different researchers have revealed that hybrid recommender system outperforms the traditional collaborative and content-based recommender systems. Knowledge-based recommender system does not need rating data for recommendation purpose. The system produces the list of recommendation according to the knowledge base of the system. The knowledge-based systems can be either categorized to case-based systems or constraint-based systems. Both case based and constraint-based systems vary in the way they use the knowledge. Demographic recommendations are based on the information provided by users considered similar according to demographic parameters such as age, gender, nationality, locality, etc.

20.2 Literature Survey

Recommender System helps the user to choose products according to their personal interests. The literature survey has included the various recommender systems for agriculture domain along with the various tree-based and fuzzy-logic based machine learning approaches. An intelligent system known as Agro Consultant, is proposed to assist the Indian farmers in making an informed decision about to select a crop according to the sowing season, soil characteristics, geographical location of the farm along with the environmental factors such as temperature and rainfall [3]. Hadoop-based agricultural product e-commerce recommender system is proposed which analyzes user's behavior data through distributed computing, discovers their interests and provides personalized recommendation service to them [4]. A recommender system using sliding window non-linear regression technique has been proposed to predict the yield of crops and the price a farmer can get from his land, by analyzing rainfall, weather, market prices, land area and past crop yield [5]. A fuzzy logic based collaborative recommender system is proposed for giving prior idea to the farmers by predicting the yield of a crop by considering the location of the farmer and the environmental factors like temperature, humidity and rain fall of that location [6]. An agriculture recommender system by using data mining techniques has been proposed which helps farmers to select particular crop in strong changing climatic conditions by understanding soil and climatic conditions [7]. A user-based collaborative recommender system has been proposed by collecting data like soil and weather conditions from experienced farmers, agricultural researchers and other stakeholders to predict a suitable crop [8]. A major role is played by precision agriculture to overcome the difficulties present among the Indian farmers. A dynamic normalized normal tree tree recommendation framework was proposed to suggest research paper using complex ontology and a large number of papers [9]. Decision trees have the capabilities to capture the dynamic aspects needed for a recommendation process. A decision tree-based recommender system has been proposed using most Popular Sampling (MPS) and matrix factorization methods [10]. Fuzzy family tree-based recommender systems recommend among the anticipatory scores for various key concepts read by online users with the highest rankings. Based on the User Key Concept Rating (UKCR) matrix, anticipatory scores are evaluated and neighbors sorted in the order of semantic and content similarities [11]. A hybrid recommender system using knowledge tree has been proposed by considering the five modules of teaching and it helps the teacher and learners to find the useful teaching resources in technology enhanced learning (TEL) [12]. A framework for multi-genre movie recommender system is proposed using neuro-fuzzy decision tree (NFDT) methodology which recommends movies in the decreasing order of preference in response to queries and profiles provided by the users [13]. A data mining technique-based recommender system has been proposed for improvising the yield of the crop by recommending appropriate crop according to the location of the farmer [14]. Based on user expectations, soil and weather conditions, a collaborative filtering recommendation framework is proposed that recommends acceptable crops using statistical data analysis and predictive modeling [15]. Machine learning also plays a key role in enhancing the recommender system's capability. A recommendation framework for precision farming is proposed to suggest a crop by using vector machines and artificial neural network by taking the soil report as input with majority voting technique [16]. Random forests act as a vital tool for recommending items to the user. An alternate framework is proposed that integrates three-way decision and random forests for building recommender systems [17]. Random forest gives better results for large dataset and the percentage of correctly classified instances increases as the number of instances of the dataset is increased [18]. A new theoretically tractable variant of random regression forests has been proposed which provide insight into the relative importance of different simplifications that theoreticians have made to obtain tractable model for analysis [19]. Random Forests identify interaction and nonlinearity without prespecification. They can be used with many correlated predictors also with the case when there are more predictors than observations [20]. Better yield depends on the soil characteristics. Using Machine learning algorithms such as Naïve Bayes and KNN algorithms, crop types are identified based on soil testing reports. Using various classification techniques such as Support Vector Machine, Principal Component Analysis, an effective model has created to suggest crop types and pesticides [21]. In agriculture, various biotic and abiotic factors such as soil characteristics, soil types, crop yield data collection were analyzed and suggested the right crop based on site-specific parameters to the farmers. Recommendation systems have been designed by means of an ensemble model with majority voting technique using Random tree, CHAID, K-Nearest Neighbor and Naive Bayes to recommend a crop with high accuracy and efficiency for the site-specific parameters [22]. Implementation of agricultural data mining and visual data mining techniques which reduce high-dimensional agricultural information to a smaller size to gain useful information related to yield and input application such as fertilizers and pesticides. Different techniques such as Self-organizing maps and Multi-dimensional Scaling techniques (Sammon's mapping) have essentially been used to reduce data. This states that Self-organizing maps are suitable for large data set and Sammon's mapping is suitable for small data set [23]. A recommender system based on SVM classification and Logistic regression has been proposed to predict the best crop and pests along with the techniques of pest control [24]. RSF, an agricultural recommender system, is proposed to recommend appropriate crops based on the location of the farmer using agro-ecological and agro-climatic data [25].

20.3   Research Gap

Agriculture plays a vital role in developing countries' economy and offers their rural populations with the primary source of food, revenue and jobs. Over the past few decades, Indian agriculture has recorded remarkable development. Over 70% of the rural household rest on agriculture. Odisha, as one of India's state, is also an agricultural economy that contributes almost 30% to the Net State Domestic Product (NSDP), with 73% of the agricultural workforce. But most of the farmers of Odisha follow the traditional process of cultivation being unaware of the new pesticides, fertilizers and new instruments available for a particular crop. Due to these reasons sometimes, they have to bear losses in their farming which in turn greatly affects our society. In this study we have proposed a recommender system which recommends the pesticides and the instruments available for a particular crop for which the farmer is interested. It also recommends the seeds for other crops which suits to the location of the farmer based on soil testing characteristics.

20.4   Problem Definitions

The proposed system takes the user's location and crop preference as input and produces a set of recommendations of pesticides, instruments for that crop as output. It also recommends seeds for other crops which suits to the location of the farmer.

20.5   Methodology

In this study we have used a questionnaire method. Initially questionnaire is distributed among the respondents. Four hundred individuals participated in this study. Three hundred ten male and ninety females with mean age (M_{age} = 35.4 years, F_{age} = 32.5 years) have participated in this study. All the respondents belong to south region of Odisha, India. The proposed system takes the user's location and crop preference as input and constructs a tree which is a skewed binary tree. We have termed this skewed tree as similarity tree because we have used this tree for similarity computation. The proposed model is shown in Figure 20.6. Similarity tree is used to find the similar farmers to the active query farmer. The structure of the similarity tree and its probable nodes are as shown in Figure 20.4. The country name to which the farmer belongs to is the root of the similarity tree. States $(ST_1, ST_2, ST_3,...STn)$ are the immediate siblings of country, places$(PL_1, PL_2,...PL_m)$ are the immediate siblings of states, seeds (S 1,S 2,...,Sp) are the immediate siblings of places, pesticides (P1) and instruments (I1) are the immediate siblings of seeds. So, for a given input active query farmer, a similarity tree will be constructed according to the above-mentioned hierarchy. The corresponding preorder traversal is found out for that farmer. The similarity trees and their corresponding preorder traversal are also evaluated for the database users. The similar users of the active query farmers are calculated by comparing the preorder traversal of the active query farmers with the preorder traversals of the database users. The database users whose preorder traversal matches with the preorder traversal of the active user are assumed as similar users. The similarity value of a database user is set as 1 if its preorder matches with the active query farmer. For example, a given active query farmer belongs to the country as India, state as Odisha and place as Jajpur and he has given his preferences in terms of crop as rice, it constructs similarity tree for that user.

The similarity tree for this active query user is shown in Figure 20.5. The similarity tree is a skewed binary search tree. The preorder traversal of the similarity tree is found out. This preorder traversal is matched with the preorder traversal of the database users. When both the preorder traversal matches with each other, the system stores the similarity value as 1, otherwise 0. Users of the database with the similarity value as 1 are presumed to be similar users to the given query user. The similar users are sorted according to the decreasing order of the rating values those they have provided for the seeds that they have purchased earlier. The top-n users from the sorted list will be used for recommendation purpose where n $\in$ N and n is the number of recommendations to the user.

20.6   Results & Discussion

20.6.1   Performance Evaluation

The performance of the proposed system is evaluated in terms of the parameters like precision, accuracy and positive predictive values (PPV).

Precision can be defined as the proportion of correct positive classifications from cases that are predicted as positive. Precision is also called as predictive positive value. Accuracy is the proportion of correct classifications from overall number of cases.

$$\text{Precision} = \frac{TP}{TP + FP} \tag{1}$$

$$\text{Accuracy} = \frac{TP + TN}{TP + TN + FP + FN} \tag{2}$$

Where, TP = True Positive
FP = False Positive
TN = True Negative
FN = False Negative

True Positives (TP) are defined as the correctly identified proportion of positive. A false negative (FN) indicates that a given condition is present when it is not. False positive (FP) is a condition which wrongly specifies that there is a specific condition or attribute. A true negative (TN) test result is one that does not detect the condition when the condition is absent. Positive predictive values (PPV) are the proportions of positive results in the tests that are true positive. The PPV describes the performance of a diagnostic statistical measure. The PPV is directly proportional to the accuracy of the system. The false discovery rate (FDR) is the predictable proportion of type I errors and a type I error is the error where we get a false positive. The FDR is related to PPV by the following equation.

$$\text{FDR} = 1 - \text{PPV} \tag{3}$$

To assess the quality of the proposed system, initially 20 types of crop are selected. Opinions of 150 users are collected in the database. The users have given opinions in terms of rating values for each seed available for different crops. We have calculated precision, accuracy, PPV and FDR values of five different users for top-5 recommendations which are listed in Table 20.1. The graph between PPV and FDR is shown in Figure 20.7 and Figure 20.8 represents the precision and Accuracy value for five different users.

Table 20.1 Precision, Accuracy, PPV & FDR values of five users.

User Id	Precision	Accuracy	PPV	FDR
1	0.6	0.8	0.6	0.4
2	0.4	0.7	0.4	0.6
3	1	1	1	0
4	0.8	0.9	0.8	0.2
5	1	1	1	0

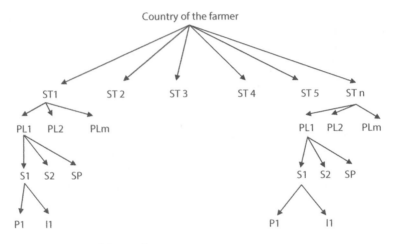

Figure 20.4 Structure of the similarity tree.

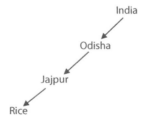

Figure 20.5 Similarity tree for a given active query farmer.

20.6.2   Time Complexity Analysis

The proposed method of finding similarity can be proved as better compared to the traditional methods of finding similarity like Cosine similarity,

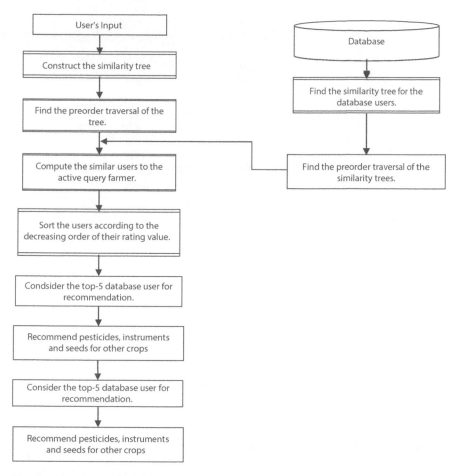

Figure 20.6 Proposed model.

Pearson correlation coefficient and Jaccard's similarity as it is efficient in terms of time. The time complexity to find the cosine similarity between two vectors is $O(n^2)$ but the time complexity to traverse the proposed skewed binary tree for recommendation is $O(n)$, where n is the size of the inputs.

20.7 Conclusion & Future Work

Recommender systems are the software solutions which are capable of predicting the users' need by analyzing their preferences from the past history. Recommender system has already shown its efficiency in all most all the domains. But countries like India whose major part of the economy

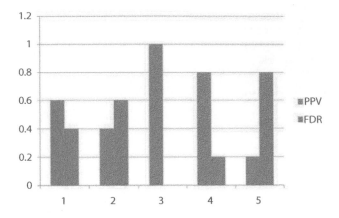

Figure 20.7 Graph for PPV & FDR.

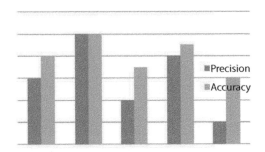

Figure 20.8 Graph for precision & accuracy.

depends on agriculture needs efficient recommender systems to help the farmers for tackling the climatic changes in the environment and also to make aware about the new pesticides and instruments available which can help them to increase the productivity of their crops. This paper recommends the farmers to decide pesticides and advanced equipments for a particular crop as per their need. It also recommends some other crops which also ensemble to the location of the farmer. The proposed method uses a tree similarity technique for finding the similar users or farmers according to a given query user. It is efficient in terms of time in compare to the other similarity measures. The efficiency of the proposed systems has been measured with precision, accuracy and positive predictive values (PPV). This study has a limitation as it considers Odisha only as geographical region. In future we may consider technology adaptation for production of crops and other geographical regions. Deep neural network is another powerful machine learning technique to increase the capability of agricultural recommender system and basically suitable for large dataset. Stacked auto-encoders can be used to pretrain deep neural networks with a tiny dataset also to optimize initial weights. Deep neural network model demonstrates better generalization performance than shallow neural network and support vector machine.

References

1. CarlKadie, J.B.D., *Empirical Analysis of Predictive Algorithms for Collaborative Filtering.* Microsoft Research Microsoft Corporation One Microsoft Way Redmond, WA, 98052 1998.
2. Delgado, J. and Ishii, N., Memory-based weighted majority prediction. *SIGIR Workshop Recomm. Syst. Citeseer*, 1999.
3. Doshi, Z., Nadkarni, S., Agrawal, R., Shah, N., AgroConsultant: Intelligent Crop Recommendation System Using Machine Learning Algorithms. *2018 Fourth International Conference on Computing Communication Control and Automation (ICCUBEA)*, pp. 1–6, IEEE, 2018, August.
4. Jiahuan, L. and Liqing, Z., *Research on Recommendation System of Agricultural Products E-Commerce Platform Based on Hadoop.* IEEE 9th International Conference on Software Engineering and Service Science (ICSESS), 1070–1073, 2018.
5. Raja, S.K.S., Rishi, R., Sundaresan, E., Srijit, V., Demand based crop recommender system for farmers. *2017 IEEE Technological Innovations in ICT for Agriculture and Rural Development (TIAR)*, pp. 194–199, IEEE, 2017, April.
6. Madhusree, K., Bikram, R., Mohanty, S., Crop Recommender System for the Farmers using Mamdani Fuzzy Inference Model. *IJET*, 7, 277, 10.14419/ijet. v7i4.15.23006 2018.
7. Dumbre, N., Chikane, O., More, G., System for Agriculture Recommendation using data mining. *IERJ*, 1, 5, 26–27, 2015.
8. Reddy, K.A. and Kumar, R.K., *Recommendation System: A Collaborative Model for Agriculture*, 2018.
9. Al Alshaikh, M., Uchyigit, G., Evans, R., A research paper recommender system using a Dynamic Normalized Tree of Concepts model for user modelling. *Research Challenges in Information Science (RCIS), 2017 11th International Conference*, on pp. 200–210, IEEE 2017, May.
10. Karimi, R., Wistuba, M., Nanopoulos, A., Schmidt-Thieme, L., Factorized decision trees for active learning in recommender systems. *Tools with Artificial Intelligence (ICTAI), 2013 IEEE 25th International Conference*, on pp. 404–411, IEEE 2013, November.

11. Perumal, S.P., Arputharaj, K., Sannasi, G., Fuzzy family tree similarity based effective e-learning recommender system. *Advanced Computing (ICoAC), 2016 Eighth International Conference,* on pp. 146–150, IEEE 2017, January.

12. Zhang, H., Ni, W., Zhao, M., Liu, Y., Yang, Y., A hybrid recommendation approach for network teaching resources based on knowledge-tree. *Control Conference (CCC), 2014 33rd Chinese,* pp. 3450–3455, IEEE 2014, July.

13. Bhatt, R.B., Neuro-fuzzy decision trees for content popularity model and multi-genre movie recommendation system over social network. *TENCON 2009-2009 IEEE Region 10 Conference,* pp. 1–6, IEEE 2009, January.

14. Nilesh, D., Omkar, C., Gitesh, M., System for Agriculture Recommendation using Data Mining. *IERJ,* 2015.

15. Reddy, K.A. and Kumar, R.K., Recommendation System: A Collaborative Model for Agriculture. *IJCSE,* 2018.

16. Rajak, R.K., Pawar, A., Pendke, M., Shinde, P., Rathod, S., Devare, A., Crop recommendation system to maximize crop yield using machine learning technique. *Int. Res. J. Eng. Technol.,* 4, 12, 950–953, 2017.

17. Zhang, H.R. and Min, F., Three-way recommender systems based on random forests. *Knowl-Based. Syst.,* 91, 275–286, 2016.

18. Ali, J., Khan, R., Ahmad, N., Maqsood, I., Random Forests and Decision Trees. *IJCSI,* 9, 5, 272, 2012.

19. Denil, M., Matheson, D., De Freitas, N., Narrowing the gap: Random forests in theory and in practice. *International Conference on Machine Learning,* pp. 665–673, 2014, January.

20. Jones, Z. and Linder, F., Exploratory data analysis using random forests. *Prepared for the 73rd Annual MPSA Conference,* 2015, April.

21. Paul, M., Vishwakarma, S., Verma, A., 'Analysis of Soil Behaviour and Prediction of Crop Yield using Data Mining Approach'. *International Conference on Computational Intelligence and Communication Networks,* 2015.

22. Pudumalar, S., Ramanujam, E., Rajashreeń, R., Nishań, J., Crop Recommendation System for Precision Agriculture. *2016 IEEE Eighth International Conference on Advanced Computing (ICoAC),* 978-1-5090-5888-4, 2016.

23. Sanghvi, Y., Gupta, H., Doshi, H., Koli, D., Gupta, U., 'Comparison of Self Organizing Maps and Sammon's Mapping on agricultural datasets for precision agriculture'. *International Conference on Innovations in Information, Embedded and Communication Systems (ICIIECS),* 2015.

24. Kumar, A., Sarkar, S., Pradhan, C., *Recommendation System for Crop Identification and Pest Control Technique in Agriculture.* International Conference on Communication and Signal Processing, pp. 0185–0189, 10.1109/ICCSP.2019.8698099 2019.

25. Mokarrama, M.J. and Arefin, M.S., RSF: A recommendation system for farmers. *2017 IEEE Region 10 Humanitarian Technology Conference (R10-HTC),* pp. 843–850, 2017.

21

Influenceable Targets Recommendation Analyzing Social Activities in Egocentric Online Social Networks

Soumyadeep Debnath[1], Dhrubasish Sarkar[2]* and Dipankar Das[3]

[1]Tata Consultancy Services Limited, Kolkata, India
[2]Amity Institute of Information Technology (AIIT), Amity University,
Kolkata, India
[3]Department of Computer Science and Engineering, Jadavpur University,
Kolkata, India

Abstract

Nowadays, Online Social Media (OSM) has vast impact on various aspects of industry, business and society along with on user's life. In an OSN platform, reaching the target users is one of the primary focus for most of the businesses and other organizations. Identification and recommendation of influenceable targets helps to capture the appropriate audience efficiently and effectively. In this paper, an effective model has been discussed in egocentric OSN by incorporating an efficient influence measured Recommendation System in order to generate a list of top most influenceable target users among all connected network members for any specific social network user. Firstly the list of interacted network members has been updated based on all activities. On which the interacted network members with most similar activities have been recommended based on the specific influence category with sentiment type. After that the top most influenceable network members in basis of the required amount among those updated list of interacted network members have been identified with proper ranking by analyzing the similarity and frequency of their activity contents with respect to the activity contents of the main user. Through these two continuous stages an effective list of top influenceable targets of the main user has been distinguished from the egocentric view of any social network.

---

*Corresponding author: dhrubasish@inbox.com

Sachi Nandan Mohanty, Jyotir Moy Chatterjee, Sarika Jain, Ahmed A. Elngar and Priya Gupta (eds.)
Recommender System with Machine Learning and Artificial Intelligence: Practical Tools and Applications in Medical, Agricultural and Other Industries, (401–416) © 2020 Scrivener Publishing LLC

Keywords: Influenceable targets, social activities, influence measurement, content categorization, sentiment analysis, recommendation system, online social media (OSM), egocentric online social networks (OSNs)

21.1   Introduction

Over the last few years Online Social Media (OSM) have drawn huge attention of its users and grown enormously. Nowadays, millions of users across the world consider these platforms as a part of their daily lives spending a huge amount of their time to create and observe many information. Through these platforms the users can create or exchange their ideas or thought through textual, visual and web contents as well as they can react, comment, share and tag others on those contents of own and other users. Hence these Online Social Media (OSM) platforms have drawn the focus of the data driven business industries to understand or gain some valuable information about the customers, their preferences, choices and various influencing parameters, etc. by analyzing their social activity contents, it's types and frequency.

There are generally two types for social network observation, such as egocentric and sociocentric [1]. In sociocentric approach the complete or whole network is considered but egocentric approach considers on individual (called ego) network with focusing the interactions among that individual person with all connected people (called alters) indirectly or directly. In our current paper, a effective algorithmic mathematical technique has been discussed by incorporating an efficient Influence Measurement [2, 3] with a significant recommendation system in order to generate a list of top most influenceable target users among all interacted network members for any specific social network user (main user) in egocentric online social network.

At first a list of interacted network members are selected based on their acitivities with the main user and then all those interacted network members are categorized based on the activity contents classification (five classes) and sentiment (two classes) analysis on them for all five types of social activities. After that the list of interacted network members (based on activities) again has been updated with a less value by the operation of a significant recommendation system of textual lexical analysis (similarity and frequency), on which the interacted network members with most similar activities have been recommended with proper ranking by analyzing the recommendation of their post contents with respect to the post contents of the target user. Then the top most influenceable network members among those updated list of interacted network members have been identified in any specific influence category with specific sentiment type based on the required amount.

The proposed model can work on three most popular social network platforms of the main user separately; Facebook*, Twitter†, LinkedIn‡ and only considers the egocentric scenario as it is useful when the research focuses on individuals in the network compared to the complete network analysis. The chapter is organized with a section in next discussed about the previous works done in this area as Literature Review. After that the following sections are covered with the Data Collection, Preprocessing, Influence and Activities Analysis, and the proposed Recommendation System. Last two sections contain the conclusion and future scope.

21.2   Literature Review

Network structure, its properties and analysis are also very much common in the various fields of business and industry. An OSN structure can be described as a graph or network structure which comprises the collection of individuals and the links or association between them. It is very much essential to identify the most important targets in a networked environment in order to address various issues and services related to the network. Primarily the graph theory concepts are used for topological or structural analysis of social networks. Social activities analysis of the connected users also helps to explore the network with insight knowledge.

Influenceable targets identification in OSNs has huge significance as far as its business applications are concerned. It can help a business or organization to reach to its target audiences. Hence this domain draws the attention of many researchers. Identifying influenceable targets is basically influence maximization problem. Many mathematical and algorithmic techniques have been proposed to identify influenceable targets or users in a network.

Domingous and Richardson [4] did the first study in this research field. In their study, instead of viewing a market as a set of independent entities, they considered it as a social network and represented it as Markov random field in their work. They developed three algorithms for determining influential users which are be used in viral ways of marketing. They have also discussed the reviews on some of the significant approaches used to identify influential targets have been presented. Kempe *et al.* [5] formulated influence maximization as a discrete optimization problem and proved that this optimization problem is NP-hard. Through experiments they showed that the proposed algorithm could significantly outperform the classic degree and centrality based heuristics in influence maximization. Bonchi [6] took his work to show the diffusion of influence using a data mining perspective. However, Saito *et al.* [7, 8] revealed that the diffusion of the different topics is not same because of the different preferences of the users that will affect their role in the spread of a specific topic. Later, Tang *et al.* [9] proposed the topic-level social influence using Topical Affinity Propagation (TAP) for large social networks. Later, Zhou *et al.* [10] proposed top-K influential nodes mining on the basis of user choices using a two-stage mining algorithm. Li *et al.* [11] proposed to consider the individual behaviors of persons to model the influence propagation in heterogeneous social networks. Marsden [12] discussed about centrality measures on egocentric and sociocentric networks. Later, Chung *et al.* [1] mentioned about egocentric and sociocentric approaches on social network analysis with highlighting the scopes or challenges for both cases.

To measure users' activities in OSNs, Debnath *et al.* [13] analyzed the lexicons and citation parameters for particularly Twitter network users' activities. In egocentric OSNs, they proposed for identification of top-k number of influencers considering only the activity behaviors [2]. In another [3], they considered the network structure of the user with its network members including analysis of activity behaviors among them and proposed a model based on egocentric OSNs in order to recognize influential users as nodes for that user.

21.3   Dataset Collection Process with Details

As the input for our algorithmic method massive amount social media contents of a longtime duration were needed for any particular user with details from different social media platforms like *Facebook, Twitter, LinkedIn*, etc. So here from past two years all social media activities data have been collected for a particular user with it's network members associated by activities and prepared nine datasets of different contents for each social network separately. The sequential process is mentioned below (shown in Figure 21.1).

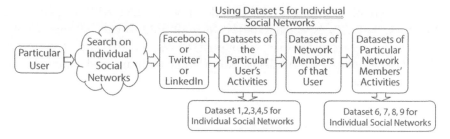

Figure 21.1 Diagram of dataset collection process.

21.3.1   Main User's Activities Data

For individual Online Social Media (OSM) platforms, from the activity log portal all activity contents with details have been collected within a long time duration for the main user. Datasets are such as; all contents of own posts, commented posts, reacted posts, tagged posts, shared posts (*Dataset 1*), all additional contents of shared posts (*Dataset 2*), all comments of commented posts (*Dataset 3*), all messages of the conversations with other network members (*Dataset 4*), the list of all the network members associated with all main user's activities like posting, reacting, commenting, sharing, tagging, messaging activities (*Dataset 5*).

21.3.2   Network Member's Activities Data

Here also for individual Online Social Media (OSM) platforms, from the activity log portal all activity contents with details have been collected within a long time duration for all network members of that main user. Datasets are such as; all contents of own posts, commented posts, reacted posts, tagged posts, shared posts (*Dataset 6*), all additional contents of shared posts (*Dataset 7*), all comments of commented posts (*Dataset 8*), all messages of the conversations with their other network members (*Dataset 9*).

21.3.3   Tools and Libraries for Data Collection

For this '*Data Collection*' stage, as mentioned by Fredrik and Stolpe [14] different libraries for data crawling from social media are useful. So from individual social media platforms (*Twitter, Facebook, LinkedIn*), all datasets (excluding *Datasets 3* and *8*) can be crawled using Twitter4J'* by Yusuke

---

* http://twitter4j.org/en/index.html

[15], 'Facebook4J'*, 'Graph API'†, 'LinkedIn4J'‡, 'REST API'§ respectively. But these libraries (specially all 4Js) are not able to get comment/reply thread directly from any particular post, therefore, for *Datasets 3* and *8* the '*Web Scraping*' method using 'jsoup'¶, a java library by Hedley [16] is forever applicable.

21.3.4 Details of the Datasets

Here firstly all post contents of individual user (main user and each inter-acted network member from dataset 5) are stored in different folders and also all network members' data are specially separated from target user's data. After that again, for all post contents of each user have been distin-guished and stored in different csv files based on the different activity types of the particular contents, such as all post contents of four different activi-ties (React, Comment, Tag and Share) have been stored in four different csv files inside that particular user folder for each user.

In these datasets, there are total eight colums of different attributes, they are; Post/Tweet ID, Post/Tweet Content, User Name, User ID, React/Favorite Count, Share/Retweet Count, Language, Time and also comments thread. A sample twitter data in text format mentioned below (shown in Figure 21.2).

21.4 Primary Preprocessing of Data

As we all know proper preprocessing works for making input data suitable based on algorithms produce better result. Therefore, four different textual preprocessing works on all datasets excluding '*Dataset 5*´ have been incor-porated here which are briefly discussed below (shown in Figure 21.3).

21.4.1 Language Detection and Translation

Using 'TextBlob'** python library by Loria *et al.* [17], for all the social con-tents languages have been detected, if there exist non-English languages then they have been translated into English language.

---

* https://facebook4j.github.io/en/index.html
† https://developers.facebook.com/docs/graph-api/
‡ https://github.com/Aristokrates/Freelancer-aggregator/tree/master/linkedin4j
§ https://developer.linkedin.com/docs/rest-api#
¶ https://jsoup.org/
** http://textblob.readthedocs.io/en/dev/quickstart.html

Figure 21.2 Snapshot of a tweet data crawled from Twitter.

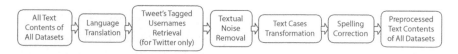

Figure 21.3 Diagram of data preprocessing process.

21.4.2   Tagged Tweeters Collection

For tweets only, all words followed by '@' symbol represents username of tagged users. So all those words have been removed from tweets and tagged users have been added in '*Dataset 5*'.

21.4.3   Textual Noise Removal

All special symbols, set of special symbols excluding the single comma and full stop, emoticons which represents emojis, unrecognized characters for the attached images and GIF files have been removed from all social contents.

21.4.4   Textual Spelling Correction

Using 'TextBlob'* python library by Loria *et al.* [17], all text cases have been converted into lowercase and all the noisy spelled words have been corrected for all social media contents.

21.5   Influence and Social Activities Analysis

Here methodologically, the influence has been tried to evaluate by analyzing the social activities of the main user and it's interacted network members from *Dataset 5* in a specific time duration. The sequential detailed process is mentioned below (shown in Figure 21.4).

---

* http://textblob.readthedocs.io/en/dev/quickstart.html

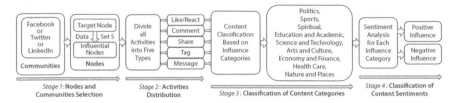

Figure 21.4 Diagram of influence and activities analysis process.

21.5.1   Step 1: Targets Selection From OSMs

Here firstly the list of all the interacted network members from *Dataset 5* have been only considered from where only the *influenceable targets* can belong because others are not associated with the *main user* throgh activities during that particular time period. This also reduced the complexity of our algorithm.

This *influenceable targets* and *OSMs* are like; friends, followers, connections for Facebook, Twitter, LinkedIn respectively with also following pages for all three OSMs. One notable point, the public and private groups can never be *influenceable targets* due to the privacy with approval feature by other known/unknow OSM user (as *admin*). The representation is mentioned below (shown in Table 21.1).

21.5.2   Step 3: Categories Classification of Social Contents

Here all the social activities data from *Dataset 1* and *4* (main user's data) and *Dataset 6* and *9* (interacted network members' data) have been classified into five classes (*Technology, Politics, Sports, Business* and *Entertainment*) by the multi-class text classification with LSTM*, a commonly used Recurrent Neural Network (RNN) using TensorFlow 2.0 framework.

This classification stage has not been applied to other dependent data from *Dataset 2* and *3* (main user's data) and *Dataset 7* and *8* (interacted network members' data) which are not owned by the post owners and dependent on *Dataset 1* and *6* respectively.

21.5.3   Step 4: Sentiments Analysis of Social Contents

Here all the social activities data from *Datasets 1, 2, 3, 4* (main user's data) and *Datasets 6, 7, 8, 9* (interacted network members' data) have

---

* https://towardsdatascience.com/multi-class-text-classification-with-lstm-using-tensor-flow-2-0-d88627c10a35

Table 21.1 Representation of influenceable targets and Online Social Media (OSM) platforms.

OSMs	Facebook	Twitter	LinkedIn
Influenceable Targets	Friends and Followers	Following Profiles	Connections and Followers
	Facebook Pages	Twitter Pages	LinkedIn Pages

been analyzed based on two sentiment classes (*Positive* and *Negative*) for each of the previous mentioned categories using VADER* (Valence Aware Dictionary and sEntiment Reasoner), a lexicon and rule-based sentiment analysis which uses the combination of sentiment lexicon and list of lexical features (example, words), labelled according to their semantic orientation; either positive or negative.

21.6   Recommendation System

In the proposed work firstly, the properties of all social activity contents of both the main user and it's interacted network members (Dataset 5) have been analyzed using the textual lexical analysis (similarity and frequency) on those activity contents.

Here the main aim was to recommend the highest similar post contents of the interacted network members with respect to all the post contents of the main user. After that a similar but short updated list of interacted network members (updated Dataset 5) with very similar activity contents with the main user has been derived. The detailed sequential stages are mentioned below (shown in Figure 21.5).

21.6.1   Secondary Preprocessing of Data

Here three different textual preprocessing works on all datasets excluding 'Dataset 5' have been implemented here using 'Natural Language Toolkit (NLTK)'†, a natural language processing package of python for only this recommendation algorithmic process. This stages are mainly responsible for removal of all unnecessary irrelevant details to get better recommended results for content analysis.

---

* https://github.com/cjhutto/vaderSentiment
† www.nltk.org

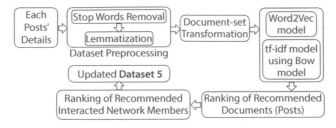

Figure 21.5 Diagram of recommendation process.

Step 1: Stop Word Removal

This stage is responsible for removal of all frequently occurred irrelevant words (*Stop Words*) from each post content which affect the recommendation indexing of post contents badly. Here all the post contents have been tokenized and all such words (example, *wh words, be and have verb forms, articles, prepositions, conjunctions,* etc.) using 'nltk.tokenize' and 'nltk.corpus' python packages respectively.

Step 2: Lemmatization without Stemming

This stage is responsible for transformation of all words retrieved from the previous stage into the root words for each post content which have reduced the word count to produce efficient recommendations. Therefore, we have applied *Lemmatization* due to its morphological analysis process on words instead of *Stemming* as it sometimes generates nonexistent or unexpected words, but lemmatization always generates actual root words. Here 'WordNetLemmatizer' has been used which has built-in morphological python function of 'WordNet'* in the 'wordnet' module at 'nltk.stem' package.

Step 3: Document-Set Transformation

After completion of previous stages, actually a new optimized dataset has been generated as *Document-Set* where each post content of this data will be considered as an individual document. This individual post content (*document*) of all users will be considered as the key input data for further recommendation process.

---

* https://wordnet.princeton.edu/

21.6.2   Recommendation Analyzing Contents of Social Activities

The recommendation process has been proposed by forwarding four sequential tasks, followed on the data of the previously preprocessed data-set (*Document-Set*) with each individual post content (*document*) analysis and made more suitable outcomes/results for the proposed recommendation system.

Step 1: Word2Vec Model Utilization
This stage is responsible for generation of *word vectors* for all words of each post content/document from the Document-set mentioned previously using Google's pre-trained 'Word2Vec'* model and retrieval of *cosine similarity* values from the *word vector pairs* considering the *pairwise distances* among them. As this is one of the crucial stages for the betterment of our recommended results, therefore, the implementation of this model has been applied using 'gensim'† a python package popular for the operations in Information Retrieval (IR) and Natural Language Processing (NLP) domains.

Step 2: BoW Model Utilization
This stage is responsible for generation of a table structure which contains the *frequencies* or *number of occurrence* for all words in individual post content/document from the Document-set mentioned previously. Here for each post content/document from Document-se, it has been tokenized and then a dictionary has been created containing the frequencies of all words of that document. This is an implementation of *bag-of-words* (BoW) model where the rows represent documents and the columns represent frequencies of unique words.

Step 3: Tf–idf Model Utilization
This stage is responsible for generation of *vector values* for all words of each post content/document from the Document-set mentioned previously based on *tf–idf* (*term frequency–inverse document frequency*) model using 'feature_extraction' module of 'scikit-learn'‡, a python package popular for the operations in Machine Learning (ML). Here the first word 'term frequency' represents the same result like *bag-of-words* (BoW) model which

---

* https://code.google.com/archive/p/word2vec/
† https://radimrehurek.com/gensim/models/word2vec.html
‡ http://scikit-learn.org/stable/

is mentioned above and the second term 'inverse document frequency' represents the amount of non-occurrence for any word in any document.

Step 4: Ranking of Recommended Users Based on Documents

Here, the output results from previous stages have been used to create a new updated list of interacted network members of the *main user* with influenceable ranking by recommending documents (post contents) based on similarity and frequency. The proposed recommendation algorithm (Algorithm 1) is explained below.

<u>Algorithm 1:</u>

Let: The total number of,

  Words in the Main user's documents (key post content) = m.
  Target users' documents (post contents) in the Document-set = N
  and Words in any of those documents (post contents) = n.
So, Key-term Word count (w) = 1 to m, Document count (d) = 1 to N, and Paper Word count (w) = 1 to n.

Let: For both the Main user's (mu) document and Target users' (tu) documents respectively,

  The vector values of any word from Word2Vec model are $Vw_{(mu)}$ and $Vw_{(tu)}$.
  The frequency values of any word from the table of BoW model are $BWw_{(mu)}$ and $BWw_{(tu)}$.
  The combined values of any word from tf-idf model are $TIw_{(mu)}$ and $TIw_{(tu)}$.
The length of tf-idf values of any document are $TIl_{(mu)}$ and $TIl_{(tu)}$.

Let: The values between the Main user's document and Target users' document,

The pairwise distance of two word vectors = Vp_d.
The cosine similarity of tf–idf = TI_{cs}.

Let: The Normalized value and Recommendation Index value of any document are N_d and R^+_d respectively.

{Main user's document Evaluation}

1:       Select each word of the Main user's document (key-term).
2:       for w = 1 to m do
3:            Evaluate, $Vw_{(mu)}$, $BWw_{(mu)}$ and $TIw_{(mu)}$.
4:       end for

5:      Repeat the same process until all done.

6:      Evaluate, $TII_{(mu)}$ using all values of $TIw_{(mu)}$.

{All Post Contents Evaluation}

7:      Select each of the Main user's documents (post contents).

8:      for d = 1 to N do

9:            Select each word of that document.

10:           for w = 1 to n do

11:                 Evaluate, $Vw_{(tu)}$, $BWw_{(tu)}$ and $TIw_{(tu)}$.

12:           end for

13:           Repeat the same process until all done.

14:           Evaluate, $TII_{(tu)}$ using all values of $TIw_{(tu)}$.

15:      end for

16:      Repeat the same process until all done.

{Rank Recommended Post Contents on Main user's document}

17:      Select each of the Target users' documents (post contents).

18:      for d = 1 to N do

19:           Comparing each word of the Main user's document and that document.

20:           for w = 1 to m with w = 1 to n do

21:           Evaluate, Vp_d using $Vw_{(mu)}$ and $Vw_{(tu)}$.

22:           Calculate, $N_d = (BWw_{(mu)} + BWw_{(tu)})/Vp_d$

23:           end for

24:           Evaluate, TI_{cs} using $TII_{(mu)}$ and $TII_{(tu)}$.

25:      Calculate, $R^+_d = (\Sigma N_d - TI_{cs})$

26:      end for

27:      Repeat this previous procedure for all other documents.

28:      Sort the R^+_d values of all the documents for all interacted network members in decreasing order.

21.7   Top Most Influenceable Targets Evaluation

Now here, all normalized recommendation indices (R^+_d) can be distinguished with both category and sentiment classes of influences separately for all Influenceable Target users with respect to the Main user and evaluated top most influenceable targets based on required amount by another algorithmic way (Algorithm 2) mentioned below where we eliminated some of the common influenceable targets having high default influence.

Algorithm 2:

Step 1: Let assume the required amount is N_{it} (50≤ N_{it} ≤Network Size), then collect first N_{it} number of *Influenceable Targets* from sorted list of Algorithm 1, as **'Selected Influenceable Targets'** based on their normalized Recommendation Indeces (R^+_d) on any categorical and sentiment classes of influence.

Step 2: Let the number of users with more than 5000 connections is D_{it}. They are removed considering as **'Default Influenceable Targets'** (example, verified pages/profiles) for already having huge influenceable impact in default.

Step 3: Consider, the remaining (N_{it} - D_{it}) number of users as **'Effective Influenceable Targets'** and replace the value of N_{it} as (N_{it} - D_{it}) by considering those as **'Top Most Influenceable Targets'**.

21.8   Conclusion

In this chapter, considering the Egocentric Online Social Networks scenario, an algorithmic model has been explained by incorporating a significant Recommendation System with an effective influence measurement process in order to generate a list of top most influenceable target users among all interacted network members for any specific social network user (main user).

At first the list of interacted network members (based on activities) has been updated with a less value by the operation of their social activities analysis based on contents classification with sentiment types and after that using the recommendation sytem of textual lexical analysis based on similarity and frequency, on which the interacted network members with most similar activities have been recommended with proper ranking by analyzing the recommendation of their post contents with respect to the post contents of the main user.

After that top most influenceable target network members (users) from that updated list of interacted network members have been identified for the main user based on any particular category and sentiment (example, influence of political category and positive sentiment) based on their social activities.

This algorithmic model can be cross validated by analyzing the results like similarly they have been justified in the previous research works [2, 3] done by us. Those testing procedures were very time consuming and also sometimes they are considered based on hypothesis [18, 19], these are some pioneering research works have already been successfully identified in these fileds.

21.9   Future Scope

Firstly in future the updated and large amount of dataset can be the most important direction for further result analysis which also can open few drawbacks or improvements for our algorithmic model with lot of eye opening justifications. This research also can be extended with more influence category classes with more sub domains and semantic analysis can be addition with sentiment analysis. Apart from that more natural language processing (nlp) analitical works such as personality analysis [3], emotion recognition etc based on social activities contents can be incorporated.

As we have considered only textual data, so considering images will be a vast field though some previously implemented methods like the *Optical Character Recognition* (OCR) on textual part recovery from images by Patel *et al.* [20] and the *Convolutional Neural Network* (CNN) for classifying patterns on images by Rakshit *et al.* [21]

Including these all above mentioned further scopes, there are also many uncovered fields which have already been mentioned in our previous research papers [2, 3], that can be great exposure for future.

References

1. Chung, K.K., Hossain, L., Davis, J., Exploring sociocentric and egocentric approaches for social network analysis, in: *Second International Conference on Knowledge Management in Asia Pacific*, pp. 1–8, New Zealand: Victoria University of Wellington, 2005.
2. Debnath, S., Sarkar, D., Jana, P., Top-k Influential Nodes Identification Based on Activity Behaviors in Egocentric Online Social Networks, in: *Computational Intelligence in Pattern Recognition*, pp. 463–475, Springer, Singapore, 2020.
3. Sarkar, D., Debnath, S., Kole, D.K., Jana, P., Influential Nodes Identification Based on Activity Behaviors and Network Structure With Personality Analysis in Egocentric Online Social Networks. *IJACI*, 10, 4, 1–24, 2019.
4. Domingos, P. and Richardson, M., Mining the network value of customers. in: *Proceedings of the Seventh ACM SIGKDD International Conference on Knowledge Discovery and Data Mining*, p. 57–66, ACM Press, San Francisco, CA, 2001.
5. Kempe, D., Kleinberg, J., Tardos, É., Maximizing the spread of influence through a social network. *Proceedings of the Ninth ACM SIGKDD International Conference on Knowledge Discovery and Data Mining*, pp. 137–146, ACM, 2003, August.

6. Bonchi, F., Influence Propagation in Social Networks: A Data Mining Perspective. *IEEE Intell. Inform. Bull.*, 12, 1, 8–16, 2011.

7. Saito, K., Kimura, M., Ohara, K., Motoda, H., Learning continuous-time information diffusion model for social behavioral data analysis. *Asian Conference on Machine Learning*, Springer, Berlin, Heidelberg, pp. 322–337, 2009, November.

8. Saito, K., Kimura, M., Ohara, K., Motoda, H., Behavioral analyses of information diffusion models by observed data of social network. *Proceedings of the 2010 International Conference on Social Computing, Behavioral Modeling, Advances in Social Computing Prediction*, (SBP10) pp. 149–158, 2010

9. Tang, J., Sun, J., Wang, C., Yang, Z., Social influence analysis in large-scale networks. *Proceedings of the 15th ACM SIGKDD international conference on Knowledge discovery and data mining*, pp. 807–816, ACM 2009, June.

10. Zhou, J., Zhang, Y., Cheng, J., Preference-based mining of top-K influential nodes in social networks. *Fut. Gener. Comp. Sy.*, 31, 40–47, 2014.

11. Li, C.T., Lin, S.D., Shan, M.K., Influence propagation and maximization for heterogeneous social networks. *Proceedings of the 21st International Conference on World Wide Web*, pp. 559–560, ACM 2012, April.

12. Marsden, P.V., Egocentric and sociocentric measures of network centrality. *Soc. Netw.*, 24, 4, 407–422, 2002.

13. Debnath, S., Das, D., Das, B., Identifying Terrorist Index (T+) for Ranking Homogeneous Twitter Users and Groups by Employing Citation Parameters and Vulnerability Lexicon. *International Conference on Mining Intelligence and Knowledge Exploration*, Springer, Cham, pp. 391–401, 2017, December.

14. Jonsén, F. and Stolpe, A., *The feasibility and practicality of a generic social media library.*, Bachelor Thesis, Linköping University, Sweden, 2017.

15. Yamamoto, Y., Twitter4j-a java library for the twitter api, (website), http://twitter4j.org/en/ (accessed on September 30, 2019).

16. Hedley, J., jsoup Java HTML Parser, with best of DOM, CSS, and jquery. (website), https://jsoup.org/ (accessed on September 30, 2019).

17. Loria, S., Keen, P., Honnibal, M., *TextBlob: Simplified text processing. Secondary TextBlob: Simplified Text Processing*, 2014. (website), https://textblob.readthedocs.io/en/dev/ (accessed on October 02, 2019).

18. Zafarani, R., Abbasi, M.A., Liu, H., *Social media mining: An introduction.*, Cambridge University Press, UK, 2014.

19. Russell, M.A., *Mining the Social Web: Data Mining Facebook, Twitter, LinkedIn, Google+, GitHub, and More.*, O'Reilly Media, Inc. USA, 2013.

20. Patel, C., Patel, A., Patel, D., Optical character recognition by open source OCR tool tesseract: A case study. *Int. J. Comput. Appl.*, 55, 10, 50–56, 2012.

21. Rakshit, S., Debnath, S., Mondal, D., *Identifying Land Patterns from Satellite Imagery in Amazon Rainforest using Deep Learning.*, arXiv preprint arXiv:1809.00340, 2018. (website), https://arxiv.org/abs/1809.00340 (accessed on September 10, 2019).

Index

Accuracy, 395
ACE model, 66–67
Action log, 76
Adaboost, 96
Algorithm, 313
Alzheimer's disease (AD), 352
Analogical learning, 226
Anonymity, 293, 295
Applicability of recommender system,
    in agriculture, 183
    in healthcare, 182
Appraisal framework (AF), 58
AQUAINT, 65
Architecture of blockchain, 317
Artificial Intelligence (AI), 122, 224, 313
Aspect-based opinion extraction,
    56–57
Automatic machine learning (aML),
    216, 217

Bag of words (BoW), 218, 219
Bagging algorithm, 96
Balanced accuracy score (BAS), 359,
    363
BAT algorithm, 315
Bayesian models (BM), 94–95
Best prediction error (BPE), 132
Bias, 259, 260, 262
Bitcoin, 295–296, 299–300, 304–305, 315
Black sheep, 84
Blockchain, 313
Blockchain architecture, 318
Blood glucose, 314
Boolean vector, 195, 197, 198, 199

Boosting technique, 96
Bootstrap aggregating, 96
BoW Model, 411–412
Breast cancer coimbra dataset
    (BCCD), 121, 124, 125
Breast cancer prediction, 121, 122, 124,
    125, 138
Breast cancer prognosis, 121

Case-based reasoning, 38
Chaining algorithm, 320
Cognitive specification language
    (CSL), 299
Cohen's kappa coefficient, 351, 362
Cold start problem, 20, 214, 230
Collaborative filtering (CF), 12, 27,
    29–30, 32, 34, 123–125, 130, 239,
    352, 354
    memory-based algorithm, 104–105,
        123
    model-based algorithm, 107, 123
Collaborative recommender system,
    214, 389
Complex item, 75
Computer tailored health
    communication (CTHC), 225
Concept-level sentiment analyses, 57
Consensus algorithm, 319
Content-based (CB), 8, 123, 124
Content-based approach, 389
Content-based health recommender
    system (CBHRS), 215
Content-based image retrieval (CBIR),
    227

Content-based recommender system (CBRS), 213, 214
Context attributes, 238
Convolutional neural network (CNN), 314, 352, 415
Correlation technique, 79–80
Cosine similarity, 10, 195, 196, 197, 198, 199, 207, 239, 396
Cosine technique, 79–80
Coverage, 227
CRBM-based model,
    algorithm, 113–114
    experiment result, 115, 116–117
    flowchart, 114
Crop disease detection & yield prediction, 159–162
Crop management,
    crop quality, 159
    disease detection, 154–156
    weed detection, 156–159
    yield prediction, 153–154
Cryptocurrencies, 315

Data collection phase, 121, 128
Data exploration, 255–256
Data imputation, 356
Data preprocessing,
    cleaning data, 252
    getting data, 252
    partition datasets, 253
Database, 313
Dataset, 354
    blood analysis, 124, 125, 128
    high body mass index (BMI), 121, 124, 126
    homeostasis model assessment-insulin resistance (HOMA-IR), 125–127, 132, 134
    UCI machine learning repository, 126
Decentralized database technology, 314
Decision logic, 27, 40
Decision tree (DT), 95, 96, 226, 344
Deep learning (DL), 122

Deep learning methods,
    adversarial networks, 109
    autoencoder, 109
    convolution neural network (CNN), 109
    restricted boltzmann machine (RBM), 109
Deep neural network (DNN), 352, 356, 358, 399
Demographic filtering, 18
Demographic recommendations, 390
Dentacoin, 300
Digital wallet, 305
Distributions,
    movie ratings, 256–257
    users distribution, 257–258
Doctor-in-loop (DiL), 216, 217, 229

Egocentric, 401–404, 414
Electronic health record (EHR), 215
Electronic medical record (EMR), 215
EmotionML, 61, 63
Ensemble learning (EL) models, 95
Entropy, 204, 222
Ether, 300
Ethereum, 300
Eucilidean distance, 11
Event extraction, 64
Example-based learning, 224
Experimental results, 377–383
Explainable recommendation model, 41
Explanation methodology,
    case-based, 36, 38–39
    collaborative-based, 36
    content-based, 29–30, 36–39
    demographic-based, 36, 39
    knowledge and utility-based, 37
Expressive statement (ES), 60

False discovery rate, 395
False negative (FN), 395
False positive (FP), 395
Feature extraction, 213, 218, 219, 220, 222

Feature selection, 127, 128, 131, 216, 218, 220, 222
    correlation matrix, 127
    dependent attribute, 127
    heatmap, 127
    independent attributes, 127
Feature vector, 220, 222
Feature weighting, 216
Feature-based opinion extraction, 56
Feedback system,
    binary, 76
    numeric, 76
    suggested text, 76
    unary, 76
Filtering, 313
Fisher's discrimination index, 222
F-measure, 83, 244
Future perspective of recommender systems, 283–286
    challenges concerning changing eating behaviour of users, 285
    challenges regarding explanations and visualizations, 286
    recommendation algorithms challenges, 284
        recipe databases, 284
    user information challenges, 283

Geo tagged-based services, 238
Gini index, 222
Global vectors for word representations (Glove), 220
Golem, 301
Gray sheep, 84
Gross value added (GVA), 90

Hamming loss (HL), 351, 355, 361
Hash function, 320
Hashing, 313
Health recommender systems (HRS), 124, 213, 215, 332, 333
HealthMudra, 313
Human–computer interaction (HCI), 225

Human-in-loop (HiL), 216, 218
Hybrid filtering, 33
Hybrid recommender system, 17, 124, 390

ICON, 300
Implementation of food recommender system using content-based approach, 276–282
    data preprocessing, 280
    dataset, 280
    information retrieval, 278
    item profile representation, 277
    obtaining word2vec embeddings, 279–280
    web scrapping for food list, 280
        cosine similarity, 281
        filtering our ingredients, 280
        final data frame with dishes and their ingredients, 281–282
        hamming distance, 281
        jaccard distance, 281
        porter stemming all words, 280
        similarity metrics, 281
Implicit and explicit feedback, 214
Indian council of medical research (ICMR), 122
Influenceable targets, 401–403, 408–409, 413–414
Information content, 205, 207
Information exchange, 49–55
    exchange of tourism objects data, 49–51
    exchange of tourism-related statistical data, 53–55
    Schema.org, 51–53
Information extraction (IE), 55–57
    opinion extraction, 56–57
    opinion mining, 57
Information filtering, 74
Information gain, 204, 206
Information technology (IT), 228
Instructive learning, 224
Integrity, 293, 295

Interactive machine learning (iML), 216, 218
Interoperability issue, 49
Inverse document frequency (IDF), 31, 220
IoTA, 300
Item features,
    fixed feature, 75
    general feature, 75
    specific feature, 75
    variable feature, 75
Item profile, 195, 197, 198, 199, 207

Jaccard similarity, 10, 239, 397

K nearest neighbor (KNN), 343
K-anonymity, 228
K-fold cross-validation, 121, 133
K-nearest neighbor (k-NN), 226, 242
Knowledge-based filtering, 18
Knowledge-based recommender
    system, 214
K-top recommendation, 227

Language detection and translation, 406
Latent dirichlet allocation (LDA), 56–57
L-diversity, 228
Learning algorithm, 320
Least squares, 259, 262–263
Lemmatization, 410
Lexicon-based natural language
    processing techniques, 57
Linked list, 319
Logistic regression, 343

Machine learning (ML), 92, 93–97, 122, 213, 214, 352, 357
Machine learning algorithms for
    Parkinson's data, 337–340
Machine learning algorithms, 145, 313
Machine learning methods,
    artificial neural network, 145–147
    decision tree learning, 148
    gradient boosted decision tree
        (GBDT), 149–150
    K-nearest neighbors (K-NN), 147–148
    matrix factorization, 107–108
    random forest, 148–149
    regularized greedy forest (RGF), 150
    singular value decomposition
        (SVD), 108
    support vector machines, 147
    variable weighted basic SVD, 108
Magnetic resonance imaging (MRI), 352, 354
Matthews correlation coefficient
    (MCC), 359, 366, 367
Mean absolute error (MAE), 19, 82, 121, 131, 132, 134
Mean square error (MSE), 365, 366, 369
Median absolute error (MAE), 359, 363
Memory-based recommendation,
    item-based approach, 81
    user-based approach, 81
Memory-based, 389
Memory-based approach, 12
Metadata tags, 58
Model fidelity, 41
Model-based algorithms, 389
Model-based approach, 16
MONERO, 301
Movie effects model, 259–260
Movielens, 253–255
Multi-class text classification with
    LSTM, 408
Multilayer perceptron, 314

Naive bayes, 226
Naive model, 258–259
National Institute of Cancer
    Prevention and Research
    (NICPR), 122
Natural language processing (NLP), 218, 222, 409, 411, 415

Natural Language toolkit (NLTK), 409
Neighborhood filters, 80
Netflix challenge, 251
Neural network (NN), 357
Neural network models, 375–377
Neural structured learning, 374–375
Normalized deviation, 222
Normalized ratings, 198

OASIS dataset, 354, 362
Observations, 283
One-hot-encoding, 354, 355, 358
Online social media (OSM), 402, 405,
    408–409
Online social network (OSN),
    401–404
Online tourism data, 55
OpinionMiningML, 59–63
Optical character recognition (OCR),
    415
Optimization process, 313
Optimization techniques/algorithms,
    199, 202, 207

Parameter vector estimation, 201
Parkinson's Disease: causes and
    symptoms, 333–334
Parkinson's Disease: treatment and
    surgical approaches, 334–335
  classification methods, 336–337
  different computational
    methodology, 337
  preprocessing techniques, 335
Pearson correlation coefficient, 397
Pearson's correlation, 11
Peer-to-peer (P2P), 295, 301–303, 307,
    315
Penalized regression, 263
Percentile bootstrap, 314
Personal health record (PHR), 215
Personalized or non-personalized
    recommendations, 214
Phrase extraction, 218, 219
Point-based services, 238

Pointer, 319
Positive predictive values (PPV), 395
Precision, 19, 82, 243, 394–395
Precision agriculture, 93
Prediction algorithms,
    alternating least squares (ALS),
        130
    baseline estimates, 130, 131
    baseline only, 130, 131, 133
    KNN basic algorithm, 130, 134
    matrix factorization methods, 131
    neighborhood models, 130, 131
    singular valued decomposition
        (SVD), 131
    stochastic gradient descent (SGD),
        130
    surprise, 129
Prediction/recommender phase, 121,
    128, 366
Preorder traversal, 394
Preprocessing phase, 121, 128
Profile health records (PHR), 213
Pros and cons of content-based
    recommender system, 185

Random forest-based decision tree,
    92–93
RBM-based model,
    algorithm, 110–111
    experimental result, 111–113
Reader class, 131
Recall, 19, 83, 243
Receiver operating characteristic
    (ROC) curve, 226
Recommendation index, 412
Recommendation process, 171
    architecture of content based
        recommender system, 172
    profile cleaner representation, 174
Recommender system,
    filtering techniques, 104–105
    phases, 103–104
Recommender system (RS), 214, 229,
    313

Recommender system for Parkinson's
   disease (PD), 341–345
   dataset for Parkinson's disease (PD),
      342
   how will one know when
      Parkinson's has progressed?, 342
Recurrent neural network (RNN),
   408
Regularization, 262–263
Regularization term, 202
Regularized model, 263–265
Reinforcement learning, 94
Residual mean square error, 257–258
Resting-state fMRI-based
   network connectivityanalysis
   (RS-fMRINC), 352
Results, 282
Ripple, 300
Root mean square error (RMSE), 19,
   82, 121, 131, 132, 134, 226
Rule-based classification, 224, 225

Schema.org, 51–53
Semantic clashes, 50
Sensitivity, 314
Sentiments analysis, 408
SentiML, 58–59, 62–64
Serendipity, 227
Shallow neural network, 399
Similarity tree, 394
Simple item, 75
Simple mean, 197
Single-user perspective in
   recommendation system, 77
Skewed binary tree, 393
Sociocentric, 402, 404
Soil health card, 90–91
Soil quality, 91
Soil testing mechanism, 91–92
Sparse information, 314
Spearman Rank correlation, 239
Specimen-based learning, 224, 225
Spelling correction, 407
Squared error, 202

Stacked auto encoders, 399
Star ratings, 198, 200, 201, 202, 207
Statistical data model exchange
   (SDMX), 53–55
Stellar, 300
Stemming, 218, 219, 410
Stop word, 410
Stop word deletion, 218
Structural clashes, 50–51
Structure of blockchain, 318
Support vector machine (SVM), 226,
   344, 399

Tamper resistant, 293, 295
TANGO, 65
Techniques used for item
   representation and learning user
   profile, 176
   representation of content, 176
   techniques for learning profiles of
      user, 178
   other methods, 181
   probabilistic method, 179
   Rocchio's and relevance feedback
      method, 180
   vector space model based on
      keywords, 177
Temporal information, 55
   extraction, 64
TensorFlow 2.0, 408
Term document matrix, 218, 220
Term frequency (TF), 31, 220
TERQAS, 65
TF-IDF, 389, 411, 412
Time complexity analysis, 396
TimeML, 65–67
Timestamp, 293, 295
Top-n recommendation, 394
TourInFrance (TIF) format, 49, 52–53,
   55
Tourism information systems (TISs),
   46
Training, testing, and validation phase,
   121, 128

Trajectory-based services, 238
Tree induction algorithm, 202, 204
True negative (TN), 395
True positives (TP), 395
Tweepy, 243
Type I error, 395
Type II error, 395
Type-I diabetes, 314
Type-II diabetes, 314

Unsupervised learning, 94
User log, 75
User profile, 195, 196, 197, 198, 207

Valence aware dictionary and sentiment
    reasoner (VADER), 409
Value of recommendation, 75
Various techniques to design food
    recommendation system,
    271–276
  collaborative filtering recommender
    systems, 271–272
  content-based recommender
    systems (CB), 272

context aware approaches, 273
different types of food
    recommender systems, 273–276
group-based methods, 273
hybrid recommender systems, 273
knowledge-based recommender
    systems, 272
Vocabulary supported solutions,
    50–53

Web scraping, 406
Weighted mean, 197
Word co-occurrence matrix (WCM),
    220
Word2Vec model, 411–412
Worst prediction error (WPE), 132
  gradient boosted decision tree
    (GBDT), 149–150
  overview, 152–153
  regularized greedy forest (RGF), 150

x2-statistic, 222
XML (eXtensible Markup Language),
    49

Printed and bound by CPI Group (UK) Ltd, Croydon, CR0 4YY

09/02/2023

03190563-0002